D1289489

# AFTER MARRIAGE EQUALITY

# After Marriage Equality

*The Future of LGBT Rights*

Edited by Carlos A. Ball

NEW YORK UNIVERSITY PRESS

*New York*

NEW YORK UNIVERSITY PRESS
New York
www.nyupress.org

References to Internet websites (URLs) were accurate at the time of writing. Neither the author nor New York University Press is responsible for URLs that may have expired or changed since the manuscript was prepared.

Library of Congress Cataloging-in-Publication Data
Names: Ball, Carlos A., editor.
Title: After marriage equality : the future of LGBT rights / edited by Carlos A. Ball.
Description: New York : New York University Press, 2016. | Includes bibliographical references and index. | Also available as an e-book.
Identifiers: LCCN 2015043573 | ISBN 978-1-4798-8308-0 (cl : alk. paper) | ISBN 1-4798-8308-5 (cl : alk. paper)
Subjects: LCSH: Sexual minorities—Civil rights—United States. | Same-sex marriage—United States. | Gay liberation movement—United States. | Sexual minorities—Civil rights. | Same-sex marriage. | Gay liberation movement. | LCGFT: Essays.
Classification: LCC HQ73.3.U6 A38 2015 | DDC 306.760973—dc23
LC record available at http://lccn.loc.gov/2015043573

New York University Press books are printed on acid-free paper, and their binding materials are chosen for strength and durability. We strive to use environmentally responsible suppliers and materials to the greatest extent possible in publishing our books.

Manufactured in the United States of America

10 9 8 7 6 5 4 3 2 1

Also available as an ebook

*To my husband Richard*

# CONTENTS

# Introduction

## The Past and the Future

CARLOS A. BALL

The question of marriage has been the subject of discussion and activism from the beginning of the LGBT rights movement in the United States. In 1953, *ONE*, the first American magazine aimed at advancing the equality rights of sexual minorities, published an essay on the question of marriage. At the time, of course, the idea that two individuals of the same sex could legally marry seemed fanciful, but the author nonetheless urged the nascent homophile movement to consider the implications of seeking marital rights.[1] Sixteen years later, during the summer following the Stonewall riots, Metropolitan Community Church ministers began conducting marriage ceremonies for same-sex couples. In the early 1970s, about a dozen same-sex couples around the country applied for marriage licenses.

After officials turned down the applications, three of the couples sued, arguing that the denials violated their constitutional rights. The courts rejected the constitutional claims out of hand, a fact that contributed to a twenty-year-long hiatus in the filing of new marriage equality lawsuits.[2] But some activists continued to push for marriage, focusing their efforts primarily on local officials. In 1975, the county clerk in Boulder, Colorado, who was also the president of the local chapter of the National Organization for Women, became the first government official in the United States to issue marriage licenses to same-sex couples (later deemed legally invalid by the state attorney general). Also in 1975, a Washington, DC, city council member introduced a marriage reform bill that called for the adoption of no-fault divorce and referred to spouses in gender-neutral terms in order to encourage a debate over marriage by same-sex couples.[3] In that same year, two members of the

Wisconsin Assembly introduced a bill that would permit same-sex couples to marry while decriminalizing sodomy and repealing a prohibition against the advertising of contraceptives.[4]

Different components of the LGBT movement had different reasons for focusing on marriage. The author of the 1953 essay worried that marriage threatened the sexual freedom enjoyed by at least some gay men at the time. For some members of the gay liberation movement in the early 1970s, the push for marriage represented an opportunity to question the sexist and heteronormative components of marriage.[5] As for liberal and reform-minded activists, rights to marriage represented a logical outgrowth of their demands for full and equal citizenship for lesbians and gay men.

Relationship-recognition advocacy during the 1980s emphasized smaller, practical steps that could be taken to provide limited forms of recognition, in particular through domestic partnership regimes. The focus on domestic partnerships was the result of different factors, including the growing clout of the social conservative movement, a political ascendancy that made marriage equality seem even less attainable than it had in the 1970s. In addition, some LGBT activists expressed concerns about expanding the institution of marriage, preferring instead to minimize its social, legal, and economic significance by pushing for alternative forms of recognition.[6]

Despite the fact that many of the movement's leading organizations did not pursue marriage during the 1980s, there remained a strong grassroots interest in marriage equality. Metropolitan Community Church ministers, for example, continued to marry dozens of same-sex couples every year. And during the 1987 gay rights March on Washington, several hundred same-sex couples participated in a collective marriage ceremony in front of the IRS headquarters as part of a rally demanding legal rights for LGBT people.[7]

The grassroots push for marriage equality also manifested itself, with significant historical consequences, in Hawai'i. In 1990, three same-sex couples, with the support of a small band of Honolulu gay rights activists, applied for marriage licenses. After officials denied the applications, the couples approached legal rights organizations, including the ACLU and the Lambda Legal Defense & Education Fund, seeking legal representation in order to constitutionally challenge the denials. The organizations, believing that a lawsuit would be futile, refused to represent them. The couples then turned to a local civil liberties attorney, who agreed to file a lawsuit on their behalf despite his lack of experience litigating LGBT rights cases.[8] To everyone's surprise, the Hawai'i Supreme Court in 1993 issued a ruling questioning the constitutionality of denying same-sex couples the opportunity to marry.[9]

After the court's ruling, social conservatives, energized by their victory in forcing President Bill Clinton to backtrack on his promise to lift the military's ban on lesbian, gay, and bisexual service members, began to sound the alarm about what was taking place on the island state. For their part, a growing number of LGBT rights organizations, facing both the surprising prospect of a possible victory in the Hawai'i courts and a growing conservative backlash against marital rights for same-sex couples, quickly turned the pursuit of marriage equality into their most important objective.

The struggle for marriage equality that began in earnest around the middle of the 1990s allowed the movement to humanize the discrimination faced by LGBT individuals in ways it had never been able to do previously. The focus on marriage put the spotlight on same-sex relationships in ways that other campaigns, such as the push for laws that prohibited discrimination on the basis of sexual orientation, had not. Through the process of demanding admission into the institution of marriage, the movement sought to establish that LGBT individuals were capable of entering and remaining in committed relationships—and, for those who had them, of raising children—in ways that did not differ fundamentally from the experiences of heterosexuals. Although some feminist and queer activists continued to criticize the embrace of marriage as an assimilationist and conservative move that would not help individuals who were not interested in, or would not benefit financially from, marriage, those voices were largely drowned out as many movement organizations, as well as an apparent majority of LGBT individuals, made marriage equality their top political priority.

The movement's prioritization of marriage was initially followed by many more defeats than victories. In Hawai'i, the progress in the courts was stymied by a constitutional amendment authorizing the legislature to define marriage as the union of a man and a woman. In addition, Congress in 1996, after conducting a vitriolic debate in which conservative legislators repeatedly claimed there was an urgent need to protect American marriages and families from LGBT people and their relationships, enacted the Defense of Marriage Act (DOMA). That law prohibited the federal government from recognizing the state-sanctioned marriages of same-sex couples (at a time when there were no such marriages). The statute also sought to exempt states from any obligation to recognize the validity of marriage licenses issued to same-sex couples by other jurisdictions. Between 1997 and 2000, fourteen states (including liberal ones such as California, Minnesota, and Washington) enacted laws prohibiting the recognition of marriages by same-sex couples.

While the marriage equality movement was experiencing a series of crushing political and legislative defeats, some of the nation's state supreme courts began accepting its constitutional claims. In 1999, the Vermont Supreme Court held that denying same-sex couples the rights and benefits that accompany marriage violated the state constitution.[10] The Vermont legislature responded the following year by enacting the nation's first civil union law, offering same-sex couples the same rights and benefits available to heterosexual married couples under state and local laws.

During the first decade of the new century, the question of whether same-sex couples should be permitted to marry became one of the mostly hotly contested political, social, and legal issues across the country. The Massachusetts Supreme Judicial Court in 2003 became the first state supreme court to hold that the government was required by a state constitution to offer same-sex couples the opportunity to marry.[11] Although the supreme courts of California, Connecticut, and Iowa soon followed with similar rulings,[12] the highest courts of Maryland, New York, and Washington upheld the constitutionality of their states' same-sex marriage bans.[13] Also during the '00s, voters in more than half the states approved constitutional amendments prohibiting the recognition of marriages by same-sex couples. One of those amendments, known as Proposition 8, received the support of a majority of California voters in 2008, bringing to an end the issuance of marriage licenses to same-sex couples that had followed the state supreme court's ruling of a few months earlier striking down the statutory marriage ban.

The fury of the political and legal debates over the issue of marriage equality only increased in the years that followed. However, several important events seemed to change the debates' dynamics, with equality proponents gaining the upper hand for the first time. It began in 2012 when President Barack Obama became the first sitting president to embrace equal marriage rights for same-sex couples. At around this time, polls showed that a majority of Americans, for the first time, supported granting same-sex couples the right to marry.[14] And marriage equality proponents, who had won only one of more than thirty ballot-box measures in the previous decade, prevailed in all four such measures—in Maine, Maryland, Minnesota, and Washington State—placed before voters in 2012.

The next year saw state legislatures in Delaware, Hawai'i, Illinois, Minnesota, and Rhode Island enact statutes granting same-sex couples the opportunity to marry. These political and legislative victories took place around the same time that the movement gained two crucial judicial victories before the Supreme Court. In the first case, the Court held that the supporters of California's Proposition 8 did not have standing to defend its constitutionality, a ruling that left in place the district court's finding that the measure violated the federal Constitution.[15] In the second case, the Court struck down the DOMA provision prohibiting the federal government from recognizing state-sanctioned marriages by same-sex couples on the ground that it violated the equality and liberty protections afforded by the federal Constitution.[16] Between that ruling in 2013 and the end of 2014, more than twenty federal courts, at both the trial and the appellate levels, struck down same-sex marriage bans. As a result, the number of states allowing same-sex couples to marry more than doubled in 2014, increasing from sixteen to thirty-five.

After same-sex marriage became a reality in most of the country, the Supreme Court in 2015 agreed to decide the question of whether the federal Constitution guarantees same-sex couples the opportunity to marry. The Court, in *Obergefell v. Hodges*, concluded that the fundamental right to marry applies in equal terms to same-sex couples. As the Court explained, laws that prohibited lesbians and gay men from marrying the individuals of their choice "are in essence unequal: same-sex couples are denied all the benefits afforded to opposite-sex couples and are barred from exercising a fundamental right."[17]

As this brief account shows, the LGBT movement concerned itself with the issue of marriage for several decades, and it made marriage equality its most important objective starting around the middle of the 1990s. In many ways, the movement has been so focused on, and driven by, the pursuit of marriage equality that there has been little time for discussing what the movement's priorities should be once the goal of nationwide marriage equality was achieved. This book brings together a diverse group of academics, consisting of political scientists, law professors, and a sociologist, to address questions related to LGBT rights following the recognition of same-sex marriages. The attainment of the long-sought goal of nationwide marriage equality provides a highly opportune moment to consider old and new challenges, as well as old and new possibilities, in promoting the political, legal, and social interests of sexual and gender-identity minorities.

It is a grave mistake to believe that the favorable resolution of the marriage equality question somehow represents the end of the struggle for LGBT equality in this country. To so think would be analogous to having believed, in the 1950s, that the Supreme Court's ruling in *Brown v. Board of Education* meant the end of any further need to grapple with questions of racial equality in the United States. It does not minimize or trivialize the importance of nationwide marriage equality to remind ourselves, for example, that LGBT individuals continue to be the subjects of violence and harassment in places ranging from schools to streets; that denying jobs, housing, and goods and services to sexual and gender-identity minorities remains legal in most states; and that, as of this writing, both houses of Congress (as well as most state legislatures) are controlled by the GOP—a political party that has traditionally been unsupportive of LGBT equality measures.

At the same time, however, the attainment of marriage equality across the country constitutes a monumental achievement by the LGBT movement. In many ways, there is no bigger or more important question facing the movement's leaders and constituents than how to respond to this historic success, an accomplishment that almost no one, a few years ago, predicted would happen as soon as 2015. That is the reason I have asked the contributors to this volume to grapple with the question of what marriage equality means for the future of LGBT rights.

In exploring what is likely to be next, Gary Mucciaroni, in chapter 1, argues that the attainment of marriage equality will not push the movement in a starkly different direction. Mucciaroni discusses several different factors that limit the movement's ability to change directions in significant ways, including its diversity and fragmentation; its organizational emphasis on professional advocacy over grassroots participation; and its identity-based civil rights orientation. Within those restraints, Mucciaroni envisions the movement, post–marriage equality, seeking to increase LGBT representation among elected and other government officials and placing greater emphasis on LGBT rights issues in other countries. He also argues that the movement would benefit from moving beyond issues of civil rights, and the *policing* of nondiscrimination obligations, in order to focus more explicitly on efforts to engage and educate institutions of civil society, such as corporations and schools, on the need to adopt policies that make LGBT individuals feel safe, secure, and respected as equals.

Donald P. Haider-Markel and Jami Taylor, in chapter 2, explore some of the challenges in *implementing* marriage equality, including resistance from some government officials; the enactment of religious-based exemptions allowing public officials and private individuals to refuse to facilitate marriages by same-sex couples; and the absence of legal antidiscrimination protections for sexual minorities and transgender individuals in most states. Haider-Markel and Taylor also discuss the possibility that the attainment of the marriage equality objective may leave progressives feeling less inclined to expend money and energy on LGBT issues. They also urge those in the movement to pay greater attention to the challenges and complexities raised by both HIV/AIDS and transgender issues. And, like Mucciaroni, they envision the American LGBT rights movement becoming more engaged with questions of international human rights and the treatment of sexual minorities in developing nations.

The divide between red and blue states is explored by Clifford Rosky in chapter 3. While legal equality is now a reality in most blue states, Rosky reminds us that such equality is still far off for LGBT individuals living in most red states, a phenomenon that remains true even though same-sex couples are now able to marry nationwide. He therefore urges that the movement turn "back to work" by prioritizing the passage of antidiscrimination laws. Rosky contends that such a prioritization will require two strategic shifts: first, an increased investment in local rather than national lobbying, and second, an increased investment in swing and red states. Rosky also flags two important questions that the movement must address when it goes "back to work": (1) whether to lobby for limited or expansive laws and (2) how to use litigation and lobbying in ways that support, rather than undermine, each other. In exploring these issues, Rosky counsels that lobbying must not entertain exemptions from antidiscrimination laws that apply only to claims brought by LGBT plaintiffs, and activists should reject proposed laws that fall short of what may be achieved through successful litigation under existing antidiscrimination laws.

In chapter 4, Nancy Knauer tackles the topic of LGBT elders and their interests, a subject that has received little attention from LGBT organizations and activists. Knauer notes that although the advent of nationwide marriage equality offers LGBT elders a much-needed measure of legal protection and security, the right to marry fails to address some of the most pressing issues facing such elders, including the legal fragility of their extended chosen families, their disproportionately high levels of financial insecurity, and their fear of encountering anti-LGBT bias across a wide range of senior services. Knauer also uses LGBT elder issues to make two broader points about the nature and future of LGBT rights advocacy. First, while emphasizing the similarities between sexual minorities and heterosexuals can be helpful in some settings, it fails to address disparities between the two groups. As Knauer explains, there are several crucial characteristics that distinguish LGBT elders, including the fact that they are more likely to be single, to live alone, and to be estranged from their families of origin, while being less likely to have children. Second, Knauer points out that LGBT elders challenge the strong claims of shared identity that undergird the contemporary LGBT rights movement. Many members of the older generation, for example, do not identify as homosexual or gay, much less as "out and proud." As a result, she argues, they stand as living examples of the historically contingent nature of LGBT identity.

While Knauer discusses the elderly, Nancy Polikoff, in chapter 5, focuses on children. Polikoff delineates the ways in which marriage equality advocates emphasized the needs and interests of primarily white and well-to-do lesbian and gay families while ignoring those of LGBT parents of color. Polikoff argues that because same-sex marriage advocacy overlooked the family circumstances of the majority, and the most disadvantaged, of children raised by gay and lesbian parents, future advocacy must put the needs of those children at the forefront. She also questions the assumption by many in the marriage equality movement that the recognition of same-sex marriages will help solve the legal parentage questions arising from the formation of LGBT families. She urges advocates not to conflate marriage with parentage. By focusing so intently on marriage, advocates have ignored the fact, for example, that children sometimes have two parents who are not interested in marriage. Polikoff also warns that there is no guarantee, post–marriage equality, that legislatures or courts, especially in conservative states, will allow nonbiological lesbian mothers to gain parentage rights through marital presumption laws. The focus on marriage rather than on parentage, Polikoff argues, has created troubling blind spots for the LGBT movement, blind spots that can be removed only if advocates recognize the need to separate parentage questions from those of marriage.

I argue in chapter 6 that the imminent attainment of the marriage equality goal offers the LGBT movement the opportunity to push for reforms that reduce the legal salience of distinct gender and sexual identities. A growing number of Americans, especially young ones, are becoming increasingly comfortable with the idea of fluid and changing notions of gender and sexuality. I contend, therefore, that the movement should prioritize encouraging the state to adopt laws and policies that recognize and protect gender and sexual fluidity and multiplicities. This objective can be pursued through political and legal campaigns that, for example, seek (1) to promote an understanding of sex and sexual-orientation antidiscrimination law that is unmoored from the protection of distinct identities and (2) to remove one of the last gender-based barriers to accessing public spaces by ending gender segregation in bathrooms and other similar facilities. I argue that these types of objectives represent reforms that are not grounded in the need to protect individuals on the basis of distinct—and ostensibly fixed and static—gender and sexual identities. Instead, the attainment of these goals would promote the equality rights of all individuals regardless of how (or even whether) they identify, or of how society identifies them, along gender and sexuality continuums.

In chapter 7, Joseph Fischel argues that, despite the contentions of marriage equality proponents to the contrary, the push for same-sex marriage has opened the door for the legal recognition of polygamous marriages. Rather than denying the likelihood or advisability of such recognition, Fischel urges the movement to embrace it as part of its commitment to relational autonomy, which he defines as the capability to codetermine intimate and/or sexual relations. In Fischel's view, the movement should shift perspectives from an identitarian to a relational one, from LGBT equality to relational autonomy, and from individualized discrimination to social transformation. In calling, in effect, for LGBT rights without the "LGBT" part, Fischel encourages the movement to offer ethically defensible approaches to pressing policy issues that it has largely sidestepped or ignored, including sexual violence and sex education. In the case of sexual violence, Fischel calls for a more nuanced approach that moves beyond demonization, ostracization, or trivialization and focuses on how sexual assaults destroy the capability of persons to codetermine their sexual and intimate relationships. He also argues that if advocates approach questions of sex education and youth sexuality from a relational autonomy perspective, they would avoid the current desexualization and singularization of the victimized gay teen while empowering and enabling young people to be skilled sexual decision makers.

Russell Robinson, in chapter 8, contends that there are important differences between lesbians and gay men in matters of relationships and monogamy, differences that have been largely ignored by both scholars and advocates. Robinson argues that the push for LGBT rights, and in particular the need to present a unified and sympathetic "gay and lesbian" subject to the courts and public in order to attain marriage equality, has led many community leaders to "closet" gender differences. On the positive side, Robinson believes that the success of the marriage equality campaign may offer greater opportunities for admitting and engaging divergent gender patterns in sexual minority communities. But he also worries that the attainment of marriage equality may lead to a renewed attack on LGBT people, gay men in particular, whose sexual relationships fall outside of traditional and monogamous ideals.

While Robinson tackles questions of gender, Katherine Franke, in chapter 9, grapples with those of race. Franke warns that same-sex couples today face the challenges of enduring bigotry; as with emancipated black people who gained the right to marry in the nineteenth century, the types of highly problematic justifications for the longstanding exclusion of sexual minorities from civil marriage will survive the repeal of that exclusion and fuel a backlash against the new rights holders. Franke argues, in other words, that homophobia, like racism, will have a significant postmarriage afterlife. In doing so, she urges same-sex couples to prepare for the ways in which access to marriage licenses will lead to new forms of state discipline and regulation driven by prejudice. Franke also points out that what the marriage equality cases have done for gay people has not been, and cannot be, accomplished for individuals bearing the signature of racial inferiority. In the marriage cases, lesbians and gay men have accomplished a kind of rebranding of what it means to be "homosexual"—they have been awarded a type of "dignity of self-definition" that law and culture still deny to African Americans. Finally, Franke cautions that the members of the gay community who have succeeded, through marriage equality gains, in lifting a badge of inferiority that marked them are those who are willing or able to present their relationships as respectable. The process of redeeming the social reputation of "good gays," Franke argues, depends on a contrast with "bad gays" who do not want to marry or discipline their sexual selves into a tidy couple form.

The United States, of course, is not the first country to grant same-sex couples the opportunity to marry nationwide. The LGBT rights movements in those other nations have gone through a process that the movement in this country is now embarking on: addressing and responding to the challenges facing sexual and gender-identity minorities in a post–marriage equality society. Although every country has social, political, and legal characteristics that impact differently on LGBT issues, we can learn from each other's experiences. For this reason, the book ends with chapters written by experts on three countries—Canada, Holland, and France—that preceded the United States in recognizing the need for nationwide marriage equality.

David Rayside, in chapter 10, explains that there is some evidence that LGBT activism in Canada post–marriage equality has declined, especially in the ability of movement groups to mobilize grassroots activism on a large scale. But he cautions that factors other than the attainment of nationwide marriage rights in 2005 probably contributed to the decline. These factors include the difficulty of sustaining volunteer-based groups over long periods of time, the diffuse character of the Canadian LGBT movement, and the increasing proportion of LGBT advocacy taking place in largely disconnected institutional settings (such as government departments, major political parties, and the courts). Rayside also explains that movement groups, since the attainment of marriage equality, have paid increased attention to other issues such as the need for greater inclusivity for sexual and gender-identity minorities in schools. He also finds that sexual-minority communities historically on the movement's margins, such as transgender people and LGBT members of the large diasporic communities in Canada's major cities, are increasingly finding ways to be heard. Finally, Rayside explains that the postmarriage movement is grappling with competing rights claims on sexual and religious grounds while paying greater attention to the challenges facing sexual minorities in other regions of the world. Although most of the LGBT issues that Rayside identifies were already rising in prominence during the push for marital rights in Canada, the expanded rights regime that accompanied marriage equality has increased their profile by exposing ongoing disparities for LGBT people in that country.

Jan Willem Duyvendak, in chapter 11, explains that the attainment of marriage equality in Holland in 2001, and the accompanying further "normalization" of homosexuality, has had two troubling effects. First, it has allowed political parties and politicians, across the political spectrum from the far Right to the far Left, to use acceptance of homosexuality as an ideological benchmark to test whether other minorities, most prominently Muslim immigrants, can ever be "truly Dutch." Duyvendak explores how, from this perspective, Muslim immigration is conceived as a threat to the stability of the Dutch progressive moral order and to Dutch cultural and sexual liberties. Gay rights and gender equality have thus become a normative framework that helps to shape a critique of Islam and multiculturalism. Second, the normalization of homosexuality has led lesbians and gay men to embrace heteronormative discourses and presentations that minimize overt expressions of sexuality and gender variance. Duyvendak points out how this mainstreaming of homosexuality leaves ongoing problems, such as the high rates of suicide attempts by LGBT youth and antigay violence in Holland, unaddressed and unchallenged.

Finally, Bruno Perreau, in chapter 12, explains that the 2013 law allowing same-sex couples to marry in France left in place many different forms of discrimination against LGBT people, including the absence of an automatic presumption that same-sex married couples are related to each other's children, a ban on surrogacy, and an insistence on medicalizing the ability of transgender individuals to legally change their gender. These policies, when coupled with the Socialist Party's tepid support for sexual-minority rights, have encouraged the continuation of the fierce resistance by religious and social conservatives to LGBT equality that took place in the months leading up to the adoption of the 2013 marriage law. Perreau details the chronology of that resistance, showing that its manifestations and motivations after the enactment of the marriage equality law are essentially the same as they were before. He also argues that the resistance is being fueled by the fear that the French society is embracing the teachings of so-called gender theory, which, in ostensibly calling for the denaturalization of sexual categories, seeks to destabilize the "traditional French family." Perreau contends that the repeated denunciations of gender theory that are part of the political resistance to LGBT rights are saturated with nationalist overtones that contain racist, anti-Semitic, and anti-American elements. He also argues that political progressives should discard the very notion of a "postmarriage" LGBT politics and the mythology of the "battle won."

It is, of course, difficult to predict with exact certainty what the priorities and challenges will be for LGBT organizations and activists in the decades to come. It is my hope, however, that the diverse perspectives, ideas, and insights contained in this book will help those who care about the rights of sexual and gender-identity minorities explore objectives and overcome obstacles in a post–marriage equality society.

NOTES

1  E. B. Saunders, "Marriage License or Just License?" *ONE*, August 1953, pp. 10–12.

2  Jones v. Hallahan, 501 S.W.2d 588 (Ky. Ct. App. 1973); Baker v. Nelson, 191 N.W.2d 185 (Minn. 1971); Singer v. Hara, 522 P.2d 1187 (Wash. Ct. App. 1974).

3  Jason Pierceson, *Same-Sex Marriage in the United States: The Road to the Supreme Court* (Lanham, MD: Rowman & Littlefield, 2013), pp. 35–36.

4  Andrea Rottmann, *Passing Gay Rights in Wisconsin, 1967–1983*, Thesis, Freie Universität Berlin (2010), p. 44.

5  Michael Boucai, "Glorious Precedents: When Gay Marriage Was Radical," 27 *Yale Journal of Law and Humanities* 1 (2015).

6  *See, e.g.*, Paula Ettelbrick, "Since When Is Marriage a Path to Liberation?" *OUT/LOOK*, Fall 1989, p. 9, reprinted in *Cases and Materials on Sexual Orientation and the Law*, William B. Rubenstein, Carlos A. Ball, Jane S. Schacter, and Douglas NeJaime, eds. (St Paul: West, 5th ed. 2014), p. 800.

7  Amin Ghaziani, *The Dividends of Dissent: How Conflict and Culture Work in Lesbian and Gay Marches on Washington* (Chicago: University of Chicago Press, 2008), pp. 120–21. In his study of relationship-recognition advocacy in California during the 1980s and 1990s, Douglas NeJaime found that activists consistently used the government's failure to recognize same-sex relationships as marital as a main justification for demanding that same-sex couples be given the opportunity to register as domestic partners. Douglas NeJaime, "Before Marriage: The Unexplored History of Nonmarital Recognition and Its Impact on Marriage," 102 *California Law Review* 87 (2014).

8  Carlos A. Ball, *From the Closet to the Courtroom: Five LGBT Rights Lawsuits That Have Changed Our Nation* (Boston: Beacon, 2010), pp. 165–66.

9  Baehr v. Lewin, 852 P.2d 44 (Haw. 1993).

10  Baker v. State, 744 A.2d 864 (Vt. 1999).

11  Goodridge v. Department of Public Health, 798 N.E.2d 941 (Mass. 2003).

12  In re Marriage Cases, 183 P.3d 384 (Ca. 2008); Kerrigan v. Commissioner of Public Health, 957 A.2d 407 (Conn. 2008); Varnum v. Brien, 763 N.W.2d 862 (Iowa 2009).

13  Conaway v. Deane, 932 A.2d 571 (Md. 2007); Hernandez v. Robles, 855 N.E.2d 1 (N.Y. 2006); Andersen v. King County, 138 P.3d 963 (Wash. 2006).

14  In 1996, Gallup found that only 27 percent of Americans believed that same-sex marriages should be legally recognized. In 2010, a majority of Americans, for the first time, told Gallup they supported the legal recognition of same-sex marriages. Gallup polls taken in later years also found that a majority of Americans supported marriage equality. *See* Jeffrey M. Jones, *Same-Sex Marriage Support Solidifies above 50% in U.S.*, Gallup Politics (May 13, 2013), http://www.gallup.com/poll/162398/sex-marriage-support-solidifies-above.aspx, accessed April 2015.

15  Hollingsworth v. Perry, 133 S.Ct. 2652 (2013).

16  United States v. Windsor, 133 S.Ct. 2675 (2013).

17  Obergefell v. Hodges, 135 S.Ct. 2584, 2604 (2015).

PART I

The American LGBT Movement after Marriage Equality

1

# Will Victory Bring Change?

*A Mature Social Movement Faces the Future*

GARY MUCCIARONI

The elimination of the remaining barriers to same-sex marriage offers an appropriate opportunity to contemplate the future of the LGBT rights movement in the United States. Undoubtedly, attaining marriage equality across the entire nation constitutes a striking achievement for the movement, particularly given how quixotic such a goal seemed even a decade ago. For better or worse, marriage in the United States grants spouses an important legal and social status and a bundle of rights and benefits. Marriage elevates the cultural legitimacy of gay and lesbian people and improves the material condition of many of their lives.[1] For the movement, the achievement of marriage equality frees up a good many resources—time, money, and organization—that it can devote to other endeavors. It may also provide a measure of political momentum that savvy movement leaders might harness to achieve additional political victories.

The questions that I address in this chapter are as follows: What difference does the attainment of marriage equality make for the future of the LGBT movement? Will it lead the movement to strike out on a different path than the one it has been following? What are the possibilities and the likelihood for major changes in the movement's mission, goals, and strategies?

The attainment of marriage equality marks the beginning of the end of a decades-long effort to achieve legal equality for gays and lesbians. The attainment of full formal legal equality could theoretically open the possibility for the movement to shift from civil rights as its dominant mission to an alternative. My central point is that we should temper our expectations about the impact of marriage on the future course of the

LGBT movement. In "The 18th Brumaire of Napoleon Bonaparte," Karl Marx famously wrote, "Men make their own history, but they do not make it as they please."[2] Marx was calling attention specifically to the weight of history upon those who act in the present. Marriage equality will not propel the movement forward or mark a turning point in the way that World War II, the Stonewall rebellion, or the AIDS crisis did. It will not constitute a "critical juncture" in the movement's history— putting the movement on a new trajectory that it would not follow in its absence. I expect the movement will continue to pursue many of the same goals that it has in the past, but pursue them somewhat differently and with different emphases. It may change its priorities and activities, but the changes will be more or less consistent with the movement's history rather than a sharp break from it.

This chapter is a cautionary note for movement observers who might see the present time as auspicious for the movement to strike out in dramatic new directions as well as for movement leaders and activists who will face strong incentives to resist fundamental change. Before activists and scholars opine about where the movement should go once it attains marriage equality, we need to be realistic about what magnitude and type of change in goals and strategies are possible. Thinking about what is likely to happen, rather than just what advocates may want to happen, forces us to confront the constraints on the LGBT movement. Some of these constraints are internal and deeply entrenched; others arise out of the broader social and political context in which the movement is embedded and over which it has little control. At the same time, continuing down the same path that the movement has been on entails opportunity costs. Specifically, if movement leaders and activists continue an emphasis on achieving, preserving, and enforcing civil rights, they may neglect education and institutional reform as alternative strategies that may be more effective in improving the lives of LGBT people than the civil rights model. These include educating the public and those who manage and lead business, nonprofit institutions, and other organizations about homophobia and heterosexism and pressing for reforms of organizational cultures and practices.

This chapter proceeds in two parts. The first takes stock of the major constraints that will block or slow down any large-scale transformation of the movement's goals and strategies. The second discusses five main tasks that I expect will occupy the postmarriage movement: (1) completing the unfinished civil rights agenda that will most likely remain after marriage is achieved, particularly adoption of the Employment Nondiscrimination Act (ENDA) and transgender rights; (2) guarding against a backlash from LGBT-rights opponents who threaten to erode the movement's victories; (3) increasing the number of openly gay and lesbian public officials; (4) devoting greater attention to the diffusion of LGBT rights across the globe; and (5) enlarging efforts to educate the public and reform the cultures and practices of civil society institutions.

The fifth task is the most distinct from the other four because it offers the chance to more fully embrace a "change-the-culture" model in place of (or in addition to) the established "civil rights model." The change-the-culture model deemphasizes regulation, litigation, and the coercive powers of the state in favor of education, persuasion, and direct engagement with citizens and those who lead and manage major institutions. Rather than policing individuals and institutions to do the right thing, changing the culture induces institutions to embrace equality as an expected standard of behavior. Enforcement of formal equality gives way to the *praxis* of normative equality.

It should go without saying that predicting the future evolution and fortunes of a social movement is a hazardous undertaking. The unexpected emergence of same-sex marriage as the dominant issue on the LGBT agenda and the dramatic progress it has made over the past decade attest to the limitation of our powers of prediction. Nevertheless, reason and evidence suggest that some outcomes are more likely to occur than others. We can find some clues about where we may be headed by looking closely at the LGBT movement's own history, the experiences of other social movements in the United States, and what LGBT movements are doing in nations that have already achieved full legal equality.

## The Constraints on Change

One reason for skepticism that the attainment of marriage will open the door to a significant change in the movement's mission, agenda, or strategies is that attainment of the movement's other longstanding goals is independent of the attainment of marriage. The issues presently on the movement's agenda, many having been there a long time, will not suddenly disappear or be resolved. One might think that policymakers who are willing to adopt same-sex marriage would easily agree to laws proscribing employment discrimination for gays, lesbians, and transgender people, but this is not the case. Similarly, marriage should have only a modest impact on how smoothly openly gay servicemen and women integrate into the military or whether rates of bullying and violence toward LGBT youth decline. Political dynamics and institutional venues vary across LGBT issues in ways that influence outcomes.[3]

Perhaps the greatest constraint on the LGBT movement will be its organizational structure, mission, and level of maturity. Four key features of the movement will shape and limit its future: (1) the diversity and fragmentation of the movement; (2) the movement's organizational emphasis on professional advocacy over grassroots participation; (3) its identity-based civil rights orientation; and (4) the likely leveling off of its organizational growth as it matures as a movement.

A number of writers have pointed out that the LGBT "movement" is more aptly conceived as several "movements," each one emerging at different points in its history and having distinctive impulses. LGBT organizations span a spectrum that runs from radical and liberationist to decidedly conservative, with a broad array of organizations built to serve particular constituencies, pursue particular causes and goals, and employ particular strategies and tactics.[4] Of course, the movement has had a central political tendency throughout most of its history. Over the long haul, it has always maintained or returned to a left-of-center, assimilationist equilibrium. Yet, even within this liberal mainstream, no single organization or cadre of leaders has exerted continuous control over the movement's present or future direction.

The movement's fragmentation and pluralism arise out of the fabric of American society and politics. The United States is a large, socially diverse nation. Diversity guarantees that any LGBT "movement" will consist of a multiplicity of diverse interests and opinions divided along demographic, political, and geographic lines, limiting the capacity for leaders at the top to develop a set of common goals and strategies. Different interests and opinions naturally arise because LGBT individuals experience discrimination and other harms in a variety of institutional and social contexts.

Further, the structure and strategies of the LGBT "movement" mirror the fragmentation and diversity of U.S. political institutions. The different levels and branches of government encourage the development of scores of national, state, and local organizations and chapters as well as strategies geared alternatively toward litigation, lobbying, protest, and electoral activities. Finally, like other social movements, large, established LGBT umbrella organizations often underrepresent and marginalize the viewpoints and interests of minorities. The movement reproduces the class, racial, and gender inequality found throughout American society. Thus, racial and ethnic groups, the transgender population, and LGBT constituencies with particular grievances (e.g., gays and lesbians serving in the military), feeling excluded or underserved, have formed their own organizations out of frustration. While diversity can produce fresh ideas and perspectives and fragmentation means that the different constituency groups under the LGBT umbrella have some representation, it makes coordination and development of a broad consensus more difficult.

A second feature of LGBT movement organizations is that they place greater emphasis on advocacy than on building inclusive, participatory grassroots organizations. Critics complain that LGBT leaders and activists assume that they know the priorities of ordinary LGBT individuals and proceed to devote greater proportions of their resources to lobbying, litigating, educating, and advertising than to grassroots organizing at the state and local levels.[5] The lack of opportunities for participation and the focus on advocacy for issues that the leadership deems are important contributes further to the fragmentation of the movement. Groups that feel underrepresented exit and form new organizations rather than work within the established ones. Here again, this situation is not peculiar to the LGBT movement, but reflects a broader systemic trend in American politics that has occurred over the past decades. The decline of civic engagement in the United States has transformed civil society organizations from venues for grassroots participation into professionally managed lobbying organizations that collect membership dues but ask little else of their members in terms of their participation.[6] The problem is not simply that the movement is internally more elitist and less democratic, but that it is not cultivating a key resource of any social movement—the ability to mobilize the masses at times when such mobilization is needed.

Third, today's LGBT movement is predominantly an identity-based civil rights movement. The African American and women's movements that preceded it, or with which it was contemporaneous, deeply influenced its formative period of development. From these movements, it took its identity-based approach to organization, its central mission to combat the evils of discrimination and violence, and its strategies of litigation, legislative lobbying, and electioneering. While organizing around identity provides a measure of unity of purpose that helps to mitigate some of the effects of diversity and organizational fragmentation, it also means that the LGBT movement is detached from broader social movements and reform goals and reinforces its dominant orientation toward civil rights rather than facilitating its adoption of other approaches to social change.

Same-sex marriage itself is a clear example of these enduring features of LGBT politics. It obviously fits into the identity-based, civil rights template. While marriage has the support of most gays and lesbians, some groups feel that it is irrelevant to their lives or that it perpetuates broader inequalities in society.[7] It reached the agenda when a handful of same-sex couples and legal strategists brought lawsuits before sympathetic judges in far-flung, gay-friendly states like Hawai'i and Vermont.[8] Neither "the movement" as a collectivity nor the leaders of any major LGBT-rights organizations decided that marriage should be high on the agenda. (Indeed, many of those organizations were reluctant to give same-sex marriage the prominent agenda status that it would come to occupy.)

Finally, we need to consider that the LGBT movement is in a highly mature stage of its development. It is almost certainly past the point when its organizations will grow significantly. Once the salient and popular issue of marriage has passed, the movement's size may even contract. Research by Nownes on the transgender movement, which is younger than the gay and lesbian movement, suggests that this has already occurred. As predicted by "density dependence" theory, movements experience robust growth as their causes gain legitimacy, but once they reach a certain level of density, organizations begin to compete with one another for finite resources. Organizational growth levels off and may decline.[9] Assuming that the entire LGBT movement has reached the leveling-off point, this means either that it will be harder for new and more dynamic organizations to emerge and compete effectively with older established ones or that the threat of competition will induce the older organizations to reinvent themselves by launching innovative initiatives and projects.

## Whither the LGBT Movement?

Having sketched how many of the LGBT movement's basic features are grounded in its history and the broader social and political constraints in which it is embedded, we are ready to entertain the question of what the movement's postmarriage future might look like. Before we turn to the likely course that the movement will follow, however, let us first consider one path that the movement will probably *not* follow.

A well-established critique of the mainstream of the American LGBT-rights movement—what I call "the social democratic wish"—is that its identity-based, civil rights approach narrows and limits its potential for building a broader, more inclusive movement and a more ambitious public policy agenda. The identity-based focus isolates the movement from other groups and movements in society based upon race, class, gender, and age. The civil rights approach fails to address a variety of forms of inequality rooted in the economy, other institutions, and power relations in a variety of social settings that are impervious to civil rights remedies. These critics call upon the movement's leaders and members to reconstitute a broader organizational vision by becoming or joining a more radical and inclusive social democratic movement, advocating more far-reaching egalitarian goals and social welfare policies that go beyond civil rights.[10] Proponents of this view have renewed these calls in light of the expected accomplishment of marriage equality.[11]

How feasible and likely would it be for the movement to refashion itself in a more social democratic image? Such aspirations should not be dismissed out of hand. For one, much of the civil rights agenda has been attained (or is not far out of reach). For another, social attitudes toward gays and lesbians have changed dramatically in recent decades. Less need exists today for continuing down the same civil rights path. While the movement will always have to be vigilant that the gains that it has made remain secure and make sure that public officials enforce civil rights laws, the objective need for the movement to be as consumed with the attainment of identity-based civil rights goals will surely lessen. At the same time, the worsening of economic inequality and persistence of unemployment mean that the concerns of gay and lesbian citizens increasingly mirror those of the rest of the U.S. population.

Second, LGBT individuals are remarkably politically homogenous and receptive to social democratic appeals. Compared to the rest of the population, they are overwhelmingly liberal in their policy preferences across the board, including policies that have little to do with civil rights.[12] They are also among the most reliable supporters of the Democratic Party, which is, for better or worse, the closest the United States has to a social democratic party of any political significance at the national level. The ideological homogeneity and partisan unity within the gay movement is critical because it acts as a counterweight to the splintering effects of class, race, and gender, which cut across the LGBT population and, unlike the African American and women's movements, might be expected to make it more difficult to gain consensus on redistributionist goals and policies that would benefit more than the LGBT population.

The greatest impediment to moving the LGBT movement in the direction of a more inclusive, social democratic movement is the movement's own established organizations and leaders. Most organizations seek to maintain themselves by avoiding what they perceive as risky, radical experiments. Proponents of the social democratic wish need to take more seriously the powerful forces that militate against large-scale changes in organizations. One source of resistance is "path dependency"—societies and the institutions within them tend to stay on the same path because the costs of getting off a path and onto an alternative one outweigh the perceived benefits.[13] Getting off the established path is possible, but not easy or typical, and not fully under the control of anyone. Consistent with the logic of path dependency is a great degree of social psychological research that suggests that people are risk averse (they discount the promise of future gains and overestimate the prospects for future losses from change). As a result, organizations are far more likely to stick with the devil they know than switch to the devil they do not know.[14]

The LGBT movement emerged as an identity movement—gays and lesbians rose up because society failed to accept their sexual orientation and gender expression, not because they were getting the short end of the economic stick. More affluent gays and lesbians might have been accorded a bit more freedom and equality than their less affluent peers, but all were vulnerable to the social opprobrium directed at people who were the least bit open about their same-sex orientation or who transgressed gender norms. The identity-based focus and civil rights mission has been highly successful in contributing to the growth of LGBT political organizations and in advancing formal legal equality. By providing a measure of common ground for diverse constituencies within the movement to rally behind, and enabling movement leaders to hone sharply focused demands for policy changes, it has attracted large membership bases and other resources and has helped the movement gain political stature and policy breakthroughs. Rights-based claims are potent for minorities because they rest on legal principles that are more or less inviolable rather than on the ability to bring political resources to bear. In addition, civil rights causes can be framed in ways that resonates with broader values in American culture like ensuring individual freedom and treating individuals on the basis of their merit and achievement rather than stereotypes and ascriptive social characteristics. Civil rights are consistent with the principle of equal opportunity, which has more support in the United States than equality of outcome.[15]

For these reasons, organizational leaders are unlikely to abandon approaches that they consider productive and that fit into their existing repertoire of goals, strategies, and tactics. The leaders of these organizations believe that they occupy an important organizational niche in the American political system and that they would have to compete with an even wider array of organizations if they emphasized a broader agenda. While LGBT voters may support social democratic positions on most issues, they may be most moved to provide the movement with resources when leaders make identity-based appeals. Leaders may perceive that turning in more social democratic directions will "dilute their message" and risk the alienation of more affluent, libertarian donors.

Even if these barriers to the emergence of a more social democratic LGBT movement did not exist, we must ask ourselves, "What results would we expect an embrace of a social democratic agenda to produce?" Gays and lesbians are a small minority of the population. A social democratic movement in the United States only has a chance to succeed when millions of workers, the vast majority of whom do not identify as LGBT, join labor unions and engage in political mobilization to demand greater economic and social justice. Social democracy is weak in the LGBT movement because it is weak in the United States. In the absence of a much broader social democratic movement, it seems unlikely that an LGBT movement that embraced social democracy would be any more successful in improving the lives of gays and lesbians than the present one is.

In the absence of a fundamental shift in the movement's vision and mission, what will occupy the movement in the coming years? Given the movement's substantial constraints, it will continue to do much of what it has been doing, but with important adjustments in its specific activities and gravitation toward newer "growth areas" of advocacy and representation. LGBT social-movement organizations will direct their efforts toward five major tasks: completing the civil rights agenda; guarding against new or renewed threats from opponents; increasing descriptive representation; helping to diffuse LGBT rights abroad; and deemphasizing civil rights in favor of alternative strategies, such as education, for changing institutions and organizational cultures.

## 1. The Unfinished Rights Agenda and Enforcement

### Completing the Rights Agenda

Now that the marriage equality objective has been achieved, what about the rest of the LGBT civil rights agenda? The overwhelming attention paid to same-sex marriage has eclipsed other civil rights goals and perhaps even slowed progress in attaining them. In 2003, when thirteen states offered gays and lesbians protection against employment discrimination, only Massachusetts permitted same-sex marriage. In 2014, nineteen states permitted same-sex marriage, only two fewer than the number of states that provide protections on the job. Many states, especially the more conservative ones, remain without hate crimes legislation and basic civil rights protections for gays and lesbians. Ironically, the movement's success in winning public support for protection against hate crimes and employment nondiscrimination has diminished the prospects for further progress in getting them approved at the state level. The lack of controversy over hate crimes and nondiscrimination measures reduces the salience of those issues, which in turn makes it easier for state legislatures to ignore them and cater to the intensely held preferences of conservative and religious anti-LGBT groups.[16]

The LGBT movement achieved marriage equality nationwide before it has attained employment nondiscrimination. The Employment Non-Discrimination Act (ENDA), first introduced four decades ago, will not become law until the Democrats retake control of both chambers of Congress and a Democratic president occupies the White House. ENDA will probably generate more partisan conflict in the future if, as expected, proponents of the legislation broaden it to include a more sweeping nondiscrimination policy that covers not just employment but also education, housing, and other domains.[17] Prospects for Democratic control of the House of Representatives are very dim for the foreseeable future given gerrymandered House districts and increased "residential sorting"—liberals clustering in urban areas and conservatives spread across the rural heartland—which favor the Republican Party in House elections. It will take a "national tide" that sweeps a large number of Republican incumbents out of office, while still keeping the Senate and White House under Democratic control, before ENDA's passage is as-sured. Another possibility, though much less certain given the continued strength of social conservatives in the Republican Party, is the election of a moderate and pragmatic Republican president with a Democratic Congress, which also could approve ENDA.

## Transgender Issues

The spread of rights and protections for transgender individuals has accelerated in the past decade. Nineteen states have fully inclusive LGBT employment nondiscrimination laws (compared to twenty-one states that cover sexual orientation). Half of the states permit indi-viduals who have undergone medical treatment for transitioning to amend their birth certificates. The federal hate crimes law passed in 2009 covers gender identity. The number of municipalities that afford civil rights protection for gender identity had risen to 154 as of 2011, and many are among the largest jurisdictions in the country.[18] The federal courts and Equal Employment Opportunity Commission have used Title VII to protect transgender employees from employment discrimination.[19]

Still, transgender equality is very far from realization and lags behind the diffusion of rights for gays and lesbians. Congress excluded gender identity from the Americans with Disabilities Act and courts have failed to recognize gender identity in employment nondiscrimination cases (in *Ulane v. Eastern Airlines*[20] and *Oiler v. Winn-Dixie*)[21] in 1984 and 2002 and other key cases (*Littleton v. Prange*[22] and *In re Estate of Gardiner*)[23] in 1999 and 2002. In some states and localities, opponents have used objections to transgender rights to block LGBT laws; in others, LGB laws have advanced without transgender inclusion.[24] Even more elusive have been policy changes that make it easier for transgender individuals to access health care for treatments related to their transitioning.

Given the challenges facing the transgender movement, the degree of progress that has been attained is noteworthy. Yet, the movement is hobbled by the minuscule size of the transgender population, its lack of resources, the stigma attached to transgender people and widespread ignorance of their issues, and the dominance of LGB concerns within the LGBT movement. Transgender-specific organizations have emerged and proliferated because of a lack of responsiveness within the LGBT movement to their demands. At the same time, the group desperately needs its LGB allies. Since the late 1990s, as transgender demands have gained legitimacy and as LGB organizations have sought to attract new members and resources, many LGB organizations have "added the T." (American organizations are ahead of the U.K.'s Stonewall in this respect.) Whether competition between transgender-specific and LGBT organizations will help propel progress for the transgender movement, or impede it, remains to be seen.

The United States is not exceptional in being further behind in advancing the interests of transgender individuals than in advancing those of gays and lesbians. Egale Canada Human Rights Trust and other Canadian organizations, for example, have continued to fight for the inclusion of gender identity and expression in employment nondiscrimination and hate crimes laws at the provincial and federal levels long after they achieved marriage and the full complement of rights for gays and lesbians.[25] Advocates for transgender interests may hope that the attainment of marriage equality and other civil rights goals for gays and lesbians will clear the way for LGBT organizations to pay greater attention to their agenda. This may not happen, however. For example, the attainment of marriage equality in Massachusetts led MassEquality to turn to assist in campaigns for marriage equality in other states rather than devote greater attention to the transgender population's concerns. Once the LGBT movement achieves full equality for gays and lesbians domestically, it may channel more resources to the international movement for gay rights or to other LGB-focused issues domestically. What is certain is that the struggle for transgender rights remains far from over.[26]

### After the Laws and Court Rulings: Enforcement

We should expect the movement's organizations to focus less upon on policy advocacy and adoption and more on monitoring and enforcing the laws in effect. As the United States moves closer to full legal equality, LGBT organizations will naturally move toward protecting what the movement has achieved, making sure that existing laws are faithfully executed, and amending statutory language, where needed, to strengthen legal guarantees. Civil rights laws may fail to deliver on their promise of affording effective protection against discrimination for a host of reasons, including poorly drafted statutes, misunderstandings in the application of new laws or concepts, or a "judicial backlash" against civil rights claims that stems from viewing them as demands for special treatment rather than demands for equality.[27] Whatever the case, LGBT groups will play a key role in monitoring enforcement and working with legislatures, courts, and agencies to strengthen statutes, regulations, and judicial interpretations. Since attaining marriage equality, Canada's Egale, for example, intervenes before Canadian courts in specific complaints of discrimination from LGBT individuals as complainants' legal representative or in support of the complaints. It pressures and advises government ministers and others in charge of enforcing laws against discrimination, hate crimes, and bullying to draft effective regulations and budget sufficient resources for this purpose. It demands action to fill gaps in the coverage of existing laws and regulations, such as the recognition of foreigners who have same-sex partnership statuses from other nations and Canadian same-sex married couples living abroad.[28]

## 2. Guarding against New and Renewed Threats

The recent experiences of African Americans and women should dispel any misapprehension that society marches toward ever greater freedom and equality without setbacks and reversals. Civil rights struggles that culminate in complete political and legal victories in one period may have to be refought at a later time. While a wholesale return to the status quo ante (for example, when same-sex marriages were banned through-out the United States) seems very unlikely, gay rights opponents will look for ways to erode the movement's gains, or contain the effects of future victories, particularly in more conservative areas of the country. The lessons from other social movements are instructive. The right wing has launched successful challenges to affirmative action to redress racial disparities in employment and academia and, more unexpectedly, has renewed its efforts to discourage African Americans and others from exercising their right to vote. We have seen a similar slowdown, if not reversal, in the advancement of women's rights, specifically reproductive rights and freedoms, medical leave, and pay equity.[29]

How serious these threats become and how well the movement ad-dresses them is contingent. Sociologists often call attention to the "po-litical opportunity structure." The fortunes of the movement will depend upon a host of political factors over which it has limited control, includ-ing whether public opinion continues to grow increasingly accepting and supportive of LGBT causes, the electoral fortunes of the Democratic and Republican parties (especially nationwide), the policy preferences, personal convictions, and leadership capabilities of the president, the composition of the courts, and a host of others.

A major question mark in this regard is whether the religious Right and socially conservative "family values" organizations will continue to prioritize their opposition to gay rights. What is more certain is that such challenges have a greater chance of happening in the United States, and with greater impact, than in most of the rest of the developed world because of the large size and politicization of the evangelical commu-nity. Thus, we should expect that gay rights will not become univer-sally accepted or "settled law" as they might be in other nations. The continued resistance to abortion rights and contraception in the United States, unusual by the standards of most other developed democracies, suggests a continued role for evangelicals in the future politics of sexual orientation.

A critical front in the backlash against the advance of same-sex marriage and other rights is well underway—the assertion of a right to discriminate based upon constitutionally protected religious liberty. The Arizona legislature passed a law in 2014 that permitted business owners to refuse service to gay men and lesbians on religious grounds. Fears about the economic repercussion of such a law led the governor to veto it, but similar efforts have continued because opponents realize that the "religious liberty" frame is resonant with the public and claims of religious liberty hold a privileged constitutional status in the First Amendment.[30] Religious liberty claims have gained traction on the Supreme Court, as *Burwell v. Hobby Lobby Stores, Inc.* clearly demonstrates.[31] It concerned only whether employers were compelled to provide insurance plans that covered contraception under the Affordable Care Act, but courts in the future may extend its holding to make it easier for businesses to discriminate on the basis of sexual orientation.[32] Because of *Hobby Lobby*, several LGBT rights groups have withdrawn their support of ENDA, noting that the religious exemptions in the bill, as currently drafted, may invite legal challenges and court decisions that permit widespread discrimination.[33]

## 3. From Interest Group Advocacy to Descriptive Representation

We should expect that the LGBT movement will place more emphasis on getting greater numbers of openly LGBT individuals elected and appointed to positions in government. As with women and African Americans, we know that greater "descriptive representation" translates into increased substantive representation. The more openly gay and lesbian individuals serve in government, the more policies to promote the interests of gays and lesbians reach the agenda and gain adoption (even when we control for other influences).[34] LGBT state legislators, for example, help get issues onto the agenda, formulate proposals, and develop legislative strategies to gain their adoption. In helping to push policies to adoption, they supply what their most ardent straight colleagues cannot: educating their peers by their mere presence and by telling stories of their personal experiences of discrimination. One might ask why striving for greater descriptive representation is needed given that gays and lesbians are already moving closer to full legal equality. As already discussed, the movement still has a way to go before it completes its rights agenda, and it may have to guard against attacks on its achievements for years to come. Second, having elected and appointed public officials who are open about their sexual orientation is important for symbolic reasons. The mere fact that openly LGBT persons hold leadership positions in government further increases the visibility and legitimacy of the LGBT population in the eyes of both the public and the LGBT population.

The number of openly gay and lesbian officeholders, just a handful a decade ago, especially at the national level, should grow. According to the Gay and Lesbian Victory Fund, the number of openly gay and lesbian public officials has risen from forty-nine in 1991 to over five hundred in 2014.[35] Seven openly gay or bisexual members joined the 113th Congress.[36] Openly gay and lesbian members of Congress are still a tiny group, but they continue to grow. LGBT representation has come a long way from the years when members were forced out of the closet because of scandals.

Even more than women and racial minorities, however, gays and lesbians remain very underrepresented. The number of gay and lesbian officials represents far less than 1 percent of all elected officials in the United States and a fraction of the proportion of gays and lesbians estimated in the population. While openly gay candidates tend to be as successful as straight ones, few have ventured to run outside the safety of gay-friendly, heavily Democratic districts. The number of openly transgendered public officials is much lower than the number of gays and lesbians. Only a handful of transgendered individuals have run for elective office, and in 2014 only one reportedly had been elected to office (the mayor of Silverton, Oregon).[37] The first presidential appointment of an openly transgender individual has occurred only very recently.[38] Clearly, the Victory Fund and others operating in this area have their work cut out for them.

## 4. "High-Profile Politics" and the Diffusion of LGBT Rights Abroad

While we should not expect the attainment of full, formal legal equality, much less marriage, to bring about a transformation in the LGBT rights movement, it might change the movement's relationship to the government and its stature in the polity as a whole. Studying LGBT movements in Europe, Ronald Holzhacker has identified three "modes of interaction" between LGBT movements and governments. Movements' relationships with their governments vary depending upon how much support they receive from elites and the public. Movements that enjoy high levels of support from *both* elites and the public are able to engage in "high-profile politics." For these countries, of which the Netherlands is the paradigmatic case, LGBT political and community organizations sponsor large, public "celebratory events" (such as parades), cooperate closely with the ruling party coalition, and undertake efforts to "export" their ideas and resources to movements abroad.[39]

Should we expect that the American movement will become more like the Dutch as it moves closer to achieving full legal equality? Already, the U.S. movement engages in celebratory public events more than it does in street protest, but whether it has met, or is on the verge of meeting, Holzhacker's other criteria for "high-profile politics" is less clear. The U.S. movement has become an increasingly important constituency within the Democratic Party ever since Bill Clinton actively and openly campaigned for the "gay vote" in 1992. The movement's ability to consult with the party in power will continue to depend critically on whether the Democrats or Republicans have a majority and control the White House and governorships, while the Dutch movement, working within a unitary system and multiparty democracy, may be able to build close relations with several parties. The American movement's ability to engage in "high-level politics" will depend critically upon the degree of legitimacy that Americans accord LGBT rights. Miriam Smith has pointed to a basic difference between the status of gay and lesbian rights in the United States compared to Canada. Canadians have tended to view gay rights as "Canadian rights," while Americans have been prone to see them as benefits bestowed upon a special interest group.[40] Whether Americans will accord gay rights a broader level of legitimacy is uncertain, but rising bipartisan support for LGBT rights in the United States is a positive sign that they may be doing so.

LGBT movements that have secured full legal equality domestically have increasingly focused their attention on promoting LGBT rights abroad, monitoring developments in other nations and bringing pressure to bear upon nations in which persecution and discrimination persist.

Some of these nations are developed communist and postcommunist states in Eastern Europe and Asia. Others are developing countries in Africa, Asia, and the Middle East, particularly former British colonies and predominantly Muslim countries.[41] Globalization has facilitated the turn of domestic LGBT movements' attention outward as globalization has diffused democratic values and fueled aspirations for greater freedom and equality. Rather than pressure recalcitrant governments directly, LGBT organizations work through their own governments, international organizations (e.g., the United Nations and supranational regional organizations like the European Union), businesses and financial institutions with investments in nations with poor human rights records, and NGOs at the national and international levels, including Amnesty International and the International Lesbian, Gay, Bisexual, and Trans Association (ILGA) of which they are usually members. Domestic LGBT organizations try to assist activists in nations where persecution of LGBT individuals is rampant by working with, and putting pressure on, these intermediaries.

The main Dutch LGBT organization, COC (Cultuur-en Ontspannings Centrum), has engaged in very public displays of support for advancing LGBT causes in Eastern Europe and Central Asia, such as sponsoring parade floats and symposia and lobbying the European Union and Amnesty International to pressure foreign governments to reduce homophobia and permit more openness for their fledgling, indigenous LGBT movements.[42] The turn toward greater international involvement is not confined to the more advanced Dutch movement but appears increasingly in nations that have lagged behind the Dutch. Stonewall U.K., for example, which has devoted four of its staff to international LGBT issues, recently announced its plans to devote more resources to that endeavor, targeting Uganda, Russia, and Eastern Europe, in particular. The organization seeks to pressure the British government and banks and firms that do business or contemplate investing in foreign nations with poor records on LGBT rights.[43] Egale Canada has undertaken similar activities.[44]

Some American LGBT rights organizations have just started to turn in this direction, but we should expect them to accelerate their pace as we get closer to the attainment of full legal equality in the United States.[45] We should not assume, however, that American LGBT organizations will embrace internationalism as avidly as their counterparts in other nations. Despite the LGBT movement's international visibility and pioneering work, the geographic isolation of the United States and many Americans' disinterest in and ignorance of developments in other parts of the world may lead American organizations to view the concerns of movements abroad as more distant and less relevant. American organizations also lack the institutional venues for influencing other nations that European members of regional, supranational organizations like the European Union enjoy.

## 5. From Changing Laws to Changing Hearts and Minds: Can the Movement Move beyond Civil Rights?

Political and legal challenges to LGBT rights are unlikely to disappear in the foreseeable future, but the passage of national legislation extending basic civil rights protections in employment, public accommodations, education, and other spheres would open the possibility for the movement to reduce the proportion of its resources that it devotes to lobbying, campaign donations, and litigation in favor of other approaches to gaining social equality for LGBT persons. Changes in law can have powerful effects on educating the public and changing attitudes within society, but our experience with fighting racism and sexism indicates that ending discrimination is a slow, long-term project that must go beyond legal remedies. Formal, legal equality will not end discrimination and hostility toward gays and lesbians. A need will remain for sustained efforts to combat homophobia and heterosexism in most institutions of American life, particularly in schools, in professional sports, and throughout much of the world of commerce. Thus we should expect LGBT organizations to devote greater resources toward prevention of discrimination and violence toward their LGBT constituents by developing programs and sponsoring projects aimed at public education and reforming key institutions in society.

A number of scholars have warned of the limitations of the civil rights model as a vehicle for social change.[46] For one thing, many people who experience discrimination decide not to pursue legal action because it entails risks and costs that stem from their loss of control over a hostile situation. The legal system turns those who have been discriminated against into victims, and "the social psychology of victimhood influences and helps maintain asymmetric power relations."[47] Rooting out homophobia and heterosexism on the job and in other settings, through the initiation of civil rights complaints, can be particularly ineffective for sexual orientation because gays and lesbians can choose to remain closeted rather than resist their oppression by initiating a complaint. Initiating a complaint may require revealing one's sexual orientation (or having to deny it), which the complainant will perceive as risky; but staying in the closet contributes to a perpetuation of the conditions that give rise to the discrimination. Further, the more hostile the work environment is, the stronger the incentive is for the victim of discrimination to remain closeted (or leave his or her job) rather than bring a complaint.

Second, the legal process transforms vexing social problems with complex and deeply rooted causes into more narrow, technical, and procedural legal issues. Courts focus on whether plaintiffs have met the technical requirements for asserting a "right" contained in a statute, which is often unrelated to the social context in which the plaintiffs experience the discrimination and fails to address social structural forces and relationships that cause the conditions that give rise to the discrimination.[48] In addition, the decentralized structure of the court system, the case-based method of decision making, the adversarial process, and focus on whether a right has been violated leads often to public policy decisions that are inconsistent across jurisdictions, incremental, and incompatible with policy solutions that take account of competing political claims and values.

Finally, because legislatures find it difficult to clearly define what particular legal concepts mean (such as a "right" or "public accommodation"), courts may construe the right in question in a way that is narrow and limited. The U.S. Supreme Court's rulings that the exclusion of gays and lesbians from the Boy Scouts and St Patrick's Day parades is constitutionally permissible illustrate some of the problems with attempting to end discrimination through civil rights litigation.[49]

A number of LGBT movement organizations have supported efforts to address problems of discrimination, bullying, violence, and social needs outside of the civil rights model. This approach recognizes that schools, the mass media, churches, civic organizations, and businesses are places where homophobia and heterosexism can remain rooted or where it can be rooted out. It is aimed at directly challenging and assisting civil society institutions to address discrimination, often through inducing voluntary reforms aimed at changing their cultures. Some of these efforts involve changing public policy, while others do not, but they all have in common an emphasis on trying to "change the culture" rather than trying to police and coerce appropriate behavior. In contrast to the "civil rights model's" emphasis on using the police powers of the state to coerce nondiscrimination and respect for LGBT persons, the change-the-culture model stresses persuasion, education, and direct engagement and pressure on institutions of civil society. The inclusion of openly gay scouts and leaders in the Boy Scouts of America demonstrates the success of such an approach. Reforming organizations' cultures may be more effective in making LGBT individuals feel safe, secure, and respected as equals because it avoids many of the limits and shortcomings of using the state's police powers. It is directed at the source of the problem, thus obviating the need for legislation and litigation.

Whether the LGBT movement can shift its focus and resources away from the civil rights model toward other strategies of education, training, and changing organizational cultures and power relations remains to be seen. We have seen that the civil rights model is deeply entrenched in the LGBT movement and in American social movements generally. If we are correct about the powerful effects of path dependency and risk aversion on organizational and individual behavior, then it is very possible that the movement will fail to take full advantage of the opportunity for change that the attainment of full legal equality will afford.

## Conclusion

Whatever its impacts on the lives of gays and lesbians, the attainment of marriage equality is a political victory of great significance for the LGBT movement. Most likely, it will provide some impetus toward completing the adoption of the rights agenda, marking an important milestone on the road to full legal equality for LGB *and* T. We should not expect the movement that helped bring it about to change all that much, however. Political organizations that have established decades-old missions, strategies, and tactics and are embedded in a broader web of durable political institutions and values do not usually change easily, quickly, or radically, particularly if they perceive themselves as reasonably successful. Nevertheless, the advent of full legal equality will provide some opportunity for movement leaders and followers to devote greater resources to goals and strategies that have until now suffered from relative neglect.

NOTES
1 While I applaud the achievement of same-sex marriage, I am cognizant that it will not address many other problems facing LGBT communities, that many LGBT individuals will not benefit from marriage, and that tying rights and benefits to marriage privileges spousal relationships above others in ways that exacerbate social inequality.
2 Karl Marx, "The Eighteenth Brumaire of Louis Bonaparte," in *Karl Marx: Surveys from Exile,* David Fernbach, ed. (New York: Vintage, 1974), pp. 143–249.
3 Gary Mucciaroni, *Same Sex, Different Politics: Success and Failure in Struggles over Gay and Lesbian Rights* (Chicago: University of Chicago Press, 2008).
4 See Craig Rimmerman, *The Lesbian and Gay Movements: Assimilation or Liberation?* (Boulder, CO: Westview, 2nd ed. 2014); Steven Epstein, "Gay and Lesbian Movements in the United States: Dilemmas of Identity, Diversity, and Political Strategy," in *The Global Emergence of Gay and Lesbian Politics: National Imprints of a Worldwide Movement,* Barry D. Adam, Jan Willem Duyvendak, and Andre Krouwel, eds. (Philadelphia: Temple University Press, 1999), pp. 30–89.
5 Frances Kunreuther, Barbara Masters, and Gigi Barsoum, *At the Crossroads: The Future of the LGBT Movement,* a report of the Building Movement Project, New York, NY, www.buildingmovement.org, 2013 (accessed July 2014).
6 Theda Skocpol, *Diminished Democracy: From Membership to Management in American Civic Life* (Norman: University of Oklahoma Press, 2003).
7 See, e.g., "Beyond Same-Sex Marriage: A New Strategic Vision for All Our Families and Relationships," http://www.beyondmarriage.org/full_statement.html, July 26, 2006 (accessed July 2014); Kenyon Farrow, "Is Gay Marriage Anti-Black?" June 14, 2005, http://kenyonfarrow.com/2005/06/14/is-gay-marriage-anti-black/ (accessed September 2014).
8 George Chauncey, *Why Marriage?* (New York: Basic Books, 2005), pp. 123–26.
9 Anthony J. Nownes, "Interest Groups and Transgender Politics: Opportunities and Challenges," in *Transgender Rights and Politics: Groups, Issue Framing, and Policy Adoption,* Jami K. Taylor and Donald P. Haider-Markel, eds. (Ann Arbor: University of Michigan Press), pp. 83–106.
10 See Urvashi Vaid, *Virtual Equality: The Mainstreaming of Gay and Lesbian Liberation* (New York: Anchor Books, 1995). For a presentation of this view from a more academic point of view, see Craig A. Rimmerman, *From Identity to Politics: The Lesbian and Gay Movements in the United States* (Philadelphia: Temple University Press, 2002). See also "Beyond Same-Sex Marriage."

11 Urvashi Vaid, "Still Ain't Satisfied: The Limits of Equality," www.prospect.org, May 2012, pp. 38–43 (accessed July 2014); Kunreuther et al., *At the Crossroads.*

12 Patrick J. Egan, Murray S. Edelman, and Kenneth Sherrill, "Findings from the Hunter College Poll of Lesbians, Gays, and Bisexuals: New Discoveries about Identity, Political Attitudes, and Civic Engagement," Hunter College, City University of New York, 2008, http://politics.as.nyu.edu/docs/IO/4819/hunter_college_poll.pdf (accessed July 2015); Patrick J. Egan, "Explaining the Distinctiveness of Lesbians, Gays, and Bisexuals in American Politics," presented at the Meetings of the American Political Science Association, Boston, MA, August 28–31, 2008.

13 Paul Pierson, "Increasing Returns, Path Dependency, and the Study of Politics," 94 *American Political Science Review* 251–67 (June 2000).

14 Daniel Kahneman and Amos Tversky, "Prospect Theory: An Analysis of Decision under Risk," 47 *Econometrica* 263–91 (1979).

15 For a discussion of the pros and cons of the "civil rights model" see Matthew Diller, "Judicial Backlash, the ADA, and the Civil Rights Model," 21 *Berkeley Journal of Employment and Labor Law* 1, 19–52 (2000).

16 Jonathan Lax and Justin Phillips, "Gay Rights in the States: Public Opinion and Policy Responsiveness," 103 *American Political Science Review* 367 (2009).

17 Katy Steinmetz, "A Comprehensive LGBT Nondiscrimination Bill Is Coming," *Time,* December 10, 2014, http://time.com/3626346/lgbt-nondiscrimination-merkley-center-for-american-progress (accessed March 2015).

18 Jami K. Taylor and Donald P. Haider-Markel, "Introduction to Transgender Rights and Politics," and Mitchell D. Sellers and Roddrick Colvin, "Policy Learning, Language, and Implementation by Local Governments with Transgender-Inclusive Nondiscrimination Policies," in *Transgender Rights and Politics: Groups, Issue Framing, and Policy Adoption,* Jami K. Taylor and Donald P. Haider-Markel, eds. (Ann Arbor: University of Michigan Press, 2014), pp. 1–5, 208.

19 Dana Beyer and Jillian T. Weiss with Riki Wilchins, "New Title VII and EEOC Rulings Protect Transgender Employees," Transgender Law Center, http://transgenderlawcenter.org/wp-content/uploads/2014/01/TitleVII-Report-Final012414.pdf (accessed March 2015).

20 742 F.2d 1081 (7th Cir. 1984).

21 U.S. Dist LEXIS 17417 (E. D. La. 2002).

22 9 S.W.3d 223 (Tx. Ct. App. 1999).

23 42 P.3d 120 (Kan. 2002).

24 Taylor and Haider-Markel, Introduction to *Transgender Rights and Politics,* pp. 4–5.

25 *See* http://egale.ca/category/trans-rights/; http://egale.ca/all/egale-demands-action-from-education-ministers-to-end-violence-and-hate-crime-against-lgbtq-youth/ (accessed September 2014).

26 Nownes, "Interest Groups and Transgender Politics," pp. 83–106.

27 Diller, "Judicial Backlash, the ADA, and the Civil Rights Model," pp. 19–52.

28 *See* http://egale.ca/category/equal-families/equal-marriage/ (accessed September 2014).

29 Adam Liptak, "Justices' Rulings Advance Gays: Women Less So," *New York Times*, August 4, 2014; Erik Eckholm, "Access to Abortion Falling as States Pass Restrictions," *New York Times*, January 3, 2014.

30 Fernanda Santos, "Arizona Governor Vetoes Bill on Refusal of Service to Gays," *New York Times*, February 26, 2014.

31 134 S. Ct. 2751 (2014).

32 Adam Liptak, "Ruling Could Have Reach beyond Issue of Contraception," *New York Times*, March 24, 2014.

33 Ed O'Keefe, "Gay Rights Groups Withdraw Support of ENDA after Hobby Lobby Decision," July 8, 2014, http://www.washingtonpost.com/blogs/post-politics/wp/2014/07/08/gay-rights-group-withdrawing-support-of-enda-after-hobby-lobby-decision/ (accessed September 2014).

34 Donald Haider-Markel, *Out and Running: Gay and Lesbian Candidates, Elections, and Policy Representation* (Washington, DC: Georgetown University Press, 2010).

35 Gay and Lesbian Victory Fund, https://www.victoryfund.org/our-story/victory-fund-brief-history (accessed September 2014).

36 Jeremy W. Peters, "Openly Gay and Openly Welcomed in Congress," *New York Times*, January 25, 2013.

37 Nownes, "Interest Groups and Transgender Politics," p. 97.

38 Taylor and Haider-Markel, Introduction to *Transgender Rights and Politics*, p. 16.

39 Ronald Holzhacker, "National and Transnational Strategies of LGBT Civil Society Organizations in Different Political Environments: Modes of Interaction in Western and Eastern Europe for Equality," 10 *Comparative European Politics* 23–47 (2012). Where elite and public opinion are opposed or badly split on LGBT equality, "morality politics" and "incremental change" occur.

40 Miriam Smith, *Political Institutions and Lesbian and Gay Rights in the United States and Canada* (New York: Routledge, 2008).

41 David John Frank, Steven A. Boutcher, and Bayliss Camp, "The Reform of Sodomy Laws from a World Society Perspective," in *Queer Mobilizations: LGBT Activists Confront the Law*, Scott Barclay, Mary Bernstein, and Anna-Maria Marshall, eds. (New York: New York University Press, 2009), ch. 7.

42 Holzhacker, "National and Transnational Strategies of LGBT Civil Society Organizations in Different Political Environments," pp. 41–42.

43 Michael K. Lavers, "British Gay Group to Expand International Advocacy Efforts," *Washington Blade*, January 6, 2014, http://www.washingtonblade.com/2014/01/06/british-gay-group-expand-international-advocacy-efforts/ (accessed August 2014).

44 *See* http://egale.ca/category/international/ (accessed September 2014).

45 *See* the Human Rights Campaign, http://www.hrc.org/resources/category/international (accessed September 2014). The National Gay and Lesbian Task Force does not seem as interested in this issue, *see* www.thetaskforce.org/ (accessed September 2014).

46 Joel F. Handler, *Social Movements and the Legal System: A Theory of Law Reform and Social Change* (New York: Academic Press, 1978); Stephen C. Halpern, *On the*

*Limits of the Law: The Ironic Legacy of Title VI of the 1964 Civil Rights Act* (Baltimore, MD: Johns Hopkins University Press, 1995); Kristin Bumiller, *The Civil Rights Society: The Social Construction of Victims* (Baltimore, MD: Johns Hopkins University Press, 1988).

47  Bumiller, *The Civil Rights Society*, p. 3.
48  Halpern, *On the Limits of the Law*, p. 4.
49  Boy Scouts of America et al. v. Dale, 530 U.S. 640 (2000); Hurley v. Irish American Gay, Lesbian, and Bisexual Group of Boston, 515 U.S. 557 (1995).

2

# Two Steps Forward, One Step Back

## *The Slow Forward Dance of LGBT Rights in America*

DONALD P. HAIDER-MARKEL AND JAMI TAYLOR

This edited collection is premised on the advent of marriage equality in the United States. However, a few years ago, that outcome seemed distant given the hurdles faced by proponents of same-sex marriage. The period between the early 1990s and 2014 saw intense political and legal battles waged over rights for same-sex couples.[1] Even within the movement for lesbian, gay, bisexual, and transgender rights (LGBT), advocates have not always agreed on movement priorities and goals, and the divisions over the pursuit of marriage equality have been significant.[2] Civil unions or domestic partnerships were enacted in some states in the 1990s and early 'oos, and the main push for state court rulings and legislation legalizing same-sex marriage did not begin in earnest until after 2001. Some authors and activists remain critical of the institution of marriage, and they argue that it reinforces heteronormative biases and devalues women.[3] Other activists have complained that the fight for marriage has detracted from the advancement of other movement goals.[4] Sometimes, advocacy groups have been concerned about the timing and selection of court cases, ballot initiatives, or particular policy fights.[5]

Beyond their internal divisions, advocates for same-sex marriage have faced determined opponents who have been willing to use a variety of tactics to block gay equality. For instance, the Republican Party has included language opposing same-sex marriage in its presidential platform since 1992.[6] Additionally, same-sex marriage has been used as a wedge issue in numerous state and national elections (e.g., Bush v. Kerry in 2004). Many states enacted statutory laws banning same-sex marriage in the 1990s,[7] and many of these same states adopted subsequent constitutional bans through referenda and ballot initiatives, such as California's Proposition 8. In the 2000s, many of the state-level constitutional bans were enacted after the 2003 same-sex marriage decision in Massachusetts (*Goodridge v. Dept. of Health*)[8] and the Supreme Court ruling overturning antisodomy laws in *Lawrence v. Texas*.[9] Interest groups such as the National Organization for Marriage (NOM) engaged in aggressive public relations campaigns to demonize gay equality. In addition, NOM and similar groups raised funds and donated to candidates who opposed same-sex marriage. Opponents initially held the upper hand through their defense of the status quo and a noted bias against pro–gay rights policymaking in the states.[10] They also made the advancement of same-sex marriage far more onerous through passage of the Defense of Marriage Act (DOMA), which forbade the national government from recognizing same-sex marriages and allowed states to ignore those marriages from other jurisdictions.[11] Same-sex marriage opponents would appeal to other courts or switch venues from the judiciary to the legislature or to ballot initiatives when faced with unfavorable state court rulings. Some pro–marriage equality state-level judges, such as those in Iowa, were targeted for defeat during electoral campaigns.[12] Congressional Republicans, via the House of Representatives' Bipartisan Legal Advisory Group, chose to defend DOMA in the courts after the Obama administration declined to do so.[13] Opponents to gay equality even attempted to invoke novel techniques, such as claiming legal standing to uphold California's marriage ban in the form of Proposition 8 when state officials refused to defend the measure.[14]

Despite the internal divisions and external opposition, beginning with Vermont's decision to enact civil unions after its supreme court ruled that gay couples were entitled to the same benefits as married couples,[15] advocates for same-sex marriage have slowly been gaining equal recognition of their relationships. With key legal victories in cases like *United States v. Windsor*[16] and Massachusetts's 2003 court decision in *Goodridge v. Dept. of Health*,[17] combined with important wins at the ballot box in states like Minnesota, Washington, and Maryland, full legal equality for same-sex couples finally arrived in June 2015 with the Supreme Court's ruling in *Obergefell v. Hodges*.[18]

In this chapter, we examine the future of LGBT rights advocacy now that same-sex couples have won full marriage rights. We will discuss potentially difficult issues in the implementation of marriage equality, such as the lack of supporting legal frameworks for gay people in many states, religious exemptions, and elder care. We try to predict what problems LGBT advocacy groups might face after marriage equality, including the side effects of pursuing a litigation strategy for LGBT mobilization, such as the potential for demobilization of activists and policy implementation problems. We will also look at other issues remaining on the LGBT rights agenda, such as HIV/AIDS, antidiscrimination policies, and tensions within the LGBT advocacy coalition on priorities. Particular attention will be paid to the policy concerns of the transgender community, which has frequently been sidelined within the LGBT movement. In short, our goal in this chapter is to offer insights into the potential future of LGBT rights advocacy in a post-same-sex-marriage country.

Although the future for LGBT equality is not entirely clear, we have outlined what we believe are some of the primary issues that are likely to be faced by the LGBT movement in coming years. It should be apparent that although important, the achievement of marriage equality does not mark the end of the LGBT rights struggle. Indeed, the push for equality is likely to become more complex as implementation issues hinder the attainment of equality, and obtaining trans and gender identity protections might be left to a politically demobilized LGBT community.

## Implementation and Resistance

### Officials and Government Resistance

Now that marriage equality has been achieved for same-sex couples, this policy change must be implemented by governments at multiple levels. The federal system, with fifty sovereign diverse states (which contain numerous local governments) and a national government, each with shared powers among a judiciary, a legislative, and an executive branch, offers potential difficulties in implementing same-sex marriage. As evidenced by the multitude of states that enacted constitutional bans on same-sex marriage and that tenaciously fought attempts to deny legal attempts to strike those bans down, there will probably be resistance by state and local governments to implementation efforts. For example, following several federal court rulings on same-sex marriage bans in

October 2014, one local judge in Johnson County, Kansas, issued an order allowing marriage licenses to be provided to same-sex couples. At the same time, the other judges in the county disagreed with the order, and the state's governor said that he would defend the will of the people; the state attorney general issued a public statement saying that the state constitutional ban on same-sex marriage was still legal.[19] Likewise, we have observed examples of county clerks refusing to issue marriage licenses and local magistrates refusing to marry same-sex couples (citing religious beliefs).[20]

State and local government resistance is likely to be strongest in states, such as those in the Deep South, where public opinion is more firmly against same-sex marriage.[21] An analogy to this potential threat could be the obstructionist Massive Resistance practiced by some southern states in the post–*Brown v. Board of Education* era.[22] And even in nonsouthern states, many localities, such as Boston, resisted implementation of *Brown*.[23] In the case of same-sex marriage, we cannot predict the precise form of resistance that might materialize, but we expect in some areas it could take the form of officials "blocking the courthouse doors" in the fashion of resistance to school integration, while in other areas it will probably be acts of individual defiance by lone officials. An example of this type of behavior occurred in Toledo, Ohio, when a municipal court judge refused to marry a same-sex couple because of his religious beliefs.[24] His action generated an outcry from other local officials.[25]

But resistance could be more systematic; in early 2015 a number of states considered legislation that would hinder the issuance of marriage licenses to same-sex couples. The Texas House considered a bill that would ban government funds from being used to "license, register or support" same-sex marriage.[26] An Idaho House committee passed a resolution that called on Congress to impeach federal judges who rule in favor of same-sex marriage.[27] And Utah adopted a law that allows officials to refuse to marry same-sex couples, provided that an alternative official is made available.[28] Key to implementation will be a willingness by the national government, particularly the courts and the executive branch, to thwart any efforts to deny marriage equality and force state and local officials to comply with the law or face removal from office.

Likewise, although abortion is legal in the United States, states have been able to place many roadblocks for women to gain access to an affordable abortion, such as mandatory twenty-four-hour waiting periods. Even if such laws do not significantly reduce the number of abortions, one can imagine that states might attempt to construct new legal methods for delaying access to marriage, even if they affect opposite-sex couples as well. For example, in the past many states required blood tests before couples could be granted a marriage license (and some still do), and in the 1980s some states also used such laws to test couples for HIV.[29] Similar laws could be resurrected where they are not already in place as a means of inhibiting same-sex couples from applying for marriage licenses or simply delaying their doing so.[30] The effect would largely be symbolic, reflecting a cost increase or "rent-seeking" aspect to marriage that simply makes it less desirable for less earnest couples. But as with many abortion restrictions, the symbolism can be more import to proponents of the law than any actual impact on the "problem" itself.[31]

## Religious Exemptions

A related component of resistance to same-sex marriage implementation is the enactment of new statutory components that might legally allow public officials and private individuals to opt out of any participation in same-sex marriages. Our view partly stems from the Supreme Court's 2014 decision in *Burwell v. Hobby Lobby*.[32] In that case, the Court found that the Religious Freedom Restoration Act of 1993 (RFRA) allowed owners of a privately held for-profit company to refuse to provide insurance coverage of contraception for employees as mandated under the Patient Protection and Affordable Care Act. Hobby Lobby argued that such coverage would be a violation of the owner's religious beliefs. Given the ruling and its justification, it is plausible that owners of closely held companies could use the same legal reasoning and attempt to deny provision of benefits to lawfully married gay or lesbian employees if such marriages are contrary to the ownership's religious beliefs. This fear is heightened given the lack of existing laws against sexual-orientation-based discrimination when the Court's decision stated,

> The principal dissent raises the possibility that discrimination in hiring, for example on the basis of race, might be cloaked as religious practice to

escape legal sanction. . . . Our decision today provides no such shield. The Government has a compelling interest in providing an equal opportunity to participate in the workforce without regard to race, and prohibitions on racial discrimination are precisely tailored to achieve that critical goal.

Here, the Court was silent about discrimination against LGBT-identified individuals. However, discrimination based on sexual orientation is currently legal under national law (for nonfederal employees) and in most states (see discussion in next section). If this type of bias was cloaked in religious terms, it is plausible that *Hobby Lobby*'s expansive view of the RFRA might override existing state nondiscrimination statutes. Whether the impact of the *Hobby Lobby* decision will affect the rights of same-sex couples or LGBT individuals will probably be litigated over the next several years.

Beyond the impact of the *Hobby Lobby* decision, state legislatures could also carve out broad religious exemptions that affect same-sex marriage rights. States commonly do not compel religious groups to participate in or recognize same-sex marriages. However, they could choose to extend the breadth of religious exemptions to allow religious exemptions to deny other services to gay couples. An example of this type of action would be Maryland and Connecticut statutes that allow religiously affiliated groups the right to deny adoption services to those in same-sex marriages. Similar denial-of-service provisions have sometimes been extended to fraternal benefit societies like the Knights of Columbus.[33]

It is also not entirely clear how states might apply or extend existing statutes typically known as Religious Freedom Restoration Acts.[34] Since the federal RFRA was passed in 1993, and its application to state and local officials has been viewed as limited, some twenty states have passed similar laws that (to varying extents) exempt public officials from performing their stated duties if such duties violate their religious beliefs. These laws typically have been understood to allow religious exemptions, "which the government must grant unless it can show that applying the laws is the least restrictive means of serving a compelling government interest."[35] In October 2014, officials in North Carolina were proposing to expand existing legislation and allow state officials to refuse to issue marriage licenses or perform weddings for same-sex couples.[36] And even though the compelling government interest has often been fairly easy to demonstrate, the burden is placed on the state, and until the state can challenge the exemption in court, the exception could be allowed to stand. It is not difficult to envision a series of cases like this in a number of states that tie up government resources and perhaps embolden opponents. In states such as Indiana, where there are no legal protections for LGBT people, expansive RFRA laws pose the greatest risk of discrimination by private or public entities against LGBT people.

In addition, states could seek to provide greater religious freedom protections for those companies and religious institutions that provide marriage-related services, such as venues, caterers, photographers, and the like. Legislation in this vein was introduced in states such as Arizona and Kansas. The controversial 2015 RFRA law adopted in Indiana (effective July 2015), may allow such discrimination. The Indiana RFRA and similar laws considered by other states in 2014–15 expand the parties that can ask for legal relief and expands the situations under which legal action to protect religious beliefs can be requested; the expanded RFRA laws also allow legal action for parties to "prevent a 'likely' burden on religious belief, even before any burden is imposed."[37] Certainly this would not stop same-sex couples from being married by a judge at a courthouse or from seeking services elsewhere, but it would provide symbolic ammunition for those hoping to embed religious beliefs in statutory code. We turn to this form of discrimination below.

## *Backlash: Additional Policy Responses*

The rapid legalization of same-sex marriage also engendered a broader backlash against the LGBT movement in several states during the 2015 legislative session. For example, the Michigan House passed a bill that would allow adoption agencies to refuse services to gay couples and would ban governments from taking action against agencies that refuse service,[38] and in Missouri the legislature considered eight bills that observers said discriminated against LGBT people, including a bill that would ban government spending on projects that included gender-neutral bathrooms.[39] Meanwhile, Texas lawmakers considered some twenty anti-LGBT bills, including bills that would ban localities from preventing LGBT discrimination.[40] Additional examples abound, and although many of these bills failed, it is also likely that it will take years to overturn similar laws in court.

## Legal Framework for Gay Individuals

Another problem for marriage equality implementation is that it will affect actors beyond government. Business, religious institutions, non-profit organizations, and other actors may be affected, depending on the exceptions carved out by the judiciary or via statute. Here, the existing legal framework for gay individuals in the United States is not helpful to marriage equality advocates. At the national level, no statute currently protects gay men or lesbian women from discrimination. However, some states and localities offer these protections via statute or local ordinance; in fact, a majority of the U.S. population is protected in one form or another by subnational antidiscrimination laws. Mostly located on the West Coast, in the upper Midwest, and in the Northeast, these states are more liberal than states that have not adopted such protections.[41] Prior to the decision in the 2013 case *United States v. Windsor*,[42] every state that adopted (or was forced by the courts to adopt) same-sex marriage already had a legal framework that supported the rights of gay individuals. These states had comprehensive laws that banned sexual-orientation-based discrimination in areas such as employment, public accommodation, housing, and education; many also had additional laws recognizing same-sex couples for a variety of circumstances, including things like hospital visitation rights and insurance benefits.

Although sexual-orientation-based prejudices might remain in those states, gay men and lesbian women had potential legal recourse against biased actions. Gay individuals in these states had the legal framework that allowed them to be equal members of society prior to marriage equality.

Table 2.1 shows the year when a state's sexual-orientation-inclusive employment nondiscrimination law was adopted. It also shows when each state adopted same-sex marriage prior to 2015. Table 2.1 demonstrates that the vast majority of states that now allow same-sex marriage do not have a legal framework that protects gay individuals from discrimination. This includes all of the former Confederate states along with other large states such as Pennsylvania and Missouri. Thus, if two gay men or two lesbian women marry and then reside in a state without legal protections from discrimination, they could be subject to biased actions such as being fired from a job. Given that most of these states also lack policies against discrimination in housing or public accommodations, it is plausible that lawfully married gay couples in these states could also be denied choices in where they want to live as a same-sex couple or be denied access to places like hotels, theaters, or restaurants.

TABLE 2.1: State Laws on Employment Discrimination and Employment Nondiscrimination

| State | Sexual Orientation Employment Non-discrimination Law | Marriage |
|---|---|---|
| Alabama | | |
| Alaska | | |
| Arizona | | |
| Arkansas | | |
| California | 1992 | 2013 |
| Colorado | 2007 | |
| Connecticut | 1991 | 2008 |
| Delaware | 2009 | 2013 |
| District of Columbia | 1977 | 2010 |
| Florida | | |
| Georgia | | |
| Hawaii | 1991 | 2013 |
| Idaho | | |
| Illinois | 2005 | 2014 |
| Indiana | | |
| Iowa | 2007 | 2009 |
| Kansas | | |
| Kentucky | | |
| Louisiana | | |
| Maine | 2005 | 2012 |
| Maryland | 2001 | 2012 |
| Massachusetts | 1989 | 2004 |

TABLE 2.1 (*cont.*)

| State | Sexual Orientation Employment Non-discrimination Law | Marriage |
|---|---|---|
| Michigan | | |
| Minnesota | 1993 | 2013 |
| Mississippi | | |
| Missouri | | |
| Montana | | |
| Nebraska | | |
| Nevada | 1999 | |
| New Hampshire | 1997 | 2010 |
| New Jersey | 1992 | 2013 |
| New Mexico | 2003 | 2013 |
| New York | 2002 | 2011 |
| North Carolina | | |
| North Dakota | | |
| Ohio | | |
| Oklahoma | | |
| Oregon | 2007 | 2014 |
| Pennsylvania | | |
| Rhode Island | 1995 | 2013 |
| South Carolina | | |
| South Dakota | | |
| Tennessee | | |
| Texas | | |
| Utah | | |
| Vermont | 1992 | 2009 |
| Virginia | | |
| Washington | 2006 | 2012 |
| West Virginia | | |
| Wisconsin | 1982 | |
| Wyoming | | |

*Source*: National Gay and Lesbian Task Force

Although gay individuals in states lacking sexual-orientation protections are subject to this current lack of legal recourse against bias, gay couples are situated differently. A gay individual may choose to disclose his or her sexual orientation to an employer or service provider like an insurance company, bank, or hospital.[43] A lawfully married gay couple is *forced* to disclose their legal status to these types of actors. Because employers withhold federal (and sometimes state or local) taxes for employees, marital status must be disclosed via mechanisms such as the Internal Revenue Service's W-4 form.[44] Employers also may offer health insurance to married couples or life insurance to employees. Attempts to obtain these benefits would almost certainly disclose marital status by listing beneficiaries and the relationship to the employee. Health care providers also commonly collect spousal information so that next of kin can be notified or for liability purposes. Creditors collect spousal information on loan documents when making lending decisions. In some states married couples have a joint type of property ownership known as "tenants by the entirety" that entail rights to survivorship. In such states, this ownership and a couple's marital status would be recorded in easily available public records. Thus, the act of marriage necessarily outs a gay couple to a society that may or may not approve of their status.

Although the majority of Fortune 500 companies have policies that offer benefits to partners in same-sex couples and policies that ban discrimination on the basis of sexual orientation,[45] not all companies have such internal protections. It is therefore a plausible scenario that a gay man could marry his partner only to then be fired by his employer for exercising this fundamental right.[46]

An additional issue for legal protections applies to all LGBT individuals. Some thirty states have hate crime laws that include sexual orientation and fifteen states, as well as the District of Columbia, include gender identity in their hate crime laws; in 2009 the national government adopted a hate crime law that includes sexual orientation and gender identity.[47] Most of these laws allow for penalty enhancement for any crimes motivated by bias, but some, such as Michigan's and Rhode Island's, only include statistics collection by police for bias-motivated crimes. The crimes can range from graffiti to violent attacks against individuals. Hate crime laws and associated implementation measures, such as hate crime task forces within police departments, help to protect

LGBT people from the often violent discriminatory actions of segments of the population.[48] Marriage equality does little to protect LGBT people from displays of hatred and in the short-term might even increase some of this activity. In the latest available statistics from the FBI, there were over eleven hundred reported hate crimes based on sexual orientation in 2012, making these crimes second only to crimes motivated by race.[49] Nevertheless, local police departments voluntarily submit these and all crime statistics to the FBI, and the underreporting of all crime, including hate crime, is common. In addition, since most hate crime laws do not cover gender identity, we know even less about these crimes. Even with a relatively small LGBT population compared to those of racial minorities, the ongoing incidence of bias-motivated crimes against legally protected groups suggests that hate crime and related victim services will continue to be a significant issue for the LGBT population, regardless of marriage equality.

## Issues for the Older LGBT Population

Another implementation issue is elder care and end-of-life issues for all LGBT people. Retirement and long-term health care issues are faced by an aging LGBT population, just as they are for the rest of the population, but LGBT individuals and couples face additional challenges as they move into their twilight years. Some individuals and couples desire to move to retirement facilities in the event that later assisted living is necessary. Others are forced to do so when faced with a health crisis.

Although marriage equality should in theory remove existing concerns regarding disparities in Social Security, Medicare, health insurance benefits, utilization of the Family and Medical Leave Act, hospital visitation, income and estate tax issues, and pension rules, there are additional considerations for the aging LGBT community.[50] Given that opposition to LGBT equality tends to be strongest among older individuals,[51] how will retirement communities and facilities respond to same-sex couples? If a facility is located in a state or locality without LGBT discrimination protections, will facilities adopt policies to deal with discrimination by residents or employees? The answer is unknown, but LGBT people seeking residence in retirement facilities will need to consider what such a move might mean for them.

We do know that LGBT individuals are more reluctant to accept services as they age given fears of discrimination or abuse,[52] and the industry itself might address this by creating LGBT-friendly or LGBT-focused facilities, much as the travel industry has done.

## LGBT Political Demobilization?

As argued by pluralist thinkers, interest groups often form and/or mobilize when they face threats to their interests as well as when they hope to expand their benefits.[53] Not surprisingly, the civil rights movement for gays and lesbians has experienced periods of intense advocacy activity in the face of existential threats like HIV/AIDS, the waves of ballot measures to repeal antidiscrimination laws or prevent new laws from being enacted, and the backlash against same-sex marriage during the early part of the twenty-first century.[54] During a mobilization effort, groups tend to form as more people become involved and two key ingredients to politics can be acquired: money and votes. However, what might happen to LGBT groups after important policy victories are achieved? Are there unforeseen risks to the advocacy groups that are fighting for LGBT equality? Are these risks more acute if the victories occur through litigation rather than legislation? For some insight into what can happen, we can turn to the experience of the state with the longest history of same-sex marriage, Massachusetts.

In that state, one of the foremost organizations involved in the fight over same-sex marriage was MassEquality. The organization was formed with a sole purpose, marriage equality. After this goal was obtained, it adjusted the organizational mission to "ensure that everyone across Massachusetts can thrive from cradle to grave without discrimination and oppression based on sexual orientation, gender identity, or gender expression."[55] MassEquality is comprised of two legal entities, a 501(c)(4) organization (MassEquality Org Campaign for Equality Inc.) and a 501(c)(3) organization (Mass Equality Education Fund Org Inc.). The 501(c)(4) organization received recognition in 2002 so that it could engage in legislative lobbying pursuant to Internal Revenue Service rules on tax-exempt organizations. The 501(c)(3) organization was formed in 2006 so that it could accept more restricted donations that would allow individuals to deduct the contribution from their taxes. This type of multiform organizational approach is fairly common in LGBT advocacy and political advocacy.[56]

MassEquality was heavily involved in the legislative campaign to block attempts to amend the state's constitution after the 2003 *Goodridge* decision. Not surprisingly, as noted in figure 2.1, contributions to the 501(c)(4) organization skyrocketed during this mobilization between 2003 and 2007. However, after marriage rights were protected following a 2007 legislative vote to keep the issue off the 2008 ballot,[57] donations to MassEquality collapsed, as shown in figure 2.1. From a high point of approximately $2.5 million in 2005 to approximately $355,000 in 2013, revenues to MassEquality's 501(c)(4) organization have dropped by about 85 percent.[58] Contributions to the 501(c)(3) revenue are also declining but not as precipitously. It is important to note that the declines in revenue highlighted in figure 2.1 are in nominal terms. If adjusted for inflation and population change, the declines in revenue would be even starker. Although it is possible that individual organization-level factors or macroeconomic factors have affected the ability of MassEquality to extract a key political resource, money, its decline in revenue is consistent with a demobilization effect (e.g., a decline in political interest and activity) of their constituency. Also consistent with this explanation is the fact that the Massachusetts gay and lesbian communities have long enjoyed comprehensive state-level nondiscrimination protections and other favorable policies like adoption rights or hate crimes laws.[59] There are few policy threats to mobilize gay and lesbian individuals or couples in Massachusetts. If the experience of MassEquality is indicative of what could happen nationally, LGBT groups should plan for ways to engage their constituencies given the remaining items on the LGBT advocacy agenda. Additionally, groups narrowly focused on same-sex marriage, such as the American Foundation for Equal Rights or Freedom to Marry,[60] should give significant attention to an evolving mission or to shutting down.

At the same time, policy success does not always lead to a significant decline in group activity or political mobilization. The effective repeal in 2011 of "Don't Ask, Don't Tell" (DADT), the ban on gays and lesbians serving openly in the U.S. military, did lead to a merger of the two main groups working on this issue (Servicemember's Legal Defense Network [SLDN] and OutServe) into OutServe-SLDN, and a decline in

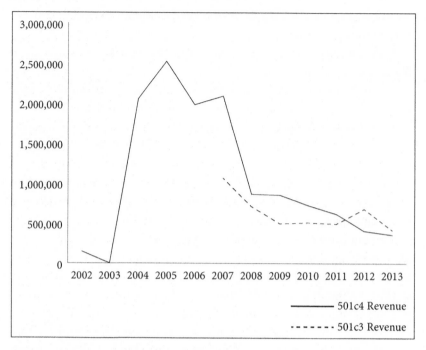

Figure 2.1. MassEquality Revenues over Time. *Source*: National Center for Charitable Statistics—IRS Reported 990 Total Revenue.

revenues for the new organization. However, the drop-off in revenues was not quite as dramatic as it had been for MassEquality. In 2003, SLDN reported revenues of just over $2 million. Revenues peaked at $3.6 million in 2010 as Congress acted at the end of the year to repeal DADT, and then dropped back to $2.3 by 2012 after DADT was fully repealed.[61] OutServe-SLDN continues to defend LGBT service members from discrimination. As its mission statement notes, the organization represents "the U.S. LGBT military community worldwide. Our mission is to: educate the community, provide legal services, advocate for authentic transgender service, provide developmental opportunities, support members and local chapters, communicate effectively, and work towards equality for all."[62] The activities of OutServe-SLDN include legal assistance for discharge reclassification for service members who were less than honorably discharged prior to the repeal of DADT. Likewise, even with marriage equality, some LGBT couples are likely to still need specialized legal assistance to help ensure that their marriages are fully recognized.

The other danger to mobilization stems from policy victories achieved via litigation rather than through legislation, or broad-based grassroots mobilization that results in legislative consideration or policy change. Policy advocacy through litigation takes considerable financial resources and legal expertise. However, while these things can be garnered through generous patrons, litigation strategies can fail to mobilize the grassroots of a community. If the grassroots does not mobilize around an issue, policy implementation can become more difficult as attention wanes over time and the ability to challenge new or additional issues in the future can be sidelined. In short, litigation does not typically invoke the type of institution building that fosters vibrant social movements.[63]

Legal change also does not equal attitude change. Support for LGBT equality, including marriage equality, has grown dramatically since the 1990s.[64] However, most polls still show bare national majorities of adults supporting same-sex marriage, and many states have less than majority support.[65] Without significant increases in support for marriage equality and LGBT equality in some states, the likelihood of new antidiscrimination protections and full and equal access to marriage remains dim in some states, especially in the South.

Likewise, years after the significant policy victories of the African American civil rights movement, African Americans still contend with racist and discriminatory attitudes in many aspects of society. And such attitudes have often been institutionalized into organizational practices and policies that are less visible and more difficult to address. For example, the institutionalized racism in the American criminal justice system is well documented and apparent to most citizens,[66] but the practices that lead to unequal outcomes, such as investigatory stops in policing, seem as prevalent as they were forty years ago.

## HIV/AIDS Policy

As noted in the previous section, the HIV/AIDS crisis that began in the 1980s provided an existential threat that mobilized gay and lesbian communities. Although a cure has not been found for HIV/AIDS, drug combination treatment regimens were developed in the 1990s that allowed management of this disease.[67] This advance saved countless lives, but access to these drug treatments is often facilitated by funding mechanisms for populations lacking adequate insurance coverage or income, such as the Ryan White CARE Act or Medicare/Medicaid.[68] In addition to domestic programs, President George W. Bush initiated and President Obama extended the foreign-aid-focused President's Emergency Plan for AIDS Relief (PEPFAR).[69] Both domestic and foreign-aid-focused HIV/AIDS treatment funding must be periodically reauthorized by Congress. LGBT advocates and their allies interested in HIV/AIDS treatment and prevention will need to remain vigilant and mobilized to secure funding at adequate levels.

Beyond funding for HIV/AIDS treatment, the Food and Drug Administration's (FDA) policy blocking blood donations by men who have had sex with other men remains partly in effect as of 2015. This ban, enacted during the height of the AIDS crisis, bars blood donations by males who have had sex with males at any point in the last year (previously this was a lifetime ban). The FDA defends this policy by arguing that men who have sex with other men constitute 61 percent of all new HIV/AIDS cases.[70] However, others argue that this ban is discriminatory and that the ban is unnecessary in light of improved laboratory testing for the virus.[71] It is also a difficult policy to enforce because some gay men fail to voluntarily comply with donation bans.[72] In 2015, the FDA relaxed the policy and reduced the time frame to one year.[73] Finally, HIV/AIDS prevention is and will probably remain an area of public controversy. Two areas of interest are sex education and the development of drugs to lessen the chance of HIV infection. Health advocates have long pushed for use of condoms and comprehensive sex education as ways to halt the spread of the disease.[74] One of the primary ways to disseminate this information is via schooling. However, sex education remains a contentious issue in public K–12 education;[75] some districts rely on abstinence-based policies while others have comprehensive sex education curriculums. Such policies are heavily influenced by state laws and district-level policymaking when discretion is passed to the local level. Of course, such public school policies ignore children educated in home schools or in private school settings. Sex education policies for public schools will probably remain a hotly contested policy area because of parental concerns about the promotion of sex, fragmented authority to make policy, divergent beliefs about sex and sexuality, and partisan differences on these issues.[76]

With respect to the second area of prevention, a recent drug, Truvada, was developed to lessen the likelihood of HIV infection. This type of treatment, pre-exposure prophylaxis (PrEP), has been controversial. By definition, prevention means that a person does not have the disease—which makes arguing for a treatment sometimes difficult. As a result, there are questions as to whether and to what degree insurance policies or publicly funded programs will cover this expensive drug.[77] Some AIDS activists have also opposed the drug because they assert that it must be appropriately taken to be effective and because it encourages people to engage in risky behavior.[78] There is also social stigma associated with taking the drug.[79] However, others have argued that it is an effective treatment to lessen the likelihood of infection.[80] LGBT activists and allies in the fight against HIV/AIDS will probably need to monitor this controversy and be alert for efforts to curtail public funding for PrEP treatment.

## Transgender Rights

The victory for same-sex marriage also provides an important policy victory for some members of the trans community. Of particular benefit would be trans individuals who have undergone sex-reassignment procedures. Such individuals have faced conflicting rulings regarding whom they can legally marry.[81] In states like Kansas and Florida, trans individuals who have undergone sex reassignment have seen their marriages to persons of the same birth sex invalidated by courts.[82] Other states, such as Ohio, have sometimes blocked similarly situated trans individuals from obtaining marriage licenses to wed members of the same birth sex.[83] Yet other states, given their statutes regarding birth certificate amendment for those who have undergone sex reassignment, have allowed such individuals to marry members of their assigned birth sex.[84] Further, Texas has seen its court system invalidate a marriage involving a trans person while later upholding a separate such marriage after a change in a state statute.[85]

The issue was complex (prior to marriage equality) in part because the patchwork of birth certificate amendment laws, threats of litigation, and uncertainty about the Full Faith and Credit Clause hindered the ability of some transgender people to marry the people they love or to reside in, or even travel to, some parts of the country.[86] These problems occurred because only about half of the states had specific statutory language that authorized birth certificate amendment in the event of sex reassignment.[87] In those states (prior to same-sex marriage), such changes were statutorily authorized and individuals had marriage rights according to the "new" gender.[88] In most other states, birth certificate rules are less clear, and while a trans person might be able to amend a birth certificate, this might later be challenged by the state or a private party (such as an insurance company or the birth family of a trans person's spouse). A state might also not recognize an amended birth certificate from another state. In these situations, a transgender person's marriage could be called into legal question and the trans individual might lose the legal ability to make decisions for an incapacitated spouse, lose standing to sue in a wrongful death, lose survivor benefits, or lose a host of other rights afforded in the marital context. Marriage equality removes a legal hurdle to some transgender individuals' full equality as citizens, but additional issues are likely to remain.

Most significantly, trans policy issues will probably be at the forefront of LGBT-advocacy group activity in the years after marriage equality. Given the long history of transgender exclusion from most laws against discrimination,[89] there will probably be many fights over this issue as gay and lesbian groups struggle for new state and federal laws banning discrimination and extending existing laws that prohibit discrimination on the basis of sexual orientation. Because laws combating discrimination are central to the implementation of same-sex marriage (as discussed earlier in this chapter), there will be significant pressure on policy actors to adopt these policies. However, in states like Maryland and New York, and during battles over the federal-level Employment Nondiscrimination Act (ENDA), on multiple occasions transgender protections have been jettisoned in order to advance bills.[90] In these cases it is often argued that legislators are "not ready" for transgender inclusion.[91] Additionally, there is not as much public awareness of transgender issues, and many groups still must focus on educating the LGBT community and the broader public on these issues.[92] Indeed, a 2011 national poll of adults conducted by the Public Religion Research Institute (PRRI) found that 30 percent of respondents had either never heard the term "transgender" or were unsure what it meant.[93]

Public opinion polls about transgender and gender-identity protections are themselves infrequently conducted. When such questions are asked in national polls, support for trans protections is typically about 10 percentage points lower than support for sexual-orientation protections. Even among Democrats, 75 percent approve a national law banning discrimination based on sexual orientation, but only 65 percent support including transgender protections in such a law (the Republican difference is 52 percent to 43 percent).[94] The 2011 PRRI poll mentioned above shows about 74 percent of Americans support congressional action to protect the rights of transgender people and about that same level of support for the 2009 congressional action that expanded hate crimes protections for the trans community. Given the pattern observed at the state level, with support for laws banning sexual-orientation discrimination often needing to reach supermajority levels before such legislation can pass,[95] we can probably expect that even with majority support for equality at the national level, trans activists are still likely to face an uphill battle in expanding discrimination protections at the state level, and a national antidiscrimination law is not expected anytime soon.

Traditionally within the LGBT movement, transgender people have had little access to power or decision-making authority in most LGBT advocacy organizations.[96] They also do not contribute large amounts of organizationally relevant resources (financial contributions, employees, numbers of volunteers) to most LGBT-rights groups.[97] Given these factors, it is fairly likely that a national government move to assist with the implementation of marriage equality by passing a sexual-orientation- and gender-identity-inclusive law against discrimination will face an attempt by some to jettison the concurrent transgender protections. This transgender exclusion may occur as part of the legislative logrolling process, and it will be presented by opponents of LGBT rights as their "victory."

Beyond the discrimination policy issue, other transgender rights priorities will remain. For instance, the end of the Don't Ask Don't Tell (DADT) policy allowed gay and lesbian individuals to serve their nation without fear. However, this change did little for transgender service members, who can still be removed from the service due to medical or psychiatric regulations.[98] In addition, as noted earlier in this chapter, the repeal of DADT does not protect LGBT service members from all discrimination. Groups like the Transgender American Veterans Association and OutServe-SLDN remain at the forefront of the fight to change these policies (such as the unequal treatment of same-sex couples stationed outside of the United States)[99] and undo the wrongs of past "less than honorable" discharges of LGBT service members. These groups are also working with the Veterans Administration to improve access to appropriate health care for transgender veterans.

Advocacy groups may also give attention to the policy that requires male-to-female transgender individuals to register for Selective Service. This same policy does not apply to female-to-male trans persons.[100] Although this may seem like a marginal issue because there currently is no draft for males or females, some policies require males to have registered for Selective Service in order to gain access to a variety of federal benefits or programs, including education benefits and federal employment opportunities. For both male-to-female and female-to-male trans individuals, confusion around this policy can result in a denial of benefits or create awkward situations like outing an individual as trans in a potentially hostile environment.

Health care access to appropriate gender-identity-related treatment is an important policy objective for transgender individuals.[101] Unlike laws against discrimination or hate crimes, this is an area where gay and lesbian individuals have no concurrent policy interest. This is problematic because many transgender policy gains have been achieved in conjunction with efforts to obtain similar protections for gay men and lesbian women.[102] Because most historically gay-centered advocacy groups, such as the Human Rights Campaign, have included transgender as part of their organizational missions[103] and due to the lack of transgender influence on the direction of these groups,[104] the lack of an overlapping interest means that trans health issues might not be prioritized by the largest and most influential LGBT rights organizations.[105] This is an issue because insurance policies commonly deny coverage to transition-related services.[106] Medicare, Medicaid, and Veterans Administration regulations do not cover sex-reassignment-related procedures.[107] There are also few doctors in the United States familiar with trans medical issues.[108] Access to trans-related health care is often problematic for incarcerated individuals given some state/federal corrections regulations.[109] Additionally, many trans individuals report negative experiences with health care workers and even instances of being denied care.[110] Given the multitude of issues related to health care and the trans community, this area of advocacy may become a major focus for LGBT rights groups in the future.

## A Global Movement?

Finally, we expect that even as the American LGBT movement deals with marriage-implementation issues, public education, and trans rights expansion, the movement is likely to become increasingly more global in its perspective. There are of course immigration issues for same-sex couples where one partner is not an American citizen. But in addition to focusing on immigration issues, we expect that the LGBT community is likely to increase its efforts in assisting LGBT movements in other countries and working at home to encourage the U.S. government and investors to apply pressure on foreign governments that have poor human rights records when it comes to LGBT citizens. For example, in March 2014 a coalition of groups, including the Human Rights Campaign and the National Gay and Lesbian Task Force, lobbied the Obama administration for a meeting to discuss the human rights violations of LGBT people in countries such as Nigeria, Uganda, and Russia. The letter recommended that the administration redirect foreign aid to nongovernmental organizations in these countries and use "the full weight of U.S. diplomatic" pressure to push for the repeal of anti-LGBT laws.[111]

We also expect that LGBT groups will continue to push the U.S. government to advocate for LGBT human rights in international organizations, such as the United Nations. Indeed, in late September 2014, the United States helped to pass a resolution against anti-LGBT violence and discrimination in the United Nations Human Rights Council. The council approved the measure in a 25–14 vote after rejecting a number of amendments that would have removed LGBT-specific language from the resolution; the measure had been introduced by Chile, Colombia, Uruguay, and Brazil and was strongly supported by the United States.[112]

Just as the anti-LGBT movement has gone global, pushing for anti-homosexuality laws in countries like Uganda, the pro-LGBT movement is likely to follow. There is evidence of increasing ties between the American

LGBT movement and LGBT activists in Latin America, and those efforts are likely to expand to Africa and Asia.[113] As the Russian government adopted anti-LGBT legislation in 2013, the Human Rights Campaign and other groups helped to spearhead a movement to support Russian LGBT activists prior to the 2014 Winter Olympic Games, which were being hosted by Russia.[114] These efforts appeared to encourage U.S. officials to speak out against the anti-LGBT Russian law and widespread anti-LGBT violence in the country. Whether existing LGBT interest groups in the United States can maintain their members and financial support by pursuing a global movement is less clear, but these groups are likely to redirect at least some of their lobbying efforts in Washington, DC, to focus on issues such as foreign aid and global human rights. Whether or not such a shift must come at the expense of lobbying for LGBT issues within the United States will depend on the resources available to LGBT interest groups and the vision of their leaders. Our sense is that global advocacy efforts by LGBT groups have recently helped enhance the profile of groups, but have mostly been symbolic in terms of goals.

## Conclusion

Although we do not intend to draw a bleak portrait of the future, it is important to remember, as the history of other movements has shown, that the struggle for equality is not one that simply ends at the courthouse steps. Even after important judicial (and legislative) victories are attained, rights and protections have to be defended as policies are implemented, and the understandings and attitudes of citizens often must still be shaped through political and educational campaigns.

In addition, we have outlined remaining challenges to the LGBT movement in the form of additional legal protections, a variety of transgender issues that remain unresolved or only partially resolved, the ongoing HIV/AIDS crisis, and the domestic versus international agenda of the LGBT movement. Whether the movement will continue to pursue stated goals in these areas is unclear, just as the future viability of an LGBT political movement is unclear. Our view is simply that there is still a large agenda for the movement and still plenty of research questions for social scientists to examine; an old saying, sometimes understood as a curse, others times as a wish, seems apt for this moment: "may you live in interesting times."

## NOTES

1 *See, e.g.*, Jason Pierceson, *Same-Sex Marriage in the United States: The Road to the Supreme Court* (Lanham, MD: Rowman & Littlefield, 2013).

2 *See, e.g.*, Craig Rimmerman, *The Lesbian and Gay Movements: Assimilation or Liberation?* (Boulder, CO: Westview, 2nd ed. 2014).

3 *See, e.g.*, Jyl Josephson, "Citizenship, Same-Sex Marriage, and Feminist Critiques of Marriage," 3(2) *Perspectives on Politics* 269–84 (2005).

4 *See, e.g.*, Jami Taylor and Daniel Lewis, "The Advocacy Coalition Framework and Transgender Inclusion in LGBT Rights," in *Transgender Rights and Politics: Groups, Issue Framing, and Policy Adoption*, Jami Taylor and Donald Haider-Markel, eds. (Ann Arbor: University of Michigan Press, 2014), pp. 108–32.

5 Margaret Talbot, "A Risky Proposal," *New Yorker*, January 18, 2010.

6 Gerhard Peters and John Wooley, "American Presidency Project: Republican Party Platforms—Republican Party Platform of 1992," n.d., http://www.presidency.ucsb. edu/ws/?pid=25847, accessed September 2014.

7 The 1990s wave of state statutory laws banning same-sex marriage followed the Hawai'i Supreme Court ruling in 1993 (*Baehr v. Miike* (originally *Baehr v. Lewin*)) that moved to allow same-sex marriage in that state. *See* Donald P. Haider-Markel, "Policy Diffusion as a Geographical Expansion of the Scope of Political Conflict: Same-Sex Marriage Bans in the 1990s," 1(1) *State Politics and Policy Quarterly* 5–26 (2001).

8 Goodridge v. Dept. of Public Health, 798 N.E.2d 941 (Mass. 2003).

9 Lawrence v. Texas, 539 U.S. 558 (2003).

10 Jeffrey Lax and Justin Phillips, "Gay Rights in the States: Public Opinion and Policy Responsiveness," 103(3) *American Political Science Review* 367–86 (2009).

11 Rimmerman, *The Lesbian and Gay Movements*.

12 A. G. Sulzberger, "Ouster of Iowa Judges Sends Signal to Bench," *New York Times*, November 3, 2010.

13 United States v. Windsor, 133 S.Ct. 2675 (2013).

14 Hollingsworth v. Perry, 133 S.Ct. 2652 (2013).

15 Baker v. Vermont, 744 A.2d 864 (Vt. 1999).

16 United States v. Windsor, 133 S.Ct. 2675 (2013).

17 Goodridge v. Dept. of Public Health, 798 N.E.2d 941 (Mass. 2003).

18 Obergefell v. Hodges, 135 S.Ct. 2584 (2015).

19 Tony Rizzo and Glenn E. Rice, "Same-Sex Couples Can Now Legally Marry in Johnson County," *Kansas City Star*, October 9, 2014. Meanwhile, some federal judges were still upholding same-sex marriage bans in October 2014, *see* Laura Raab, "Puerto Rico's Gay Marriage Ban Upheld by Federal Judge," *Los Angeles Times*, October 21, 2014.

20 *See, e.g.*, Joseph Mark Stern, "Magistrates Who Refuse to Grant Gay Marriages Are Law-Breakers," *Slate Magazine*, October 14, 2014. Alabama became the center of resistance in March 2015 when the state supreme court ordered probate judges

to stop issuing marriage licenses to same-sex couples. Many counties complied, even refusing to issue marriage licenses to any couple. With a number of lawsuits pending, the issue was unresolved as of this writing.

21 Lax and Phillips, "Gay Rights in the States: Public Opinion and Policy Responsiveness."

22 *See, e.g.*, Numan Bartley, *The Rise of Massive Resistance: Race and Politics in the South During the 1950s* (Baton Rouge: Louisiana State University Press, 1979).

23 *See, e.g.*, D. Garth Taylor, *Public Opinion and Collective Action: The Boston School Desegregation Conflict* (Chicago: University of Chicago Press, 1986).

24 Kim Palmer, "Toledo Judge Refuses to Perform Same-Sex Marriage," *Columbus Dispatch*, July 8, 2015 http://www.dispatch.com/content/stories/local/2015/07/08/0708-Toledo-judge-refuses-to-perform-gay-marriage.html, accessed July 29, 2015.

25 Lauren Lindstrom, "Public Officials: Gay Marriages are Judge's Duty," *Toledo Blade*, July 15, 2015 http://www.toledoblade.com/Courts/2015/07/15/Public-officials-Gay-marriages-are-judge-s-duty.html, accessed July 29, 2015.

26 *See* http://dfw.cbslocal.com/2015/03/25/texas-bill-seeks-to-ban-gay-marriage-licenses/, accessed April 2015.

27 *See* http://www.idahopress.com/community/panel-backs-federal-judge-impeachment-resolution/article_0d2d2b9e-cd16-11e4-9fa8-e7924f5647db.html, accessed April 2015.

28 *See* http://www.standard.net/Government/2015/03/20/Utah-OKs-bill-for-officials-to-refuse-to-officiate-marriages-1.html, accessed April 2015. Notably, Utah did pass new sexual- orientation-discrimination protections in housing and employment in 2015.

29 Mary Ann Glendon, *The Transformation of Family Law: State, Law, and Family in the United States and Western Europe* (Chicago: University of Chicago Press, 1989).

30 The imposition of new restrictions on opposite-sex couples might not be resisted very forcefully since this is an unorganized group and fewer adult Americans are married now than ever before—under 50 percent—and the percentage is even lower in many conservative southern states. *See* Hunter Schwartz, "For the First Time, There Are More Single American Adults Than Married Ones, and Here's Where They Live," *Washington Post*, September 15, 2014.

31 *See, e.g.*, Amy Fried, "Abortion Politics as Symbolic Politics: An Investigation into Belief Systems," 69(1) *Social Science Quarterly* 137–54 (1988); Kenneth J. Meier, Donald P. Haider-Markel, Anthony J. Stanislawski, and Deborah R. Mcfarlane, "The Impact of State-Level Restrictions on Abortion," 33(3) *Demography* 307–12 (1996).

32 Burwell v. Hobby Lobby Stores Inc., 134 S.Ct. 2751 (2014).

33 David Masci, "States That Allow Same-Sex Marriage Also Provide Protections for Religious Groups and Clergy Who Oppose It," Pew Research Center, http://www.pewresearch.org/fact-tank/2013/11/20/states-that-allow-same-sex-marriage-also-

provide-protections-for-religious-groups-and-clergy-who-oppose-it/, accessed
September 2014.

34  *See, e.g.*, Rachel Zoll, "Conservatives Are Clinging onto Religious Exemptions
to Fight Same-Sex Marriage," *Huffington Post*, October 15, 2014, http://www.
huffingtonpost.com/2014/10/14/gay-marriage-religion_n_5983756.html, accessed
October 2014.

35  Eugene Volokh, "What Is the Religious Freedom Restoration Act?" *Volokh Conspiracy*, December 2, 2013, http://volokh.com/2013/12/02/1a-religious-freedom-
restoration-act/, accessed October 2014; see also Hunter Schwarz, "19 States
That Have 'Religious Freedom' Laws like Indiana's That No One Is Boycotting,"
*Washington Post*, March 27, 2015, http://www.washingtonpost.com/blogs/the-fix/
wp/2015/03/27/19-states-that-have-religious-freedom-laws-like-indianas-that-no-
one-is-boycotting/, accessed April 2015.

36  *See* Michael Biesecker, "GOP Leader: NC Officials Can Refuse to Marry Gays,"
*News and Observer*, October 21, 2014.

37  Erik Eckholm, "Religious Protection Laws, Once Called Shields, Are Now Seen as
Cudgels," *New York Times*, March 30, 2015.

38  Alisha Green, "House Poised to Approve Religious-Objection Adoption Bills,"
*Morning Sun News*, March 18, 2015, http://www.themorningsun.com/general-
news/20150318/house-poised-to-approve-religious-objection-adoption-bills,
accessed April 2015.

39  Shannon Halligan, "Eight 'Anti-LGBT Bills' Filed in Missouri Legislature," March
20, 2015, http://www.kshb.com/news/political/eight-anti-lgbt-bills-filed-in-
missouri-legislature, accessed April 2015.

40  Jay Michaelson, "The Texas-Sized Anti-Gay Backlash," *Daily Beast*, March 29,
2015, http://www.thedailybeast.com/articles/2015/03/29/the-texas-sized-anti-gay-
backlash.html, accessed April 2015.

41  *See, e.g.*, Donald P. Haider-Markel and Kenneth J. Meier, "The Politics of Gay and
Lesbian Rights: Explaining the Scope of the Conflict," 58(2) *Journal of Politics*
332–49 (1996); Jami Taylor, Daniel Lewis, Matthew Jacobsmeier, and Brian DiS-
arro, "Content and Complexity in Policy Reinvention and Diffusion: Gay- and
Transgender-Inclusive Laws against Discrimination," 12(1) *State Politics & Policy
Quarterly* 75–98 (2011).

42  United States v. Windsor, 133 S.Ct. 2675 (2013).

43  However, we do recognize that marriages are public records and are often listed in
local newspapers, making it possible for employers and others to independently
discover a person's sexual orientation if that person is in a same-sex marriage.

44  Form W-4, Internal Revenue Service, http://www.irs.gov/pub/irs-pdf/fw4.pdf,
accessed September 2014.

45  Human Rights Campaign, Corporate Equality Index 2014, http://www.hrc.org/
campaigns/corporate-equality-index, accessed September 2014.

46  If the scenario seems implausible, consider another situation where national
laws allow for private policies that can conflict with state laws; for example, in

Colorado and Washington, residents are allowed to legally purchase and use marijuana. Partly encouraged by national laws, private companies in those states have policies that allow for termination for the use of marijuana; such cases were reported in 2014. Even with the legal protection the state offers, it appears as though private companies can still invoke such policies.

47  *See* the National Gay and Lesbian Task Force website on hate crime: http://www. thetaskforce.org/reports_and_research/hate_crimes_laws, accessed October 2014; and the Human Rights Campaign website on hate crime laws: http://www.hrc. org/resources/entry/maps-of-state-laws-policies, accessed October 2014.

48  Donald P. Haider-Markel, "Regulating Hate: State and Local Influences on Law Enforcement Actions Related to Hate Crime," 2(2) *State Politics and Policy Quarterly* 126–60 (2002).

49  *See* the FBI Hate Crime Statistics web page at http://www.fbi.gov/about-us/cjis/ucr/hate-crime/2012, accessed October 2014.

50  Services & Advocacy for Gay, Lesbian, Bisexual, and Transgender Elders, "Marriage Equality," http://www.sageusa.org/issues/marriage.cfm, accessed September 2014.

51  Paul Brewer, *Value War: Public Opinion and the Politics of Gay Rights* (Lanham, MD: Rowman & Littlefield, 2008).

52  Loree Cook-Daniels, "Lesbian, Gay Male, Bisexual, and Transgendered Elders: Elder Abuse and Neglect Issues," 9(2) *Journal of Elder Abuse & Neglect* 35–49 (1998).

53  *See, e.g.*, David Truman, *The Governmental Process: Political Interests and Public Opinion* (New York: Knopf, 1951).

54  *See, e.g.*, M. Kent Jennings and Ellen Anderson, "The Importance of Social and Political Context: The Case of AIDS Activism," 25(2) *Political Behavior* 177–99 (2003).

55  Jami Taylor, *The Adoption of Gender-Identity-Inclusive Legislation in the American States* (doctoral dissertation, North Carolina State University, 2008, ProQuest Theses and Dissertations, Accession Order No. 3306647); MassEquality "Our Work" website at http://www.massequality.org/ourwork, accessed October 2014.

56  State of the States Report 2011, Equality Federation, http://equalityfederation.org/sites/default/files/downloads/SoS2011-final.pdf, accessed October 2014.

57  Frank Phillips and Andrea Estes, "Right of Gays to Marry Set for Years to Come— Vote Keeps Proposed Ban off 2008 State Ballot," *Boston Globe*, June 15, 2007, A1.

58  National Center for Charitable Statistics, search Active Organizations-MassEquality, http://nccsweb.urban.org/PubApps/search.php, accessed September 2014.

59  Maps of State Laws & Policies, Human Rights Campaign, http://www.hrc.org/resources/entry/maps-of-state-laws-policies, accessed September 2014.

60  American Foundation for Equal Rights, "About Us," http://www.afer.org/about/the-foundation/, accessed September 2014.

61  Revenue data are from the OutServe-SLDN website at http://www.sldn.org/pages/finance-and-governance, accessed September 2014.

62  OutServe-SLDN website at http://www.sldn.org/pages/about-sldn-vision-mission-and-goals, accessed September 2014.

63  *See* Robert J. Hume, *Courthouse Democracy and Minority Rights: Same-Sex Marriage in the States* (New York: Oxford University Press, 2013).

64  Robert P. Jones, Daniel Cox, and Juhem Navarro-Rivera, *A Shifting Landscape: A Decade of Change in American Attitudes about Same-Sex Marriage and LGBT Issues* (Washington, DC: Public Religion Institute, 2014).

65  Jones et al., *A Shifting Landscape*; Lax and Phillips, "Gay Rights in the States.: Public Opinion and Policy Responsiveness."

66  For a good overview, see Nazgol Ghandnoosh, *Race and Punishment: Racial Perceptions of Crime and Support for Punitive Policies* (Washington, DC: Sentencing Project, 2014), http://sentencingproject.org/doc/publications/rd_Race_and_Punishment.pdf, accessed October 2014.

67  Timeline, AIDS.gov, http://www.aids.gov/hiv-aids-basics/hiv-aids-101/aids-timeline/, accessed October 2014.

68  "Legislation," United States Department of Health and Human Services, http://hab.hrsa.gov/abouthab/legislation.html, accessed October 2014.

69  PEPFAR Stewardship and Oversight Act of 2013, http://www.gpo.gov/fdsys/pkg/PLAW-113publ56/pdf/PLAW-113publ56.pdf, accessed October 2014.

70  Food and Drug Administration, "Blood Donations from Men Who Have Sex with Other Men Questions and Answers," http://www.fda.gov/BiologicsBloodVaccines/BloodBloodProducts/QuestionsaboutBlood/ucm108186.htm, accessed October 2014.

71  *See, e.g.*, Charlene Galarneau, "Blood Donation, Deferral, and Discrimination: FDA Donor Deferral Policy for Men Who Have Sex with Men," 10(2) *American Journal of Bioethics* 29–39 (2010).

72  P. Grenfell, W. Nutland, S. McManus, J. Datta, and K. Soldan, "Views and Experiences of Men Who Have Sex with Men on the Ban on Blood Donation: A Cross-Sectional Survey with Qualitative Interviews," *BMJ* 343: d5604 (2011).

73  Rob Stein, "FDA Lifts Ban on Blood Donations by Gay and Bisexual Men," *National Public Radio*, December 22, 2015.

74  *See, e.g.*, Douglas Kirby, B. A. Laris, and Lori Rolleri, "Sex and HIV Education Programs: Their Impact on Sexual Behaviors of Young People throughout the World," 40(3) *Journal of Adolescent Health* 206–17 (2006); D. Kirby, L. Short, J. Collins, D. Rugg, L. Kolbe, M. Howard, B. Miller, F. Sonenstein, and L. S. Zabin, "School-Based Programs to Reduce Sexual Risk Behaviors: A Review of Effectiveness," 109(3) *Public Health Reports* 339–60 (1994).

75  *See, e.g.*, Janice Irvine, *Talk about Sex: The Battles over Sex Education in the United States* (Berkeley: University of California Press, 2004).

76  Irvine, *Talk about Sex.*

77  Michael Horberg and Brian Raymond, "Financial Policy Issues for HIV Pre-Exposure Prophylaxis," 44(1) *American Journal of Preventive Medicine* S125–28 (2013) (Supplement 2).

78  *See, e.g.*, David Tuller, "A Resisted Pill to Prevent H.I.V.," *New York Times*, December 30, 2013.

79  Tuller, "A Resisted Pill to Prevent H.I.V."

80  Food and Drug Administration, "FDA Approves First Drug for Reducing the Risk of Sexually Acquired HIV Infection," 2012, http://www.fda.gov/NewsEvents/Newsroom/PressAnnouncements/ucm312210.htm, accessed October 2014.

81  Jami Taylor, "Transgender Identities and Public Policy in the United States: The Relevance for Public Administration," 39(7) *Administration Society* 833–56 (2007).

82  In re Estate of Gardiner, 42 P.3d 120 (Kan. 2002); Kantaras v. Kantaras, Case no. 2D03–1377 (Fla. App. 2004).

83  In re Application for Marriage License for Nash, 2003-Ohio-7221.

84  In re Jose Mauricio Lovo-Lara, 23 I&N Dec. 746 (BIA 2005); Jami Taylor, Barry Tadlock, and Sarah Poggione, "State LGBT Rights Policy Outliers: Transsexual Birth Certificate Laws," 34(Winter) *American Review of Politics* 245–70 (2014).

85  Littleton v. Prange, 9 S.W.3d 233 (Tex. App 1999); In the Estate of Thomas Trevino Araguz III, Deceased, Number 13-11-00490-CV (Tex. App 2014).

86  Julie Greenberg, "When Is a Same-Sex Marriage Legal? Full Faith and Credit and Sex Determination," 38(2) *Creighton Law Review* 289–307 (2005); Julie Greenberg and Marybeth Herald, "You Can't Take It with You: Constitutional Consequences of Interstate Gender-Identity Rulings," 80(4) *Washington Law Review* 819–85 (2005).

87  Taylor et al., "State LGBT Rights Policy Outliers: Transsexual Birth Certificate Laws."

88  In re Jose Mauricio Lovo-Lara, 23 I&N Dec. 746 (BIA 2005).

89  Taylor and Lewis, "The Advocacy Coalition Framework and Transgender Inclusion in LGBT Rights."

90  Taylor and Lewis, "The Advocacy Coalition Framework and Transgender Inclusion in LGBT Rights."

91  Taylor and Lewis, "The Advocacy Coalition Framework and Transgender Inclusion in LGBT Rights."

92  Barry Tadlock, "Issue Framing and Transgender Politics: An Examination of Interest Group Websites and Media Coverage," in *Transgender Rights and Politics: Groups, Issue Framing, and Policy Adoption*, Jami Taylor and Donald P. Haider-Markel, eds. (Ann Arbor: University of Michigan Press, 2014), pp. 25–48; Jacob Longaker and Donald P. Haider-Markel, "Transgender Policy in Latin American Countries: An Overview and Comparative Perspective on Framing," in *Transgender Rights and Politics*, pp. 49–80.

93  *See* http://publicreligion.org/research/2011/11/american-attitudes-towards-transgender-people/, accessed October 2014.

94  Alex Roarty, "Poll: End Workplace Discrimination against Gays," *National Journal Daily*, December 10, 2013, p. 1.

95  Lax and Phillips, "Gay Rights in the States: Public Opinion and Policy Responsiveness."

96  Taylor and Lewis, "The Advocacy Coalition Framework and Transgender Inclusion in LGBT Rights."

97  Taylor and Lewis, "The Advocacy Coalition Framework and Transgender Inclusion in LGBT Rights."

98  Department of Defense Instruction 6130.03–Medical Standards for Appointment, Enlistment, or Induction in the Military Services, United States Department of Defense, 2011, http://www.dtic.mil/whs/directives/corres/pdf/613003p.pdf, accessed September 2014; see also "Report of the Transgender Military Commission," Palm Center, 2014, http://www.palmcenter.org/files/Transgender%20Military%20Service%20Report_0.pdf, accessed October 2014.

99  Status of Current Issues, Out Serve-SLDN, 2014, http://www.sldn.org/page/-/Website/Fact%20Sheets/Advocacy%20and%20Policy%20Committee%20Report.pdf, accessed October 2014.

100 "Fast Facts," Selective Service System, 2014, https://www.sss.gov/fswho.htm, accessed September 2014.

101 Jaime Grant, Lisa Mottet, and Justin Tanis, *Injustice at Every Turn: A Report of the National Transgender Survey* (Washington, DC: National Gay and Lesbian Task Force, 2011), http://www.thetaskforce.org/downloads/reports/reports/ntds_full.pdf., accessed March 2012.

102 Jami Taylor, Daniel Lewis, Matthew Jacobsmeier, and Brian DiSarro, "Content and Complexity in Policy Reinvention and Diffusion: Gay and Transgender-Inclusive Laws against Discrimination," 12(1) *State Politics & Policy Quarterly* 75–98 (2011).

103 Anthony Nownes, "Interest Groups and Transgender Politics: Opportunities and Challenges," in *Transgender Rights and Politics: Groups, Issue Framing, and Policy Adoption*, Jami Taylor and Donald P. Haider-Markel, eds. (Ann Arbor: University of Michigan Press, 2014), pp. 83–107.

104 Taylor and Lewis, "The Advocacy Coalition Framework and Transgender Inclusion in LGBT Rights."

105 Indeed, a 2013 poll of the LGBT population indicates that only 29 percent of LGBT adults believe that transgender health issues should be "a top priority for the movement." *A Survey of LGBT Americans: Attitudes, Experiences, and Values in Changing Times* (Washington, DC: Pew Research Center, 2013).

106 Daphna Stroumsa, "The State of Transgender Health Care: Policy, Law, and Medical Frameworks," 104(3) *American Journal of Public Health* e31–e38 (2014).

107 Stroumsa, "The State of Transgender Health Care."

108 Stroumsa, "The State of Transgender Health Care."

109 Stroumsa, "The State of Transgender Health Care." However, courts have sometimes ruled that prisoners must have access to appropriate hormonal and/or surgical treatments.

110 Grant et al., *Injustice at Every Turn*; Ryan Combs, "Key Issues in Transgender Health Care Policy and Practice," in *Transgender Rights and Politics: Groups, Issue*

*Framing, and Policy Adoption*, Jami Taylor and Donald P. Haider-Markel, eds. (Ann Arbor: University of Michigan Press, 2014), pp. 231–51.

111 *See* http://www.hrc.org/blog/entry/coalition-calls-for-white-house-meeting-on-human-rights-violations-in-niger, accessed September 2014.

112 Michael K. Lavers, "U.N. Human Rights Council Adopts LGBT Resolution," *Washington Blade*, September 26, 2014.

113 *See* Javier Corrales and Mario Pecheny, *The Politics of Sexuality in Latin America: A Reader on Lesbian, Gay, Bisexual, and Transgender Rights* (Pittsburgh, PA: University of Pittsburgh Press, 2010).

114 *See, e.g.*, http://www.hrc.org/blog/entry/hrc-announces-100000-contribution-to-support-the-russian-lgbt-movement, accessed September 2014.

3

# Still Not Equal

## *A Report from the Red States*

CLIFFORD ROSKY

When I moved from San Francisco to Salt Lake City to begin teaching law, I knew that I was moving to one of the country's most conservative states—indeed, to the headquarters of the Church of Jesus Christ of Latter-day Saints, an organization widely known for promoting conservative values. I did not realize, however, that I was moving to the next battleground in the struggle for LGBT rights.

But a few weeks after I arrived, the LDS Church transformed the geography and the trajectory of the LGBT movement. On June 29, 2008, the church announced that it was joining the campaign to pass Proposition 8, a ballot initiative to prohibit same-sex marriage in California. In a letter read aloud to Mormons during Sunday services in California, the church called upon followers to "do all you can to support the proposed constitutional amendment by donating of your means and time" and explained that "Local Church leaders will provide information about how you may become involved in this important cause."[1] By helping to repeal one of the LGBT movement's crowning achievements, the church invited attention and scrutiny from LGBT advocates across the United States.

Proposition 8 is history now, and the church stayed out of ballot initiatives in Maine, Maryland, and Minnesota in 2012.[2] But since the church's announcement, Utah has remained at the vanguard of the country's debates about LGBT rights. In December 2013, a federal court in Salt Lake City ruled that Utah's ban against same-sex marriage was unconstitutional—making it the first state law to fall in the wake of *United States v. Windsor*.[3] In the next seventeen days, more than twelve hundred same-sex couples were married in Utah, before the Supreme Court issued a temporary stay pending appeal.[4] In 2014, the

Tenth Circuit upheld the lower court's ruling,[5] along with the validity of the twelve hundred marriages already performed.[6] In 2015, the Supreme Court vindicated the reasoning of the Tenth Circuit, granting same-sex couples the freedom to marry in all fifty states.[7]

As a result, LGBT activists and scholars across the country are asking "what's next" for the LGBT movement—what issues LGBT organizations should pursue now that marriage equality has been secured. Increasingly, the LGBT movement's leaders have begun to rally behind the banner of "lived equality."[8] While *legal* equality is defined as the equal protection of LGBT people in policies and laws, *lived* equality is measured by reference to "equality of outcomes and community well-being"[9]—the "lived experiences" of LGBT people.[10] Drawing on "the history of civil rights struggles in the United States," one scholar warns that "formal legal equality does not provide more resources, greater political power or better lives."[11]

Although the LGBT movement's interest in lived equality is greater than ever, the idea itself is not new. Twenty years ago, Urvashi Vaid described the options now confronted by LGBT activists in terms that are still apt:

> We can choose in this moment to follow the path our predecessors paved—of pursuing incremental legal and legislative reform, increasing gay and lesbian visibility, pressing for fair treatment in all aspects of life. . . . But we do have the choice of reaching beyond the civil rights framework of mainstream integration, and beyond the partial equality that it delivers, to imagine and create a different movement whose goal is genuine social change.[12]

Needless to say, the contents of concepts like "lived equality" and "genuine social change" depend heavily on the particular organizations or individuals who invoke them and the particular purposes and contexts in which they are invoked. In general, however, the LGBT movement's new calls to pursue lived equality include many of the most familiar items on the progressive agenda—namely, immigration, homelessness, education, criminal justice, and health care reforms.[13] Rather than focusing on the LGBT movement's traditional goals—most obviously, the passage of antidiscrimination laws—lived equality focuses on the intersection of LGBT identity with race, class, ethnicity, and age.[14] As a result, lived equality would require LGBT organizations to prioritize broader issues and form coalitions with a wider range of other groups—not only the NAACP, La Raza, and the National Organization for Women, but also the the AFL-CIO, Sierra Club, and Occupy Wall Street.[15]

Before I raise any strategic questions about the wisdom of this shift, I want to be very clear about where I stand on the political values that underlie it: I wholeheartedly agree with this vision of what the LGBT movement should be fighting for. By definition, the pursuit of lived equality is vital work; the movement should not press forward without it. As the phrase suggests, equality is not worth nearly as much when it is not lived in everyday life—when it exists only in law, or only on paper. The freedom to marry is a valuable right, but it doesn't mean nearly as much when you're unemployed, homeless, uninsured, or imprisoned. Unless LGBT organizations support progressive causes, LGBT people will continue to suffer from pervasive, structural inequalities—and so will many others. (In this respect, it is worth remembering that non-LGBT people are no less equal than LGBT people, regardless of whether they are allies.) This type of work was important long before same-sex marriage and will continue to be important long after.

Yet I am a Utahn now. As an activist and scholar working in one of the country's most Republican states, I cannot resist raising a red flag about the possibility of presenting "lived equality" as a new paradigm for the LGBT movement. After all, it is a model developed by LGBT activists living and working in places like Boston, New York, San Francisco, and Washington, DC—the country's most liberal enclaves. In these settings, the LGBT movement has already achieved full legal equality for LGBT people, and there is already substantial support for the broader progressive agenda. Under such circumstances, a wholesale shift toward lived equality makes perfect sense. It's the only thing left to do, and it seems likely to be successful.

But that is not where I live, and it is not where I work. As activists and scholars anticipate the dawn of marriage equality, we must remember that even the most basic conditions of legal equality still have not been achieved in most U.S. states. Although the Supreme Court has granted same-sex couples the freedom to marry, there are still twenty-eight states without inclusive antidiscrimination laws and another twenty states without inclusive hate crimes laws. In these states, same-sex couples can marry, but LGBT people have no specific protections from being fired from their jobs, evicted from their homes, denied public services, targeted in public schools, and assaulted or murdered—all because of who they are and who they love. Under such circumstances, exercising the freedom to marry may well exacerbate these risks, rather than mitigating them: By marrying a person of the same sex, LGBT people risk outing themselves to employers, landlords, and others, which could trigger a broad range of retaliation against them.[16]

At this historic moment, it is worth remembering that legal equality—no less than lived equality—is among the LGBT movement's unfinished business. As we emphasize the vitality of the progressive agenda, we must not forget or dismiss the value of finishing the work that we started. From this perspective, it is both puzzling and troubling to hear antidiscrimination laws described as merely "formal" or "legal" protections—as if they have no meaningful impact on the lived experiences of LGBT people. Without doubting the value of lived equality, we can insist that legal equality is no less lived and no less important. As Vaid herself warned twenty years ago, "This work, of securing and broadening civil equality, is in itself a lifetime's work, in which there is indeed very little choice; all of us who support gay rights must engage in it."[17]

To be sure, even the achievement of full equality under the law would not be perfect. Nothing is. If critical theory has taught us anything about law, it is that claims based on rights and identities are always perilous, as they are implicated in a larger system of inequality that law sanctifies and structures.[18] For present purposes, we can use legal protections against employment discrimination as a case study of legal equality's limits. To win a claim under such a law, you would have to start by hiring a lawyer. This is already going to be difficult, because you have just been fired from your job, so you're out of work now. You've got bills to pay, and plenty of other pressing issues to worry about. Even if you find a lawyer, then you would still have an uphill battle, because you'll have to prove that your employer fired you because you are lesbian, gay, bisexual, or transgendered. This is going to be difficult, too, because very few employers are foolish enough to give illegal reasons for firing you. In light of these kinds of obstacles, it is not surprising that workplace protections are no panacea for structural inequalities. Fifty years after the passage of the Civil Rights Act of 1964, our country still has massive wealth and income disparities based on race and sex.[19]

Yet even after we take law down a peg, there are still compelling reasons to work for legal equality, limited and flawed as it may be. For many years, studies have shown that LGBT people face discrimination in many settings—not only at work and at home but in the provision of public goods and services, and in the playgrounds and hallways of schools. When the government bans discrimination in these spheres, it reaches into the heart of everyday life, striking directly at the problems of unemployment, homelessness, and the provision of everyday needs.

Recent studies suggest that antidiscrimination laws have actually reduced discrimination against gay applicants and helped to reduce the wage gaps between gay and heterosexual workers.[20] Of course, there will always be complicated causal questions behind the assessment of any law's impact. But even if we assume that law is likely to lag behind public opinion, we might still believe that legal reforms might be used to secure and solidify social gains—and that in some circumstances, legal and social progress might support and reinforce one another.

Moreover, even when antidiscrimination laws are not enforced, they remain potent symbols. Among other things, they signal the public inclusion of LGBT people within the community itself, and they acknowledge the profound harm that discrimination inflicts upon LGBT people. In short, we should work for the right to work because we want it, and because we deserve it. When this principle is codified in our laws, it does not end discrimination altogether, but it gives us one more tool in our arsenal—one more source of power in our political, social, and cultural struggles. At the margins, it may make it a little bit harder for employers to discriminate, and a little bit easier for employees to come out.

Finally, there is little reason to think that legal equality and lived equality are mutually exclusive options for the LGBT movement. If anything, the two goals seem to complement one another: They call upon activists to engage in many of the same kinds of work, and they depend on many of the same ideals. Indeed, the LGBT movement's track record in blue states illustrates that the labor required to secure the passage of local and statewide antidiscrimination laws—i.e., grassroots campaigns to persuade and support community leaders, municipal officials, and state legislators—establishes the social, political, and financial foundation that allows activists to pursue more progressive, ambitious reforms in future years.

Indeed, it would be both ironic and tragic if marriage, of all things, were taken as legal equality's crowning achievement. For many years, left-leaning activists have criticized the LGBT movement for pursuing the right to marry at the expense of more basic protections, which would benefit many of the LGBT community's most vulnerable members.[21] At the same time, right-leaning critics have long objected to the LGBT movement's emphasis on litigation, rather than legislation, on the ground that so-called judicial activism is undemocratic.[22] While advocates and scholars have offered thoughtful responses to these objections, the LGBT movement has little reason to ignore them now that marriage equality has been secured. By achieving the passage of laws that directly address problems like unemployment and homelessness, the movement can address criticisms from the Right and the Left.

As LGBT activists and scholars ponder what's next, we must be realistic about the opportunities and obstacles for successfully exporting the paradigm of lived equality beyond the blue states. Among other things, we will confront challenges in framing and funding this work. Because legal equality appeals to values that are widely shared by a majority of Americans, it has traditionally been more effective at attracting supporters, persuading the moveable middle, and neutralizing opponents than other issues on the progressive agenda. In swing states and red states, activists cannot afford to dismiss or ignore these advantages. Conversely, the barriers to lived equality are more structural, more entrenched, and more persistent in swing states and red states, where progressives do not enjoy electoral majorities.

In light of these concerns, this chapter considers how the LGBT movement might pursue legal equality—alongside lived equality—now that same-sex couples enjoy the freedom to marry across the United States. In particular, it focuses on the passage of antidiscrimination laws in swing states and red states. While this objective may sound familiar—perhaps even passé—the political dynamics and strategic dilemmas that it presents are unprecedented. As one activist admits, the challenges now facing LGBT people in swing states and red states are "unlike anything we've faced before."[23]

The chapter begins by explaining why the LGBT movement is likely to turn "back to work" after marriage equality by focusing on the passage of antidiscrimination laws. Next, it argues that the LGBT movement will undergo two strategic shifts in pursuing this work—first, an increased investment in local rather than national lobbying, and second, an increased investment in red states and swing states, as opposed to blue states. Finally, the chapter claims that the LGBT movement will confront two strategic dilemmas in pursuing this work—whether to lobby for piecemeal bills or package deals, and how to use litigation and lobbying in ways that support each other. Without attempting to resolve the first dilemma, it argues that lobbyists must not entertain exemptions that apply only to claims brought by LGBT plaintiffs—or more broadly, any protections that fall short of what might reasonably be achieved through litigation under existing antidiscrimination laws.

## After Marriage: Back to Work

If we can safely assume that what's past is prologue, then what's next for the LGBT movement is already clear: After marriage, the passage of antidiscrimination laws is likely to attract the greatest investment of time and money from activists and donors. It is one of the oldest items on the LGBT movement's agenda—and to date, it has been one of the most successful.

In 1972, East Lansing, Michigan, passed the country's first law prohibiting discrimination based on "affectional or sexual preference."[24] Within five years, antidiscrimination ordinances had already been adopted in more than forty municipalities across the United States.[25] Today, laws protecting lesbian, gay, and bisexual people from discrimination have been adopted by twenty-two states and more than three hundred municipalities. In recent years, nearly all of these laws have included parallel protections for transgender people.[26]

Until the Supreme Court's ruling in *Windsor*, the LGBT movement's progress on employment and marriage had followed a consistent trend—first comes work, then comes marriage.[27] Before any state had granted official recognition to same-sex relationships—by legalizing same-sex domestic partnerships, civil unions, or marriages—that jurisdiction had previously adopted a law prohibiting employers from discriminating based on sexual orientation.[28] In seventeen of these twenty-two states, workplace protections were passed at the same time as fair housing and public accommodations laws.

By striking down the Defense of Marriage Act (DOMA) before Congress passed federal employment protections for LGBT people,[29] the Supreme Court broke this historical trend: Although federal law now recognizes the validity of same-sex marriages, it still does not specifically prohibit employers from discriminating against LGBT workers. Now that the Supreme Court has invalidated state laws against same-sex marriage, twenty-eight states find themselves in similar circumstances.

Now that same-sex marriage has been legalized, the LGBT movement seems likely to experience significant losses in funding and staffing. In comparison to other LGBT issues, same-sex marriage has demonstrated a truly astonishing ability to mobilize resources. In 2008, the campaign against California's Proposition 8 attracted more than $44 million in contributions, including more than $13 million from other states.[30] Although ballot initiatives are relatively expensive, same-sex marriage has also proved to be an exceptionally powerful fundraising tool for litigation and lobbying efforts.[31]

As a matter of popular opinion and political support, there are good reasons to predict that after marriage equality, the LGBT movement will seek to sustain momentum by lobbying for federal and state antidiscrimination laws with renewed vigor. First, such laws are widely supported by the American public: While Americans remain roughly divided on the legalization of same-sex marriage, more than two-thirds support the adoption of federal laws banning discrimination against gay and transgender workers.[32] Second, and relatedly, such laws enjoy an impressive degree of support among legislators: Although Congress has not passed federal employment protections for LGBT people, it has come relatively close in recent years. In 2014, for example, the bill known as the Employment Non-Discrimination Act (ENDA) boasted 55 supporters in the Senate and 190 supporters in the House.[33] Because of this widespread appeal, antidiscrimination has a greater potential than other issues to galvanize the LGBT movement's supporters, capture undecided voters, and neutralize or marginalize the movement's opponents.

Finally, there are more tactical, defensive reasons for the LGBT movement to reinvest in the passage of antidiscrimination laws after marriage. Given the path toward marriage equality in red states—through courts, instead of legislatures—the legalization of same-sex marriage was likely to trigger a legal and cultural backlash against LGBT people.[34] Capitalizing on the Supreme Court's ruling in *Burwell v. Hobby Lobby*,[35] this backlash has been framed as a defense of so-called religious liberties—e.g., the bakers, florists, and photographers who object on religious grounds to serving same-sex weddings.[36] Without a robust investment in antidiscrimination work, the LGBT movement will lose the opportunity to reframe this backlash in more favorable terms—as an attack against the equality and liberty of LGBT people, rather than a defense of religious freedom.

## Federal Legislation: Betting on ENDA

In our federal system, there are always two options for pursuing legislative reforms—state and federal. If we take the push for same-sex marriage as a case study, then we might assume that the federal government offers the best way to bring legal equality to swing states and red states.

For many years, the campaign for same-sex marriage has followed a carefully orchestrated framework: The earliest cases were brought in state courts, under state constitutions, in the country's most favorable states. After a few early losses during the 1970s, this strategy yielded short-lived victories in Hawai'i and Alaska, followed by civil unions in Vermont and New Jersey and same-sex marriage in Massachusetts, Connecticut, California, Iowa, and New Mexico.[37] By bringing these early cases in favorable forums, litigators laid the groundwork for favorable rulings in other courts and favorable legislation in other states.[38] As momentum built, lobbyists were able to bring along the president and the attorney general,[39] and litigators have now achieved a nationwide victory in the Supreme Court. This "Roadmap to Victory" was most explicitly laid out by Evan Wolfson of Freedom to Marry,[40] but it required the cooperation of countless activists, litigators, and organizations over the course of more than twenty years.

Using marriage as a model, one might wonder whether antidiscrimination law is now poised for a national moment—namely, whether Congress is ready to pass antidiscrimination protections for LGBT people in the near future. Of course, predicting the behavior of Congress is always a risky business. But in light of recent experience, it does not seem likely that Congress will pass new antidiscrimination protections for LGBT people in the short term.

During the two decades between 1994 and 2014, many LGBT organizations had been working hard to secure the passage of ENDA, a bill that would have prohibited discrimination based on sexual orientation (and more recently, gender identity) in employment.[41] Although ENDA had many supporters in both houses of Congress, it was never able to overcome three major obstacles—partisan politics, legislative gridlock, and gerrymandering. Because all of these obstacles are still present, the passage of federal antidiscrimination legislation may remain a long shot for the foreseeable future.

## Partisan Politics

First, partisan politics: Of ENDA's 254 supporters in the House and the Senate, only a handful were Republicans—eight in the House and ten in the Senate.[42] This is hardly surprising. While the Republican Party's platform opposes "discrimination based on sex, race, age, religion, creed, disability, or national origin," it makes no mention of discrimination based on sexual orientation or gender identity.[43] Indeed, in a remarkable demonstration of retrograde rhetoric, the party's platform still speaks derisively of the administration's attempt to impose "the homosexual rights agenda" on foreign countries.[44] By contrast, the Democratic Party's platform opposes "discrimination on the basis of . . . sexual orientation, [and] gender identity," among other characteristics—and it explicitly supports "marriage equality" and "the movement to secure equal treatment under law for same-sex couples."[45] In November 2014, Republicans expanded control of the House, while picking up control of the Senate.[46]

## Legislative Gridlock

Second, legislative gridlock:[47] In most instances, the Republican House has followed the "majority of the majority" rule, commonly known as the "Hastert Rule," which prohibits a vote on any bill that is not supported by a majority of Republicans.[48] And now that Democrats have lost control of the Senate, they would need fourteen Republicans to join them to invoke cloture, breaking a filibuster.[49] To satisfy these rules, ENDA would have needed to garner support from at least 110 more Republicans in the House and four more Republicans in the Senate.

## Gerrymandering

Third, gerrymandering: After the 2010 census, Republicans controlled redistricting in a majority of states. As a result, the newly established boundaries of electoral districts heavily favor Republicans, creating a larger number of districts that are "safe" for the party's incumbents. In 2012, for example, Republican House candidates lost the national vote by more than one million votes but still managed to hold onto 220 of 228 seats.[50] In 2014, Republicans won the national vote by more than four million votes, so they now hold a majority of 247 to 188—the largest Republican majority in the House since the Great Depression.[51]

## Party Primaries

Finally, the combination of these three factors presents a fourth obstacle to the passage of antidiscrimination laws: When Republicans run in safe districts, they are more vulnerable in primaries than general elections. If they were to support ENDA, Republican incumbents would expose themselves to Tea Party challengers. In Republican primaries, voters are more likely to be libertarian, conservative, and religious—in short, Tea Party voters—and as a result, they are more likely to oppose the passage of antidiscrimination laws that protect LGBT people. As a result of this electoral dynamic, it remains challenging for LGBT lobbyists to win over Republicans and secure the passage of antidiscrimination laws.

## State Legislation: Beyond the Blue States

If antidiscrimination work is stalled out in Congress, then perhaps it's time to return to the states? Until recently, however, the LGBT movement's progress on antidiscrimination laws had been strictly limited to state legislatures controlled by Democrats—specifically, to twenty-one of the country's bluest states.[52] In 2012, for example, the map of President Obama's victory included every state that had adopted an antidiscrimination law to protect LGBT people.[53]

To sustain the progress of this work after marriage equality, the LGBT movement will be forced to invest in working with Republicans—venturing into more hostile territory, beyond the blue states. Presumably, the movement will begin by focusing on the remaining swing states that lack antidiscrimination laws, such as Pennsylvania, Virginia, Ohio, and Florida. As further victories are tallied, the work seems likely to proceed along the political spectrum from swing states to red states, such Alabama, Idaho, Oklahoma, and Wyoming. Indeed, national LGBT organizations such as the Gill Foundation, the Human Rights Campaign, the Gay and Lesbian Victory Fund, and the American Civil Liberties Union's LGBT Project have already announced multi-million-dollar campaigns to win the passage of antidiscrimination laws in southern and western states.[54]

### A Movement Divided

I have already indicated the most obvious impact of this new dynamic: After marriage equality, the objectives and operations of LGBT organizations will diverge in blue states and red states. In fact, this shift started years ago. Once the first blue states succeeded in passing antidiscrimination laws and legalizing same-sex marriage, local LGBT groups in these states began to consider what type of work to do next.

The most striking example of this shift came from Connecticut, where the state's LGBT group (known as Love Makes a Family) closed down shortly after same-sex marriage was legalized.[55] More subtle shifts occurred in Massachusetts and Maine, where organizations have pivoted toward the pursuit of "lived equality," based on the recognition that "discrimination lives on, often in subtle ways."[56] At MassEquality, for example, the organization adopted a new tagline, "Equal, safe, and free, from cradle to grave."[57] Under this banner, MassEquality has moved into "new policy areas that focus on community well-being rather than specific protections for LGBTQ people."[58]

By contrast, LGBT groups in swing states and red states will still have much work left to do after marriage, and much of that work will seem all too familiar. In such states, same-sex couples will have the freedom to marry, but they will not have specific protections under the state's antidiscrimination laws.

## Post–Marriage Equality PACs

To protect LGBT people from discrimination at work, at home, and in the market, LGBT groups will have to reach out to Republicans in swing states and red states. Sadly, in contemporary U.S. politics, "reaching out" to politicians involves offering political endorsements and campaign contributions through Political Action Committees. Indeed, some national LGBT organizations have already helped state organizations support Republican candidates, in an effort to win new legislative victories at the state level. In 2012, for example, the *New York Times* reported that "[g]ay rights advocates from Wall Street to Hollywood poured donations into the coffers of four little-known Republican state senators after the lawmakers provided the decisive votes for same-sex marriage in New York."[59]

Yet this model is not so easily replicated in swing states and red states. Now that same-sex marriage has been elevated to the top of the LGBT community's agenda, it is rarely tenable for LGBT PACs to endorse Republicans in general elections. In most cases, the local LGBT community will not stand for it. The dividing line is that most Democrats are willing to publicly support same-sex marriage, as the party's national platform indicates. In liberal and moderate districts, viable Republican candidates have been willing to support employment and housing protections, and perhaps civil unions. But for now, most Republicans are still opposed to same-sex marriage in red states—or at least, they are still unwilling to publicly support it. Even if a Republican candidate personally believes in marriage equality, the political benefits of publicly acknowledging that stance as a Republican are likely to be outweighed by the political costs.

Now that same-sex marriage is legal in all fifty states, this dynamic may shift, as moderate Republicans feel free to accept same-sex marriage as a *fait accompli*. But the dynamic is not likely to disappear altogether. Barring any sea change in party platforms, Democrats will still be more likely than Republicans to support broader protections for LGBT people in the vast majority of electoral contests. Even though the validity of same-sex marriage is resolved, this tension between the LGBT community and the Republican Party will resurface in debates over more ambitious, progressive LGBT issues—e.g., public accommodations, safe schools, and perhaps affirmative action for LGBT people.

To resolve this dilemma, the LGBT movement will have to find ways to support Republicans without alienating the LGBT community that it claims to represent, or the donors on which it has come to depend. If existing LGBT organizations cannot support this effort, then new LGBT organizations may be formed to pursue it.

Today, the most prominent example of such an organization is American Unity PAC. Founded in 2012 by a $1 million donation from a major Republican donor, American Unity is a so-called Super PAC "focused exclusively on protecting and promoting candidates for U.S. House and U.S. Senate who support freedom for all Americans, regardless of their sexual orientation."[60] Putting aside this organization's particular limitations,[61] American Unity represents a strategic framework that may be vital to the LGBT movement's success in a two-party system: In order to secure the passage of pro-LGBT reforms, LGBT activists must identify pro-LGBT Republicans and donors who are willing to support them.

### Better Dead Than Red?

Given the Republican Party's mistreatment of LGBT people, the prospect of building such relationships may well be challenging (not to mention distasteful) for many of the current leaders of the LGBT movement. And in principle, at least, there is another way out of this dilemma: After marriage equality, the LGBT movement can wed itself to the fate of the Democratic Party, as it has effectively done for so many years. In this scenario, LGBT PACs would work to bring state legislatures across the country under Democratic control, as a way of regaining control of the redistricting process in a majority of states by 2020. Unless LGBT PACs can find ways to support Republican candidates, then redistricting in 2020 may well turn out be the most consequential item on the LGBT movement's agenda in the near future. Once we step back from single issues, it is hard to imagine a single political achievement that is more likely to improve the overall welfare of LGBT people.

The danger of this approach is that Democrats have a long history of taking the LGBT community for granted. As Urvashi Vaid recently quipped, "the Democrats see us as an ATM; the Republicans, as a punching bag."[62] Yet even in today's landscape, an ATM may still be better than a punching bag. After all, a party that newly embraces the legal equality of LGBT people is a far cry from a party that continues to reject it. As long as Republicans decry the advancement of "the homosexual rights agenda," the best hope for LGBT people may be the long-term project of turning red states purple and swing states blue.

## Strategic Dilemmas: Piecemeal Reforms, Package Deals, and the Delicate Relationship between Lobbying and Litigation

Beyond party politics, the LGBT movement will confront two additional dilemmas in pursuing antidiscrimination reforms: whether to present antidiscrimination bills as piecemeal reforms or package deals, and how to manage the delicate relationship between lobbying and litigation. Without attempting to resolve the first dilemma, this part of the chapter argues that LGBT lobbyists should not entertain exemptions that apply only to claims brought by LGBT plaintiffs—or more broadly, any protections that fall short of what might realistically be achieved through litigation under existing antidiscrimination laws.

### All Aboard: HRC's Omnibus Bill

The first issue is illustrated by a recent announcement from Chad Griffin, the president of the Human Rights Campaign (HRC).[63] For the last twenty years, HRC has been one of the country's leading lobbyists for the passage of ENDA. In September 2014, Griffin told a gathering of transgender activists "how many thousands of hours and millions of dollars we put into the campaign for a fully inclusive ENDA."[64] Looking ahead, Griffin promised that HRC would remain committed to the passage of ENDA: "First things first: an inclusive ENDA. . . . It will change millions of lives for the better. And as an organization, HRC will continue to invest in and fight for an inclusive ENDA."[65]

In the very next sentence, however, Griffin candidly admitted that "even a broad, inclusive ENDA isn't enough."[66] Stressing the importance of fair housing and safe schools, he explained, "If you're trans, a fully-inclusive ENDA doesn't do much good if you're living on the street because you've been kicked out of your apartment . . . [or] if you haven't been able to finish school."[67]

To address these broader concerns, Griffin then announced a significant addition to HRC's legislative agenda: "That's why, in the next session [of] Congress, HRC will lead the campaign for a fully inclusive, comprehensive, LGBT civil rights bill."[68] This bill, Griffin explained, will include "non-discrimination protections that don't stop at employment, but that finally touch every aspect of our lives—from housing, to public accommodations, to credit, to federal funding, to the education we all need to succeed and thrive."[69] On July 23, 2015, the Human Rights Campaign joined Democratic legislators and other national LGBT organizations to announce the introduction of the Equality Act, a bill to add sexual orientation and gender identity to the protections of the Civil Rights Act of 1964 and other federal antidiscrimination laws.[70]

In the abstract, it's impossible to say which proposal is a better strategy for the LGBT movement: an employment-only bill or an omnibus bill. On the one hand, an employment-only bill is more feasible, because it's more modest, and it may well pave the way for more ambitious bills in subsequent years. On the other hand, an omnibus bill is more inspiring precisely because it's more ambitious. Even if the passage of an omnibus bill "is not going to be an easy fight," it might more effectively mobilize the LGBT community and educate the general public about the many legal inequalities that persist now that same-sex marriage is legal. In this respect, even the legislative defeat of an omnibus bill may prove helpful.[71]

If we look at the history of antidiscrimination laws, the LGBT movement's track record does not weigh clearly in favor of package deals or piecemeal reforms. In seventeen of the twenty-two states that have adopted inclusive antidiscrimination laws, the legislature passed employment, housing, and public accommodations laws in the same year, as a package deal. In the remaining five states, the legislature initially passed an employment law, while deferring passage of housing and public accommodations laws.[72] In the long run, these piecemeal reforms seem no less successful than package deals: In all but one of these states, the legislature subsequently passed housing and public accommodations laws.[73]

Moreover, as Griffin's speech implies, it may be possible to gain the benefits of each strategy while minimizing each strategy's drawbacks. Rather than introducing all of the movement's objectives within a single bill, LGBT organizations could launch public education campaigns that push multiple bills under the umbrella of a single, unified theme. For example, a campaign for the passage of antidiscrimination protections might be framed not only as providing LGBT people with a chance "to earn a living" and "pay the rent," but as giving all Americans a chance to participate in the free market, contribute to the economy, and pursue the American Dream.[74] Even when bills address a diverse range of separate subjects, they can still be presented as advancing the LGBT movement's broader goals.

However this dilemma is resolved, it is important to recognize that it is qualitatively different than an earlier dilemma faced by the LGBT movement—whether to include protections for gender identity, in addition to sexual orientation, within antidiscrimination bills. In 2007, the House of Representatives passed a version of ENDA that included only sexual-orientation protections, because some members of the House majority were not willing to support gender-identity protections.[75] ENDA's primary sponsor, Representative Barney Frank, attempted to justify this proposal as a piecemeal reform that would pave the way for gender-identity protections in subsequent years.[76] As many LGBT organizations recognized, however, this justification was problematic, because the bill failed to protect a particular class of persons, namely, transgender workers. It is one thing to pursue protections in one domain (e.g., employment), while putting off protections in other domains (e.g., housing); it is quite another to pursue protections for one group (e.g., lesbian, gay, and bisexual workers), while putting off protections for other groups (transgender workers). So long as the LGBT movement insists upon equal treatment for LGBT people, there is no obvious reason why it must insist upon the passage of all antidiscrimination laws in one package deal.

## Legislation, Litigation, and Symbiosis

In the struggle for same-sex marriage, legislation and litigation have often paved the way for each other.[77] In some states, courts have relied on the legislature's adoption of antidiscrimination laws as a basis for concluding that sexual orientation is legally irrelevant—and thus, for invalidating the state's laws against same-sex marriage.[78] In other states, the failure of same-sex marriage litigation has triggered legislative responses—not only limited partnerships in Hawai'i but full marriage equality in New York. More generally, a string of high-profile judicial and legislative victories in states like Massachusetts, Iowa, California, and New York established a sense of momentum, which likely bolstered subsequent ballot initiatives in states like Maine, Maryland, and Minnesota.

As Douglas NeJaime has shown, however, the relationship between legislation and litigation has not always been symbiotic.[79] To secure the passage of statutes that recognize same-sex relationships, LGBT lobbyists have accepted religious exemptions that would not otherwise exist. In 2011, for example, Rhode Island passed a law permitting civil unions, but the law allowed all religious organizations—including hospitals, schools, and community centers—to refuse to treat any civil union "as valid."[80] In a similar vein, the laws of several other states now "exempt religious entities from providing 'services, accommodations, advantages, facilities, goods, or privileges' relating to 'the solemnization or celebration of a marriage.'"[81]

In a recent article in the *Stanford Law Review*, Mary Anne Case identified a similar tension between lobbying for the passage of ENDA and litigating sex discrimination claims under Title VII.[82] As Case observed, the most recent version of ENDA included a handful of troubling exemptions: Most notably, it contained language suggesting that employers may impose "dress codes" that distinguish between males and females, and it included an exemption for religious employers. Depending on how these clauses were interpreted, they might have been used to carve out sweeping exceptions to Title VII. This would have been especially unfortunate, because transgender employees have recently begun winning sex discrimination claims under Title VII.[83] The irony is evident: After fighting so hard with gay lobbyists to be included in ENDA's protections, transgender litigants may fare better off without them.

In her article, Case acknowledged that lesbian and gay plaintiffs have been less successful than transsexual plaintiffs under Title VII—but she found "some reason for optimism" in recent rulings from the Equal Employment Opportunity Commission, the agency charged with enforcing federal antidiscrimination laws.[84] In the past few years, the EEOC has begun to reverse the dismissal of sex discrimination claims brought by lesbian and gay plaintiffs—even when the plaintiff's claim is based only on the "choice of a same-sex partner," or the plaintiff's "homosexual orientation."[85] More recently, the EEOC issued a formal decision holding that "sexual orientation is inherently a 'sex-based consideration'" and that "discrimination based on sexual orientation is necessarily . . . sex discrimination under Title VII."[86]

Whether or not federal courts end up adopting this framework, Case's analysis offers a powerful indictment of the exemptions in ENDA, and a cautionary tale about the kinds of compromises that lobbying so often entails. At the very least, it now seems clear that the LGBT movement should not support the passage of antidiscrimination laws that would significantly jeopardize the progress that LGBT plaintiffs have already made, or the progress that plaintiffs seem likely to make in the near future. In particular, Case's analysis tips the scales against accepting any new exemptions that apply specifically to claims based on sexual orientation or gender identity, or any other exemptions that are not already recognized under well-settled interpretations of existing federal or state antidiscrimination laws. If litigation still harbors the hope of full inclusion within the country's antidiscrimination laws, then legislation should not settle for anything less.

## Conclusion

Now that marriage equality exists across the United States, the LGBT movement is confronted with two Americas—one blue and one red. In a minority of states, LGBT people enjoy legal equality, but not lived equality: They have formal equality under our laws, but they do not experience themselves as equal in many aspects of everyday life. But in a majority of states, LGBT people do not enjoy equality of any kind, beyond equality in marriage itself. Although the goals of legal equality may seem old-fashioned, they are still unfilled for most LGBT Americans.

This chapter has argued that for the near future, the passage of antidiscrimination laws is an attractive target for the LGBT movement to pursue. Because this issue has widespread appeal, it seems likely to energize the movement's base, win over moderate voters, and neutralize the movement's most strident opponents. But after marriage equality, this work will be transformed in two ways—first, it will shift from national to local legislatures, and second, it will shift from blue to red and swing states. In order to successfully navigate this political transition, the LGBT movement will need to build relationships with Republican legislators, or rewrite the electoral map across the United States. Unless and until the movement achieves at least one of these goals, LGBT people will not be equal in law or life.

## Epilogue

As this book was going to press, Utah generated more headlines in the struggle for LGBT rights: On March 11, 2015, the Utah legislature passed SB 296, a law that prohibits discrimination against LGBT people in employment and housing.[87] Utah is the first state in which a Republican-controlled legislature passed an antidiscrimination law that protects LGBT people. With a Republican majority of 89 percent in both chambers, it is one of the country's most Republican legislatures. In addition, it is one of the country's most religious and conservative states.

Because I was personally involved in drafting and lobbying for SB 296, I will let others decide the extent to which it lives up to (or falls short of) the standards of advocacy that I have articulated in this chapter. In light of my involvement, it seems more useful to share a few lessons that I learned from my experience, rather than to attempt a detailed explanation or justification of the bill's provisions.

First, the passage of Utah's law illustrates that LGBT organizations can capitalize on popular backlash against anti-LGBT campaigns, reforms, and initiatives. Shortly after the Church of Jesus Christ of Latter-day Saints (LDS Church) joined the campaign to pass Proposition 8, the church began issuing a series of statements responding to "allegations of bigotry and persecution."[88] In these statements, the church attempted to distinguish between "opposition to same-sex marriage" and "hostility toward gays and lesbians."[89] Specifically, the church noted that it did not object to "rights for same-sex couples regarding hospitalization and medical care, fair housing and employment rights, or probate rights, so long as these do not infringe on the integrity of the traditional family or the constitutional rights of churches."[90]

Although the LDS Church had acknowledged that these rights were "already established in California,"[91] they were still vitally needed by LGBT Utahns. To publicize the church's new statement, Equality Utah launched the "Common Ground Initiative"—a package of bills based on the church's positions that garnered overwhelming support in opinion polls.[92] In 2009, Salt Lake City adopted municipal ordinances prohibiting employment and housing discrimination against LGBT people, after receiving the church's official endorsement.[93] In each of the following years, new antidiscrimination ordinances were adopted by more cities and counties. In March 2015—five months after same-sex marriage became legal in Utah—SB 296 was passed by overwhelming margins in both houses of the Utah Legislature, after another official endorsement from LDS leaders.[94]

As the timing of SB 296 suggests, marriage litigation is shaping the way that lobbying is conducted in state legislatures—for good and for ill. On the one hand, the astonishing success in federal marriage litigation since *Windsor* has instilled the LGBT community with a new sense of empowerment and inevitability—and a new set of aspirations and expectations for the LGBT movement. Because marriage litigation takes place in courts, within a constitutional framework, it is an all-or-nothing endeavor: In contrast to legislation, it offers advocates and opponents less room for compromises and fewer opportunities to negotiate incremental gains. (For example, compare how frequently courts granted same-sex couples the right to marry, rather than offering the half-measure of civil unions or domestic partnerships.)[95] After witnessing so many unmitigated victories in federal courts, many LGBT people now seem emboldened to insist upon equally unmitigated victories in state legislatures. It remains to be seen how long this fortitude will last, especially if legislative victories do not materialize early and often in the next several years.

On the other hand, the LGBT movement's rapid gains in federal marriage litigation have already precipitated a backlash from opponents. In

Indiana and Arkansas, state legislatures have passed so-called Religious Freedom Restoration Acts (RFRAs), which were expressly crafted as measures to legalize discrimination against LGBT people.[96] Fortunately, the legislatures amended both laws in response to public pressure,[97] which is further evidence of the movement's ability to capitalize on backlash against anti-LGBT measures. But both laws remain problematic—especially the Arkansas law—and neither state has adopted any laws to protect LGBT people from discrimination of any kind.[98] Similar "religious freedom" bills are still pending in many states—all of them swing states or red states.[99]

In this emerging contest between LGBT rights and religious liberties, symbolism may turn out to be as significant as substance: In addition to negotiating the language of bills, LGBT organizations will be forced to negotiate how bills are presented to legislators and voters, many of whom have different concerns than most LGBT people. In Utah, for example, the LDS Church presented SB 296 as a "compromise" that "balances religious freedom and antidiscrimination"—a "fair, balanced approach" that achieves "fairness for all."[100] Meanwhile Equality Utah, the state's leading LGBT advocacy group, presented the same legislation as a bill that "adds the words 'sexual orientation' and 'gender identity' to Utah's anti-discrimination laws in order to establish workplace and housing protections for LGBT Utahns"—without creating "new exemptions for religious individuals or businesses owned by religious individuals," or "any exemptions that apply only to LGBT people."[101] While both of these messages were valid, the tension between them allowed misinformation to spread about what the bill provided, how it would be interpreted, what it signified, and whether it could be adopted as a model by other states. Similar tensions surfaced in Arizona, Arkansas, and Indiana when LGBT groups described state RFRAs as granting a "license to discriminate," while opponents described them as protecting "religious liberties." The question of how the LGBT movement might organize public education campaigns to address these challenges is not any less complex—nor any less vital—than the other strategic dilemmas explored in this chapter. In order to establish full equality for LGBT Americans the LGBT movement will need to tackle each of these new challenges in swing states and red states.

NOTES

1 Letter from First Presidency of Church of Jesus Christ of Latter-day Saints to Church Leaders in California, http://www.mormonnewsroom.org/article/california-and-same-sex-marriage, accessed April 2015.

2 *See* Luke Perry, *Mitt Romney, Mormonism, and the 2012 Election* (New York: Palgrave, 2014), pp. 67–69.

3 Kitchen v. Herbert, 961 F. Supp. 21 1181 (D. Utah 2013).

4 Evans v. Utah, 21 F.Supp.3d 1192 (D. Utah 2014).

5 Kitchen v. Herbert, 755 F.3d 1193 (10th Cir. 2014).

6 Evans v. Utah, No. 14–4060 (10th Cir. July 11, 2014).

7 Obergefell v. Hodges, 135 S.Ct. 2584 (2015).

8 *See, e.g.*, Rebecca Isaacs, "The LGBT Movement after Marriage," Advocate.com, June 12, 2014, http://www.advocate.com/commentary/2014/06/12/op-ed-lgbt-movement-after-marriage, accessed April 2015.

9 Fran Hutchins, "What's Next? Building Stronger LGBTQ Organizations beyond the Marriage Milestone," Equality Federation Institute 2014, http://equalityfederation.org/sites/ default/files/Whats_Next.pdf, accessed April 2015.

10 *See, e.g.*, Isaacs, "The LGBT Movement after Marriage."

11 Lisa Duggan, "Beyond Formal Equality," in "What's Next for the LGBT Movement?" *Nation*, June 27, 2013.

12 Urvashi Vaid, *Virtual Equality: The Mainstreaming of Gay and Lesbian Liberation* (New York: Doubleday, 1995), p. 2.

13 *See, e.g.*, Hutchins, "What's Next?" p. 4; Urvashi Vaid, "Be Transformative, Not Transfixed!" in "What's Next for the LGBT Movement?" *Nation*, June 27, 2013; Hayley Gorenberg, "Beyond Marriage: What's Next for the LGBT and HIV Rights Movement," April 13, 2013, http://www.lambdalegal.org/blog/beyond-marriage, accessed April 2015.

14 *See* Hutchins, "What's Next?" pp. 4, 5, 17; Gorenberg, "Beyond Marriage."

15 *See* Vaid, *Virtual Equality*, p. 285–303; Duggan, "Beyond Formal Equality."

16 *See* Michael Paulson, "Gay Marriages Confront Catholic School Rules," *New York Times*, Jan. 23, 2014, at A1 (describing "a wave of firings and forced resignations of gay men and lesbians from Roman Catholic institutions across the country, in most cases prompted not directly by the employees' sexuality, but by their decisions to marry as same-sex marriage becomes legal in an increasing number of states"); Bob Shine, "Catholic Jobs Lost over LGBT Issues on the Rise," *National Catholic Reporter*, Sept. 25, 2014 (noting that "[f]ive dioceses have revised teacher contracts explicitly banning employees from supporting same-sex relationships in both their professional and their personal lives").

17 Vaid, *Virtual Equality*, p. 2.

18 *See, e.g.*, Wendy Brown, *States of Injury: Power and Freedom in Late Modernity* (Princeton, NJ: Princeton University Press, 1995).

19 To add insult to injury, such laws are often invoked to justify the same disparities that they were intended to target: If you have the right to work, the logic goes, then problems like homelessness and unemployment must be your fault. And finally, campaigning for employment discrimination laws often masks the intersection of LGBT identity with other traits. For simplicity's sake, these campaigns often focus on the singular injustice of being fired "just for being gay" or "just for being transgendered." While this rhetoric is effective with the moveable middle, it presents a very narrow, privileged picture of who "we" are. If we're being fired "just for being gay," then we must be white, wealthy, male, young, and able—i.e., people who are not subject to other forms of discrimination based on race, class, sex, age, or disability, among other things.

20 Marieka Klawitter, "Multilevel Analysis of the Effects of Antidiscrimination Policies on Earnings by Sexual Orientation," 30 *Journal of Policy Analysis and Management* 334–58 (2011); Gary Gates, "The Impact of Sexual Orientation Anti-discrimination Policies on the Wages of Lesbians and Gay Men," 2009 (unpublished), available at http://papers.ccpr.ucla.edu/abstractphp?preprint=544, accessed April 2015.

21 *See, e.g.*, Paula Ettelbrick, "Since When Is Marriage a Path to Liberation?" *Out/Look*, Fall 1989, pp. 9, 14–17.

22 *See, e.g.*, Robert P. George, "Gay Marriage, Democracy, and the Courts," *Wall Street Journal*, Aug. 3, 2009.

23 Hutchins, "What's Next?" p. 24.

24 Lillian Faderman et al., eds., *Great Events from History: Gay, Lesbian, Bisexual, and Transgender Events, 1848–2006* (Ipswich, MA: Salem Press, 2007), p. 228.

25 William Eskridge Jr., *Gaylaw: Challenging the Apartheid of the Closet* (Cambridge, MA: Harvard University Press, 1999), pp., 328–37, 356–61.

26 No state has passed a law that bans discrimination based on sexual orientation, but not gender identity, since 2002. N.Y. Exec. Law § 296 (2003). In 2008, however, the U.S. House of Representatives passed a version of ENDA that did not include gender identity protections. *See* Final Vote Results for Roll Call 1057, H.R. 3685. And in 2011, Massachusetts banned discrimination based on gender identity in employment and housing, but refused to ban discrimination based on gender identity in public accommodations. *Compare* Mass. Gen. Laws ch. 151B, § 4 (1989), *with* Mass. Gen. Laws ch. 272 § 92A (1989).

27 Indeed, the same pattern has been repeated in European countries. Kees Waaldijk, "Eight Major Steps in the Legal Recognition of Homosexual Orientation: A Chronological Overview of National Legislation in the Member States of the European Union," https://openaccess.leidenuniv.nl/handle/1887/12684, accessed April 2015.

28 In Maine, the sequence of these events was unusual. In 1997, the legislature passed an employment law, but it was then narrowly repealed by voters. In 2004, the state legalized civil unions. In 2005, the state passed a comprehensive antidiscrimination law. Me. Rev. Stat. Ann. tit. 5, § 4572, § 4582, § 4592 (2005).

29  DOMA was a federal law that defined marriage as the union of one man and one woman, thereby banning the federal government from recognizing same-sex marriages. Pub.L. 104–199, 110 Stat. 2419, enacted September 21, 1996, 1 U.S.C. § 7 and 28 U.S.C. § 1738C. The most recent bill to include federal employment protections for LGBT people was known as the Employment Non-Discrimination Act (ENDA). See 113th Congress, H.R. 1755; S.B. 815. ENDA was a federal bill to prohibit employment discrimination based on sexual orientation and gender identity. See 113th Congress, H.R. 1755; S.B. 815.

30  Although the Prop 8 campaign was more costly than others, similar campaigns in other states have attracted impressive contributions. In 2012, supporters of same-sex marriage raised $12 million in Minnesota, $9 million in Washington, and $4 million in Maryland, which helped secure successful ballot initiatives in these states.

31  See, e.g., Annual Report of American Foundation for Equal Rights; Danny Hakim, "Money Flows to G.O.P. Backers of Same-Sex Marriage," New York Times, Jan. 17, 2012, http://www.nytimes.com/2012/01/18/nyregion/money-flows-to-gop-backers-of-gay-marriage-in-new-york.html, accessed April 2015.

32  Maggie Haberman, "Poll: Big Support for Anti-Discrimination Law," Politico, Sept. 30, 2013.

33  See U.S. Senate Roll Call Votes, 113th Congress—1st Session, Vote Summary, on Passage of the Bill (S. 815 As Amended), Nov. 7, 2013; U.S. House of Representatives, 113th Congress—2nd Session, Discharge Petition No. 0011, Motion to Discharge a Committee from the Consideration of House Resolution 678, providing for the consideration of Senate Bill 815, Sept. 17, 2014. In 2013, sixty-four senators voted in favor for ENDA, but nine of these senators were Democrats subsequently replaced by Republicans.

34  See Michael Klarman, "Brown and Lawrence (and Goodridge)," 104 Michigan Law Review 431 (2005).

35  134 S.Ct. 2751 (2014).

36  See, e.g., Elane Photography v. Willock, 296 P.3d 491 (N.M. 2012).

37  Baehr v. Lewin, 852 P.2d 44 (Hawai'i 1993); Brause v. Bureau of Vital Statistics, 1998 WL 88743 (Alaska Sup. Ct. Feb. 27, 1998); Baker v. State, 744 A.2d 864 (Vt. 1999); Lewis v. Harris, 908 A.2d 196 (N.J. 2006); Goodridge v. Department of Public Health, 798 N.E.2d 941 (Mass. 2003); Kerrigan v. Commission of Public Health, 957 A.2d 407 (Conn. 2008); In re Marriage Cases, 183 P.3d 384 (Cal. 2008); Varnum v. Brien, 763 N.W.2d 862 (Iowa 2009); Griego v. Oliver, 316 P.3d 865 (N.M. 2013).

38  Thomas M. Keck, "Beyond Backlash: Assessing the Impact of Judicial Decisions on LGBT Rights," 43 Law and Society Review 151 (2009).

39  Letter of United States Attorney General Eric Holder to Speaker John A. Boehner dated February 23, 2011, available at http://www.justice.gov/opa/pr/letter-attorney-general-congress-litigation-involving-defense-marriage-act, accessed April 2015.

40 *See* Roadmap to Victory, Freedom to Marry, http://www.freedomtomarry.org/pages/roadmap-to-victory, accessed April 2015.

41 Alex Reed, "Abandoning ENDA," 51 *Harvard Journal of Legislation* 277, 281–82 (2014).

42 Lauren Fox, "GOP House Leaders Still Oppose ENDA: Republicans who Support ENDA Urge Leaders in the House to Act," *U.S. News & World Report*, June 16, 2014.

43 Republican National Platform 2012, "We Believe in America," at 9.

44 Republican National Platform 2012, "We Believe in America," at 46.

45 Democratic National Platform 2012, "Moving America Forward," at 17–18.

46 Jonathan Weisman & Ashley Parker, "G.O.P. Takes Senate," *New York Times*, Nov. 5, 2014, at A1.

47 *See generally* Michael J. Teter, "Congressional Gridlock's Threat to the Separation of Powers," 2013 *Wisconsin Law Review* 1097.

48 Molly Ball, "Even the Aide Who Coined the Hastert Rule Says the Hastert Rule Isn't Working," *Atlantic*, July 21, 2013.

49 *See* Senate Comm. on Rules & Admin., Standing Rules of the Senate, S. Doc. No. 110–9, R. XXII.2, at 15–16 (2007).

50 *See* Federal Election Commission, Federal Elections 2012, Elections Results for the U.S. President, the U.S. Senate, and the U.S. House of Representatives, at 11, available at http://www.fec.gov/pubrec/fe2012/federalelections2012.pdf, accessed April 2015.

51 *See* Jonathan Martin, "Voters' Second Thoughts on Hope and Change," *New York Times*, Nov. 4, 2014, at P6 (observing that "the Republican hold on the House may be impregnable until after district lines are redrawn again in the next decade—largely because of the party's enlarged majority and gerrymandered seats").

52 As this chapter was going to press, Utah became the first state in which a Republican-controlled legislature passed an antidiscrimination law that protects LGBT people. This development is described in the epilogue.

53 In a remarkable demonstration of this link, Colorado passed antidiscrimination laws in 2007 and 2008, shortly before it flipped from red to blue in November 2008. *See* Colo. Rev. Stat. § 24–34–402 (2007) (employment); Colo. Rev. Stat. § 24–34–502 (2008) (housing); Colo. Rev. Stat. § 24–34–601 (2008) (public accommodations); Rob Witwer & Adam Schrager, *The Blueprint: How the Democrats Won Colorado (and Why Republicans Everywhere Should Care)* (Golden, CO: Fulcrum Publishing, 2010).

54 *See* Nicholas Confessore & Jeremy W. Peters, "Gay Rights Push Shifts Its Focus South and West," *New York Times*, Apr. 27, 2014.

55 Hutchins, "What's Next?" p. 15.

56 Hutchins, "What's Next?" p. 13.

57 Hutchins, "What's Next?" p. 12.

58 Hutchins, "What's Next?" p. 12.

59 Danny Hakim, "Money Flows to G.O.P. Backers of Same-Sex Marriage," *New York Times*, Jan. 17, 2012, http://www.nytimes.com/2012/01/18/nyregion/money-flows-to-gop-backers-of-gay-marriage-in-new-york.html, accessed April 2015.

60  *See* www.americanunitypac.com, accessed April 2015.

61  A few limitations stand out: First, the PAC's contributions are exclusively limited to candidates who support same-sex marriage. Second, the PAC's contributions are largely limited to Republican candidates running in blue states. Third, and most troubling, the PAC's materials support only the rights of "gay and lesbian Americans," while making no mention of the rights of bisexual or transgender Americans. *See* www.americanunitypac.com, accessed April 2015.

62  Urvashi Vaid, "Be Transformative, Not Transfixed!" in "What's Next for the LGBT Movement?" *Nation*, June 27, 2013.

63  Rebecca Juro, "Transcript: HRC President Chad Griffin Apologizes to Trans People at Southern Comfort," Advocate.com, Sept. 5, 2014, http://www.advocate.com/print/politics/ transgender/2014/09/05/transcript-hrc-president-chad-griffin-apologizes-trans-people-speech, accessed April 2015.

64  Juro, "Transcript."

65  Juro, "Transcript." Admittedly, it was not clear precisely what Griffin meant by "ENDA" in this speech. On July 8, 2014—two months before Griffin spoke—several of the country's leading organizations had already issued a joint statement withdrawing support for the current version of ENDA, because of the bill's broad exemptions for religious organizations that applied only to LGBT workers. *See* American Civil Liberties Union et al., Joint Statement on Withdrawal of Support for ENDA and Call for Equal Workplace Protections for LGBT People, available at https://www.aclu.org/sites/default/files/field_document/ joint_statement_on_enda.pdf, accessed April 2015.

66  Juro, "Transcript."

67  Juro, "Transcript."

68  Juro, "Transcript."

69  Juro, "Transcript."

70  Sophia Tesfaye, "'The Equality Act': Democrats Push Bill Banning LGBT Discrimination," *Salon*, July 23, 2015.

71  Cf. Douglas NeJaime, "Winning through Losing," 96 *Iowa Law Review* 941 (2011); Thomas M. Keck, "Beyond Backlash: Assessing the Impact of Judicial Decisions on LGBT Rights," 43 *Law & Society Review* 151 (2009).

72  *See* Haw. Rev. Stat. § 378-2 (2011) (employment, originally passed in 1991); Haw. Rev. Stat. § 515-3 (2011) (housing, originally passed in 2006); Haw. Rev. Stat. § 489-3 (2011) (public accommodations, originally passed in 2011); Cal. Gov't Code § 12940 (employment, originally passed in 1993); Cal. Gov't Code § 12955 (housing, originally passed in 1999); Cal. Civ. Code § 51 (public accommodations, originally passed in 2005); Nev. Rev. Stat. § 613.330 (2011) (employment, originally passed in 1999); Nev. Rev. Stat. § 118.100 (2011) (housing, originally passed in 2011); Nev. Rev. Stat. § 651.070 (2011) (public accommodations, originally passed in 2009); Colo. Rev. Stat. § 24-34-402 (2007) (employment); Colo. Rev. Stat. § 24-34-502 (2008) (housing); Pa: Colo. Rev. Stat. § 24-34-601 (2008) (public accommodations).

73 The only exception is Utah, which passed employment and housing protections while this book was going to press. Utah's antidiscrimination law is addressed in the epilogue of this chapter.

74 I thank Troy Williams, executive director of Equality Utah, for suggesting this theme for the organization's post–marriage equality agenda.

75 *See* 110th Congress, House Resolution 3685.

76 "ENDA to Be Separated into Two Bills: Sexual Orientation and Gender Identity," *Advocate*, Sept. 28, 2007 (quoting Rep. Barney Frank's prediction that "moving forward on this bill now will also better serve the ultimate goal of including people who are transgender than simply accepting total defeat today").

77 Thomas M. Keck, "Beyond Backlash: Assessing the Impact of Judicial Decisions on LGBT Rights," 43 *Law & Society Review* 151 (2009).

78 *See, e.g.*, Varnum v. Brien, 763 NW 2d 862, 890–892 (Iowa 2009).

79 Douglas NeJaime, "Marriage Inequality: Same-Sex Relationships, Religious Exemptions, and the Production of Sexual Orientation Discrimination," 100 *California Law Review* 1169 (2012).

80 NeJaime, "Marriage Inequality," p. 1188.

81 NeJaime, "Marriage Inequality," p. 1187.

82 Mary Anne Case, "Legal Protections for the 'Personal Best' of Each Employee: Title VII's Prohibition on Sex Discrimination, the Legacy of *Price Waterhouse V. Hopkins*, and the Prospect of ENDA," 66 *Stanford Law Review* 1333 (2014). *See also* Reed, "Abandoning ENDA."

83 Smith v. City of Salem; Glenn v. Brumby; Macey v. EEOC.

84 Case, "Legal Protections," p. 1353.

85 Case, "Legal Protections," p. 1353.

86 Baldwin v. Foxx, Appeal No. 0120133080 (July 15, 2015), available at http://www.eeoc.gov/decisions/0120133080.pdf.

87 Senate Bill 296, Antidiscrimination and Religious Freedom Amendments, available at http://le.utah.gov/~2015/bills/static/SB0296.html. The bill was signed by the governor of Utah on March 12, 2015, and went into effect on May 11, 2015.

88 "Church Responds to Same-Sex Marriage Votes," Nov. 5, 2008, http://www.mormonnewsroom.org/article/church-responds-to-same-sex-marriage-votes, accessed April 2015.

89 "Church Responds to Same-Sex Marriage Votes."

90 "Church Responds to Same-Sex Marriage Votes."

91 Carrie A. Moore, "LDS Church Issues Statement on Same-Sex Marriage," *Deseret News*, Sept. 10, 2008 (quoting LDS Church statement, "The Divine Institution of Marriage," posted on Aug. 13, 2008).

92 Lisa Duggan, "What's Right with Utah," *Nation*, June 24, 2009.

93 Statement Given to Salt Lake City Council on Nondiscrimination Ordinances, Nov. 10, 2009, http://www.mormonnewsroom.org/article/statement-given-to-salt-lake-city-council-on-nondiscrimination-ordinances, accessed April 2015.

94 Niraj Chokshi, "Gay Rights, Religious Rights, and a Compromise in an Unlikely Place: Utah," *Washington Post*, Apr. 12, 2015; "Utah Lawmakers Introduce Bill Balancing Religious Freedom and Nondiscrimination Protections," Mar. 4, 2015, http://www.mormonnewsroom.org/article/utah-lawmakers-introduce-bill-balancing-religious-freedom-and-nondiscrimination-protections, accessed April 2015.

95 Only two courts have held that the legalization of civil unions is constitutional, because it provides equal benefits to same-sex couples. *See* Baker v. State, 744 A.2d 864 (Vt. 1999); Lewis v. Harris, 908 A.2d 196 (N.J. 2006). By contrast, dozens of federal and state courts have now found that anything less than marriage is unconstitutional, typically because it denies same-sex couples the equal protection of the laws.

96 Garrett Epps, "The Next Steps in the Battle over Religious-Freedom Laws," *Atlantic*, Apr. 2, 2015.

97 Monica Davey et al., "Indiana and Arkansas Revise Rights Bills, Seeking to Remove Divisive Parts," *New York Times*, Apr. 2, 2015.

98 Arkansas' law is especially problematic because it does not clarify whether it can be invoked as a license to discriminate against third parties. Moreover, Arkansas recently passed another law that repeals existing antidiscrimination ordinances passed by municipalities, and prohibits municipalities from adopting such ordinances in the future. *See* Jeff Guo, "Everything You Need to Know about the Gay Discrimination Wars in 2015," *Washington Post*, Feb. 25, 2015.

99 *See* American Civil Liberties Union, "Anti-LGBT Religious Refusals Legislation around the Country," available at https://www.aclu.org/anti-lgbt-religious-refusals-legislation-across-country?redirect=lgbt-rights/anti-lgbt-religious-refusals-legislation-across-country, accessed April 2015.

100 Church of Jesus Christ of Latter-day Saints, "Church Applauds Passage of Utah Senate Bill 296," available at http://www.mormonnewsroom.org/article/church-issues-statement-on-utah-house-bill-296, accessed April 2015.

101 Equality Utah and the ACLU of Utah, "FAQ: SB 296, Utah's New Law Protecting LGBT People from Discrimination," available at http://www.equalityutah.org/images/docs-pdfs/FAQ_SB296_Digital.pdf., accessed April 2015.

PART II

LGBT Issues after Marriage Equality

4

# LGBT Elders

*Making the Case for Equity in Aging*

NANCY J. KNAUER

The LGBT-rights movement has been largely silent on the topic of LGBT elders and issues related to aging. The recent push for marriage equality has been no exception. As marriage eclipsed other issues and became the pathway to equality, little attention was paid to its limitations in the context of LGBT aging. Although the advent of nation-wide marriage equality offers LGBT elders a much-needed measure of legal protection and security, marriage equality may be a bit of a mixed bag financially for LGBT elders. More importantly, marriage equality fails to address some of the most pressing issues facing LGBT elders, such the legal fragility of their extended chosen families, their disproportionately high levels of financial insecurity, and their fear of encountering anti-LGBT bias across a wide range of senior services.

One reason why the concerns of LGBT elders have not been well represented by the LGBT-rights movement is that they do not fit within the prevailing advocacy paradigm that works hard to portray LGBT individual as not only a deserving minority but also *the same as* non-LGBT individuals. This paradigm is based on claims of shared group identity and equivalence that have been deployed quite effectively in a number of recent campaigns, including the campaigns for marriage equality, for the repeal of the military's "Don't Ask, Don't Tell" policy, and, to a lesser extent, for employment nondiscrimination. It is ill equipped, however, to address the more problematic and complicated aspects of the lives of LGBT elders, such as the aging process, the fluidity of identity, and the persistence of the closet.

From a strategic standpoint, there is no question that reliance on claims of identity and equivalence in the early stages of a civil rights struggle has definite advantages. Any newly constituted and unfamiliar minority will be more intelligible and less threatening to the extent that its members are explained to be the same as the majority culture. But, these strategies are also exclusionary projects that fail to address disparities that are rooted in difference, even when resulting from marginalization and subordination. The example of LGBT elders can help demonstrate the limitations inherent in such claims and underscore the importance of building an advocacy program that embraces difference.

In many important respects, LGBT elders are very different from their non-LGBT peers. They are more likely to be single, live alone, and be estranged from their families. They are also much less likely to have children. These factors place them at a significant disadvantage in a number of respects, but most notably in the area of caregiving because the vast majority of caregiving in the United States is performed on an informal basis by younger relatives. LGBT elders, on the other hand, overwhelmingly rely on single-generational "chosen families" for their caregiving and support. Marriage equality will not protect these families and may further marginalize them, as same-sex marriage becomes increasingly the norm.

LGBT elders also challenge the strong claims of shared identity that undergird the contemporary LGBT-rights movement. As members of the pre-Stonewall generation, their identities and worldviews were formed at a time when homosexuality was criminalized and pathologized and gender variance was strictly policed. Many members of this generation do not identify as homosexual or gay—let alone LGBT. They are not the same as their "out and proud" post-Stonewall progeny, but stand instead as living examples of the historically contingent nature of LGBT identity.

This chapter explores the longstanding silence surrounding LGBT aging and examines ways to advocate on behalf of LGBT individuals who are sixty-five years of age or older. After providing an overview of the current challenges facing LGBT elders, it then demonstrates how claims of equivalence fail to address challenges that are rooted in difference. It also makes the case that advocacy on behalf of LGBT elders must start with an understanding of their difference, while asserting that they are nonetheless entitled to equal treatment, recognition, and opportunity. A final section engages the historical contingency of identity and argues that a civil rights project based on strong claims of shared identity necessarily rests on an unstable foundation and risks early obsolescence as future generations forge new iterations and understandings of self and community.

## LGBT Elders and Challenges to Successful Aging

LGBT older adults are a resilient population—they are long-time survivors of homophobia, transphobia, and, for some, HIV/AIDS. They have weathered many storms in their lifetimes and created new forms of family and community within what was at times an openly hostile society. Referred to as "Gen Silent,"[1] LGBT elders still grapple with the legacy of pre-Stonewall views on homosexuality and gender variance. For example, LGBT elders are frequently estranged from their families (and communities) of origin, are more likely to be closeted, and report a high level of distrust of the medical profession. They are often alienated from their natural allies in both the broader LGBT community and the senior community due to pervasive ageism within the LGBT community and homophobia/transphobia within the mainstream senior community.

Over the years, the failure of advocates and policy makers to address the concerns of LGBT elders has produced a stark disconnect. At a time when LGBT individuals enjoy an unprecedented degree of social acceptance and legal protection, many LGBT older adults face the daily challenges of aging isolated from family, detached from the larger LGBT community, and ignored by mainstream aging initiatives.

### The Importance of Pre-Stonewall History

The 2013 U.S. Supreme Court case of *U.S. v. Windsor*[2] highlighted the significance of pre-Stonewall history in the lives of LGBT elders. Recognized as one of the most important civil rights case in recent years, *U.S. v. Windsor* successfully challenged the constitutionality of section 3 of the Defense of Marriage Act (DOMA).[3] It opened the door for the federal recognition of same-sex marriage and later served as the basis for overturning the state marriage bans. The case was brought by Edie Windsor, an eighty-four-year old widow, who received a $363,000 federal estate tax bill solely because, as she explained, she was married to a woman and not a man.[4] In her Supreme Court brief, Edie told the Court about what it was like to be gay in the United States in the 1950s and 1960s after she graduated from college and later met her future spouse, Thea Spryer.[5] Edie first struggled to find community and then lived in fear of discovery, such as when she justifiably thought she would lose her job with the Atomic Energy Commission after being interviewed by the FBI.[6] Instead of an engagement ring, Edie wore a diamond broach in order to avoid potentially prying questions.[7] Edie and Thea's engagement lasted over forty years until they traveled to Canada in 2007 to marry legally after Thea received a life-threatening diagnosis.[8]

Edie's brief provides a glimpse of pre-Stonewall America, but it does not address the lingering effect that these experiences have on many LGBT older adults. Researchers suggest that pre-Stonewall experiences complicate the relationships LGBT elders have with medical professionals and normalize the closet as a coping mechanism or adaptive strategy.[9] Pre-Stonewall views on homosexuality and gender variance necessitated what anthropologists refer to as "fictive kin" or "chosen family" networks.[10] Such views may also be a contributing factor in the high level of health disparities and financial insecurity reported by LGBT elders. It has also been suggested that one of the reasons LGBT elders do not advocate on their own behalf is that they do not believe they deserve better treatment because, many years ago in pre-Stonewall America, they had been warned that if they chose this life they would die friendless and alone.[11]

To provide some historical context, it is important to remember that the worldview of today's LGBT elders was formed long before the 1969 Stonewall riots heralded the radical transformations that would take place in the 1970s concerning sexuality and gender. LGBT elders came of age at a time when homosexuality was criminalized and classified as a severe sociopathic illness and gender variance was strictly policed. Medical intervention to treat homosexuality included electroshock therapy, aversion conditioning, and even lobotomy. There was no concept of "coming out" to family and friends because disclosure risked institutionalization. Homosexuals were disqualified from most employment, and they were considered unfit parents. For this generation, concealing one's sexual orientation—being "closeted"—was simply a way of life, a matter of survival. By the time homosexuality was finally declassified as a mental illness in 1973, the youngest of the LGBT elders who turned sixty-five in 2015 were already twenty-three years of age. As one researcher observed, today's LGBT elders are "the last generation to have lived their adolescence and young adulthood in hiding."[12]

Over the years, many members of this pre-Stonewall generation, like Edie and Thea, responded to increasing social and legal acceptance by living more openly, but others remained deeply closeted. As they have aged, however, even those LGBT elders who chose to live openly now find themselves returning to the closet in order to avoid the perceived threat of experiencing anti-LGBT bias on the part of service providers and non-LGBT peers. They report that the pressure to "re-closet" and conceal their identities is especially intense when they are faced with the prospect of entering a long-term care facility. Reflecting on his future, one openly gay older adult explained, "as strong as I am today . . . when I am in front of the gate of the nursing home, the closet door is going to slam shut behind me."[13]

## An Overview of the Current Generation of LGBT Elders

Not only are LGBT elders an underserved population, but they are also understudied and underresearched, further compounding their invisibility. Most of what is known about LGBT elders comes from incomplete census data on self-reporting same-sex elder couples; small, largely nonrandom academic samples; advocacy and industry surveys; and an increasing store of anecdotal accounts. There continues to be very little information on transgender elders and LGBT elders with intersecting identities. With those caveats, the provisional picture that emerges suggests numerous disparities between LGBT elders and their non-LGBT peers, many of which can directly impede successful aging.

Estimates of the current number of LGBT elders range from between 1.6 million and 2.4 million.[14] The wide variation is the result of wildly differing estimates on the number of LGB individuals more generally and the lack of statistics on the number of transgender elders.[15] Regardless of the estimate used, however, it is clear that the number of LGBT elders will increase remarkably as the Baby Boom generation transitions to senior status, and the total elder population in the United States doubles by 2030.[16]

According to census data, same-sex elder partnered households are geographically diverse and broadly distributed across the United States. Elder same-sex partnered households reside in 97 percent of the counties in the United States, with 15 percent of these couples residing in areas that are classified as rural.[17] The largest concentrations of elder same-sex partnered households are not located in the traditionally LGBT-friendly jurisdictions, but rather in states with high concentrations of elders generally, such as Florida and Arizona.[18]

Studies indicate that LGBT elders are more likely than their non-LGBT peers to be single and to live alone.[19] They are also much less likely to have children.[20] These factors increase their risk of social isolation, including the fact that it is common for LGBT elders to be estranged from their family of origin. Partially as a result of this estrangement, LGBT elders overwhelmingly rely on "chosen family" for emotional, physical, and financial support.[21] LGBT elders also report higher levels of disability, and they lag well behind their non-LGBT peers on all economic indicators.[22] Elder female same-sex partnered households, in particular, are nearly twice as likely to live below the poverty level as different-sex married households.[23]

In lieu of a traditional multigenerational family formed through marriage, biology, or adoption, LGBT individuals have historically created alternative family or fictive kinship networks based on affinity rather than biology or marriage. Although these chosen family structures represent a creative way to form relationships and community in the face of a disapproving family and society, they have two major shortcomings: (1) chosen families are legally very fragile, and (2) their members tend to be from the same generation. These families are at a disadvantage because of the many ways in which the law privileges "next of kin" to the exclusion of all others in terms of property rights and decision making. They also have limitations with respect to their ability to provide the necessary levels of caregiving. Currently, U.S. aging policy rests on an intergenerational support system of "informal" (i.e., unpaid) caregiving, and 80 percent of all caregiving in the United States is performed at no cost often by younger relatives.[24] Single-generational chosen families, however, will experience reciprocal and overlapping caregiving responsibilities as their members age together.

A number of these demographic characteristics may be specific to today's generation of LGBT elders. For example, the LGBT older adults who now are approaching senior status have benefited more directly from greater freedom and recognition—not to mention expanding legal protections. Younger generations of LGBT individuals are less likely to be estranged from their families and more likely to parent by creating intentional LGBT families. However, even with these changes, the experiences of LGBT older adults who are approaching retirement age suggest that the aging process may compromise their ability to withstand and navigate bias, making them more vulnerable to anti-LGBT bias.

## The Reported Fear of Anti-LGBT Bias

LGBT elders report deep concern that they will experience anti-LGBT bias at the hands of a wide range of service providers. This fear of anti-LGBT bias causes LGBT elders to re-closet, be less than candid with medical providers, and underutilize supportive services. They are especially fearful of congregate senior living facilities, but they are reluctant to access the supportive services that are designed to help people "age in place." When combined with the lack of informal caregivers, their fear of senior-specific housing and their unwillingness to access senior services place LGBT elders at an increased risk of self-neglect and social isolation.

Surveys indicate that this apprehension is not limited to LGBT individuals who are sixty-five and older.[25] LGBT individuals generally are more fearful about growing older than their non-LGBT counterparts, particularly as they approach their senior years. [26] They express distrust over the care they will receive from medical providers and concern that they will not be able to be "out" in senior living facilities. These results suggest that fear of experiencing anti-LGBT bias or discrimination may increase with age. It makes intuitive sense that incidents of bias and discrimination that one may have successfully weathered at age thirty-five may appear much more menacing when experienced by a frail, housebound eighty-five-year-old. Accordingly, the aging process may amplify feelings of difference, as well as of vulnerability.

Unfortunately, the fear expressed by LGBT older adults that they will experience anti-LGBT bias as they age is not misplaced. LGBT elders encounter anti-LGBT bias at the hands of service providers that can range from simple ignorance to outright hostility and violence. They may also be subject to anti-LGBT bias from their non-LGBT peers, whose age cohort has the highest reported level of anti-LGBT views.[27] In long-term care facilities, anti-LGBT bias can manifest in a variety of forms.[28] For example, service providers may fail to respect long-term partners or other chosen family by deferring to the wishes of next of kin and separating partners. Long-term care facilities have required transgender residents to wear inappropriate clothing, and staff may address the residents by the wrong name and use incorrect pronouns. Non-LGBT peers sometimes engage in shunning and bullying behaviors. LGBT elders have also received inadequate care and abusive treatment from health care workers on account of their sexual orientation or gender identity. Some workers have openly expressed distaste over having to touch an LGBT person. Religiously motivated workers have been known to harangue LGBT elders who are in their care and urge them to repent before it is too late.[29]

In 2007, the *New York Times* reported that long-term care facilities have moved residents who are perceived to be LGBT to secure "memory" or dementia wards in order to placate the complaints of other residents or their family members.[30] The dementia wards are considered the perfect place to stash an LGBT elder because the residents of the dementia ward will not complain. The same *New York Times* article reported that this practice led to tragic results when an elder gay man without close family was confined to a dementia ward without cause and eventually hanged himself.[31]

In 2008, Sonoma County, California, used secure "memory" wards to separate long-time partners Harold Scull and Clay Greene. At the time, Clay was seventy-six years of age, and Harold was eighty-eight. They had been committed partners for over twenty-five years and had lived together for twenty years. They shared with their cats, Sassy and Tiger, a small house that they had filled with treasures from their travels and Hollywood memorabilia from their days in the entertainment industry. When Harold fell on the front porch steps of their home, Clay called 911, over Harold's objections.[32] Suspecting violence, the county immediately took both men into care and separated them. According to Clay, Harold was taking medication that made him unsteady on his feet, and he was still bruised from an earlier fall. Without the necessary medical screening and against his will, Clay was placed in a secure facility for individuals suffering from dementia. Four months later, Harold died alone in a "board and care" facility, and Clay was not told until "several days after the fact."[33] By the time Harold died, the county had removed Sassy and Tiger to an uncertain fate, sold all of the couple's possessions, and assumed control of their finances. Clay continued to be held in the secure facility until early 2009, when his court-appointed attorney was finally able to secure his release. Even after his release, his lawyer reported that Clay remains fearful that county workers will come to his home and harm him.[34]

In 2010 Clay and Harold's estate sued Sonoma County and related defendants alleging that the defendants' actions were motivated by antigay bias and the desire for financial gain.[35] Clay further alleged that he was verbally harassed and demeaned by the defendants, who "expressed displeasure at having to deal with expressions of grief by a gay man who had lost his partner."[36] Shortly before the trial was scheduled to begin, the defendants settled the claims against them for an amount in excess of six hundred thousand dollars.[37] Sonoma County denied any discrimination or breach of fiduciary duty, but agreed to modify its conservatorship procedures to prevent similar incidents in the future.

Although Clay and Harold were not registered domestic partners under California law, they had taken steps to secure their relationship by executing reciprocal wills and durable powers of attorney that the county allegedly disregarded.[38] In an interview with the *New York Times*, Clay articulated the fear of many LGBT elders when he said, "I was trash to them. I am going to end up in the dumpster."[39]

### "Gen Silent" and the Continuing Pull of the Closet

The closet continues to loom large in the lives of many LGBT elders. As noted earlier, some members of the pre-Stonewall generation have remained deeply closeted their entire lives, whereas others have responded to the changing times by living more openly. Many of these elders are now faced with the prospect of "re-closeting" as they age in order to protect themselves from the perceived risk of anti-LGBT bias, especially when faced with the prospect of entering a long-term care facility.

The demands of the closet subject LGBT elders to the daily pressure of pretending to be someone they are not and can exact a heavy emotional toll. To manage the closet successfully, LGBT elders have to censor many important details of their lives and choose their memories carefully. If they are in a long-term care facility or receiving health care aides in their home, they must also hide all tangible evidence that might give away their secret, including photographs, books, and mementos. Some LGBT elders report that they create an alternate set of memories to share with others, such that a same-sex partner might become a brother or simply a "best friend."[40] When LGBT elders are denied the opportunity to retell stories and revisit past events, it is not a stretch to conclude that the re-sulting isolation can literally leave them alone with their memories.

In addition to the dignitary harm of having to hide an essential part of one's identity, the closet also has adverse health consequences. The chief of geriatric psychiatry at a large New York City hospital told the *New York Times* that closeted LGBT elders face "a faster pathway to de-pression, failure to thrive and even premature death."[41] She explained that "there is something special about having to hide this part of your identity at a time when your entire identity is threatened."[42] When viewed from this perspective, the re-closeting of LGBT elders is a public health concern, as well as a civil rights issue.

For transgender elders, the closet is not always an option because many pre-Stonewall transgender individuals transitioned without med-ical intervention. Even transgender individuals who transition with medical assistance often do not have "bottom surgery."[43] As a result, a transgender elder's physical characteristics may not conform to his or her gender identity and performance, making the elder vulnerable to the prejudice and hostility of personal health aides. Transgender elders may also have difficulty navigating sex-segregated senior facilities. As noted earlier, transgender elders in long-term care facilities have been forced to wear the "wrong" clothes and to room with members of the oppo-site sex because the facility refused to honor the elder's gender identity. There have also been reports of service providers who refused to wash or provide personal care assistance for transgender elders because they objected to having to touch a transgender elder.

## Substituting Arguments of Sameness for an Appreciation of Difference

Over the past decade, the three signature issues of the LGBT rights movement have been marriage equality, the repeal of the military's Don't Ask, Don't Tell Policy, and passage of employment nondiscrimination protections. When viewed together, this slate of policy initiatives sends the clear message that LGBT individuals are just like everyone else. They want to marry, have children, go to work, and serve their country. The problem with this formulation is not that it is necessarily untrue, but that it is necessarily underinclusive. The needs of LGBT elders are not reflected in this heteronormative, youth-oriented version of the American Dream. Marriage equality will not protect their chosen family. LGBT elders are well past the age of active military service. And, as they are leaving the workforce, they are more concerned with the prospect of encountering bias and discrimination in senior-specific contexts, including medical care, supportive services, and housing.

Addressing the concerns of LGBT elders requires a more nuanced understanding of LGBT identity that extends across the life course and embraces not only the sameness of LGBT individuals but also their differences. To some extent, the recent emphasis on LGBT youth has opened up a discussion regarding how individuals experience LGBT identity over the lifespan. Interventions on behalf of LGBT youth include antibullying protections and anticonversion laws, as well as a popular public education effort to inspire and motivate LGBT teens and preteens. Many celebrities, politicians, sports figures, and policy makers have made *It Gets Better* videos to assure LGBT youth that things will improve as they move into young adulthood.[44] Of course, these videos do not mention that many of the issues LGBT youth face also present in older age—bullying, fear of anti-LGBT bias, the closet, self-neglect, and self-harm. Otherwise, the message would be more truthfully "It Gets Better and Then It Gets Worse"—potentially much worse.

### The Limits of Marriage Equality for LGBT Elders

Marriage equality is a prime example of the mismatch between the interests of LGBT elders and the mainstream LGBT agenda. As the major focus of the LGBT rights movement, marriage equality has captured the attention of the general public and dominated the media coverage of LGBT issues. The singular emphasis on marriage equality has led many members of the media to conflate marriage equality with the broader goals of the LGBT-rights agenda, leading some to declare "victory."[45] This declaration of victory is premature for many reasons, not the least of which is that marriage in and of itself is not sufficient to cement the types of fundamental protections and rights that are necessary to ensure dignity, opportunity, and safety for LGBT individuals. Marriage equality mandates access to the institution of marriage and its attendant rights, obligations, and benefits. Apart from its normalizing influence, however, marriage equality does not directly address a host of other pressing issues, including bullying in schools, health disparities, and anti-LGBT bias or discrimination. For LGBT elders and older adults, marriage equality does little to allay many of their chief concerns, such as income insecurity, the legal fragility of chosen family, and the existence of anti-LGBT bias and discrimination in medical care, senior services, and housing options.

Marriage equality offers partnered LGBT elders a much-needed measure of legal protection and security, but it may not be a wise financial move for some LGBT individuals.[46] LGBT elders who are receiving benefits must determine whether marriage will adversely affect their eligibility, including elders who are receiving benefits through a former or deceased spouse or who are receiving any sort of means-tested benefits. Accordingly, LGBT individuals have to weigh the benefits of marriage and their new-found equality against its attendant costs. Marriage may also be simply irrelevant for some LGBT elders and older adults who are not partnered or for whom marriage does not fit with their individual beliefs or worldview. For these individuals, the intense focus on marriage equality misses the mark entirely. Marriage equality also does little to mitigate the legal fragility of chosen families. Although marriage equality allows a same-sex partner to be considered "next of kin," the other members of a chosen family will remain legal strangers.

In short, marriage equality will not help LGBT elders tackle many of the obstacles they face when trying to navigate the challenges of aging. Fully addressing these challenges will require comprehensive legal reform and social change that includes greater recognition for chosen family, legal protections that span the life course, and broad-based cultural competency awareness with respect to LGBT aging and related issues. As attitudes on high-profile issues such as marriage equality continue to "evolve," it is likely that anti-LGBT bias will continue to decrease, but systemic legal and social change may take decades.

## Constructing Claims Based on Sameness

The success the LGBT rights movement has achieved with respect to its three signature issues—marriage equality, Don't Ask, Don't Tell, and employment nondiscrimination—has been the result of a two-part strategy to (1) establish LGBT individuals as a deserving minority, who are just the same as everyone else, and (2) then argue for inclusion. This strategy has worked quite effectively not only in state and federal courts but also in the court of public opinion. For example, in the case of marriage equality, polls first showed that a majority of Americans supported same-sex marriage in 2011, which was well in advance of *U.S. v. Windsor*.[47] A strong majority also supports nondiscrimination protections in employment despite the continuing lack of nation-wide federal protections.[48]

As the litigants in the marriage cases argued for heightened judicial scrutiny for sexual orientation, they found support in the contemporary understanding of sexual orientation as both an inborn and an unchangeable characteristic. Often referred to as the "ethnic" or "identity" model of sexuality, this model imagines sexual orientation as an immutable, unchosen, and benign characteristic. The identity model establishes gay men and lesbians as a valid minority group organized around a benign characteristic (i.e., sexual orientation). When sexual orientation is understood from this perspective, it is possible to advance equality measures by asserting that gay men and lesbians are *the same as* their nongay peers because everyone is born with an unchangeable sexual orientation. The moral force behind such equality assertions is an implied claim of equivalence—given that gay men and lesbians are *the same as* everyone else, they deserve equality of treatment and opportunity, including the right to marry.

This understanding of sexuality differs fundamentally from the model advanced by the gay liberationists in the early 1970s that stressed the role of agency and choice in the definition of sexual identity.[49] The liberationist model forever changed the way society discussed concepts of sexuality and gender, but was quickly displaced by the identity model, which has successfully won over the hearts and minds of many gay and nongay individuals alike.[50] The identity model introduced the American public to a new minority who are just like them, with the exception of one insignificant characteristic—sexual orientation. Other than that one minor detail, the members of this new and deserving minority are just like everyone else.

The identity model also fits nicely within existing equal protection jurisprudence and seems to position gay men and lesbians as the ideal suspect category—politically powerless, historically disadvantaged, and united by an inconsequential and immutable trait. Despite numerous attempts, however, the federal courts have been decidedly lukewarm to the idea that classifications based on sexual orientation warrant a heightened level of scrutiny. In many instances, equality gains have been made without the assistance of enhanced judicial scrutiny, and were based instead on a rational-basis standard, which is the lowest level of review. Although these decisions have fallen short of establishing that gay men and lesbians constitute a category worthy of added judicial protection and oversight, they have invalidated measures directed against gay men and lesbians on the basis that antigay laws and policies lack a rational relationship to a legitimate state interest. Arguably, such rulings send the stronger message that discrimination on the basis of sexual orientation fails any standard of review, not merely the heightened level of review necessary to protect a vulnerable minority.

### Appreciating Difference

The LGBT rights movement has successfully introduced mainstream America to a new minority—LGBT individuals—who are united by a single insignificant characteristic of sexual orientation/gender identity, and who share the hopes and dreams of all Americans to grow up, get a good job, and serve their country. The next challenge is to explain how the social meaning attached to this one insignificant characteristic can derail those shared dreams by limiting opportunity and placing entire populations at risk. In the case of LGBT elders, their family patterns, financial difficulties, and fear of encountering bias all trace their roots to that single insignificant characteristic of sexual orientation or gender identity. It has stigmatized them and set them apart from their non-LGBT peers. Advocacy on their behalf must openly acknowledge this difference while asserting that LGBT elders are nonetheless entitled to equal treatment and opportunity.

LGBT elders survived a dark period in American history. Over the course of their lifetimes, LGBT elders were simultaneously labeled as mentally ill, degenerate, and criminal. Their employment options were greatly curtailed due to officially sanctioned anti-LGBT bias, and the closet was a fearful place where the threat of disclosure was constant. Today, LGBT elders frequently rely on single-generational chosen families for support and are more likely than their non-LGBT peers to be single and less likely to have children. They experience greater levels of financial insecurity than their non-LGBT peers, as well as significant health disparities. They underutilize senior services and are much less likely to be open about their identity than younger LGBT adults. They also express great fear over encountering LGBT bias, especially in health care settings.

Their concerns require a more holistic approach to LGBT identity *and* advocacy—one that acknowledges the differences among LGBT individuals, as well as the fact that, in some instances, LGBT individuals are indeed different from their non-LGBT peers. These points of difference need not be points of division, nor should the fact of difference serve to invalidate claims for equality. Although claims of equivalence and sameness make sense in the early stages of a civil rights struggle, there are times when the moral force of a claim for equity is not grounded in sameness. Approximation to the majority culture may make a minority more familiar and less politically threatening, but it is not what makes a minority deserving.

LGBT elders are a deserving minority because their life choices were and are constrained by the social meaning attached to a characteristic that does not otherwise impair their ability to contribute to society or experience love or loss or rejection. They bear the scars from the days when sexual orientation and gender variance were pathologized and criminalized. These experiences set them apart from the post-Stonewall generations with respect to their family relationships, financial opportunities, and coping stratagems. As a result, policy interventions on their behalf need to focus on their points of difference and seek recognition for their chosen families, compensation for decades of state-sponsored discrimination in the workplace, and the eradication of anti-LGBT bias in senior-specific venues through competency training and legal protections.

## The Historical Contingency of LGBT Identity

The understanding that the worldview of LGBT elders continues to be informed by their experiences in pre-Stonewall America demonstrates the importance of historical context to LGBT identity formation. It also destabilizes the notion of a fixed, shared identity that is at the core of the identity model. Simply put, the pre-Stonewall generation is not the same as the post-Stonewall generations. Their identities and worldviews were formed at different times under dramatically different circumstances. When the pre-Stonewall generation came of age, there was no public pro-gay narrative, and science offered elaborate explanations and treatments for homosexual tendencies. After Stonewall, the increasingly vocal gay rights movement provided an alternative and affirming way of understanding sexuality and gender. For the post-Stonewall generations, the rate of social and political change has been so rapid that some sociologists suggest that the LGBT community is comprised of a number of highly compressed age cohorts that are defined by relatively narrow social and political periods.[51] These observations upend the identity model of LGBT identity, which is premised on a static, and largely ahistorical, immutable characteristic. It illustrates that LGBT identity, as it is lived and experienced, is highly contingent and uniquely a product of the historical context.

There is nothing especially remarkable about this observation to the extent that identity categories and classifications are socially constructed, but it does make visible an important and unspoken dimension of LGBT identity. The prism of intersectionality has provided a useful perspective for understanding the interplay of identity categories such as gender, race, ethnicity, and sexual orientation. However, it has not expressly addressed the crucial longitudinal or historical component of identity formation—a component that represents more than just another point of intersection. To illustrate, take the example of a man who is in a relationship with another man. His understanding of his self and place in the world will vary considerably depending not only on his age but also on whether the date is 1915, 1965, or 2015. An unspoken temporality exists at the intersection of all identity.

The practice of intersectionality uses a familiar and compelling three-dimensional metaphor of the traffic intersection to carve out a sense of place for those on the margin and, in so doing, make that place accessible to others. The metaphor reduces even the most complex iteration of self to a common, everyday experience. As the traffic swooshes by in every direction, the metaphor invites the reader to feel the confusion, fragmentation, and power of contemporary identity categories as they collide and coalesce. The explanatory power of the metaphor, however, is limited by the very spatial properties that make it so effective. Whether conceptualized as crossroads, roundabout, or cloverleaf, the point of intersection represents a position in space that is also a snapshot of a discrete point in time—past, present, or future. The traffic may be coming from all directions, but it only moves in one direction through time.

Every intersection is necessarily located within time as well as space. The coordinates of this fourth dimension represent an indelible "time stamp" that exists on every rendering of intersecting identities and carries significant explanatory value, especially in the case of LGBT elders. A seventy-five-year-old African American man in a long-term relationship with a white man stands at a complex intersection of race, gender, age, and sexual orientation, but his experience will differ considerably if the snapshot captured the intersection in 1965, 2015, or 2065.

Along the axis of time, existing identity categories will change and evolve, as will modes of bias and subordination. An individual's sense of self and worldview will also change, but, as is clear from the pre-Stonewall generation, an individual's sense of self may not be entirely in synch with the broader patterns of social and political change. The man standing at the intersection in 2015 may not identify as homosexual or gay or LGBT for a variety of reasons that may be both historical and personal, but that fact is most likely irrelevant to the traffic gunning for him in the intersection where he may be perceived as LGBT.

In the case of LGBT elders, it is tempting to feel sorry for those who have remained deeply closeted and removed from the LGBT community despite tremendous social and political gains. It is easy to perceive them as being stuck in the past or perhaps suffering from false consciousness.

But, it is not clear that individuals should be required to continually reinterpret themselves in order to correspond with the prevailing popular understanding of their presumed identity. A more nuanced view of identity formation over the life course would suggest that individuals who appear out of synch may nonetheless still be true to themselves. Although individuals should not have to hide or conceal their identities, they are still the authors of their own identities.

Given that identity is necessarily in the act of becoming, social movements based on tightly defined identity politics run the risk of becoming restrictive and exclusionary projects, unless they acknowledge the inevitable ebb and flow of identity. A movement that responds to emerging and related identities by attempting to police and shore up its initial boundaries will exhibit strong essentializing tendencies, resulting in the production of an "official" movement identity. The endorsement of an official (and probably static) version of identity will simultaneously marginalize and exclude emerging identities, even those with a strong family resemblance. A contemporary example of this dynamic would be the tension that has sometimes existed over the incorporation of lesbian and gay rights and transgender rights within a single agenda. An appreciation for the temporality of identity would urge social movements to organize around values and goals rather than an official and most likely outmoded rendition of identity. For example, in the case of LGBT elders, efforts to create LGBT-friendly senior housing in large urban centers will address the needs of some LGBT elders, but not those who do not identify as members of the LGBT community.[52] For these elders, it may be more appropriate to advocate along a platform that emphasizes inclusion and cultural competency while more broadly working toward ensuring equity and security in aging regardless of sexual orientation or gender identity.

On the macro level, the historical contingency of identity suggests a process of identity formation involving constant reinterpretation and reinvention that neither individuals nor social movements may be able to achieve across time. This observation also has direct implications for legal strategies and advocacy. The enactment or recognition of equality-based nondiscrimination protections is generally the result of lengthy and hard-fought civil rights battles. However, by the time an identity category has been recognized at law, it is entirely possible that its parameters have already changed. For example, the early nondiscrimination laws protected individuals on the basis of their "sexual or affectional preference," but such protections quickly gave way to those based on "sexual orientation," as the popular understanding of same-sex attraction shifted from a liberation ideology that emphasized concepts of autonomy to an ideology based on claims of immutability and genetics. Accordingly, historical contingency should sound a cautionary note in attempts to secure class-based protections because identity categories necessarily provide an unstable foundation for civil rights claims and protections. The shifting sands of identity have the potential to render any policy based on the existing identity model both obsolete and incomplete before it is ever enacted or even proposed.

## Conclusion

This volume asks us to look beyond marriage equality to assess the future of LGBT rights. Focusing on LGBT aging, this chapter makes the case that the current LGBT advocacy paradigm is based on claims of sameness that are ill equipped to respond to the unmet needs of LGBT elders, who are very different from both their non-LGBT peers and younger LGBT generations. LGBT elders face significant barriers to successful aging that demand a broad range of legal and policy reforms, including increased protections for chosen family, antidiscrimination protections in senior-specific venues, cultural competency training, and antibullying policies. Clearly, even "after marriage" there remains much to be done to address the unmet needs of LGBT elders and ensure equity in aging regardless of sexual orientation or gender identity.

Efforts on behalf of LGBT elders, however, should be part of a larger project that seeks to develop a more holistic approach to LGBT identity and advocacy that embraces difference rather than prioritizing sameness. An appreciation for difference will enable advocacy and policy initiatives to address the more complicated and less heteronormative aspects of LGBT lives. Such an approach would move beyond the exclusionary claims of identity and equivalence to target existing disparities while affirming the multiplicity of LGBT lives and experiences.

LGBT elders present a living example of the historical contingency of LGBT identity. The temporal nature of identity explains the lingering effect of pre-Stonewall history and illustrates the limitations intrinsic to attempts to define identity categories. It also has a wider applicability that extends past specific contemporary iterations of LGBT identity. The insight that identity is both multivalent *and* historically contingent has implications for social theory, movement building, policy interventions, and future legal reforms.

NOTES

1 *Gen Silent.* Dir. Stud Maddox. Interrobang Productions, 2011. Film.

2 United States v. Windsor, 570 U.S. ___ (2013).

3 Defense of Marriage Act, Pub. L. No. 104–199, 110 Stat. 2419 (1996), *codified at* 1 U.S.C. § 7.

4 Andrew M. Harris, "Widow's $363,000 Tax Bill Led to Obama Shift on Marriage Act," *Bloomberg*, Feb. 28, 2011, http://www.bloomberg.com/news/2011–02–28/a-363–000-tax-bill-to-widow-led-to-obama-shift-in-defense-of-marriage-act.html, accessed October 2014.

5 Brief of Respondent in Response in Support of Writ of Certiorari before Judgment at 9, U.S. v. Windsor, No. 12–307 (S.Ct. Oct. 10, 2012).

6 Brief of Respondent in Response in Support of Writ of Certiorari before Judgment at 10, U.S. v. Windsor, No. 12–307 (S.Ct. Oct. 10, 2012).

7 Brief of Respondent in Response in Support of Writ of Certiorari before Judgment at 9, U.S. v. Windsor, No. 12–307 (S.Ct. Oct. 10, 2012).

8 Richard Wolf, "Gay Marriage Case: A Long Time Coming for Edie Windsor," *USA Today*, Dec. 8, 2012, http://www.usatoday.com/story/news/nation/2012/12/07/edie-windsor-gay-marriage-supreme-court/1737387/, accessed October 2014.

9 Metlife, *Out and Aging: The Metlife Study of Lesbian and Gay Baby Boomers*, November 2006, https://www.metlife.com/assets/cao/mmi/publications/studies/mmi-out-aging-lesbian-gay-retirement.pdf, accessed October 2014.

10 Kath Weston, *Families We Choose* (New York: Columbia University Press, 1997).

11 Nancy J. Knauer, "LGBT Elder Law: Toward Equity in Aging," 32 *Harvard Journal of Law & Gender* 1, 18 (2009).

12 Ski Hunter, *Midlife and Older LGBT Adults: Knowledge and Affirmative Practices for the Social Services* (New York: Routledge, 2012), p. 14.

13 Jane Gross, "Aging and Gay, and Facing Prejudice in Twilight," *New York Times*, Oct. 9, 2007, p. A1.

14 Nancy J. Knauer, "Gen Silent: Advocating for LGBT Elders," 19 *Elder Law Journal* 289, fn. 55 (2011).

15 Jaime M. Grant, et al., Nat'l Gay and Lesbian Task Force Policy Inst., *Outing Age 2010: Public Policy Issues Affecting Lesbian, Gay, Bisexual, and Transgender Elders*, 2010, pp. 91–92 *at* http://www.thetaskforce.org/downloads/reports/reports/outin-gage_final.pdf, accessed October 2014.

16 Administration on Aging, *Aging Statistics*, http://www.aoa.gov/Aging_Statistics/, accessed October 2014.

17  Gary Gates, *Gay and Lesbian Families in the Census: Gay and Lesbian Seniors*, Urban Institute, May 30, 2003, http://www.urban.org/url.cfm?ID=900627, accessed October 2014.

18  Grant et al., *Outing Age 2010*, p. 33.

19  Brian de Vries and John A. Blando "The Study of Gay and Lesbian Aging: Lessons for Social Gerontology," in *Gay and Lesbian Aging: Research and Future Directions*, Gilbert Herdt and Brian de Vries, eds. (New York: Springer, 2004), pp. 3, 7 (describing how gay men and lesbians are more likely to be single); *see also* Sean Cahill, Ken South, and Jane Spade, Pol'y Inst. of the Nat'l Gay & Lesbian Task Force Foundation, *Outing Age: Public Policy Issues Affecting Gay, Lesbian, Bisexual, and Transgender Elders*, 2000, p. 10, http://nwnetwork.org/wp-content/uploads/2012/08/2000-NGLTF-Outing-Age.pdf, accessed April 2015 (stating gay and lesbian elders are more likely to live alone than are heterosexual elders); Gary J. Gates, *Aging and the LGBT Community*, June 2014, http://williamsinstitute.law.ucla.edu/wp-content/uploads/CAAgingGates2014.pdf , accessed October 2014.

20  Vries and Blando, "The Study of Gay and Lesbian Aging: Lessons for Social Gerontology," p. 5.

21  Randy Albelda, M. V. Lee Badgett, Alyssa Schneebaum, and Gary J. Gates, Williams Inst., *Poverty in the Lesbian, Gay, and Bisexual Community*, p. ii, March 2009, http://williamsinstitute.law.ucla.edu/wp-content/uploads/Albelda-Badgett-Schneebaum-Gates-LGB-Poverty-Report-March-2009.pdf, accessed October 2014.

22  Albelda et al., *Poverty in the Lesbian, Gay, and Bisexual Community*.

23  Barbara Coleman and Sheel M. Pandya, AARP Pub. Policy Inst., *Family Caregiving and Long-Term Care*, p. 1, 2002, http://assets.aarp.org/rgcenter/il/fs91_ltc.pdf, accessed October 2014.

24  "SAGE: New York City's Pioneer Organization for LGBT Elders," in *Lesbian, Gay, Bisexual, and Transgender Aging: Research and Clinical Perspectives*, Douglas Kimmel, Tara Rose, and Steven David, eds. (New York: Columbia University Press, 2006), p. 266.

25  Metlife, *Out and Aging: The Metlife Study of Lesbian and Gay Baby Boomers*, p. 4.

26  Metlife, *Out and Aging: The Metlife Study of Lesbian and Gay Baby Boomers*, p. 4.

27  Pew Research Center for the People and the Press, *Growing Support for Gay Marriage: Changed Minds and Changing Demographics*, March 20, 2013, http://www.people-press.org/2013/03/20/growing-support-for-gay-marriage-changed-minds-and-changing-demographics/, accessed October 2014.

28  National Senior Citizens Law Center, *LGBT Older Adults in Long-Term Care Facilities: Stories from the Field*, 2011, p. 11, http://www.lgbtlongtermcare.org/wp-content/uploads/NSCLC_LGBT_report.pdf, accessed October 2014.

29  National Senior Citizens Law Center, *LGBT Older Adults in Long-Term Care Facilities: Stories from the Field*, p. 11.

30  Gross, "Aging and Gay, and Facing Prejudice in Twilight."

31  Gross, "Aging and Gay, and Facing Prejudice in Twilight."

32 First Amended Complaint, Green v. Cnty. of Sonoma, p. 2 (Cal. App. Dep't Super. Ct. Mar. 22, 2010) (No. SPR-81815), http://www.nclrights.org/site/DocServer/Greene_v_Sonoma_County.pdf?docID=7461, accessed October 2014.

33 First Amended Complaint, Green v. Cnty. of Sonoma, p. 16

34 Scott James, "An Unlikely Plaintiff: At Issue? He Dares Not Speak Its Name," *New York Times*, May 7, 2010, p. A19.

35 First Amended Complaint, Green v. Cnty. of Sonoma, pp. 1, 9, 14, and 17.

36 First Amended Complaint, Green v. Cnty. of Sonoma, p. 9.

37 Bob Egelko, "Suit by Elderly Gay Couple to Be Settled," *San Francisco Chronicle*, July 25, 2010, p. C2.

38 Paul Payne, "Guerneville Man Settles Suit against Sonoma County for $600,000," *Press Democrat*, July 22, 2010, http://www.pressdemocrat.com/article/20100722/ARTICLES/100729795?p=3&tc=pg, accessed October 2014.

39 James, "An Unlikely Plaintiff: At Issue? He Dares Not Speak Its Name."

40 Gross, "Aging and Gay, and Facing Prejudice in Twilight."

41 Gross, "Aging and Gay, and Facing Prejudice in Twilight."

42 Gross, "Aging and Gay, and Facing Prejudice in Twilight."

43 John Eligon, "Suits Dispute City's Rule on Recording Sex Changes," *New York Times*, March 22, 2011.

44 James Montgomery, "Dan Savage Explains Why He Started 'It Gets Better' Project," *MTV News*, September 30, 2010, http://www.mtv.com/news/1649114/dan-savage-explains-why-he-started-it-gets-better-project/, accessed October 2014.

45 Linda Hirshman, *Victory: The Triumphant Gay Revolution* (New York: HarperPerennial, 2012).

46 Scott Squillace, *Whether to Wed: A Legal and Tax Guide for Lesbian and Gay Couples* (Boston, MA: Squillace & Associates, 2014).

47 Frank Newport, "For First Time Majority of Americans Favor Legal Gay Marriage," Gallup, May 20, 2011, http://www.gallup.com/poll/147662/first-time-majority-americans-favor-legal-gay-marriage.aspx, accessed October 2014.

48 Maggie Haberman, "Poll: Big Support for Anti-Discrimination Law," *Politico*, September 30, 2013.

49 Annamarie Jagose, *Queer Theory: An Introduction* (New York: New York University Press, 1997), pp. 30–43.

50 Lydia Saad, "Americans' Acceptance of Gay Relations Passes 50% Threshold," Gallup, May 25, 2010, http://www.gallup.com/poll/135764/Americans-Acceptance-Gay-Relations-Crosses-Threshold.aspx, accessed October 2014.

51 Glenda M. Russell and Janis S. Bohan, "The Gay Generation Gap: Communicating across the LGBT Generational Divide," 8 *The Policy Journal of the Institute for Gay & Lesbian Strategic Studies* 3 (2005), http://drglendarussell.com/wp-content/uploads/2013/05/Angles_GayGenerations.pdf, accessed October 2014.

52 Michael Winerip, "Rainbow-Hued Housing for Gays in Golden Years," *New York Times*, March 12, 2014.

5

# Marriage as Blindspot

*What Children with LGBT Parents Need Now*

NANCY D. POLIKOFF

Lesbian and gay parents figured prominently in the most visible gay rights issue of our time—access to marriage. Although only about 16–18 percent of same-sex couples are raising children,[1] of the plaintiff couples in the cases decided by the Supreme Court in 2015, about 68 percent were parents.[2] Opponents argued, largely without recent success, that gay and lesbian couples should not be allowed to marry because their children don't turn out as well as children of married biological parents, and because same-sex marriage hurts the prospects of all children. Supporters argued that same-sex couples had to be allowed to marry for the benefits that marriage would confer on their children. The disproportionate number of parent plaintiffs in the litigation showed that supporters expected this argument to be quite persuasive.

With marriage equality now a legal mandate, advocates for LGBT families will need to turn their attention to supporting the needs of all children with lesbian, gay, bisexual, and transgender parents. Because arguments about children became intertwined with marriage, this will sometimes prove difficult. In this chapter, I explain how we arrived at this moment and make suggestions for moving forward.

Support for a wide diversity of family forms and relationships was a tenet of the LGBT-rights movement for four decades. This included advocacy for unmarried same-sex couples adopting children together; for access to assisted reproductive technology regardless of marital status or sexual orientation; and for the ability of lesbian and gay parents who come out after a heterosexual marriage ends to continue raising their children, often with new, same-sex partners.

Inherent in such advocacy was opposition to the claim that there was anything intrinsically superior about marriage as a family form for adult relationships or for raising children. But during this same period, conservatives began blaming the decline of life-long heterosexual marriage, and especially the increase in nonmarital childrearing, for a vast array of social problems, including poverty, violence, homelessness, illiteracy, and crime. They posited marriage as the solution to those problems. They targeted women raising children outside of marriage, a group that is disproportionately women of color, for the greatest disapproval.[3]

Initially, opposition to same-sex marriage was part of the conservative canon. But over time, some conservatives revised their position to encompass support for same-sex marriage precisely because it was *marriage*.[4] To capture or solidify this support, LGBT advocates made decisions both about the rhetoric they would employ and about the legal positions they would assert. Often, explicitly or implicitly, both the rhetoric and the legal positions acquiesced to a preference for childrearing by married parents—as long as same-sex couples could marry.

In the first part of this chapter, I argue that the focus on marriage as a way to improve the lives of children raised by LGBT parents disrespected other family structures and especially disregarded the circumstances of LGBT parents of color and those with limited economic resources. Attributing greater social welfare to married families is tantamount to blaming Black and Latina women and their unmarried male partners for social problems. This serves as a wedge within LGBT activism itself, whereby LGBT parents of color, who overwhelmingly live in neighborhoods with those unmarried heterosexual parents of color, are bound to feel alienated from rhetorical arguments antithetical to the communities in which they are embedded. In addition, LGBT people of color are substantially more likely to be raising children than their White counterparts, and they are significantly more likely to be living in or close to poverty. The well-being of children within those families is therefore indelibly bound up with issues of racial and economic justice, which marriage equality will not bring.

Most children living with same-sex couples were born in prior heterosexual relationships, and LGBT parents of color are disproportionately raising those children. The parents among the marriage-equality plaintiffs, however, were disproportionately White and well off, and disproportionately raising either adopted children or children conceived through donor insemination. The narratives about children told in the context of same-sex marriage advocacy, therefore, overlooked the family circumstances of the majority, and the most disadvantaged, of children being raised by gay and lesbian parents. Future advocacy should put the needs of these children at the forefront.

My second set of criticisms centers on the conflation of the legal definition of parentage with marriage. The law must accurately identify a child's parents, as numerous critical consequences flow from parentage. Some involve economic well-being, including the obligation of a parent to support a child; the ability of the child to inherit; the availability to the child of state support through child Social Security payments if a parent becomes disabled or dies; and the ability to recover in tort for a parent's wrongful death. Others involve the parent's right to care for a child; control the child's upbringing; and make decisions on behalf of the child. For the past three decades, advocates for gay and lesbian parents and their children have been developing legal theories for accurately defining who is a parent in such families.

Conflation of marriage and parentage constituted a detour from those three decades of progress in two distinct ways. Arguments for marriage equality, and court opinions overturning marriage bans, emphasized the importance to the children of having two parents. But the benefits to children of having two parents flow from legal recognition of the two adults as parents. For more than forty years, government policy and constitutional law have demanded that the legal benefits of parentage for children not depend upon their parents' marriage. Until recently, the LGBT movement has fervently advocated for the ability to adopt irrespective of marriage and for parentage rules grounded in the parent-child relationship, not in the relationship between the two adults. Marriage-equality advocacy changed course by demonstrating a willingness to accept distinctions based on marriage as long as same-sex couples can marry.

At the same time that advocates for lesbian and gay families became more accepting of marriage as necessary to establish parentage, they portrayed marriage as sufficient to establish parentage. In doing so, they made a sweeping and unqualified promise they will be unable to keep. The argument that same-sex couples should be allowed to marry so that their children will have two parents misled those who heard such arguments, including the couples themselves. This rhetoric presupposed that the child born to a married same-sex couple would be considered the child of both spouses. While that will be true in some states under some circumstances, it will often, perhaps usually, not be true.

Marriage in every state creates the presumption that the birth mother's husband is the child's other parent, but the applicability of the presumption to a female spouse will turn on the resolution of numerous questions. These include whether the presumption ever attaches to a spouse who cannot be the child's biological parent; whether the applicability of the presumption varies according to method of conception or the presence of an identified man whose sperm contributed to the child's conception; whether, even if the presumption attaches, it can be rebutted by factors that will be routinely present when the spouses are both women; and whether there are statutes governing assisted conception and what they say. Furthermore, because the marital presumption attaches to the spouse of a woman who gives birth, it has no bearing on parentage for male same-sex couples. It also has no bearing for the large number of step-families in which same-sex couples are raising a child born in a previous heterosexual context.

The focus on marriage led many gay rights advocates to take their eyes off twin goals that are critical to the well-being of children being raised by lesbians and gay men: ensuring that no child faces either deprivation or discrimination due to the form of his or her family, and accurately determining who counts as legal parents. Now that marriage equality is the law, those are the goals to which advocates for lesbian and gay families should return.

## Prologue 1996: Parenting by Same-Sex Couples before Marriage Was on the Table

The early years of planned lesbian and gay families generated a strategy to achieve recognition of both of a child's parents as a matter entirely distinct from recognition of the parents' relationship to each other. Advocates urged courts to allow second-parent adoptions, an adoption analogous to a step-parent adoption but without the requirement that the couple be married. When one partner was the biological or adoptive parent of a child, second-parent adoption allowed the other partner to adopt the child without terminating the first parent's parental rights. Similarly, advocates urged courts to allow an unmarried couple to adopt a child jointly.

To achieve this result, advocates asked the state courts to interpret adoption statutes using the principle of the best interests of the children. A court did not need to address the parents' relationship to each other at all; it was determining only whether the child would have one legal parent or two. The Vermont Supreme Court expressed it as follows:

> We are not called upon to approve or disapprove of the relationships between the appellants. Whether we do or not, the fact remains that Deborah has acted as a parent of BLVB and ELVB from the moment they were born. To deny legal protection of their relationship, as a matter of law, is inconsistent with the children's best interests and therefore with the public policy of this state. . . .[5]

Before the first full trial on marriage equality in 1996, trial courts in numerous states, and appellate courts in five states and the District of Columbia, approved such adoptions. Today they are available in most, but not all, states.[6]

## The Misguided Focus on Marriage as Better for Children

### Parenting by Same-Sex Couples Once Marriage-Equality Litigation Began

The relationship between childrearing and same-sex marriage became firmly linked beginning with the 1996 trial mandated by *Baehr v. Lewin,* the Hawai'i Supreme Court ruling requiring the state to provide a compelling reason for its same-sex marriage ban.[7] From that moment through the present, opponents of same-sex marriage have always justified their position by asserting the well-being of children, but the articulation of why the well-being of children depended upon keeping gay and lesbian couples from marriage evolved over time. Marriage-equality supporters met head on each distinctly different child-welfare-based allegation. It is in this point/counterpoint over the well-being of children that the advocacy linking marriage and parentage solidified.

Opponents of same-sex marriage have always argued that the optimal setting for raising children is that provided by married biological parents. Over time, however, they shifted their articulation of why that claim required same-sex couples to be excluded from marriage. In the Hawai'i litigation, opponents asserted that children faced increased likelihood of harmful consequences if raised by gay or lesbian parents. At the forefront of those arguments stood the children of same-sex couples, whose numbers would presumably increase if those couples could marry. By this reasoning, the marriage exclusion was justified to limit the number of children who would suffer such bad outcomes.

It was simple enough for marriage-equality supporters to respond to arguments that focused on the relative harm to children of being raised by gay or lesbian parents; no such harm existed, nor has any indication of such harm emerged from three decades of research. Every major mental health and child welfare organization has articulated unequivocal support for childrearing by same-sex couples.[8] Dr. Michael Lamb, a world-renowned child development expert, offered the following summary of the research:

> Children and adolescents raised by same-sex parents are as likely to be well-adjusted as children raised by different-sex parents, including "biological" parents. Numerous studies of youths raised by same-sex parents conducted over the past 25 years by respected researchers and published in peer-reviewed academic journals conclude that children and adolescents raised by same-sex parents are as successful psychologically, emotionally, and socially as children and adolescents raised by different-sex parents, including "biological" parents. Furthermore, the research makes clear that the same factors, as elaborated below, affect the adjustment of youths, whatever the sexual orientation of their parents.
>
> It is beyond scientific dispute that the factors that account for the adjustment of children and adolescents are the quality of the youths' relationships with their parents, the quality of the relationship between the parents or significant adults in the youths' lives, and the availability of economic and socio-emotional resources. These factors affect adjustment in both traditional and nontraditional families. The parents' sex or sexual

orientation does not affect the capacity to be good parents or their children's healthy development. There also is no empirical support for the notion that the presence of both male and female role models in the home promotes children's adjustment or well-being.[9]

Notice that the above articulation disassociated child outcome entirely from family form. It contained no claim that marriage is a better family structure within which to raise children or that the children raised by gay men and lesbians were harmed by their parents' exclusion from marriage. To the contrary, the children were not harmed by anything in their upbringing, presumably including the absence of marriage.

Opponents of marriage equality next asserted that the marriage exclusion was justified because the children of same-sex couples are planned and wanted, and the purpose of marriage is to provide structure for the children who result from "accidental procreation." By this way of thinking, the children of same-sex couples did not need their parents to be married, and the state could limit marriage to those relationships that needed the incentive of marriage to promote stability.[10] Same-sex marriage supporters responded to this (patently ludicrous) reasoning by noting that making marriage available to an additional group of people would not in any way decrease the incentive for heterosexuals to marry.

Defenders of the marriage exclusion then further refined their claim on behalf of the children of heterosexuals by lauding marriage, and by decrying no-fault divorce and increased rates of nonmarital birth and cohabitation for making marriage more optional and less tied to the bearing and rearing of children. Marriage-equality opponents argued that same-sex marriage would be one more step in changing marriage by disassociating it from procreation.

They reasoned as follows: Because the sexual relationship of a same-sex couple does not result in procreation, same-sex marriage makes a statement that marriage is about the well-being of adults rather than about the well-being of the children who come from heterosexual sexual intercourse. In addition, when same-sex married couples do raise children, they send the message that children do not need both a mother and a father. Taken together, they argued, this revised picture of marriage, unmoored from a structure whose alleged purpose is to provide stable, two-parent, dual-gendered homes for the natural consequences of heterosexuality, would contribute to the decline in marriage by heterosexuals. More children of heterosexuals would thereby suffer the effects of being raised by never-married or divorced mothers, without the allegedly indispensable presence of fathers.

Marriage-equality supporters responded to this reasoning by combining aspects of their responses to the previous two rationales. The well-accepted consensus research demonstrated that the presence of a male and a female parental role model was not necessary for child well-being. And given that the decline in marriage was admittedly the work of heterosexuals, an argument for continuing to exclude same-sex couples in order to stem that decline was as illogical as the "accidental procreation" rationale. Furthermore, the availability of marriage to infertile and elderly couples, as well as Supreme Court reasoning on the benefits of marriage even when consummation is impossible because one spouse is incarcerated,[11] provided excellent rebuttal to the claim that procreation was the sole purpose of marriage.

But marriage-equality advocates did not counter the part of opponents' argument that posited marriage as the preferred family structure for children. Instead, they praised marriage as "majestic," "unique," and "hallowed."[12] They articulated, sometimes quoting earlier court rulings, that "the structure of society itself largely depends upon the institution of marriage"[13] and that "excluding same-sex couples from civil marriage . . . prevent[s] children of same-sex couples from enjoying the immeasurable advantages that flow from the assurance of a stable family structure in which the children will be reared, educated, and socialized."[14]

### Marriage Is Better: The 2015 Version

By the time marriage equality reached the U.S. Supreme Court, supporters were arguing that children of same-sex couples were harmed because their parents could not marry. Sometimes they listed the injury to children in terms of legal consequences, such as economic support and the right to make decisions. Later in this chapter, I explain that these legal consequences flow from a legally recognized parent-child relationship for which marriage is neither necessary nor, in many instances, sufficient.

Advocates also argued that marriage would provide economic benefit to the household and for that reason, children were harmed by its absence, but the economic-benefit argument is not always true. Two individuals earning close to the same annual income will pay more in income taxes if they marry than if they remain unmarried. This "marriage penalty" might or might not be offset by economic benefits, such as access to the other spouse's low-cost, employer-provided health insurance. For poor couples, marriage may reduce eligibility for means-tested public assistance with no corresponding economic benefit. The couples most likely to see financial benefits from marriage are those who have a single earner and a stay-at-home spouse.[15]

Although legal and economic consequences vary by individual family circumstance, marriage-equality advocates could claim that all the children of same-sex couples suffered a dignitary harm because their parents were unable to marry. The least problematic of the harm-to-children arguments was the one that focused on exclusion from marriage as legally sanctioned discrimination that sent a message of the inferiority of same-sex relationships. Banning same-sex couples from marriage *is* a statement that heterosexual relationships, and therefore heterosexuals, are morally and socially superior. Like a vote against banning sexual-orientation discrimination in the workplace, it sends the message that the government approves of discrimination.

It is a different matter to assert the superiority of marriage as a family form in which to raise children and to claim harm to children of same-sex couples because they are required, against the wishes of their parents, to live in unmarried family units. When marriage-equality advocate Mary Bonauto criticized the ban on same-sex marriage because it "means that you are increasing the number of children who are raised outside of marriage,"[16] she was going after support from those who judge it bad to raise children outside marriage.

In his majority opinion in *United States v. Windsor*, Justice Anthony Kennedy wrote that the section of the Defense of Marriage Act (DOMA) denying federal recognition of valid same-sex marriages made it "difficult for the children to understand the integrity and closeness of their own family and its concord with other families in their community and in their daily lives."[17] "Concord with other families"—all other families—sounds like a desirable condition for building schools and neighborhoods where people feel that they share a common interest in the well-being of their community. That is not what Kennedy was referring to in this statement. Rather, he was referring to "concord" with other families in which married parents are raising children.

In the same paragraph, Justice Kennedy said denial of marriage recognition "humiliates tens of thousands of children now being raised by same-sex couples."[18] "Humiliates" is a powerful verb. In *Windsor* it was used in reference to children whose parents were married under state law but considered unmarried for federal law purposes. After *Windsor*, lower federal court judges used these parts of Kennedy's reasoning to strike down state same-sex marriage bans themselves, often further elaborating upon the stigmatizing effect of having unmarried parents.[19]

Briefs filed by advocates in the cases that made up *Obergefell v. Hodges*, the 2015 Supreme Court cases seeking marriage equality, consistently argued that "marriage brings 'social legitimization' and stability to families";[20] that there is harm to children from their parents' inability to provide the "stable family structure" of marriage;[21] and that marriage is necessary to spare children "the stigma of being in a family without the social recognition that exists through marriage."[22] In his opinion for the Court, Justice Kennedy reiterated his reasoning in *Windsor* and concluded that the laws barring same-sex marriage "harm and humiliate the children of same-sex couples."[23]

Notice the odd inconsistency of arguing that thirty years of research on children shows no harm to them from being raised by gay or lesbian parents—who were not married—while also arguing that those same children *are* harmed by having unmarried parents. Researchers and advocates necessarily devoted much time and energy to proving and arguing that children are not disadvantaged by having gay or lesbian parents. It was a change of direction to construct the argument that the children *are* harmed because their parents cannot marry. That advocates who had previously championed family diversity were willing to do this is a testament to the rhetorical power of embracing the marital norm.

Yet a minority of children—46 percent—live with their married heterosexual parents in a first marriage.[24] Another 9 percent live with their married heterosexual parents but one or both of the parents have been married before. A full 45 percent of all children do not live with their married parents: 34 percent live with a parent who is single or cohabiting with an unmarried partner; 6 percent live with a parent and a step-parent; 5 percent live with someone other than a parent, such as a grandparent. This includes the majority of children with a lesbian or gay parent, as most of those children were born in prior heterosexual relationships and will not be living with their married parents even if their gay or lesbian custodial parent subsequently marries a same-sex partner. The majority of African American children, 55 percent, live with a single parent, as do 31 percent of Hispanic children, compared with about 20 percent of White children and 13 percent of Asian American children.[25]

The higher incidence of nonmarital childrearing by African American and Latina women is not just a statistical fact. Conservatives view it as a largely negative fact, causally responsible for numerous social problems. Rather than address racism, education deficits, lack of well-paying jobs, overcriminalization, income inequality, and other structural problems, they lay blame at the feet of unmarried mothers, especially women of color, as well as their unmarried male partners, for what they call a lack of "personal responsibility." The primary solution they propose is marriage.

Law professor Melissa Murray has analyzed the "racial undertones" of marriage-equality advocacy in the name of ending the "illegitimacy" of the children of same-sex couples.[26] The paradigmatic, and stigmatized, single mother is young, poor, African American, and receiving public assistance. The public face of LGBT rights is affluent, White, and often male. Marriage- equality advocacy on behalf of the children of White, economically comfortable, same-sex couples creates a distance between marriage-seeking gay and lesbian parents and those *others*, who are permitted to marry but choose a different family form.

There is a longstanding critique of the LGBT rights movement for insufficient attention to issues of racial and economic justice. A 2013 report on poverty among lesbians, gay men, and bisexuals documented increased risk of economic hardship and greater use of public assistance programs among LGB individuals and same-sex couples, but also identified subcommunities—such as those who are young, of color, parents, and living in rural and noncoastal regions of the country—who are at even greater risk of poverty. The authors concluded that their study indicated "the need for anti-poverty organizations and LGBT organizations to include considerations of poor LGBT people in their work."[27]

In this chapter, I identify marriage-equality advocacy in the name of children of same-sex couples as a choice that obscured the real picture of families in which same-sex couples are raising children. The parent-plaintiff couples in the marriage equality litigation were not representative of the vast majority of same-sex couples raising children. Test case litigation usually relies on plaintiffs chosen for characteristics that will make them appealing, and for stories that will garner support for the remedy they seek. The marriage-equality litigation was no different, and by all measures the plaintiffs accomplished those goals. But looking ahead at what policies are necessary for the well-being of children being raised by same-sex couples must begin with correcting the inaccurate picture those parent-plaintiffs presented.

Eleven of the sixteen families who made up the marriage-equality plaintiffs in the U.S. Supreme Court—about 68 percent—were parents. As I indicated at the beginning of this chapter, the vast majority of same-sex couples are not raising children. Married same-sex couples are more likely to be raising children than are unmarried couples, 27 percent compared with 15 percent, but even the 27 percent figure is significantly below the percentage of plaintiffs who became the public face of the fight for marriage equality.[28] Advocates expected the children these parents were raising to paint a compelling picture of why the marriage bans should be struck down. They selected families that were demographically unrepresentative, however, thereby obscuring the importance of racial and economic justice for the well-being of the children being raised by same-sex couples.

The parent-plaintiffs were not representative of the racial demographics of same-sex couples raising children. Of the twenty-two individuals in the eleven parent-plaintiff couples, five (23 percent) were people of color—one African American couple and three biracial couples, two White and Latina/o and one White and Filipino. Yet nationally, 34 percent of individuals in same-sex couples raising children are people of color.[29] Forty-one percent of African American individuals in same-sex couples are raising children. The figure for Latinos/as is 30 percent. Only 16 percent of White individuals in same-sex couples are raising children.[30] Among same-sex couples raising children, the African American childrearing rate is 2.4 times that of Whites. Among different-sex couples, African Americans are only 1.3 times more likely than Whites to be raising children.[31] African Americans comprise 14 percent of same-sex couples raising children, a figure that greatly exceeds the 8 percent of different-sex couples raising children who are African American. In other words, African American same-sex couples are disproportionately raising children when compared with both White same-sex couples and African American different-sex couples.

Furthermore, African American parents in same-sex couples live not in enclaves of gay-friendly communities with statistically higher numbers of lesbian and gay individuals and couples, but in the parts of the country, and the urban neighborhoods, where there are higher proportions of African Americans.[32] Their neighbors and relatives are among the targets of the hostility directed at unmarried parents. The fight to raise children within marriage neither comes from this group nor speaks to its needs.

Children living with same-sex couples are much more likely to be poor (24 percent) than their counterparts living with different-sex couples (14 percent), and race plays a substantial role in identifying who those poor children are. Twelve percent of the children of White same-sex couples are poor. For African American children, the statistics are dire; data from numerous sources between 2006 and 2012 reveal a poverty rate of 52 percent for those raised by male same-sex couples and 38 percent for those raised by female same-sex couples.[33] These are largely the biological children of one member of the couple.

In fact, most same-sex couples with children are raising children born to one partner while in an earlier different-sex marriage or relationship, but only one of the eleven plaintiff couples fit this profile. Such children usually have two parents prior to the same-sex-couple relationship, putting them in the large category of children who do not live with their married parents. If the same-sex couple marries, the child will still not be living with his or her married parents; the child, like millions of other children, will be living with a parent and a step-parent.

In addition to being disproportionately White, the parent-plaintiffs were disproportionately male and disproportionately adoptive parents. Of the eleven couples with children, six (55 percent) were female and five (45 percent) were male. Yet 77 percent of the same-sex couples raising children are female. Even among same-sex married couples raising children, 71 percent are female couples.[34] The five male couples all adopted their children, as did one of the female couples. The remaining four female couples used donor insemination to conceive.

Although same-sex couples are more likely to adopt children than different-sex couples, only 4 percent of all same-sex couples, and 8 percent of married same-sex couples, have an adopted or foster child. Even among same-sex couples raising children, only 22 percent have an adopted or foster child; 28 percent of married same-sex couples with children have an adopted or foster child.[35] Roughly double that percentage of the parent-plaintiffs in the marriage equality litigation, 55 percent, were raising adopted children.

Same-sex couples raising adopted children differ substantially from those raising biological children. A large overrepresentation of adoptive parents therefore creates a dramatically distorted picture. White same-sex couples are almost twice as likely (18 percent compared with 9.6 percent) as couples with at least one person of color to be raising an adopted child.[36] Individuals in same-sex couples with adopted children are twice as likely as those raising biological or step-children (62 percent to 31 percent) to have college degrees or higher. This contrasts with the disparity among different-sex couples raising adopted children, which is relatively small. Same-sex couples with adopted children have 200 percent the median household income of same-sex couples with biological or step-children ($124,440 vs. $62,000). Again, this is very different from different-sex couples, whose households with adopted children have median incomes only slightly above that of households with biological or step-children. According to 2013 census data, the median household income of married, male, same-sex couples with adopted children dwarfs that of all other same-sex-couple households.[37]

Data from the 2013 American Community Survey permits for the first time a comparison between married and unmarried same-sex couples.[38] Family researchers have long noted that marriage is more common, and more lasting, among those who are more affluent and who wait to marry and have children until they complete higher education. The census data suggests this may turn out to be also true for same-sex marriages. In the 2013 data, one-third of all the children living with same-sex couples, approximately seventy-one thousand, were being raised by married same-sex couples. Their poverty rate was low, 9 percent, compared with the 32 percent poverty rate for children of unmarried same-sex couples. Married same-sex couples with children also had higher median household income and a higher percentage of home ownership than their unmarried counterparts. At this rate, marriage might exacerbate inequality within the population of children being raised by same-sex couples.

In a 2013 presentation, Williams Institute demographer Gary Gates described "two paths to parenting," one for disproportionately White same-sex couples raising adopted children in high-income households in gay-supportive regions of the country; and the other for disproportionately racial-minority same-sex couples raising biological children in low-income households in regions of the country more hostile to LGBT families. Marriage-equality advocacy chooses to forefront families from the former group.

Marriage equality mandated by the Supreme Court will not make the most hostile regions of the country more welcoming, nor will it remedy racism or economic inequality. It is the children in the families of the latter group, therefore, whose needs LGBT policy and legal advocates should forefront going forward.

## The Misguided Focus on Marriage Equality as the Way to Recognize a Child's Two Parents

In the first part of this chapter, I addressed the urgency of meeting the needs of all children being raised by LGBT parents, including those born from earlier heterosexual relationships. Starting with this part, I turn to the doctrine necessary to appropriately confer the legal status of parentage on adults who are raising children but who are not their married biological mother and father. The children that same-sex couples add to their families, often through adoption or through assisted conception, fall into this category. The lens of marriage equality has led advocates astray, and now is the time to return to a path independent of the marital status of adults raising a child.

### Adoption Should Not Be Limited to Married Couples

April DeBoer and Jayne Rowse wanted both to be the legal parents of their children.[39] Between them, the two women had adopted three children from the state child welfare system. But Michigan did not allow them to adopt jointly, so April was the legal parent of two and Jayne was the legal parent of the third. Faced with this roadblock to what they knew was best for their children, the couple filed a federal lawsuit challenging the constitutionality of denying their children the benefit of having two parents through second-parent adoption.

Pointing out that if they were married the state would permit them to complete step-parent adoptions, the trial court judge assigned to the case urged them to challenge the state law prohibiting same-sex marriage.[40] According to the judge, that ban was the reason they could not adopt. Although the couple all along desired second-parent adoptions, not marriage, they amended their lawsuit. The team of attorneys representing the couple subsequently abandoned the argument that prohibiting second-parent adoption unconstitutionally infringed upon the rights of both the women and their children.

In 2012, the ACLU LGBT Rights Project filed a constitutional challenge to North Carolina's refusal to allow second-parent adoption.[41] All the plaintiffs were same-sex couples. After the *DeBoer* trial judge turned that case into one focused on same-sex marriage, the ACLU lawyers amended their complaint to challenge North Carolina's ban on same-sex marriage. After the Fourth Circuit U.S. Court of Appeals struck down Virginia's same-sex marriage ban and, in October 2014, the U.S. Supreme Court denied review,[42] the district court judge signed a consent order declaring North Carolina's marriage ban unconstitutional. The same order, with the consent of the ACLU, dismissed the challenges to the state's second-parent adoption ban as moot; the couples could now marry and complete step-parent adoptions.

Much is lost when the goal of achieving second-parent adoption disappears into marriage equality. Same-sex couples lose the right to *choose* marriage.[43] Leaders in the marriage-equality movement have insisted that their efforts do not contain the message that same-sex couples *must* marry. They have spoken instead in the register of choice.[44] But April and Jayne lost their right to *choose* marriage the moment it became the sole way they could both be parents of their children, as did the North Carolina plaintiffs. At the moment, couples in several states, including Wisconsin, Nevada, and Arizona, also lack this choice and must marry before they can both be the legal parents of the children they are raising.

The other possibility that is lost is the ability to recognize the creative family structures in which children can thrive. Second-parent adoption has never been a same-sex-couple-only solution. For example, the first second-parent adoption in Maryland was one in which a woman adopted a child who had previously been adopted by her twin sister. The two sisters lived in the same home and were raising the child together.[45] A lesbian or gay man who knows parenthood will not come in the usual planned or unplanned way must consider his or her alternatives. Those alternatives go substantially beyond the exclusive, sexually linked parents who populate marriage-equality litigation.

For example, in 2013, a New York trial court judge approved a second-parent adoption by the close gay male friend of a woman who had adopted a child in Ethiopia.[46] The two friends, K.L. and L.L., had known each other for years when they decided to become parents by inseminating L.L. with K.L.'s sperm. After two years of trying with no success, they turned to adoption. They selected Ethiopia and traveled there together to meet the child identified for them. Because they were not married, Ethiopia permitted only one to adopt, and L.L. returned to Ethiopia and completed the adoption there. When she returned to New York, she and K.L. petitioned for a second-parent adoption.

The trial judge noted that had their insemination succeeded, they would have both been the parents of their biological child.[47] The judge then went on to find that K.L. and L.L. met the definition of "intimate partners" in the statute identifying when two unmarried people could adopt together. Although K.L. and L.L. did not live together, by that time they had fully coparented for two years. The judge found the adoption to be in the best interest of the child.

The distinct circumstances within which lesbians and gay men become parents can also lend themselves to a family structure in which more than two adults function as a child's parents. Although lesbian couples often choose an unknown sperm donor, or a known donor who will have limited involvement with the resulting child, some couples choose to fully parent with the child's genetic father (and perhaps his partner). When it is in the child's best interests to recognize more than two parents, adoption should be available to solidify this result. The first lesbian-couple "second-parent" adoption in the country, granted in Alaska in 1985, was actually a third-parent adoption, as the parental rights of neither biological parent were terminated.[48] Lawyers representing lesbian and gay families around the country report an increasing number of states in which judges have been willing to grant an adoption to a third parent, usually after a period of successful coparenting has taken place. Confining adoption to married couples forecloses this possibility.

It also forecloses the possibility of adoption when a couple starts raising a child while married but separates and divorces before an adoption takes place. This may happen when the couple becomes foster parents and the child does not become available for adoption for a substantial period of time. Or it may happen when one spouse is the biological parent but the couple delays a second-parent adoption and then separates. If the parents are in conflict, an adoption might not at that point be in the child's best interests. But if they are coparenting successfully, and both welcome the prospect of establishing joint legal parentage, prohibiting such a result leaves the child without the benefits that flow from recognition of her parents.

Law professor Angela Mae Kupenda wrote almost twenty years ago about the importance of allowing two unmarried African Americans to pool financial and emotional resources to become adoptive parents of African American children.[49] She was not, of course, suggesting that this mechanism should be available only to African Americans. Rather, she focused on certain distinctive characteristics of African American communities that, she argued, gave this tool an especially significant means for providing for the welfare of children.

*Assisted Reproduction Laws Should Not Be Limited to Married Couples*

The path to parentage through assisted reproduction should similarly not turn on the marital status of the parents. When a lesbian couple plans for, welcomes, and raises a child together, the child and all those around her may believe she has two mothers. In some marriage-equality states, however, including Massachusetts and New York, the child has two mothers only if those mothers were married when the child was born. Those states are among about twenty that enacted a model statute written in the 1970s naming a husband the father of his wife's child if he agreed to the conception of the child with donor semen. Massachusetts and New York courts have applied their statutes to a female spouse. If the couple isn't married, however, the child has only one mother unless and until there is a second-parent adoption.[50] In 2010, the New York Court of Appeals reaffirmed the rule it established almost twenty years earlier that when such a couple separates, the one legal parent may entirely obliterate the other parent from the child's life.[51]

Marriage equality may precipitate statutory reform integrating same-sex couples. Advocates for gay and lesbian families should not accept a rewrite of donor-insemination statutes that simply makes them applicable to married lesbian couples. Five states and the District of Columbia now have insemination statutes based on twenty-first-century model laws that extend parentage on a gender-neutral and marital-status-neutral basis to any person who consents to a woman's insemination when both persons intend that they will both be parents.[52] Those statutes should be the models going forward. Advocates working in states considering surrogacy statutes should also ensure that surrogacy not be restricted to intended parents who are married couples.

## The Misleading Focus on Marriage as the Gateway to Parentage for a Nonbiological Mother

### A Same-Sex Spouse May Not Get the Marital Presumption of Parentage

Many states have no statutes on assisted conception, in which case all questions of legal parentage are decided according to statutes and court rulings that define parentage more generally. Married men in all states become legal fathers because a statute or common law rule extends to them a presumption of parentage based on marriage. Advocates for same-sex marriage have acted as though this presumption will extend to the wife of a woman who bears a child, but I'm not so sure this will turn out to be true. One state appeals court has already found its marital presumption inapplicable to a woman, ruling instead that the marital presumption was a statute of presumed *biological* paternity. The court wrote that it could not apply to a female spouse because, "for the presumption of parentage to apply, it must be at least possible that the person is the biological parent of the child."[53] Another state's trial court made a similar ruling that a woman's female spouse was not her child's other parent because the statute used the terms "husband" and "father," and a female could be neither.[54]

If a state interprets its own constitution to protect gay men and lesbians from discrimination, there may be a better outcome. A case from Iowa is illustrative. The Iowa Supreme Court ruled that the state's ban on same-sex marriage violated the state constitution.[55] After that ruling, Melissa and Heather Gartner married.[56] Heather got pregnant through donor insemination, and when the child was born the state refused to put Melissa's name on the birth certificate. The state argued that Melissa needed to adopt the child, and then the state would issue a new birth certificate naming both parents. Melissa argued that the marital presumption of parentage applied to her. The state argued that it did not because she was not a biological parent. The statute read that "if the mother was married . . . the name of the husband shall be entered on the certificate as the father of the child unless paternity has been determined otherwise by a court of competent jurisdiction."

The Iowa Supreme Court concluded that those words meant what they said, that "only a male can be a husband or father. Only a female can be a wife or mother." Therefore, Melissa was not a parent under that statute. Because the court had previously held the marriage ban unconstitutional, however, it said that this statute, excluding a married woman's female spouse from the presumption of parentage, was also unconstitutional.

Here is the problem. In states that have allowed same-sex couples to marry without a constitutionally based mandate from the state courts, and in states that do not have good constitutional law for sexual-orientation-based classifications, there is reason for grave concern that courts will find that marriage does not create a parentage presumption for a female spouse who is not biologically related to the child. With the Supreme Court imposing marriage on hostile states, we cannot expect those states to go any farther than constitutionally required. There is reason to believe that many courts in those states will find the marital presumption inapplicable to a clearly nonbiological parent.[57] Without supportive state constitutional doctrine, that will be the final word.

Iowa had (and still has) no statute governing assisted reproduction. Melissa and Heather Gartner's child was born through the use of unknown donor insemination. Iowa also had (and still has) no statutory definitions of "parent." Rather than explore the possibility of law reform with Iowa family law practitioners and scholars, Lambda Legal approached the Gartners' problem as one dependent upon a more robust recognition of their marriage. They were successful, but only because sexual orientation receives heightened scrutiny under the Iowa constitution. Their success provides no benefit to those couples who do not marry.

No marital presumption will ever apply to a same-sex male couple. This is the case because no marital presumption applies for heterosexuals to the wife of a man who becomes the biological father of a child born to another woman. Rather, the woman is the child's mother, and, if she is married, it is *her* husband who gets the marital presumption. The same rule will apply to a married gay male couple that uses one spouse's sperm to conceive a child. For the most part, without a surrogacy statute in place, the woman bearing the child is the child's mother, and, if she has a husband, he is the presumed father.

### Conception through Sex Will Bring Additional Legal Challenges

Marriage will also be a problematic path to parentage when one of the lesbian spouses conceives not through insemination but through sexual intercourse. Consider the facts of one 2014 case from California.[58]

After a number of years together, a married lesbian couple, Julia and Victoria, decided they wanted a child, and they agreed that Victoria would ask a coworker, Sam, if he would be willing to be a sperm donor. The three discussed the arrangement, and all agreed that Sam would donate semen so that Julia and Victoria could raise a child together, and that he would have no parental rights or responsibilities. They downloaded a sperm donor agreement from the internet, made a few changes, and signed it

Over a two-month period, Sam gave the couple semen samples, and Julia inseminated Victoria at home. Unbeknownst to Julia, Victoria and Sam had begun a sexual relationship a few months before the first insemination. As soon as Victoria became pregnant, her sexual relationship with Sam ended.

Julia participated in all prenatal activities and was present when Baby Marta was born. Both women are named as parents on the birth certificate, and Marta's last name is the hyphenated last names of her mothers. The two mothers shared in child care and financial support. Sam paid no support, had no relationship with the child, and, in fact, had a girlfriend he didn't want to upset and a son with that girlfriend.

When Marta was eight months old, Julia and Victoria split up, but they continued to share custody, and Julia paid child support to Victoria. Marta called both women "Mommy." Several months later, Victoria and Sam resumed their sexual relationship. Sam moved in with Victoria, and Victoria told Julia that although she originally intended to raise Marta with her, she now intended to raise her with Sam.

Julia filed for partial custody, alleging that Marta was conceived during the marriage by donor insemination. Victoria's response revealed to Julia for the first time that during the relevant period, Victoria was also having sexual intercourse with Sam. She opposed Julia's custody request, and she and Sam joined in a petition to declare him the father of the child.

The court had to identify Marta's legal parents. The trial court chose Julia over Sam. On appeal, the majority upheld Julia's parentage but also sent the case back to the trial judge to determine if all three should be considered parents under a new California statute—unique in the country—explicitly allowing such a finding.[59] One appellate judge dissented, reasoning that Marta had a biological mother and father who wanted to raise her together and that, therefore, only they should be her legal parents. The approach of that judge is most likely representative of judges across the country in states with laws less favorable than California's to lesbian couples raising children.

It would be a mistake to consider the facts of this case anomalous. An increasing number of cases have reached the courts in which the child raised by a lesbian couple was conceived through sexual intercourse. Sometimes that is not an issue in the case but simply part of the factual background. Sometimes, as in the case above, it matters greatly.

According to Williams Institute demographer Gary Gates, the 2008–2012 General Social Survey showed that 13.8 percent of women who identify as lesbian had had sex with a man in the preceding five years; 4.3 percent had had sex with a man in the preceding year.[60] Gates's most recent demographic analysis suggests that there were approximately 756,000 lesbians aged eighteen to forty-four in the United States, which estimate translates into 32,508 lesbians aged eighteen to forty-four who had slept with a man in the preceding twelve months. Gates's analysis of bisexuals suggests that there are approximately 1,557,500 bisexual women aged eighteen to forty-four, 92.9 percent of whom said they had had sex with a man in the preceding five years, and 91.4 percent of whom—over 1.4 million—said they had had sex with a man in the preceding year.

In the 2012 American Community Survey, 3.5 percent of women in same-sex couples reported giving birth to a child in the previous year. The 2013 American Community Survey counts approximately 351,900 female same-sex couples, which translates to an estimate of over 12,000 children born to lesbian couples in a year. While some number of those births are certainly the result of assisted conception, the General Social Survey data suggests that many of those children were conceived—intentionally or unintentionally, with or without a same-sex partner's consent—through sex with a man.

## The Way Ahead

Some same-sex marriage advocates have on marriage blinders when it comes to parentage. If there are bumps ahead in what marriage brings to the families of same-sex couples, they expect to get marriage to do more work rather than seek results for a wider range of families. The experience with the *Gartner* case in Iowa may be a precursor of what is to come.

I cringe when I think about the resources that advocates for gay and lesbian families will expend trying to make the marital presumption work across the country. But the fact that one spouse is not the child's biological parent—something that will continue to distinguish same-sex marriage from the vast majority of different-sex marriages—means that this process will have somewhat of a square-peg/round-hole quality to it. There will be successes, but these will probably derive from case law involving nonbiological husbands.

Advocates for gay and lesbian parents should work for parentage laws that apply regardless of marital status. They need to remove their marriage blinders and look around at the paths to parentage that have proven capable of protecting a more diverse set of gay and lesbian families. Some have required statutory changes forged through work with a wide range of stakeholders, and successes have not been limited to traditionally gay-friendly states. As a result of a statute enacted in Nevada in 2013, for example, a gay male couple, married or unmarried, may become parents through surrogacy. And when a woman conceives through donor insemination, with the consent of her female or male partner, married or unmarried, they both are parents of the resulting child.[61]

One of the architects of marriage equality, Mary Bonauto, stands as an excellent example for future advocacy. In addition to pursuing marriage equality, including representing same-sex couples seeking marriage in the United States Supreme Court, she served on the Family Law Advisory Commission in Maine that drafted a comprehensive proposal for a Maine Parentage Act.[62] The resulting law, which goes into effect July 1, 2016, will facilitate determination of a child's parentage for lesbian and gay parents in a variety of family arrangements not dependent upon marriage.

The evolution of parentage law in California is a case study for protecting children of same-sex couples through existing statutes and without any reference to marriage. In 2005, the California Supreme Court in *Elisa B. v. Superior Court* extended to the female partner of a woman who bore twins the statutory presumption of parentage that attaches to a man who receives a child into his home and openly holds the child out as his natural child.[63] The path to that victory was not paved by married heterosexuals, but by diverse family structures.

In *In re Nicholas H.*, the name of a woman's unmarried male partner was placed on the birth certificate even though the couple knew he was not the biological father.[64] He raised the child for many years. The issue of his legal status arose when the child's mother could no longer care for the child. The appeals court ruled that the "holding out" presumption was rebutted by his lack of biological paternity, but the California Supreme Court reversed, reasoning that it was discretionary, not mandatory, to rebut the presumption based on lack of biology.

In a subsequent case, *In re Karen C.*, a mother who bore a child in a hospital misidentified herself as Letitia C.[65] Karen's birth mother wanted Letitia to raise the child, and by using Letitia's name, she ensured that Karen had a birth certificate that named Letitia as her mother. Letitia raised Karen as her own child and told Karen she was adopted. Ten years later, when the issue of Karen's legal parentage arose, a California appeals court cited *Nicholas H.,* and the principle of gender-neutral statutory interpretation, for the proposition that a woman could not lose her status as a presumptive parent solely on the basis of a lack of biological tie.

A year after *Karen C.,* a California appeals court refused to rebut the holding out parentage presumption of Monica, the adult half-sister of Salvador, whom Monica had helped care for since birth.[66] Their (common) mother died when Salvador was three, and Monica raised him as her son alongside her other children. Monica said that "[Salvador] thinks of me as his mother and I think of him as my son. Our family knows of the actual relationship between Salvador and me and I have been truthful in official matters such as school registration, but to the rest of the world, Salvador is my son."[67] The court applied the holding out presumption and ruled that it would be inappropriate to rebut Monica's parentage because doing so would "sever this deeply rooted mother/child bond."

Twenty-five years ago, before *Nicholas, Karen,* and *Salvador,* advocates for a nonbiological mother in California thought the holding out presumption could not apply to her. They thought that to hold the child out as her "natural" child, she would have to think the child was her biological child. But less than fifteen years later, with no intervening statutory changes, the very same holding out presumption guaranteed protection for the parent/child relationships formed by both lesbian and gay male couples and their children.[68]

It's worth remembering what made that result possible. It was not the married heterosexuals with whom marriage-equality advocates always compare same-sex couples, but an unmarried man and woman, an unmarried woman wanting her child to be raised by an unmarried woman friend, and an unmarried woman who raised her half-brother as her son.

Seeking broad statutory reform or favorable court rulings will take substantial effort. But so will trying to gain parentage through the marital presumption. It isn't a question of the amount of work there is to do; it's about whether that work will focus on protecting only married same-sex couples or the broader range of LGBT family arrangements.

Two principles emerge from this chapter:

1. The well-being of a disproportionately large segment of the children being raised by LGBT parents depends upon remedying racial and economic inequality as much as it depends upon ending the discrimination their parents face as gay, lesbian, bisexual, and transgender adults. Marriage will not bring them justice.
2. Children with LGBT parents thrive in a variety of nonmarital family forms. They require rules that do not revolve around marriage to give them the legal parents they need.

These are the principles that should guide future advocacy on behalf of children raised by LGBT parents.

NOTES

1 Jonathan Vespa, Jamie M. Lewis, and Rose M. Kreider, "America's Families and Living Arrangements: 2012, Population Characteristics," U.S. Census Bureau, August 2013 [hereinafter Census Report 2012] (16.4 percent, comprised of 10.5 percent of male couples and 21.6 percent of female couples); Gary J. Gates, "LGB Families and Relationships: Analysis of the 2013 National Health Interview Survey," Williams Institute, October 2014 [hereinafter Gates, 2013 NHIS] (18 percent of married same-sex couples and 19 percent of unmarried same-sex couples).

2 *See* Obergefell v. Wymyslo, 962 F. Supp. 2d 968 (S.D. Ohio 2013) (one of two plaintiff couples); Bourke v. Beshear, 996 F. Supp. 2d 542 (W.D. Ky. 2014) (three out of four plaintiff couples); Tanco v. Haslam, (M.D. Tenn. 2014) (two out of three plaintiff couples); DeBoer v. Snyder, 973 F. Supp. 2d 757 (E.D. Mich.) (one out of one plaintiff couples), *rev'd*, 772 F.3d 388 (6th Cir. 2014), *cert. granted*, 83 U.S.L.W. 3315 (U.S. Jan. 16, 2015) (No. 14–574).

3 *See, e.g.*, Barbara Dafoe Whitehead, "Dan Quayle Was Right," *Atlantic Monthly*, April 1993; Charles Murray, "The Coming White Underclass," *Wall Street Journal*, October 29, 1993.

4 The paradigmatic about-face was that of David Blankenhorn, who wrote a book opposing same-sex marriage in 2007 and testified in favor of California's ban on same-sex marriage in 2010 but then publicly switched his position. David Blankenhorn, "How My View on Gay Marriage Changed," *New York Times*, June 23, 2012.

5 In re Adoption of BLVB and ELVB, 628 A. 2d 1271, 1276 (Vt. 1993).

6 The most updated list of states allowing second-parent adoption can be found on the website of the National Center for Lesbian Rights: "Legal Recognition of LGBT Families," http://www.nclrights.org/wp-content/uploads/2013/07/Legal_Recognition_of_LGBT_Families.pdf, accessed April 2015.

7   852 P.2d 44 (Haw. 1993) (finding the ban to be a classification based on sex, a suspect classification under the state constitution, and requiring the state to show that the ban was necessary to achieving a compelling state interest).

8   The statements of numerous organizations have been assembled by the Human Rights Campaign as "Professional Organizations on LGBT Parenting" and can be found at http://www.hrc.org/resources/entry/professional-organizations-on-lgbt-parenting, accessed April 2015.

9   Declaration of Michael Lamb, Ph.D., *Sevcik v. Sandoval*, Case No. 2:12-CV-00578-RJC-PAL, United States District Court District of Nevada, filed Sept. 12, 2012.

10  As professor Courtney Joslin summarized, "rather than arguing that marriage can be limited to heterosexual couples because heterosexual couples make better parents, the claim is essentially that marriage can be limited to heterosexual couples because, without the inducement of marriage, heterosexual couples are more likely to be unstable and unhealthy parents." Courtney G. Joslin, "Searching for Harm: Same-Sex Marriage and the Well-Being of Children," 46 *Harvard Civil Rights–Civil Liberties Law Review* 81, 90 (2011).

11  Turner v. Safely, 482 U.S. 78 (1987).

12  Respondents' Supplemental Brief, *In re* Marriage Cases, 183 P.3d 384 (Cal. 2008) (No. S147999) online at http://www.courts.ca.gov/documents/08Rymer_Supplemental_Brief.pdf [hereinafter NCLR marriage brief]. This brief was prepared by lawyers for the National Center for Lesbian Rights and Lambda Legal in the challenge to California's ban on same-sex marriage; Brief *Amicus Curiae* of Bay Area Lawyers for Individual Freedom et al., in *Obergefell v. Hodges,* the U.S. Supreme Court same-sex marriage case, online at http://www.supremecourt.gov/ObergefellHodges/AmicusBriefs/14–556_Bay_Area_Lawyers_for_Individual_Freedom.pdf, accessed April 2015 [hereinafter BALIF brief]. This brief was submitted on behalf of several LGBT bar associations from around the country.

13  NCLR marriage brief, p. 24.

14  BALIF brief, p. 15.

15  Kyle Pomerlau, "Understanding the Marriage Penalty and Marriage Bonus," Tax Foundation Fiscal Fact, 2015, available at http://taxfoundation.org/sites/taxfoundation.org/files/docs/TaxFoundation_FF464_0.pdf, accessed April 2015.

16  Nina Totenberg, "Legal Battle over Gay Marriage Hits the Supreme Court Tuesday," NPR, April 27, 2015, available at http://www.npr.org/blogs/itsallpolitics/2015/04/27/402456198/legal-battle-over-gay-marriage-hits-the-supreme-court-tuesday, accessed April 2015.

17  133 S. Ct. 2675, 2694 (2013).

18  133 S. Ct. at 2694.

19  *See, e.g.,* Obergefell v. Wymyslo, 962 F. Supp. 2d 968 (S.D. Ohio 2013); Campaign for Southern Equality v. Bryant, 2014 US Dist LEXIS 165913; *Bostic v. Schaefer,* 760 F.3d 352 (4th Cir 2014).

20  Briefs of Petitioners, *DeBoer v. Snyder*, p. 37, filed in U.S. Supreme Court, available at http://www.supremecourt.gov/ObergefellHodges/PartyBriefs/14–571_Brief_Of_DeBoer.pdf, accessed April 2015.

21  *See, e.g.*, Brief *Amicus Curiae*, Garden State Equality, p. 29, in *Obergefell v. Hodges*, the U.S. Supreme Court same-sex marriage case, available at http://www.supremecourt.gov/ObergefellHodges/AmicusBriefs/14–556_Garden_State_Equality.pdf, accessed April 2015.

22  BALIF Brief, p. 15.

23  192 L. Ed. 2d 609, 627 (2015).

24  The data in this paragraph is from the Pew Research Center analysis of census data. Gretchen Livingston, "Less Than Half of U.S. Kids Today Lives in a 'Traditional' Family," Pew Research Center, December 22, 2014, available online at http://www.pewresearch.org/fact-tank/2014/12/22/less-than-half-of-u-s-kids-today-live-in-a-traditional-family/, accessed April 2015.

25  Census Report 2012, figure 8, p. 27.

26  Melissa Murray, "What's So New about the New Illegitimacy?" 20 *American University Journal of Gender, Social Policy & Law* 387 (2011).

27  M. V. Lee Badgett, Laura E. Durso, and Alyssa Schneebaum, "New Patterns of Poverty in the Lesbian, Gay, and Bisexual Community," Williams Institute, June 2013, p. 24 [hereinafter Poverty Report 2013].

28  Gary J. Gates, "Demographics of Married and Unmarried Same-sex Couples: Analyses of the 2013 American Community Survey," p. 5, Williams Institute, March 2015 [hereinafter Gates 2013 ACS].

29  Gates 2013 ACS, p. 7.

30  Angeliki Kastanis and Bianca D. M. Wilson, "Race/Ethnicity, Gender, and Socioeconomic Well-being of Individuals in Same-sex Couples," Williams Institute, p. 2.

31  Gary J. Gates, "Family Formation and Raising Children among Same-sex Couples," National Council of Family Relations, Family Focus, Winter 2011, p. F3 [hereinafter Gates, "Family Formation"].

32  Angeliki Kastanis and Gary J. Gates, "LGBT African-Americans and African-American Same-sex Couples," Williams Institute, p. 3

33  Poverty Report 2013, p. 16.

34  Gates 2013 ACS, p. 6.

35  Gates 2013 ACS, pp. 7–8.

36  Gates, "Family Formation," p. F3

37  Gates, Power Point presentation, UCLA, April 2015.

38  Gates, 2013 ACS.

39  The extensive facts of the case are contained in *DeBoer v. Snyder*, 772 F.3d 388 (6th Cir. 2014) (dissenting opinion).

40  Christine Ferretti, "Judge Tells Couple to Consider Challenging State's Gay Marriage Ban," *Detroit News*, August 29, 2012.

41  Fisher-Borne v. Smith, Case No. 1:12CV589, United States District Court for the Middle District of North Carolina. This case arose after the North Carolina

Supreme Court, in 2010, ruled that a second-parent adoption granted five years earlier was void because the court lacked subject matter jurisdiction to enter such an order. Boseman v. Jarrell, 704 S.E.2d 904 (N.C. 2010). That decision simultaneously invalidated every second-parent adoption ever granted in North Carolina.

42  Bostic v. Schaefer, 760 F.3d 3352 (4th Cir. 2014), *cert. denied*, 135 S. Ct. 316 (2014).

43  And of course different-sex couples as well. In the New York litigation approving second-parent adoption in that state, Lambda Legal represented both a lesbian couple and an unmarried different-sex couple who did not wish to marry. *In re Jacob*, 86 N.Y.2d 651 (NY 1995).

44  For example, Evan Wolfson, "Crossing the Threshold: Equal Marriage Rights for Lesbians and Gay Men, and the Intra-Community Critique," 21 *New York University Review of Law & Social Change* 567 (1994).

45  Information about this adoption is found in a June 9, 2000, letter from Assistant Attorney General Kathryn M. Rowe to Maryland General Assembly Delegate Sharon Grosfeld. The letter can be found at http://www.oag.state.md.us/Opinions/2010/Grosfeld.pdf, accessed April 2015.

46  In re Matter of Adoption of G., 42 Misc. 3d 812 (N.Y. Surr. Ct. 2013).

47  Under federal and state law, when an unmarried woman gives birth and the biological father of the child is present, the couple is offered the opportunity to sign a voluntary acknowledgment of paternity that has the force of a court judgment declaring the man the legal father of the child.

48  In re A.O.L., discussed in Nancy D. Polikoff, "This Child Does Have Two Mothers: Redefining Parenthood to Meet the Needs of Children in Lesbian-Mother and Other Nontraditional Families," 78 *Georgetown Law Journal* 459, 522 (1990).

49  Angela Mae Kupenda, "Two Parents Are Better Than None: Whether Two Single African American Adults—Who Are Not in a Traditional Marriage or a Romantic or Sexual Relationship with Each Other—Should Be Allowed to Jointly Adopt and Co-Parent African American Children," 35 *University of Louisville Journal of Family Law* 703 (1996–1997).

50  I discuss this issue in depth in Nancy D. Polikoff, "The New 'Illegitimacy': Winning Backward in the Protection of Children of Lesbian Couples," 20 *American University Journal of Gender, Social Policy & Law* (2012).

51  Debra H. v. Janice R., 930 N.E.2d 184 (NY 2010).

52  I describe the enactment of one such law in Nancy D. Polikoff, "A Mother Should Not Have to Adopt Her Own Child: Parentage Laws for Children of Lesbian Couples in the Twenty-first Century," 5 *Stanford Journal of Civil Rights and Civil Liberties* 201 (2009).

53  Shineovich v. Kemp, 214 P.3d 29 (Ore. App. 2009).

54  Opinion and Order, Conover v. Conover, 21-C-13–046273 (Circuit Ct for Washington Cty, Maryland), currently on appeal to the Maryland Court of Appeals

55  Varnum v. Brien, 762 N.W.2d 862 (2009).

56 Gartner v. Iowa Department of Public Health, 830 N.W.2d 335 (Iowa 2013).

57 There are a handful of cases determining parentage when the egg of one partner in a lesbian couple is fertilized *in vitro* with donor semen and the embryo is implanted in the other woman. For example, *D.M.T. v. T.M.H.*, 129 So. 3d 320 (Fla. 2013). Because one woman has a parentage claim based on giving birth to the child and the other based on genetic parentage, courts have found that both women are parents under existing statutes. It is unlikely that many lesbian couples will choose this expensive and medically invasive method of conception.

58 These facts are based on the reported opinion and the briefs in S.M. v. E.C., 2014 Cal. App. Unpub. LEXIS 4574 (2014). The case refers to all the individuals by initials. To minimize confusion, I have selected names for them.

59 Cal. Fam. Code §7612 (c).

60 The General Social Survey data is from an analysis Gates conveyed to me by e-mail. The estimate of total U.S. population aged eighteen to forty-four is from *Age and Sex Composition: 2010*, United States Census Bureau, May 2011, found at http://www.census.gov/prod/cen2010/briefs/c2010br-03.pdf, accessed April 2015. Estimates of percentages of the population who are lesbians and bisexual women are from Gary J. Gates, "LGBT Demographics: Comparisons across Population-Based Surveys," October 2014, found at http://williamsinstitute.law.ucla.edu/wp-content/uploads/lgbt-demogs-sep-2014.pdf, accessed April 2015. A 1999 study of 6,935 self-identified lesbians found that 5.7 percent reported one or more male sexual contacts in the preceding year. Alison L. Diamant et al., "Lesbians' Sexual History with Men: Implications for Taking a Sexual History," 159 *Archives of Internal Medicine* 2730, 2732 (Dec. 13/27, 1999). Women who were not White, were younger than fifty, had not graduated from college, and had annual income of less than twenty thousand dollars were more likely to be in this category.

61 Statutes and cases achieving these results are listed in a publication of the National Center for Lesbian Rights, "Legal Recognition of LGBT Families," http://www.nclrights.org/wp-content/uploads/2013/07/Legal_Recognition_of_LGBT_Families.pdf, accessed April 2015.

62 The text of the law is available at http://www.mainelegislature.org/legis/bills/get-PDF.asp?paper=SP0358&item=3&snum=127 accessed August 2015.

63 Elisa B. v. Superior Court, 117 P.3d 660 (Cal. 2005).

64 In re Nicholas H., 46 P.3d 932 (Ca. 2002).

65 The facts of this case are contained in *In re Karen C.*, 124 Cal. Rptr. 2d 677 (Ct. App. 2002).

66 4 Cal. Rptr. 3d 705 (Ct. App. 2003).

67 4 Cal. Rptr. 3d at 707.

68 I describe this evolution in detail in Nancy D. Polikoff, "From Third Parties to Parent: The Case of Lesbian Couples and Their Children," 77 *Law & Contemporary Problems* 195 (2014).

6

# A New Stage for the LGBT Movement

*Protecting Gender and Sexual Multiplicities*

CARLOS A. BALL

It is common for social movements to shift priorities in the face of both policy victories and changed social circumstances. In the early days of the civil rights movement, for example, its top priorities were ending racial segregation in education and eliminating voting restrictions. After some initial successes in these areas, the movement added other priorities, such as the enactment of antidiscrimination statutes and the elimination of antimiscegenation laws. For its part, the early women's movement prioritized the lifting of voting bans and contraception restrictions. The later movement has focused on issues such as educational and employment opportunities for women and the right to choose an abortion.

The LGBT-rights movement's priorities in the United States have also shifted through the decades, from an early focus on getting the government to leave lesbians and gay men alone to a later emphasis on equality and antidiscrimination protection to a more recent focus on marriage and the pursuit of social acceptance. The attainment of the marriage-equality goal offers movement leaders and constituents an opportunity to consider new priorities. One of those priorities should be encouraging the state to adopt laws and policies that recognize and protect gender and sexual fluidity and multiplicities. This objective can be pursued through political and legal campaigns that, for example, seek (1) to promote an understanding of sex and sexual orientation antidiscrimination law that is unmoored from the protection of distinct identities and (2) to remove one of the last gender-based barriers to accessing public spaces by ending gender segregation in bathrooms and similar facilities. These types of objectives represent reforms that are not grounded in the need to protect individuals on the basis of distinct—and ostensibly fixed and static—gender and sexual identities. Instead, the attainment of these objectives would promote equality rights for all individuals regardless of how (or even whether) they identify, or of how society identifies them, along gender and sexuality continuums.

Although the movement framed the struggle for marriage equality as one that implicated the basic rights of lesbians and gay men, the reality is that marriage equality opens up marriage to all couples regardless of their gender and sexual identities. The attainment of marriage equality means that the way individuals identify according to gender and sexual orientation is irrelevant in determining whom they can marry. Under this understanding of marriage equality (which is admittedly not the one promoted by the marriage equality movement), the state lacks the authority to deny marriage licenses to any two individuals regardless of how (or even whether) they identify, or of how society identifies them, along gender and sexuality continuums. From this perspective, for example, a bisexual intersex individual is as free to marry a transgender female asexual as a heterosexual man is free to marry a heterosexual woman and a lesbian woman is free to marry another lesbian woman.

As a practical matter, the rendering of gender and sexual orientation as irrelevant criteria in the distribution of marital rights benefits all individuals who choose to marry regardless of how they identify according to gender and sexuality. As a result, this is a particularly opportune time to explore other legal and policy reforms that have the potential for promoting gender and sexual fluidity and multiplicities.

The so-called left critique of the marriage equality movement, as reflected in the writings of many feminists and queer theorists, has raised important questions about the privileging of marriage in our society and whether the push for marriage equality reinforces the second-class status of those who choose to lead lives outside of state-sanctioned monogamous or committed intimate relationships. It is difficult to determine whether, as a whole, LGBT individuals and other gender and sexual minorities would be better off today had the movement chosen not to focus so intently on marriage equality. Obviously, it is not possible to reset the clock to circa 1995 and then proceed along a different advocacy track, one that does not prioritize marriage equality. Nonetheless, it is worth noting that there have been significant LGBT rights advances on nonmarriage issues during the last two decades, including the issuance of executive orders prohibiting sexual-orientation and gender-identity discrimination in the federal civilian workforce and by federal contractors; the repeal of the military's discriminatory policy excluding openly lesbian, gay, and bisexual service members; the amendment of the federal hate crime law to include the actual or perceived sexual orientation or gender identity of crime victims; the enactment by fifteen states (up from zero in 1995) of school antibullying laws that focus on issues of sexual orientation and gender identity; and the enactment by twenty states (up from zero in 1995) of laws prohibiting employment discrimination on the basis of gender identity.

It is possible, of course, that progress on these nonmarital fronts would have been greater had the movement not prioritized marriage rights to the extent that it did. But it is also possible that the greater visibility and acceptance of sexual minorities that has resulted from the push for marriage equality contributed to these other legal reforms. Either way, the nonmarital gains during the marriage equality era cannot easily be dismissed as insubstantial or insignificant.

It is also worth noting that the prioritization of marriage equality may have had more transformative effects on social policies than are recognized by the left critique. For example, Douglas NeJaime, in exploring family law issues, persuasively explains how the push for marriage equality reinforced efforts to reduce the salience of biology, gender, sexual orientation, and, paradoxically, *marital status* in legally determining who is a parent.[1] In a similar vein, I believe that marriage equality has the *potential* to reduce the legal and policy salience of distinct gender and sexual identities. Whether that potential turns into reality will depend on the priorities movement leaders and constituents set for themselves going forward. My hope, now that the objective of nationwide marriage equality has been achieved, is that the movement will consider other ways to encourage the state to adopt laws and policies that recognize and promote gender and sexual fluidity and multiplicities.

## A Brief Look Back

The first political and legal objective of the LGBT movement in the United States was to protect lesbian and gay men from government campaigns to harass, intimidate, and imprison them. The government witch hunts aimed at gay people began in earnest in 1950 when a U.S. Senate committee issued a report titled *Employment of Homosexuals and Other Sex Perverts in Government* calling on federal agencies to investigate the presence of lesbians and gay men among their work forces.[2] Three years later, President Eisenhower issued an executive order authorizing the investigation of "sexual perverts" in the federal government, leading to the expulsion of hundreds of lesbian and gay employees.[3] At around this time, district attorneys and police commanders routinely authorized the raiding of bars where lesbians and gay men congregated, while so-called vice squads in cities across the country set out to entrap men in public places in order to charge them with sex solicitation of other men.[4]

It is hardly surprising that the early movement, operating in this highly repressive atmosphere, focused on demands that the government essentially leave lesbians and gay men alone. What the early movement of the 1950s and 1960s asked of the state was that it refrain from coercively intervening in the lives of sexual minorities. Specific manifestations of these demands included the decriminalization of sodomy between consenting adults, the end of bar raids and entrapment campaigns, and the unencumbered distribution of lesbian and gay publications, both political and erotic.[5]

The early movement's demands clearly fit within a liberal theoretical framework that emphasized the importance of state neutrality in matters of sexuality and of carving out spaces for individuals to express and pursue their sexual and romantic interests free of state coercion. In the 1970s, as a result of both a decrease in overt manifestations of governmental repression and an increase in the political power and visibility of lesbians and gay men, the movement's relationship with the state entered a new phase. At this time, activists began demanding not only that LGBT individuals be protected *from* the government but also, in many instances, that they be protected *by* the state. This protection was particularly necessary in order to address rampant discrimination against sexual minorities by both public and private entities in employment, housing, and the provision of goods and services.[6]

The movement's political and normative realignment, which placed greater emphases on considerations of equality, complicated the relationship between the state and LGBT communities and individuals. The relatively simple mantra of "keep the government out of our lives" no longer satisfactorily captured all of the movement's demands—while sexual minorities still wanted the government out of their bars and bedrooms, they also wanted the state to protect them from discrimination by both public and private parties. This objective was reflected in the push by activists for the enactment of federal, state, and local laws prohibiting discrimination on the basis of sexual orientation. The need for antidiscrimination protections grew even more urgent with the arrival, in the 1980s, of the AIDS epidemic and the corresponding intensification of irrational fears—often expressed through invidious discrimination—about the sexuality of gay men in particular.

The movement's increasing attention to the question of marriage, beginning in the 1990s, represented yet another political and normative realignment.[7] The push for marriage was in many ways consistent with earlier efforts to guarantee basic equality for individuals regardless of their sexual orientation. The government, by not allowing same-sex couples to marry, denied lesbians and gay men access to the thousands of rights and benefits that it distributes through the institution of marriage. But the struggle for marriage equality was, from the beginning, about more than legal rights and benefits. If the goal had been simply to attain formal equality under the law, then the movement would have been largely satisfied with civil union and domestic partnership regimes that offered registered same-sex couples the same rights and benefits provided to married heterosexuals. The fact that the movement demanded not just the rights and benefits that accompany marriage but also the social respect and recognition afforded to married couples showed that it was pursuing more than just de jure equality—it was also seeking social acceptance.

The push for marriage further complicated the relationship between the LGBT movement and the state. The demand for access to the institution of marriage was, in effect, a request that the government *regulate* (and not just ignore) the intimate relationships of lesbians and gay men. The movement now contended that full equality for, and complete social acceptance of, sexual minorities was impossible unless the government offered same-sex couples the opportunity to have their relationships acknowledged and regulated through the institution of marriage.

The attainment of the marriage equality objective brings with it the opportunity to reflect on how the movement, as it has done previously, should modify its priorities and objectives in the face of policy victories and changed social circumstances. Now that the movement has attained many (though by no means all) of its objectives in matters related to privacy, equality, and social acceptance, it should include among its priorities encouraging the government to respect and protect sexual and gender fluidity and multiplicities.

## Gender and Sexual Fluidity and Multiplicities

The quest for civil rights in the United States has focused on traits-based protections (on the grounds, for example, of race, sex, and sexual orientation) that have been understood by rights proponents, somewhat paradoxically, to be both central to the self-identity of individuals *and* largely irrelevant to the setting of social policy. The prioritizing of a handful of traits that merit protection from discrimination has been accompanied by understandings of identities that are largely binary (e.g., individuals are either black or white, female or male, and gay or straight) and static (i.e., individuals do not shift from one identity to another). However, as many critics have pointed out, the traits that undergird contemporary identity politics are neither binary nor static. In actuality, individuals fall along continuums of race, sex/gender, and sexual orientation that resist easy and simplistic "either/or" categorizations. In addition, gender and sexual identities, far from being "natural" or "predetermined," can be highly fluid depending on factors such as social cues, norms, and expectations.[8]

The limitations that inhere in binary and rigid understandings of gender and sexual identities are reflected in the challenges that the American LGBT-rights movement has faced in fully incorporating the needs and perspectives of transgender and bisexual individuals. From a strategic/advocacy perspective, it may seem advantageous to divide the population into two gender and sexuality categories, respectively, in order to emphasize the harm inflicted by one group (e.g., men) when it subordinates another (e.g., women). But the lived experiences of transgender and bisexual individuals show that gender and sexual identities are more fluid and open-ended than is evident from most political and legal discussions.

The debates over same-sex marriage, for example, largely assume that individuals are either straight or lesbian/gay, with little attention paid to bisexuals. The question of transgender individuals and marriage, while the subject of a few lawsuits, has also received relatively little attention compared to the raging national debates over the rights of lesbian and gay couples to marry.

It is important to note that full recognition of the fluidity and multiplicities of gender and sexual identities cannot be achieved simply by adding "transgender" and "bisexual" identities to the already widely recognized identities of "men," "women," "straights," "lesbians," and "gay men." As an article in the New York Times explains, a growing number of young Americans are becoming increasingly comfortable with the idea of fluid notions of gender and sexuality, notions that might shift according to changing dispositions, perspectives, and attractions.[9] For these young individuals, even terms like "transgender" and "bisexual" are unduly restrictive because they insufficiently account for the fluidity and malleability of gender and sexual identities. It is not surprising, therefore, that Facebook now offers its users more than fifty gender-identity options, including gender neutral, androgynous, bi-gender, intersex, gender fluid, and transsexual.[10] For its part, OKCupid, the popular online dating service, not only allows users to choose among more than fifty gender-identity categories but also offers sexual-orientation choices that include—in addition to the traditional categories of straight, lesbian, gay, and bisexual—asexual, demisexual (sexual attraction driven by emotional attachment), heteroflexible, homoflexible, pansexual (sexual attraction to individuals of any sex or gender identity), queer, questioning, and sapiosexual (sexual attraction driven by the intelligence of potential partners).[11]

The fact that some individuals are intersex, while others are asexual, while yet others identify as queer or questioning or polyamorous or androgynous further reflects the multiplicity of gender and sexual identities.[12] The movement, in grappling with these identity multiplicities, has two principal choices. The first option is to treat the large and ever-growing number of identities as distinct ones that deserve social respect and support in their own right. This approach is reflected in the understandable push by many in the movement to add initials to "LGBT" (as in, for example, "LGBTQIA") to account for up-until-now largely ignored identities, such as queer, intersex, and asexual.

One advantage of this approach is that it allows for the making of rights claims on behalf of the "new" (or up-until-now ignored) identities based on the state's recognition of rights for the "old" (or traditionally recognized) identities. It makes it possible, for example, to contend that if the state protects lesbians and gay men from discrimination, it should provide the same protection to intersex and asexual individuals. However, there is a disadvantage to this approach: no matter how inclusive it tries to be, it still depends, at the end of the day, on the privileging of some gender and sexual identities over others. To put it simply, decisions (both normative and strategic) must still be made as to which initials to add, and which not to add, to "LGBT."

The second option available to the movement in grappling with the multiplicity of gender and sexual identities is to emphasize not the constitutive characteristics or elements of the distinct identities that deserve protection (a process that inevitably privileges some identities over others) but the fluidity and malleability of all such identities. This alternative approach avoids the problematic consequences of privileging some identities over others. By adopting this second option, the movement would not be asking that the state recognize and protect a list of predetermined gender and sexual identities; instead, it would be demanding, more generally, that the state respect and protect fluidity and multiplicities in gender and sexual identities.

The goal under this approach would not be to provide particular gender and sexual minorities with a menu of rights and benefits that the state already provides to majority groups. Instead, the objective would be to encourage the state to adopt and implement laws and policies in ways that give individuals wide latitude in expressing or performing gender and sexual identities, identities that do not necessarily track traditional or existing categories.

There is some overlap between the political and normative shift that I am urging the LGBT rights movement to make and the critique of identity politics raised by many queer theorists. Like queer theory critics, my vision for the movement is skeptical of seemingly static, and highly essentialized, notions of identity. Identities are not predetermined categories that exist independently of the social forces that constitute them. Individuals do not "discover" their identities so much as they adopt them as mechanisms and strategies for making sense of the social world around them.

My vision for the movement, however, contains several characteristics of liberal theory. First, my vision allows room for autonomous individuals to play a role—sometimes large, sometimes small—in choosing both which identities to adopt and how to express or perform them. Although individuals cannot completely free themselves from social forces in deciding which identities to adopt, they are capable, if society gives them the necessary freedom and support, of expressing or performing those identities in a variety of different ways. At its core, therefore, my vision is a liberal one that emphasizes both the capability of individuals to exercise some autonomy (or agency) and the obligation of society to facilitate and make possible that exercise.[13]

Second, my vision for the movement's future does not follow from the queer theory (and feminist) critique of the push for marriage equality. That critique is based on the view that the pursuit of marriage rights for same-sex couples is ultimately an assimilationist effort that prioritizes access to an intrinsically hierarchical and patriarchal institution, precluding or displacing more radical and transformative changes in legal and social policies in matters related to families and relationship recognition.[14] I do not view the pursuit of marriage rights for sexual minorities in such critical terms. Instead, I view the struggle for marriage equality as a necessary and helpful step in setting the stage for broader and more important conversations about questions of gender and sexuality in our society. In the same way that the homophile movement of the 1950s and 1960s paved the way for the Stonewall riots and the gay liberation movement, and in the same way that the push for the decriminalization of sodomy laws and the enactment of sexual-orientation antidiscrimination laws during the 1970s and 1980s paved the way for the marriage equality struggle, that struggle—and the increasing social acceptance of same-sex relationships, families, and intimacy that has followed in its wake—has created political, social, and legal conditions that make it possible for movement leaders and constituents, if they so choose, to focus on more transformative policies that recognize and value the fluidity and malleability of gender and sexual identities.

I recognize that it is easier to build political movements around considerations of identity than it is to build them around notions of fluidity and multiplicity. But the very success of the LGBT identity-based movement in getting society to start thinking differently (and more open-mindedly) about sexual orientation and gender identity makes a more expansive focus on questions of fluidity and multiplicities politically feasible, at least on some issues and in some settings. It is admittedly neither realistic nor politically advisable for the movement to eschew relying on identity-based claims overnight. But it is possible to begin reframing some questions of equality and nondiscrimination in ways that universalize rather than minoritize, that is, in ways that account both for the fact that we all have (or are perceived to have) gender and sexuality identities and for the fact that those identities are (or could be) expressed or performed in a myriad of different ways.

It may be objected that the political and legal goals that I discuss in this chapter may be attained by normatively emphasizing the *irrelevance* of gender and sexual-orientation identities rather than their fluidity and multiplicity. While that may be true as a conceptual matter, I worry that emphasizing the notion of irrelevance leaves undisturbed current assumptions about the limited number of categories of gender and sexuality identities. Although many Americans, as a result of the LGBT movement's political and legal campaigns over the last four decades, now see sexual orientation as a benign trait comparable to skin color, most Americans continue to have a narrow understanding of gender, limited to only two categories, and of sexual orientation, limited to questions of attraction depending on the sex of sexual partners. I fear that a continued and exclusive focus on the irrelevance of gender and sexual orientation will reinforce rather than challenge those narrow understandings.

## Antidiscrimination Laws: Looking beyond Distinct Identities

My discussion, so far, of which direction the movement should pursue post–marriage equality has been fairly theoretical. I now want to shift gears by providing two specific examples of the types of reform efforts I have in mind, efforts that acknowledge and promote fluidity and multiplicities in gender and sexual identities.

Although antidiscrimination statutes do not usually define "race" or "sex,"[15] they almost always define "sexual orientation"—and they do so, almost exclusively, in terms of heterosexuality, homosexuality, and bisexuality.[16] This legal definition of sexual orientation improperly limits the protection to only three "orientations," leaving out a panoply of others, including asexuality and polyamory, as well as the preferences of those who do not have, or refuse to identify around, a sexual orientation.

It is not clear why American antidiscrimination laws do not usually define race. This omission may be a consequence of the highly problematic ways in which government officials used earlier statutory definitions of race, such as the so-called one-drop provisions contained in some antimiscegenation laws (which considered anyone with any trace of African ancestry to be "colored" or "Negro"), to promote white supremacy. But it may also be that such a definition is thought to be unnecessary because the statutes are generally understood to protect individuals from race discrimination *regardless of their particular race* (or, to put it differently, regardless of how they self-identify or how society identifies them according to race). The definition of race, in this sense, is irrelevant to the attainment of the antidiscrimination objectives. Indeed, to limit the protection against race discrimination to only particular racial identities would seem to be entirely inconsistent with the laws' central purpose.[17]

As for the general absence of definitions of sex in antidiscrimination laws, it may be that legislators have not bothered to include them because of the traditional consensus which holds that (1) there are only two of them (male and female) and (2) everyone is either one or the other. This traditional understanding of "sex" is analogous to the prevailing statutory definition of sexual orientation in antidiscrimination laws; under both, protection is limited to a set number of categories (two in the case of "sex," three in that of "sexual orientation") and it is strongly presumed that all individuals fit comfortably into one (and only one) of those categories.

The LGBT movement should push for an understanding of antidiscrimination law that is closer to the race model by moving away from the current focus on protecting distinct sexual-orientation identities. Rather than seeking protection exclusively for the three traditional sexual-orientation categories, the movement should push for statutory language that prohibits discrimination on the basis of any emotional or sexual attachment (or lack thereof) to other adults, whether that attachment is actual or perceived.

Under the approach proposed here, the objective would not be to protect employees, for instance, from discrimination simply because the employer was motivated by animus against those who sexually identify in certain ways, for example, as gay or bisexual; instead, the objective would be to prevent employers from impermissibly making assumptions about an employee's abilities based on *any* judgments or expectations grounded in matters related to sexuality. Under this approach, sexual-orientation antidiscrimination law would clearly cover discrimination motivated by animus toward, for example, lesbian women and bisexual men. But it would also protect, among others, asexuals, the polyamorous, and those who are simply unsure of what their sexuality is or should be.

Part of the challenge presented by the normative shift that I am suggesting is that both the movement and the broader society have become accustomed to thinking of sexual orientation solely in terms of sexual attraction or conduct as linked to the sex of the parties. But there are many different ways in which sexual orientation can be understood or defined, including through other traits (such as age, intelligence, body types, and gender identity) that may impact on emotional and sexual attraction, as well as through other factors such as the willingness to be in more than one intimate relationship at the same time with the consent of everyone involved, as is true of those who prefer polyamorous relationships.

While expanding the meaning of sexual orientation in existing antidiscrimination laws would require statutory amendments that broaden their coverage beyond the three traditional categories, the question of how "sex" in antidiscrimination law should be defined is likely to remain—given the general absence of statutory guidance—one of judicial interpretation. As has been recognized in antidiscrimination circles, legal advocates in this area have made considerable progress in securing some protection for gender and sexual minorities under sex antidiscrimination laws. What has not been sufficiently recognized is the extent to which this progress has been grounded in the decoupling of sex antidiscrimination law from particular identities.

During the two decades following the enactment of Title VII of the Civil Rights Act of 1964, the federal law that prohibits employment discrimination on the basis of sex (as well as race, color, religion, and national origin), courts generally interpreted the prohibition of discrimination on the basis of "sex" under the statute to mean, as a federal appellate court put it in a ruling rejecting a discrimination claim brought by a transgender woman, "that it is unlawful to discriminate against women because they are women and against men because they are men."[18] Such a cabined understanding of the protection against sex discrimination afforded by Title VII offered little to employees whom employers treated differently because of the way they expressed or performed their gender. After all, under the appellate court's understanding of the statute, employers could always contend that when they took negative employment actions against gender-variant individuals, they did so not because the employees were men or women but because they were gender nonconforming.

In 1989, the Supreme Court called for a more expansive understanding of sex discrimination in *Price Waterhouse v. Hopkins*.[19] The employer in *Hopkins* denied the plaintiff the opportunity to become a partner at the accounting firm because she was perceived as too assertive and masculine. As one of the male partners bluntly put it, if she wanted to become a partner, she had to "walk more femininely, talk more femininely, dress more femininely, wear make-up, have her hair styled, and wear jewelry."[20] The Court in *Hopkins* embraced the plaintiff's legal theory that employers engage in "sex" discrimination within the meaning of Title VII when they assess their employees' abilities according to how closely they comply with traditional gender expectations.

*Hopkins*, which recognized Title VII claims under the theory of "gender stereotyping," has meant that the statute can, in at least some circumstances, protect LGBT individuals from discrimination even though it does not explicitly include either "sexual orientation" or "gender identity" as protected categories. While pre-*Hopkins* rulings consistently rejected discrimination claims brought by LGBT plaintiffs, some courts have more recently held that such plaintiffs have actionable Title VII claims when employers make negative employment decisions based on gender stereotypes.

This developing case law is notable for at least two reasons. First, the viability of a gender-stereotyping claim is not dependent on either the plaintiff's sexual orientation or gender identity. In other words, whether the plaintiff identifies as lesbian, gay, bisexual, straight, transgender, or cisgender (nontransgender) is (or should be) entirely irrelevant to the analysis.[21] Instead, what matters is whether the employer imposed on the employee or applicant certain gender-based expectations related to performance or abilities.

Second, implicit in the holding that gender stereotyping constitutes unlawful discrimination is the notion that it is for individuals, and not their employers, to determine which gender and sexual identities to adopt, and how to express or perform them. The legal doctrine of gender stereotyping, in other words, is consistent with the notion of fluid and multiple gender and sexual identities. The doctrine does not look for the expression of particular and predetermined identities in order to offer them protection; instead, it permits individuals to express or perform their identities (whatever they may be) without fear that employers will hold it against them.

It bears noting that the ability of the legal theory of gender stereotyping to provide protection to a multiplicity of gender and sexual identities is not limited to the context of Title VII and other employment antidiscrimination laws. In interpreting the Constitution's Equal Protection Clause, the Supreme Court has left little doubt that it is constitutionally impermissible for the government to set policy with the objective of encouraging individuals to pursue particular priorities and preferences depending on their gender.[22] Furthermore, although the Supreme Court has not discussed gender stereotyping in the context of sexual orientation or gender identity, a federal appellate court, in an employment discrimination case involving a transgender plaintiff, has held that government officials violate the Equal Protection Clause when they engage in gender stereotyping.[23]

The Supreme Court cases, as well as the lower court ruling, have significant implications because they limit the ability of government officials to make decisions in response to the way individuals express or perform their gender in all matters, not just those related to employment. In addition, the federal appellate court's reasoning was not limited to cases involving transgender individuals. The plaintiff's transgender identity was relevant only to the extent that it explained her supervisor's discomfort with the way she performed or expressed her gender; the identity, as such, was legally irrelevant.

This is the kind of understanding of antidiscrimination law that the LGBT movement should explicitly and purposefully promote. The movement needs to move away from the idea that only certain categories of individuals (e.g., gay, lesbian, bisexual, and transgender) are entitled to discrimination protection on the basis of gender and sexual orientation. Instead, as with the legal theory of gender stereotyping, the movement should focus on ways to decouple antidiscrimination protections from the particular gender and sexual-orientation identities of the victims of discrimination.

Interestingly, the definition of "gender identity" in the Employment Non-Discrimination Act (ENDA), a federal bill that would have prohibited employment discrimination on the basis of "sexual orientation" and "gender identity," did not limit its proposed protection to individuals who identified as transgender. That definition was as follows: "The term 'gender identity' means the gender-related identity, *appearance*, or *mannerisms* or other gender-related *characteristics* of an individual, with or without regard to the individual's designated sex at birth."[24]

This broad definition makes clear that the protection would be afforded not only to gender-related identities but also to "appearance, or mannerisms or other gender-related characteristics" that may be disconnected from, or go beyond, the distinct gender identities of potential ENDA plaintiffs. As called for by the discrimination theory of gender stereotyping, the proposed definition of "gender identity" would unmoor the antidiscrimination protection from any particular identity. *All* gender-variant or nonconforming individuals, regardless of whether they identify as transgender, would be covered under the statute.[25]

Unfortunately, the same bill's definition of "sexual orientation" was not nearly as capacious because it defined that term to mean only "homosexuality, heterosexuality, and bisexuality."[26] As already noted, this type of definition, which tracks the definition of sexual orientation contained in almost all the existing state laws prohibiting discrimination on that basis, improperly limits the protection to three categories of individuals, leaving out a panoply of others, including asexuals, the polyamorous, and those without a defined sexual orientation.[27]

It is true that Congress, like many state legislatures, has been unwilling to enact even a traditional antidiscrimination law that protects individuals on the basis of well-established identities such "homosexuality" and "bisexuality." It could be argued, therefore, that Congress and most state legislatures are unlikely to adopt the expansive understanding of sexual orientation that I am suggesting.

I have two responses to this possible criticism. The first is that it might be politically necessary to first enact laws with identity-specific definitions of "sexual orientation," and to return later to seek more expansive forms of legislation. Such piecemeal reform efforts are sometimes necessary to gradually build the types of majorities and coalitions that can bring about additional reforms in the future.

My second response is that even when antidiscrimination laws that rely on traditional sexual-orientation categories represent the only realistically achievable short-term objective given conservative political environments, there are long-term advantages to framing questions of sexuality (and gender) more broadly by deemphasizing rigid and predetermined identities and focusing instead on informing legislators, policymakers, and the general public about the fluidity and malleability of those identities. If such an approach seems misguided because it is unlikely to succeed, then we need to remember that, a decade ago, almost no one predicted that the marriage equality objective would be attainable nationwide in only a few years. But the fight for marriage equality was about more than simply seeking what was politically possible; more fundamentally, it was about what was right. Similarly, focusing on fluid and multiple notions of gender and sexual identities is normatively the right thing to do because it allows for the protection of individuals who—despite the fact that society has grown increasingly tolerant of lesbians and gay men—remain vulnerable to discrimination based on the ways in which they express or perform their gender and sexuality.

It bears noting that some of the movement's educational and outreach efforts in this regard will have to be aimed not only at the broader society but also at those members of LGBT communities who view notions of gender and sexual fluidity and malleability with skepticism. There are some transgender individuals, for example, who view gender in strongly binary terms. There are also some lesbians and gay men who, as Kenji Yoshino puts it, believe that "bisexuality endangers the immutability defense and effective political mobilization."[28] The existence of these types of views means that any concerted push to emphasize notions of fluidity and malleability will require extended, and perhaps uncomfortable, intracommunity discussions about the movement's normative goals.

## Gender Segregation in Bathrooms

Our society no longer tolerates de jure segregation in the use of public facilities on the basis of race. The country has also dispensed with many of its policies and norms that kept women out of privileged spaces, such as corporate boardrooms and the floors of legislatures. However, there is one type of public space that remains highly segregated along gender lines: bathrooms (and similar facilities such as locker and dressing rooms). The LGBT rights movement should promote the degendering of public bathrooms as part of a broader effort to encourage the state to adopt laws and policies that protect gender and sexual fluidity and multiplicities. For reasons I will explain, this push should go beyond current campaigns to allow transgender individuals to have access to the gendered bathrooms of their choice.

It may seem at first that bathrooms are places of little social or political importance. The truth, however, is that public bathrooms in the United States have long been the subject of civil rights struggles. Under the Jim Crow regime, public bathrooms, like most other facilities, were racially segregated. The push for racial integration, therefore, included a push to make public bathrooms accessible to everyone regardless of race. The women's movement advocacy for greater opportunities in employment and higher education has included demands that more women's bathrooms be made available in workplaces and educational settings.[29] The disability rights movement has long made accessibility to public bathrooms one of its primary goals. Similarly, the LGBT rights movement has pushed government agencies, employers, and places of public accommodation to adopt policies that permit transgender individuals to use the bathrooms of their choice instead of having to use bathrooms that correspond to the sex category they were assigned at birth.[30]

Despite the fact that requiring transgender individuals to use bathrooms according to their birth sex can subject them to physical and psychological harm, the bathroom advocacy campaigns have faced strong resistance from some and general indifference by others. In addition, the ability of antidiscrimination law to remedy the problem has been relatively limited.[31] For many in our society, including legislators and judges, the segregation of bathrooms according to so-called biological sex seems both natural and benign. Those views are reflected in the panoply of state and local laws that mandate sex-segregated public restrooms, which, unlike the ones that mandated race-segregated facilities, are still on the books.[32]

Recently, there have been some legal successes in requiring officials to permit transgender girls to use girls' bathrooms in public schools.[33]

These successful lawsuits have led some schools to adopt policies allowing transgender girls to use the bathrooms in which they feel most comfortable, while avoiding the psychological harm, stigma, and harassment that comes with being forced to use either boys' bathrooms or specially designated bathrooms (such as single-stall ones).

These types of legal victories, however, have at least two significant limitations. First, they place the burden on the transgender adult or child to identify as such and to request what is essentially an accommodation of the nearly universal gender-segregation policy that requires individuals to use bathrooms according to the sex they were assigned at birth. This process places the spotlight on transgender individuals by requiring them to explain and justify the accommodation before being deemed eligible. This burden is often accompanied by intrusive and demeaning inquiries by employers, school officials, and others as they try to determine the "true" gender of the individual seeking the accommodation.

Second, even when an accommodation is an option, it is available only to those who identify as transgender. As a result, individuals who are gender variant but do not identify as transgender—for example, those who identify as both male and female, or as neither—are not likely to be able to use the bathrooms in which they are most comfortable.

Both of these limitations would be addressed by the complete degendering of bathrooms. If all bathrooms were gender neutral—as a growing number of activists, in particular on college campuses, are pushing for—then there would be no room for exclusion on the basis of gender or sexuality.[34] This would benefit not only those who identify as transgender but also those who express their gender and sexuality identities in other ways.

The literature in this area is replete with disturbing incidents of gender policing (by, for instance, employers, business owners, police officers, and security guards) of bathroom use.[35] To provide just one example, an employee at a New York City restaurant physically removed a lesbian, cisgender woman who expressed her gender in masculine ways from the establishment's female-designated bathroom because the employee believed she "looked too much like a man."[36] Victims of the physical and verbal harassment that often accompanies the gender policing of bathrooms are not limited to transgender individuals; instead, victims fall under different categories of gender-variant identities, including those who identify, for example, as queer, intersex, androgynous, or butch.

Instituting a policy of gender-neutral bathrooms would take away from government agencies, employers, and places of public accommodation the ability to engage in the policing of gender and sexual boundaries through bathroom assignation rules and norms. The policy would allow everyone—regardless of how they self-identify in terms of gender and sexuality—equal access to all bathrooms (and similar spaces such as locker and dressing rooms).[37]

Those who have called for the end of bathroom segregation have done so on the basis of either sex equality or transgender rights.[38] My suggestion is that the LGBT movement seek the same objective on a different ground: the importance of implementing policies that recognize and support gender and sexual fluidity and multiplicities. The purpose behind this different approach was succinctly explained by a self-identified nontrans queer femme who told a researcher that "if we were to desegregate gendered bathrooms we would have to have a public social conversation about the fact that . . . the majority of folks fall somewhere in between the signs on bathroom doors."[39]

Persuading society to abandon the long-held custom of gender bathroom segregation will not be easy. Indeed, as with seeking more expansive statutory definitions of "sexual orientation," it is important to acknowledge the challenges that the movement will confront if it pursues gender desegregation for public bathrooms as a policy objective. For many people, that type of segregation seems both natural and necessary, in ways that are similar to the way most people, until recently, believed it was natural and necessary to limit marriage to individuals of different genders.

Furthermore, it is in many ways easier to argue, for example, that a transgender school girl is a *girl* and that therefore she should be permitted to use the girls' bathroom than it is to argue that bathrooms should no longer be segregated according to gender. The former claim is easier to make because it falls more neatly under the identity-based discrimination-protection paradigm with which policymakers and judges are increasingly familiar and comfortable. That paradigm holds that individuals should not be treated differently on the basis of a finite number of identities, including the female one.

Despite these challenges, it is important that the LGBT movement seek to gain greater legal protections for a greater number of individuals by pursuing policies that are not dependent on particular (and, therefore, to some extent, privileged) gender and sexuality identities. Such an approach is needed in order to afford equality rights to more than just lesbians and gay men.

## Conclusion

Although the marriage equality movement framed the issue as one involving the rights of same-sex couples to marry, the reality is that removing the gender barrier to marriage opens up the institution to *any* two individuals, regardless of their gender and sexual identities. As a result, the benefits of marriage equality can potentially accrue to a much wider segment of the population than cisgender lesbians and gay men. As LGBT movement leaders and constituents ponder which objectives to pursue next, they should consider advocating for other reforms that delink the allocation of rights and benefits from the way individuals identify according to gender and sexuality. These new laws and policies would make it possible for a greater number of individuals, if they so wish, to explore a wider range of gender and sexual identities. They would also make it possible for individuals, if they so wish, to transition back and forth between different identities, with less fear of discrimination, stigma, and harassment.

I noted earlier how the push for marriage equality represented a political and normative realignment on the part of the LGBT-rights movement, as it placed less importance on considerations of state neutrality and the right to "be left alone" and more importance on gaining social respect, support, and acceptance. The attainment of the marriage equality goal offers the movement the opportunity to consider another political and normative realignment, one that moves away from calls for the protection of particular classes of gender and sexual minorities and toward the protection of the many different ways in which gender and sexual identities can be expressed or performed. The LGBT movement, going forward, needs to focus less on promoting the rights and interests of a handful of gender and sexual groups and more on encouraging the state to adopt laws and implement policies that promote equal treatment in ways that are disconnected from traditional, rigid, and binary understandings of gender and sexuality.

NOTES

I would like to thank Mary Anne Case and Douglas NeJaime for providing me with extremely helpful comments and suggestions on an earlier draft of this chapter.

1 As NeJaime explains,

> by integrating developments in family law governing different-sex and same-sex couples, biological and nonbiological parents, and marital and nonmarital families, . . . marriage equality was enabled by—and in turn enables—significant shifts in the law's understanding of parenthood. More specifically, . . . the claim to marriage both seized on and extended the very model of parenthood forged by LGBT advocates in earlier work on behalf of unmarried parents. That model of parenthood is premised on intentional and functional, rather than biological and gendered, concepts of parentage. . . . [R]ather than affirming traditional norms . . . , marriage equality and the model of parenthood it signals are transforming parenthood, marriage, and the relationship between them—for all families.

> Douglas NeJaime, "Marriage Equality and the New Parenthood," 129 *Harvard Law Review* 1185, 1187 (2016).

2 Subcommittee on Investigations of the Senate Committee on Expenditures in the Executive Department, "Interim Report: Employment of Homosexuals and Other Sex Perverts in Government" (1950).

3 On the efforts by the federal government to identify, harass, and dismiss lesbian and gay employees during the 1950s, see David K. Johnson, *The Lavender Scare: The Cold War Persecution of Gays and Lesbians in the Federal Government* (Chicago: University of Chicago Press, 2004).

4 John D'Emilio, *Sexual Politics, Sexual Communities: The Making of a Homosexual Minority in the United States, 1940–1970* (Chicago: University of Chicago Press, 1983), pp. 49–50.

5 The first two cases involving issues of sexual orientation that reached the Supreme Court, *see* One, Inc. v. Olesen, 355 U.S. 371 (1958); Manual Enterprises, Inc. v. Day, 370 U.S. 478 (1962), resulted from government efforts to censor gay publications. For an exploration of the two cases, *see* Carlos A. Ball, "Obscenity, Morality, and the First Amendment: The First LGBT Rights Cases before the Supreme Court," 28 *Columbia Journal of Gender and Law* 229 (2015).

6 I am not suggesting that issues related to employment discrimination were completely foreign to LGBT rights activism prior to the 1970s. This was clearly not the case. *See, e.g.*, Norton v. Macy, 417 F.2d 1161 (D.C. Circ. 1969); Kameny v. Brucker, 282 F.2d 823 (D.C. Cir. 1960). My point is simply that it was not until the 1970s that the movement was able to start making realistic demands for the adoption of laws and regulations that protected sexual minorities from discrimination.

7 Although as I note in the introduction to this book, there was some marriage activism early on, especially during the 1970s, LGBT activists paid relatively little attention to marriage equality before the mid-1990s.

8  For particularly influential critiques of essentialized, rigid, and binary under-
    standings of gender and sexuality, see Judith Butler, *Gender Trouble: Feminism
    and the Subversion of Identity* (New York: Routledge, 1990); Janet E. Halley,
    "Sexual Orientation and the Politics of Biology: A Critique of the Argument from
    Immutability," 46 *Stanford Law Review* 503 (1994).

9  Michael Shulman, "Generation LGBTQIA," *New York Times*, January 10, 2013, E1.

10  Martha Mendoza, "Facebook Offers New Gender Options for Users," *Associated
    Press: The Big Story*, www.bigstory.ap.org/article/apnewsbreak-new-gender-
    options-facebook-users (accessed April 2015).

11  Emmanuell Grinberg, "OKCupid Expands Options for Gender and Sexual
    Orientation," *CNN*, Nov. 18, 2014, http://www.cnn.com/2014/11/18/living/okcupid-
    expands-gender-orientation-options (accessed April 2015). To help its users choose
    a sexual-orientation category, OKCupid provides a "Sexual Orientation Test." *See*
    http://www.okcupid.com/tests/the-sexual-orientation-test-1 (accessed April 2015).

12  On intersexuality, see Julie A. Greenberg, *Intersexuality and the Law: Why Sex
    Matters* (New York: New York University Press, 2012); on asexuality, see Elizabeth
    F. Emens, "Compulsory Sexuality," 66 *Stanford Law Review* 303 (2014); on poly-
    amory, see Elizabeth F. Emens, "Monogamy's Law: Compulsory Monogamy and
    Polyamorous Existence," 29 *N.Y.U. Review of Law & Social Change* 277 (2004);
    Ann E. Tweedy, "Polyamory as a Sexual Orientation," 79 *University of Cincinnati
    Law Review* 1461 (2011).

13  I have elsewhere explored how a liberal feminist understanding of autonomy,
    as articulated by thinkers such as Marilyn Friedman, *see* Marilyn Friedman,
    *Autonomy, Gender, Politics* (New York: Oxford University Press, 2003), can be
    particularly helpful to those who want to promote the rights of sexual minorities.
    *See* "This Is Not Your Father's Autonomy: Lesbian and Gay Rights from a Feminist
    and Relational Perspective," 28 *Harvard Journal of Gender & Law* 345 (2005).

14  For particularly trenchant critiques of the LGBT-rights movement's prioritiza-
    tion of marriage rights, see Paula Ettelbrick, "Since When Is Marriage a Path to
    Liberation?" *OUT/LOOK*, Fall 1989, p. 9, reprinted in William B. Rubenstein,
    Carlos A. Ball, Jane S. Shacter, and Douglas NeJaime, eds., *Cases and Materials
    on Sexual Orientation and the Law* (5th ed., Minneapolis: West, 2014), p. 800;
    Katherine Franke, "The Domesticated Liberty of *Lawrence v. Texas*," 104 *Columbia
    Law Review* 1399 (2004); Nancy D. Polikoff, "We Will Get What We Ask For: Why
    Legalizing Gay and Lesbian Marriage Will Not 'Dismantle the Legal Structure of
    Gender in Every Marriage,'" 79 *Virginia Law Review* 1535 (1993).

15  Title VII of the Civil Rights Act of 1964 does not contain a definition of "race."
    Although the original version of the statute also did not define "sex," a later
    amendment, in response to a Supreme Court ruling holding otherwise, *see*
    General Electric Co. v. Gilbert, 429 U.S. 125 (1976), made clear that discrimina-
    tion "because of sex" under Title VII includes discrimination due to pregnancy.
    Pregnancy Discrimination Act, Pub. L. No. 95–555, 92 Stat. 2076 (1978) (codified
    as amended at 42 U.S.C. § 2000e(k) (2014)).

16  A survey of sexual-orientation antidiscrimination laws in the twenty-one states that had them in 2010 found that eighteen defined "sexual orientation" in terms of heterosexuality, homosexuality, and bisexuality. The three remaining provisions did not include a definition of "sexual orientation." Tweedy, "Polyamory as a Sexual Orientation," pp. 1463–64.

17  As the Supreme Court has noted, Title VII's prohibition of race discrimination "is not limited to discrimination against members of any particular race." McDonald v. Santa Fe Trail Transp. Co., 427 U.S. 273, 278–79 (1976).

18  Ulane v. Eastern Airlines, Inc., 742 F.2d 1081, 1085 (7th Cir. 1984).

19  Price Waterhouse v. Hopkins, 490 U.S. 228 (1989).

20  *Hopkins*, 490 U.S. at 235.

21  *See, e.g.*, EEOC v. Boh Brothers Construction Co., 731 F.3d 444 (5th Cir. 2013) (en banc) (involving plaintiff of unspecified sexual orientation); Prowel v. Wise Business Forms, 579 F.3d 285 (3rd Cir. 2009) (involving self-identified gay plaintiff); Smith v. City of Salem, 378 F.3d 566 (6th Cir. 2004) (involving self-identified transgender plaintiff). I say "should be" in the text because some courts unfortunately continue to point to the sexual orientation and gender identity of LGBT plaintiffs, and the fact that neither trait is protected under Title VII, in rejecting their claims of gender stereotyping under that statute. *See, e.g.*, Dawson v. Bumble & Bumble, 398 F.3d 211 (2nd Cir. 2005).

22  For a discussion of this case law, see Carlos A. Ball, *Same-Sex Marriage and Children: A Tale of History, Social Science, and Law* (New York: Oxford University Press, 2014), pp. 99–102.

23  Glenn v. Brumby, 663 F.3d 1312 (11th Cir. 2011).

24  Employment Non-Discrimination Act of 2013, S. 815, 113th Cong. §3(a)(7) (2013) (as referred to the House of Representatives, Nov. 12, 2013) (emphases added).

25  Mary Anne Case has raised the concern that the definition of "gender identity" under ENDA is so broad that judges may find it obscure or confusing. Mary Anne Case, "Legal Protections for the 'Personal Best' of Each Employee: Title VII's Prohibition on Sex Discrimination, the Legacy of *Price Waterhouse v. Hopkins*, and the Prospect of ENDA," 66 *Stanford Law Review* 1333, 1366 (2014). Case's point is well taken and suggests that if the definition becomes part of federal antidiscrimination law, advocates will have to explain to courts how such a definition is consistent with the theory of gender stereotyping under Title VII that they are already familiar with, one that disconnects questions of sex discrimination from a plaintiff's distinct gender and sexual identities.

26  Employment Non-Discrimination Act of 2013, S. 815, 113th Cong. §3(a)(10) (2013) (as referred to the House of Representatives, Nov. 12, 2013).

27  An expansive definition of sexual orientation could still include specific exemptions from antidiscrimination protection for certain groups, such as those who claim to have a sexual orientation toward minors.

28  Kenji Yoshino, "The Epistemic Contract of Bisexual Erasure," 52 *Stanford Law Review* 353, 428 (2000).

29  *See, e.g.,* Sarah Moore, "Facility Hostility? Sex Discrimination and Women's Restrooms in the Workplace," 36 *Georgia Law Review* 599 (2002).

30  *See, e.g.,* Jennifer Levi and Daniel Redman, "The Cross-Dressing Case for Bathroom Equality," 34 *Seattle University Law Review* 133 (2010).

31  For two leading cases holding that employers do not violate antidiscrimination laws when they prohibit transgender employees from using bathrooms that correspond to their gender identity, *see* Etsitty v. Utah Transit Authority, 502 F.3d 1215 (10th Cir. 2007); Goins v. West Group, 635 N.W.2d 717 (Minn. 2001).

32  For a historical exploration of these laws, *see* Terry S. Kogan, "Sex-Separation in Public Restrooms: Law, Architecture, and Gender," 14 *Michigan Journal of Gender & Law* 1 (2007).

33  *See* Doe v. Regional School District 26, 86 A.3d 600 (Me. 2014); Mathis v. Fountain-Fort Carson School District, Colorado Division of Civil Rights, Charge No. P20130034X, June 17, 2013.

34  For an account of the activism in favor of gender-neutral bathrooms, *see* Izzy Rode, "No More Women's Rooms: Why All Bathrooms Should Be Gender Neutral," *Slate*, December 26, 2013, www.slate.com/blogs/outward/2013/12/26/gender_neutral_bathrooms_all_bathrooms_should_be_open_to_all_users.html (accessed April 2015).

35  *See, e.g.,* Kath Browne, "Genderism and the Bathroom Problem: (Re)materialising Sexed Sites, (Re)creating Sexed Bodies," 11 *Gender, Place, and Culture* 331 (2004); Sheila L. Cavanagh, *Queering Bathrooms: Gender, Sexuality, and the Hygienic Imagination* (Toronto: Toronto University Press, 2010), ch. 2.

36  Jennifer Lee, "Woman Wins a Settlement over Her Bathroom Ouster," *New York Times*, May 14, 2008.

37  The type of reform I have in mind is consistent with the step taken by the White House to create an "'all-gender restroom' in the Eisenhower Executive Office Building, where many of the White House staff members work, to provide an additional option for transgender individuals who are not comfortable using either the men's or women's bathrooms." Michael D. Shear, "Obama to Call for End to 'Conversion' Therapies for Gender and Transgender Youth," *New York Times*, April 4, 2015.

38  For a sex-equality perspective on unisex bathrooms, *see* Mary Anne Case, "Why Not Abolish Laws of Urinary Segregation?" in *Toilet: Public Restrooms and the Politics of Sharing*, Harvey Molotch and Laura Noren, eds. (New York: New York University Press, 2010), p. 211. For a transgender-rights perspective, *see* Olga Gershenson, "The Restroom Revolution: Unisex Toilets and Campus Politics," in *Toilet: Public Restrooms and the Politics of Sharing*, p. 191.

39  Cavanagh, *Queering Bathrooms*, p. 56.

7

# A More Promiscuous Politics

## LGBT Rights without the LGBT Rights

JOSEPH J. FISCHEL

This chapter is promiscuous in style and substance. Its eye-wandering politics breeds a wantonness of form. Beholden in the end neither to "rights" nor to "LGBT" identities, this chapter is not marriage material. It is not ready to settle down.

Part 1 responds to right-wing objections that same-sex marriage will devolve into the statutory recognition of polygamy. I argue that the reactionaries are right, or could be—and it is the very litigation and public relations strategies of gay rights advocates that have made the slope to polygamy not just slippery but lubricated.[1]

Part 2 argues not only that the marriage equality movement has accelerated the potential constitutionalization of polygamy but that this development is also *ethically right*, however politically noxious. This development is ethically right not because of its doctrinal rationale—a fundamental right to marriage, discussed below—but because the LGBT movement is committed to a principle of relational autonomy, which I elaborate as the capability to codetermine intimate and/or sexual relations. Such a capability, were it enshrined into liberal law, would implicate a "leveling down" of state recognition: states would support and route benefits and obligations through citizens' chosen intimate arrangements, irrespective of gender, numerosity, or affective attachment. "Marriage" would be left to the jurisdiction of private, religious institutions.[2] In the political present of the United States, this possibility is but dimly imaginable.

Despite this impossibility, or rather because of it, relational autonomy portends divorcing our gay social selves from our political selves. If we redraft what binds us (in the streets, not in the sheets)[3]—sexual and relational determination, rather than gender of object choice—a different field of political emergencies comes into view, emergencies that offer prospects of a coalitional activism affecting a larger constituency. Part 3 briefly examines two sites of social contestation—sexual violence and sex education—and suggests that the U.S. LGBT movement ought to be taking on these pressing issues.

Shifting perspectives from an identitarian frame to a relational one, from gay equality to relational autonomy, and from individualized discrimination to social transformation, we must break up with, or relax our allegiance to, three pivotal symbolic figures: the heroic homosexual, the recidivistic sex offender, and the bullied gay teenager. An ethically defensible approach to sexual justice requires glossing gayness as but one form of minoritized sexuality; an ethically defensible approach to sexual violence requires more nuanced thinking and politicking than demonization, ostracization, or trivialization; an ethically defensible approach to youth sexuality requires more than desexualizing and singularizing the suffering gay teen, but instead enabling young people to be skilled sexual decision makers.

My proposals for the after-marriage future of LGBT rights are nonexclusive. But given that the national LGBT movement has achieved remarkable public acceptance and legal victories, this chapter asks, modestly, if we might harness some of our newfound capital to broker a more capacious politics of sexual justice. Less modestly, this chapter asks what our movement might look like if we weren't, as Kate Bornstein elegantly puts it, "so fucking selfish."[4]

## I. Gays and Polys Sitting in a Tree . . .

Polygamy is the bugaboo of marriage equality. Like clockwork, opponents of same-sex marriage raise the specter of multiplicity, among other horrors. As Brian Brown, president of the National Organization for Marriage, warns,

> People in polygamist, plural marriages are just a short step away now from winning official marriage rights. Adult incest practitioners will have similar claims, as will adult siblings. . . . Lost in this disastrous push to transform marriage into the satisfaction of adult sexual desires are the interests of children and their right to the love of one mother and one father.[5]

This argument is known colloquially as the slippery slope. If we slide from marriage defined exclusively as, and reserved for, one man and one woman, then we sink so much closer to moral depravity: men will marry multiple women, women will marry their cats or toasters, sisters will marry brothers. For Brown, the unrepentant hedonism of gays and lesbians ushers in social degradation, thereby trampling over children who were otherwise doing swell under the regime of conjugal, dyadic heterosexuality.

Advocates for same-sex marriage ridicule the slippery slope argument. Freedom to Marry founder and president Evan Wolfson denounces comparisons to polygamy as "scare tactics."[6] He assures, "One thing [polygamy] has nothing to do with the other [same-sex marriage]. . . . [I]f the only good reason you can give to deny something is to change the subject to something else, it's kind of a hint, as the courts have found, that you really don't have a good reason."[7] But does polygamy really have "nothing to do" with gay marriage? Or might Wolfson be performing the rhetorical move he is exposing: changing the subject on a changed subject to avoid substantive discussion of the poly charge?

As law professor Geoffrey Stone delineated—before *Obergefell v. Hodges*, the 2015 Supreme Court landmark decision guaranteeing same-sex couples the right to marry under the United States Constitution—district and appellate courts had, by and large, struck down statewide same-sex marriage bans through one or more of the following three arguments: (1) the bans unconstitutionally infringe a "fundamental right" to marry; (2) the discriminatory bans serve neither a "compelling" nor an "important" state interest; and (3) the discriminatory bans do not even serve a "legitimate" state interest.[8]

Prior to *Obergefell*, four federal appeals courts had struck down statewide marriage bans as unconstitutional, and one[9] had upheld them. The Ninth Circuit Court of Appeals premised its decision on argument number 2.[10] The Seventh Circuit premised its decision on argument number 3.[11] The Fourth and Tenth Circuits premised their decisions on argument number 1, the argument that proved triumphant in *Obergefell*.[12] And it is this first argument—a constitutionalized, fundamental right to marry—that slicks the slope for multiple-partner intimate arrangements.

How so? The doctrinal argument for marriage-as-a-fundamental-right plays out this way: *Loving v. Virginia* declares marriage a "fundamental freedom" and invalidates interracial marriage prohibitions. *Zablocki v. Redhail* finds marriage to be a fundamental right that the state cannot withdraw on the basis of one's record of paying child support. *Turner v. Safley* strikes down a categorical ban against prison inmates marrying. *United States v. Windsor*, requiring federal recognition of state same-sex marriages, neared us that much closer to making sex as immaterial to marriage entry (and exit) as criminal status, "deadbeat dad" status, or race. Finally, *Obergefell v. Hodges*, extolling marriage as a "fundamental right" and "a keystone of our social order," holds that the Constitution "does not permit the State to bar same-sex couples from marriage on the same terms as accorded to couples of the opposite sex."[13] Combined, these cases establish a constitutional right to marry.

If a constitutional right is fundamental, then a state needs a "compelling interest" to restrict that right. The compelling-interest standard mops up some of the slipperiness of the slippery slope: men cannot marry children because of the state interest in child welfare. Women cannot marry their cats because cats cannot execute the duties and obligations of the marriage contract.

But as Judge Paul Niemeyer asks in his dissent from the Fourth Circuit holding, if adults hold a fundamental right to marry, what prevents polygamy?[14] What makes numerosity different from race, sex, prisoner status, or "deadbeat dad" status? These questions were pressed by Justice Sonia Sotomayor—no right-wing ideologue—during the oral arguments of *Hollingsworth v. Perry*: "If you say that marriage is a fundamental right, what State restrictions could ever exist? Meaning, what State restrictions with respect to the number of people. . . . I can accept that the State has probably an overbearing interest on—on protecting a child until they're of age to marry, but what's left?"[15] Not much. Chief Justice John Roberts echoes Judge Niemeyer and Justice Sotomayor in his *Obergefell* dissent. Does not the constitutional denial of plural marriage, he asks, likewise "disrespect and subordinate people who find fulfillment in polyamorous relationships?" If children of gay and lesbian couples suffer from their parents' marital nonrecognition by the State, would not children of multiple-person relationships suffer similarly?[16]

These questions remained unanswered in the *Obergefell* majority opinion, and to my mind, as a constitutional matter, they are unanswerable. "The legal arguments against polygamy," comments Martha

Nussbaum, "are extremely weak."[17] Moreover, it is the same-sex marriage cases themselves, along with other gay rights and women's rights cases, that have neutralized objections to the statutory recognition of polygamy. What are some of those objections? Here are four common and uncompelling ones.[18]

## A. Polygamy Harms Children

A main objection against polygamy is that the progeny of such marriages may suffer neglect or abuse.[19] But marriage, as we have learned from same-sex marriage cases, has no necessary connection to procreation.[20] Just as plenty of heterosexual and homosexual couples are childless and married, multiple-partner intimate arrangements do not *per se* entail begetting and raising children, let alone abusing them.

If anything, excluding polygamists (or polyamorists) from marriage harms children more than including them does. As one judge after another has pointed out, bans on same-sex marriage harm the children raised by gay and lesbian couples.[21] If children develop better with married parents than with unmarried parents, this augurs for permitting, not proscribing, same-sex marriage. Surely, the same principle holds for the children of polygamous, polyamorous, and other multiple-partner intimate relations: would not these children be more dignified, better respected, and better protected if their parents' partnerships were sanctioned by the state, and if their family arrangements were seen as equally legitimate? Moreover, if we are worried about child exploitation or neglect, legalization may offer rights and formal recourse, whereas criminalization may drive polygamy further underground, dissuading parties from reporting abuse to authorities.[22]

## B. Polygamy Harms Women

Opponents protest that polygamy subordinates women. To that end, same-sex marriage heralds a more egalitarian division of labor, whereas polygamy reinstalls patriarchy.[23] But as John Stuart Mill explained over 150 years ago, dyadic marriage is not so sanguine either on the sex-equality front.[24] Historically, opposition to polygamy has more to do with religious chauvinism and anti-Mormonism than with protecting women.[25] If we are concerned about the subordination of women, we should place less energy on criminalizing and scapegoating polygamy and place more energy on violent gender norms attendant to everyday heterosexuality and "normal" marital relations.[26]

And "polygamy," which typically refers to the union of one man and multiple women, is but one form of intimate plurality. Imagine the Court telling three women seeking a marriage license that their relationship harms women.

Post-*Obergefell*, Judge Richard Posner has argued that polygamy harms *men*: "Suppose a society contains 100 men and 100 women, but the five wealthiest men have a total of 50 wives. That leaves 95 men to compete for only 50 marriageable women."[27] This supposition is not only farcically speculative but also sexist (women's only relevant criterion for marriage is apparently wealth, and women must marry into money, rather than earn it) and ironically heterosexist (all two hundred people in Posner's society wish to marry, and marry someone of a different sex). Further, the rationale contravenes Posner's heartfelt Millian rejection of laws criminalizing conduct that does not demonstrably harm others.[28]

## C. Polygamy Is Gross

Marriage among one man and many women, or three women, or anything other than dyadic and different-sex couples, may be queasiness inducing. But as *Planned Parenthood v. Casey, Romer v. Evans, Lawrence v. Texas*, and many of the same-sex marriage cases have firmly established, your moral disgust is not a legitimate basis for the regulation of sexual conduct, or for discriminating against sexual minorities.[29] If you don't like abortion, don't have one; if you don't want to marry your two or three friends, then don't. But your moral code is just that: yours.

## D. Polygamy Is Complicated

If any argument will be victorious in withholding marriage from multiple partners, it will be that polygamy is complicated. This complexity may be the way multiple-partner marriage is most distinguishable from same-sex marriage.[30] Who gets the dog in the divorce? How is an estate split up after the breadwinner dies? But if marriage is a fundamental right, remember, the state needs a compelling interest to interfere. In the landmark case *Reed v. Reed*, complexity did not rise to the level of a legitimate state interest for discriminating based on sex (argument number 3), let alone a compelling or important one (argument number 2).[31] On the other hand, the "complexity" before the Court in *Reed* was in fact not so complex at all—whether Idaho could constitutionally default to husbands over wives as the administrators of estates (no). In the case of polygamy, complexity becomes much more, well, complicated. This is especially true because of polygamy's "ongoing entrances and exits."[32] Must all marital partners consent to the addition of a new partner? How are rights, responsibilities, reciprocities, and benefits negotiated given the "serial and open-ended nature of polygamy's multiplicity"?[33] Still, insofar as compelling state interests tend to be priorities like "national security," "political stability," "education," "child welfare," and "antidiscrimination," it is unlikely that "complexity" will merit overrunning a now constitutionally protected fundamental right.[34]

I have shown that one line of reasoning in favor of marriage equality—found in litigation strategies, court decisions, and public relations campaigns ("love is love"; "freedom to marry")—commits us to endorsing the statutory recognition of polygamous and other multiple-partner intimacy arrangements. Not all lines of reasoning commit us this way. Judge Posner, writing for the Seventh Circuit, held that same-sex marriage bans unlawfully discriminate against gays and lesbians on equal protection grounds, thus explicitly sidestepping the marriage-as-a-fundamental-right question.[35] He sidesteps the question, I believe, because he knows the inevitable answer: the constitutionalization of nearly all adult intimacy arrangements.

My hunch was that the Supreme Court would follow Judge Posner's lead, in part to batten the conjugal hatches against the poly charge. I was wrong. *Obergefell* is a veritable encomium for marriage as both a central human right and a fundamental constitutional right.[36] Unsurprisingly therefore, *Obergefell* instigated a flurry of legal and journalistic hand-wringing as to whether the ruling opens the door (even wider) to a constitutional right to plural marriage.[37]

Amplified if not initiated by the Supreme Court's fundamental-rights analysis in adjudicating marriage equality, the poly charge opens out to an even more challenging predicament than the social collateral of legal logic:[38] it is not simply that we, as an LGBT movement, might be doctrinally obliged to endorse poly relations. Rather, we, as an LGBT movement, should be ethically committed to endorsing poly relations and other experiments in intimacy.[39]

## II. LGBT Rights without the LGBT

Why should the LGBT movement endorse the statutory recognition of multiple-partner intimacy arrangements? The first set of reasons, empirical and more immediately cognizable, is grounded in what we might call "queer good." This substantive argument—retrieving the ethical stuff of (some) poly relations—provokes a conceptual reason for defending plural intimacies: relational autonomy, or what we might call "queer right."

### A. Poly Relations and the Queer Good

What are some of the "queer goods" scholars have retrieved in their research on poly relations? In her essay "Monogamy's Law: Compulsory Monogamy and Polyamorous Existence," law professor Elizabeth Emens excavates five ethical principles from the writings and testimonies of practicing polys. Those principles are *self-knowledge* (reflecting upon one's desires, aspirations, and relational ambitions), *radical honesty* (as counterpoint to the dissemblance attendant to monogamous fidelity; as everyday practice), *consent* (as shorthand for commitment to open negotiation and information sharing; emphasis on individual choice over unthinking subscription to norms), *self-possession* (a sense of self unmerged into the other; love as indexed by independence and mutuality rather than fusion and mastery), and *privileging love and sex* (as ends, not means; as requiring emotional maintenance and sustenance).[40]

Sociologist Elisabeth Sheff, in her interviews with seventy-one people who "identified as poly,"[41] discovered "many similarities between polyamorous and lesbigay families."[42] Among those similarities are special priority given to constructing family, kin, and community, rather than defaulting to blood relations; the innovation of familial roles and responsibilities; and emphasis on clear communication regarding those roles and responsibilities.[43] Polys place ethical primacy on the "prolif-eration of choices."[44] Whether or not we take a constructivist or natural-ist position on homosexuality, lesbian and gay *coupledom* is premised upon the "proliferation of choice" too—that social convention need not determine the gender identities of the couple form. So too, writes Sheff, "polyamorous families demonstrate an elasticity that allows complicated families to manage daily life and navigate intricate relationships," thus modeling ways other "blended families" (e.g., families with children from prior marriages) might successfully negotiate the obstacles of ev-eryday life.[45] Sheff argues that poly families slick the slope not morally downward to incest and the end of civilization but morally upward, "to-ward individuality, tolerance of diversity, and gender equality."[46] Sheff thus advocates state recognition of poly families.[47]

Dossie Easton and Janet W. Hardy's *Ethical Slut* corroborates and ex-tends these "queer goods"—the avowals, honesty, emotional processing, and positivity toward sex and intimacy—of poly relations. In addition to *honesty* and *consent*, Easton and Hardy suggest that poly relations may help their practitioners unlearn jealousy and offer opportunities to navigate jealousy and dissociate love from control of others.[48] Part of what makes "ethical sluthood" ethical, for these authors, is "setting boundaries"—for one's self and one's relations—rather than reverting to gendered social convention;[49] "embracing conflict"—owning up to and expressing vulnerabilities, frustrations, and disappointments that otherwise register as personal failures to the romance narrative;[50] and modeling love and sex as "abundant" and shared rather than scarce and zero-sum.[51]

Nor is it just *queer* poly relations that promise queer goods. Courtney Bailey's critical review of the TLC show *Sister Wives* exposes the reso-lutely queer heterosexuality on display in the program.[52] *Sister Wives* chronicles the Browns, a Mormon family consisting of husband Kody, his four wives, Meri, Christine, Janelle, and Robyn, and their seventeen children.

The Browns and their show reflect a "queer image of family."[53] *Sister Wives* queers heterosexuality itself, "making it strange and opening it up in democratic ways."[54] What viewers witness is a surprisingly intense female homosociality among the wives, who support, care, and advocate for one another. They also help raise one another's children, and share domestic responsibilities, so as to be more fully participatory in civic and social life.[55] This observation recalls one of Emens's informants, a Mormon wife who reports that the presence of other wives permits a more equitable and manageable distribution of household, emotional, and occupational labor.[56]

Gender is troubled by the Browns too. Kody, a self-proclaimed "metrosexual," is demonstrably concerned with his sartorial style and hair, disrupting the association of male "femininity" with gayness.[57] And the wives range widely in their body types, some defending their curvier, heavier bodies as healthy and desirable.

Bailey points out that these subversive representations of intimacy, family, gender, and desire are neither consistent nor without contradiction—most if not all of the erotic and affective energies are circuited toward the husband, and whiteness and class privilege make culturally digestible the Browns' endless offspring. But who of us live our intimate lives consistently and without contradiction?

What the Browns help us see, as do Bailey, Emens, Sheff, and Easton and Hardy, is that any singular gloss on multiple-partner intimacy arrangements, like any singular gloss on same-sex relations, is premature and probably bigoted. The plural relations documented in these accounts cultivate a consciousness and communicativeness among their participants, which serve as antidotes to the uncritical assumption of gendered, biologically determined roles, the indexing of love through jealousy, and the equating of love with possession. These sorts of challenges to the conventions of the couple form have been critical to and componental of LGBT relational flourishing.

## B. Poly Relations and the Queer Right

One might counter that I have cherry picked the polygamy data to make polygamy queer, as in ethically supportable from an LGBT-rights perspective. Certainly, there are multiple-partner intimacy arrangements that confirm what we thought we knew: these relations are patriarchal, abusive, and culty.[58] Yet, what even this small aggregation of poly testimony and description reveals is a premium on individual choice in determining the structure of one's sustaining, stabilizing intimate relations. These poly stories are stories of people codetermining their relations, families, and intimacies. It is this premium on relational choice that is a good presuppositional to any other goods we might discover in the content of such relations (upending gender norms, more equitable distributions of labor, collectivized childrearing, etc.). And it is this pre-suppositional *good* that lesbians and gays have sought to enshrine as a constitutional *right* to marry their partners. As Carlos Ball explains in this volume, gayness, in many crucial respects, is incidental rather than elemental to same-sex marriage. What is at stake, and what has maybe always been at stake in the marriage equality movement, is relational autonomy:

> Although the movement framed the struggle for marriage equality as one that implicated the basic rights of lesbians and gay men, the reality is that marriage equality opens up marriage to all ~~couples~~ [multiples] regardless of their gender and sexual identities. . . . Under this understanding of marriage equality (which is admittedly not the one promoted by the marriage equality movement), the state lacks the authority to deny marriage licenses to any ~~two~~ [number of] individuals. . . . [A] bisexual intersex individual is as free to marry a transgender female asexual as a heterosexual man is free to marry a heterosexual woman and a lesbian woman is free to marry another lesbian woman [and a transgender female asexual].[59]

Following feminist theoretical reconstructions of the concept, I understand relational autonomy as the *capability to codetermine sexual and/or intimate relations.* I develop a similar concept of *sexual autonomy* more thoroughly elsewhere,[60] but a few remarks here should suffice to show what I do and do not intend by "relational autonomy." The notion of relational autonomy, which I believe underwrites the marriage equality movement, neither requires nor presumes a Kantian rational agent impeccably deliberative and preference-calculating, uninfluenced by emotions or dependence.[61] Nor is this version of autonomy exhausted through negative liberty, a right to be free from others' interference. Relational autonomy posits the self as constituted through relations, intimate and otherwise; a self sustained by, not despite, emotional attachments and material dependence. Relational autonomy is a capability because it demands more than noninterference. "The state does not contribute to autonomy, in other words, only by leaving individuals alone."[62]

This version of autonomy sounds in *Obergefell* itself: "There is dignity in the bond between two [or three?] men or two [or three?] women who seek to marry and in their autonomy to make such profound choices."[63]

For its cultivation, relational autonomy requires social contexts, material provisions, and informational resources that engender persons with the capability to structure their intimate relations in ways that are sustaining and stabilizing. If the withholding of marriage to same-sex couples represents a "failure to create the necessary conditions that make the realization of autonomy by lesbians and gay men possible,"[64] then we must also ask (1) what other statutory or structural conditions are necessary for the realization of relational autonomy and (2) how effectively does marriage equality cultivate relational autonomy?

The following part sketches the beginning of an answer to the first question. As for the second: once we understand that what we wanted from marriage equality was the autonomy to structure our intimate relations as we choose, and with the requisite material provisions to do so, then we can appreciate how state-sponsored marriage so terrifically fails this promise for everyone else. Let us assume that the liberal state has a "compelling interest" in "recognizing and subsidizing the family";[65] it is not *ipso facto* justified in designating some of those arrangements "marriage" and others not so. More justifiable is "a universal 'civil union' status" conferred on adult intimate and family formations.[66] To put this directly: why should the United States Customs and Immigration Services officer need to review my wedding album for my Brazilian husband to receive his green card? What if my husband were instead my cousin? Why is love the criterion, not choice, and why is marriage the conferred status, not civil union? Relational autonomy portends that rights and responsibilities be distributed with (or among) those with (or among) whom we choose to distribute them. Modern "marriage," as a status designation of love and romance, is properly the jurisdiction of private institutions, not secular, democratic states. Under political liberalism, the content of my intimate relations ("intimate" is synonymous neither with "amatory" nor "sexual") should be immaterial to the rights and responsibilities I wish to channel through those relations, thereby sustaining and stabilizing them.[67]

In the historical present, divorcing state from marriage is all but a political pipe dream, which is one reason I propose we look elsewhere to vitalize projects of relational autonomy.

Before we look elsewhere, a final note on the parameters of relational autonomy. Relational autonomy need not and should not reduce to first-person choice, willy-nilly. A relational autonomy right might augur for, not against, third-party intervention in a severely abusive but consensual relationship,[68] just as a relational autonomy right might augur for, not against, prohibiting teenagers from having consensual sex with their high school teachers.[69] We might determine that relational autonomy, as the capability to codetermine present and *future* intimate and sexual relations, is better protected and promoted by overriding the present-tense choices of the abused spouse and the desiring teenager. This paternalistic claim requires much more conceptual armature than I am providing here,[70] but I point to these scenarios to emphasize that a right to relational autonomy is not summarily about the satisfaction of immediate choice, but about creating and maintaining conditions that allow us to cultivate and be cultivated by our intimate relations. If we are committed to *that* kind of relational autonomy, where might the LGBT movement turn?

## III. LGBT Rights without the Rights; or, Relational Autonomy and Social Transformation

Poly relations, insofar as they presume no particular gender identities, and relational autonomy, insofar as it prioritizes material relations over abstracted subject positions, both point towards gay rights without the gay. Poly, practically, and relational autonomy, conceptually, remind us that the capability to structure our intimate relations is the filament of gay justice.[71] Even more, insofar as a commitment to relational autonomy entails generating material and cultural conditions for people to exercise meaningful choices about how to structure their intimate and sexual relations, we are directed to gay rights without the rights. A movement organized around relational autonomy cannot be dispatched through the codification of an actionable right in an otherwise unjust world; it also must build worlds more hospitable to sexual and intimate pluralism.[72]

This part thus distinguishes itself from more familiar queer criticisms of marriage, which tend to cut one of three ways: first, marriage is assimilationist, and it is our queer birthright, living and loving "diagonal"[73] to social order, to contravene assimilation; second, marriage affects a small population of LGBT individuals, and we should instead focus on issues that impact larger, more vulnerable LGBT populations;[74] and lastly, we should be committed to nonidentitarian social justice more broadly.[75]

The first criticism has always been radically seductive and seductively radical, but disingenuous as a matter of justice. We might think U.S. democracy a sham, but that does not mean we ought to exclude women from the franchise.[76] The second and third criticisms are right on, but underdemanding and overdemanding, respectively. The second criticism—what about most queers?—runs into the very identitarian cul-de-sac that "queer" promised to dispel.[77] If what binds us politically is a commitment to relational autonomy, why should we care only for self-described queers? Why should we not be concerned that many folks—straight people too—are impeded from sexual and intimate flourishing?[78] The third criticism—what about the revolution?—has wanting hortatory appeal. It is unlikely enough that the mainstream gay rights movement will direct time, intellect, or money to sexual injustices not identifiably taxonomic (L, G, B, or T). The notion that the movement will redirect its energies to redistributive justice writ large defies credulity.

My proposal for movement priorities then—beholden to relational autonomy, not sexual identity—keeps us in the orbit of sexual justice, but queerly. I suggest that we extend our resources, energies, and time to scenes where sexual and intimate relations are undernourished or damaged. I survey two sites of sexual life and political emergency in the United States: sexual violence and sex education.

## A. Sexual Violence

> The problem with rape is presumed to be with the force used, not with the victim's loss of *autonomy* or lack of consent.[79]

The dominant,[80] national sociolegal responses to sexual violence are largely ineffective, often counterproductive, and decidedly not feminist. Our legal remedies are also contradictory, structured by assumptions of sexual violence as either uniquely heinous and shattering, on the one hand, or as unserious and falsely accused, on the other.

## SEXUAL VIOLENCE AS HEINOUS

Starting in the 1990s, following several incidents of horrid sex crimes committed against children, the states and federal government enacted sex offender registration and notification regulations (SORN), heralding the "most significant changes to rape law in the past two decades."[81] I will not discuss SORN and other postconviction—or alternative-to-conviction[82]—regulations in detail here,[83] but in short, states and the federal government subject "sex offenders" to a barrage of unparalleled restrictions. Perhaps most well known, hundreds of thousands of sex offenders are placed on state sex offender websites, where all sorts of identifying information—name, local address, place of employment, conviction details—is made publicly available. SORN and other regulatory requirements are premised on a host of seemingly unimpeachable assumptions: that sexual violence is committed by deranged strangers; that these deranged strangers are recidivistic; that registration, notification, residency restrictions, and other regulatory measures will be both effective deterrents and useful surveillance tools.

Because the assumptions are so misguided, SORN and other requirements have been resounding policy failures—they are not effective preventative measures, and they do not make communities safer from sexual violence.[84] What SORN offers us is a repository figure, the recidivistic sex offender, on whom we can offload all sorts of social, political, and sexual anxieties.[85] But "recidivism rates for sex offenders are lower than for the general criminal population," and recidivism varies widely by particular sex crime.[86] Likewise, SORN and its premises belie what feminists have insisted upon for over forty years: sexual violence is committed most often by family members and acquaintances; sexual violence is more a function of eroticized dominance, gender inequality, and dependence (of the victims) than of outlier, demonic men; hyperpunitive remedies for rape and sexual assault probably deter victims' reporting, and deter police and prosecutors from vigorously pursuing, perpetrators of sexual violence.[87]

## SEXUAL VIOLENCE AS UNSERIOUS

Rose Corrigan's devastating *Up against a Wall: Rape Reform and the Failure of Success*, chronicles the many ways in which contemporary medical and legal institutional responses to rape are insufficient and underwhelming.[88] Despite feminist-led legislative reforms of the 1970s (elimination of the corroboration and "utmost resistance" requirements, scaling back of marital exemptions, gradation of sex offenses, etc.), Corrigan shows, through extensive interviews with rape crisis center (RCC) staffers and other stakeholders, how implementation has largely failed. Corrigan tracks the "leaky pipeline"[89] of institutional responses to rape, from initial complaint onward, and finds that "the attitudes of health care providers, police, and prosecutors work together to force victims out of the criminal justice pipeline by making rape reporting so unpleasant and difficult that victims are persuaded, ignored, intimidated, and bullied into withdrawing complaints."[90] Medical providers regularly delay or refuse care; many are untrained to administer rape kits.[91] Patrol officers readily disbelieve victims or pressure them to withdraw their complaints, and they refuse to file or downgrade reports if the victim is not a "good girl" (if she is nonwhite, a sex worker, etc.) or if the alleged assailant is esteemed in the community.[92] Prosecutors plea down or drop rape cases to ensure high conviction rates, amounting to "wide-scale refusal to move ahead with sexual assault charges."[93] Corrigan summarizes: "[V]oluntary and criminal justice reforms have failed not because they were poorly designed or inherently ineffective, but because of the massive and continuing resistance of nurses, doctors, police, and prosecutors to taking rape seriously."[94] On the other end, rape crisis centers are underfunded, politically alienated, and severed from the feminist analysis of gender inequality and sexual violence that led to their institutional emergence; RCCs mostly offer individualized, therapeutic, necessary, but uneven assistance to victims.[95]

What does "taking rape seriously" entail, if we can resist the temptation to synonymize seriousness with punitiveness? And why should our national failures to remediate sexual violence be of concern to the LGBT movement? Because what sexual violence violates is neither children's innocence nor women's chastity, but relational autonomy. Sexual assault inhibits persons from codetermining sexual and intimate relations; if sexual relations are dialogic, sexual violence is monologic, disbarring people from collaborating in their sexual lives. In combination, SORN and the "leaky pipeline" of responses to rape configure sexual violence as a spectacular, uncommon, heinous assault on innocence, rather than an all-too-common, all-too-gendered denial of autonomy.

If we understand sexual violence as violence against relational autonomy, LGBT community leaders, organizers, and members might involve themselves more fully in, contribute to, and expand the agenda of RCCs. We might serve as volunteers, fundraisers, and staffers of RCCs that have been so politically and financially cut off.[96] We might participate more seriously in restorative justice programs committed to eliminating sexual violence.[97] We might demand that states and the federal government direct more of their funds to victim services, prevention, restorative justice, and sex education than to criminal justice remedies and ever-expansive SORN schemes.[98] And if sexual violence is so often perpetrated because victims are financially dependent on spouses, parents, or guardians, then we should be more vocal in our demands for state and federal job-training programs, robust welfare assistance, and funded after-school activities; these are the kinds of material resources that make the capability to codetermine sexual and intimate relations actually realizable.[99]

In the past few years, sexual violence on college campuses has reemerged as a national concern. LGBT student groups, in my admittedly armchair perspective, ought to be at the forefront of campaigns to stop campus sexual assault. Activist campaigns to eliminate campus sexual assault, and federal agencies that have stepped up enforcement to hold colleges and universities accountable, are operating under the auspices of Title IX of the Education Amendments of 1972, which "prohibit[s] discrimination on the basis of sex in education programs or activities operated by recipients of Federal financial assistance."[100] What is so promising about these recent efforts is that they conceive sexual violence not as an unspeakable harm worse than death, but as an impediment to equal participation in the curricular and extracurricular life of the university. In other words, under a Title IX register, sexual violence and institutional indifference violate something akin to students' autonomy. Because of this commitment to autonomy, however implicit, campaigns against campus sexual assault emphasize better reporting procedures, proper training for advocates, bystander intervention, the administration of sexual climate surveys, and the codification of affirmative consent in sexual misconduct policies.[101] These strategies are imperfect, but they are, at root, about cultivating an environment free of sex discrimination and gendered inequality, an environment in which all students[102] are able to codetermine their intimate and sexual relations. This sort of climatic aspiration should find affinity with LGBT advocates, who might create generative coalitions with campus sexual educators and antisexual violence organizers. Indeed, the Obama administration sees in Title IX the very cross-identitarian solidarity I am proposing, recognizing gender-identity discrimination, sexual-orientation discrimination, and sexual violence as all symptomatic of institutional environments hostile to equal participation.[103]

Ultimately, stopping sexual violence requires a transformation in our discussions and practices around gender, sex, sexuality, and sexual decision making. Critical, comprehensive, and feminist sex education is a necessary (but insufficient) ingredient for such a social transformation.

## B. Sex Education

The state of sex education in the United States is abysmal. When it arose as a national issue in the late 1970s (amidst concerns of teen pregnancy) and early 1980s (amidst concerns of HIV/AIDS), the Religious Right quickly and effectively hijacked sex education.[104] First federally funded in 1981 under the Reagan administration, Abstinence Only Until Marriage (AOUM) sex education programs have prevailed in public schools. "Funding for these unproven programs grew exponentially from 1996 until 2009, particularly during the years of the George W. Bush Administration, and to date Congress has funneled over one-and-a-half billion tax-payer dollars into abstinence-only-until-marriage programs."[105] AOUM programs are ineffective against their own success metrics (pregnancy prevention; deferral of sexual initiation) and riddled with scientific inaccuracies.[106] A "disaster prevention"[107] model of sex education, AOUM synonymizes sex with disease, presumes and reiterates norms of male sexual aggression and female passivity, and erases or degrades queer sexualities.[108]

Starting in 2009, federal funding streams for sexual education were no longer conditioned on AOUM, but the current snapshot is still dim.[109] Most sex education programming remains abstinence-only or "abstinence-plus"—where abstinence and delay of sexual initiation are prioritized, but contraceptives are reluctantly mentioned.[110] According to a *Time* special report on sexual education, "[A] recent CDC study showed that among teens ages 15–17 who have had sex, nearly 80% did not receive any formal sex education before they lost their virginity. Or, if they did, it was only to discourage them from being sexually active."[111]

Moreover, what gets titled "comprehensive sexuality education" (CSE) is rarely comprehensive in any reasonable sense of the term. While CSE programs may acknowledge and defend minority sexual orientations as legitimate and worthy of respect, and while they may present more scientifically accurate information about contraceptives, sex, reproduction, and disease, they too, for the most part, run on the "disaster prevention model," stressing the deferral of sex and the prevention of infection and pregnancy.[112] Almost nonexistent are programs in which sexual desire is understood as a "force for good"[113] and sexual pleasure is positively valued; in which sex acts of all kinds—what they are, why they feel good, how to refuse them, how to initiate them, how to perform them well, how to perform them safely—are discussed with candor;[114] in which students are taught by trained educators to be informed, competent sexual decision makers; in which young people are taught to more perceptively navigate their often exhilarating, but sometimes hostile and misogynist, online worlds; in which the "plumbing" lessons of sex education are integrated with critical lessons around, for example, gender normativity, gender policing, dominant cultural discourses around sex (boy-as-pedal, girl-as-brake), the generation of one's sexual values, and healthy, least-damaging ways to make and break intimate relationships.[115] In other words, almost nonexistent are programs invested in developing the sexual, relational autonomy of young subjects.

How might the LGBT movement be involved in transforming sexual education to develop the relational autonomy of young persons?

As parents and community members, we might participate more extensively in local school boards. Local school boards are where sex education programs get gutted or die.[116] Minoritized but no longer as marginalized, LGBT persons are uniquely positioned to advocate for youth sexuality, to defend critical, comprehensive, and feminist sex education programs, and to steer the conversation (not entirely) away from pregnancy and disease and toward sexual competency, literacy, and autonomy.

We might collaborate with the Future of Sex Education (FoSE) initiative. Spearheaded by the organizations Advocates for Youth, Answer, and Sexuality Information and Education Council of the U.S. (SIECUS),

FoSE aims to "create a national dialogue about the future of sex educa-tion and to promote the institutionalization of comprehensive sexuality education in public schools."[117] FoSE partners advocate comprehensive sexuality education as pre-K through twelfth-grade curricula focused on the sexual health and well-being of public school students.[118] FoSE has no formal LGBT organizational involvement; we should be a part of this courageous project.

It bears noting that FoSE is not immune to cultural pressure. Priority is placed upon "avoid[ing] negative health consequences," and there is almost no discussion of desire and pleasure as *sui generis* goods. "Au-tonomy" is equated with "saying no" rather than saying "yes" or "let's try this instead." And LGBT kids are prefigured exclusively as vulnerable victims, rather than as incipient sexual agents.[119] LGBT involvement principled on relational autonomy might help generate an even more capacious vision for FoSE and sexual education in our nation.

Part of the reason why abstinence programs are such futile endeavors is that teens get so much of their information about sex, gender, and sexuality from online platforms.[120] Rather than insist on the endless and hopeless project of monitoring and restricting youth Internet participa-tion, LGBT activists might spearhead or affiliate with online projects that provide opportunities for young people to learn about, discuss, and share information around sex, gender, and sexuality.

We ought to encourage teenagers to participate in the creation of sexual education programs. Shared across abstinence, abstinence-plus, and comprehensive-sexuality-education programs is a lack of curricular input from teenagers themselves.[121] As Nancy Kendall so persuasively points out, allowing young people to help select, design, debate, and administer sex education curricula would radically reframe the peda-gogic goals of such programs. Sex education might be a site of "civics education" and citizen training for teens, who might then be figured not as "dangerous and endangered"[122] data recipients of omniscient adults, but as becoming-autonomous subjects, reflective of cultural contexts, normative constraints, sexual pressures, and sexual possibilities.[123]

More significant LGBT politicking around sex education would gen-erate a competing figure of the "gay teen,"[124] too. At present, the gay teen of our advocacy efforts, funding streams, and legislation is suffering, bullied, and innocent. While I do not seek to downplay the prevalence, severity, or consequences of antigay bullying and cyberbullying, my concern is that the political and narrative magnetism of this helpless youth currently predominates the national conversation.[125] Focalizing sex education may enable us to see queer adolescence more accurately, in all its richness. We can observe instead resilient, digitally dexterous, dependent but desiring, and sometimes "unseemly" teens.[126] While the bullied gay teen is invoked for the passage of protective, punitive legislation—legislation that may very well trouble or bar queer teens' access to online and offline materials that have made their lives livable[127]—the sexually agentive gay teen invokes something else from us, an altogether different political response.[128] What do queer teens, or all teens, need to develop the capability to codetermine their sexual relations? Accessible and affordable safer sex materials. Good lube. Explicit, accurate information on sexual anatomy, particularly regarding those otherwise mystified vulvas and vaginas.[129] Online spaces for queer youth.[130] Offline spaces less saturated by heteronormativity, where teens can play with gender identity and expression.[131] Critical literacy of gender roles, sexual violence, pornography, and gendered media representations.[132] Trained educators who can speak openly and knowledgeably with young people.[133] This list is not exhaustive; but enabling queer teens to be relationally autonomous subjects, rather than protecting gay teens from a hostile world, generates a more thrilling, less gloomy sexual justice politics.

## Conclusion

This chapter has made the case that a commitment to relational autonomy portends LGBT advocacy for the statutory recognition of poly relations, for anti–sexual violence campaigns, and for feminist, sex-positive, democratic sex education. One might wonder if I am a saboteur, given these rallying cries: embrace the polys with whom the opponents of same-sex marriage have associated us; undermine the construction of the sex offender, for whom homosexuals have long been metonymic; enable the sexual agency of children, whom homosexuals have long been accused of recruiting.[134] And yet, the advantage of assimilation is the avoidance of association. Now that many of us are upstanding, presentable, and married, perhaps we might risk a queerer world, and a more promiscuous politics.

## NOTES

1 A version of part 1 of this chapter was published as Joseph Fischel, "Bigger Love? Same-Sex Marriage and the Poly Problem," *Bilerico Project*, September 18, 2014, http://www.bilerico.com/2014/09/bigger_love_same-sex_marriage_and_the_poly_problem.php, accessed December 2014. For a meticulous argument in favor of the constitutional right to plural marriage, similarly structured but much further elaborated than the argument I provide in part 1, *see* Ronald C. Den Otter, *In Defense of Plural Marriage* (Cambridge: Cambridge University Press, 2015).

2 *See* Andrew F. March, "What Lies beyond Same-Sex Marriage? Marriage, Reproductive Freedom, and Future Persons in Liberal Public Justification," 27 *Journal of Applied Philosophy* 39, 40–41 (2010); Andrew F. March, "Is There a Right to Polygamy? Marriage, Equality, and Subsidizing Family in Liberal Political Justification," 8 *Journal of Moral Philosophy* 246, 253–56 (2011); *see also*, "Beyond Same-Sex Marriage: A New Strategic Vision for All Our Families & Relationships," *beyondmarriage.org*, July 26, 2006, http://www.beyondmarriage.org/full_statement.html, accessed December 2014; and *infra*, part 2.

3 Marxist on the Street/Foucauldian in the Sheets Tee Shirt, *Zazzle*, http://www.zazzle.com/marxist_on_the_street_foucauldian_in_the_sheets_tshirt-235239033628620742, accessed December 2014.

4 *Kate Bornstein Is a Queer & Pleasant Danger* (dir. Sam Feder, 2014).

5 National Organization for Marriage, "The National Organization for Marriage Reacts to Federal Judge Legalizing Polygamy, Cites Same-Sex Marriage Rationale," *NOM BLOG*, December 16, 2013, http://www.nomblog.com/38639/, accessed December 2014.

6 Evan Wolfson, "Countering a Right-wing Claim to the Slippery Slope Argument," *Freedom to Marry*, October 12, 2005, http://archive-freedomtomarry.org/evan_wolfson/by/countering_a_right-wing_claim.php, accessed December 2014.

7 "Same-Sex Marriage in the U.S.," *C-SPAN*, October 11, 2014, http://www.c-span.org/video/?322045-4/washington-journal-brian-brown-evan-wolfson-samesex-marriage, accessed December 2014. Margaret Denike argues that polygamy figures as the rhetorical *cum* constitutive *cum* queer outside of assimilationist gay politics. *See* Margaret Denike, "What's Queer about Polygamy?" in *Queer Theory: Law, Culture, Empire*, Robert Leckey and Kim Brooks, eds. (New York: Routledge, 2010), pp. 137–53.

8 Geoffrey R. Stone, "Justice Kennedy Opened the Door to Same-Sex Marriage," *Daily Beast*, August 3, 2014, http://www.thedailybeast.com/articles/2014/08/03/justice-kennedy-opened-the-door-to-same-sex-marriage-will-he-walk-through-next.html, accessed December 2014.

9 DeBoer v. Snyder, No. 14–1341 (6th Cir. 2014).

10 Latta v. Otter, No. 14–35420, 2014 WL 4977682 (9th Cir. 2014).

11 Baskin v. Bogin, 766 F.3d 648, 656 (7th Cir. 2014). Although Judge Posner argues that discrimination against gays and lesbians triggers stricter judicial review than

"rational basis" (argument number 2), heightened scrutiny is nevertheless not required because "discrimination against same-sex couples is irrational."

12   Bostic v. Schaefer, 760 F.3d 352 (4th Cir. 2014); Kitchen v. Herbert, 755 F.3d 1193 (10th Cir. 2014); Obergefell v. Hodges, 576 U.S. ___ (2015). *Obergefell* held that state prohibitions on same-sex marriage violated both the Due Process Clause and the Equal Protection Clause of the Fourteenth Amendment, but the core of the ruling is located in the former (marriage as a nearly infrangible fundamental right), not the latter (the denial of marriage as a "grave and continuing harm" against gays and lesbians).

13   Loving v. Virginia, 388 U.S. 1, 12 (1967); Zablocki v. Redhail, 434 U.S. 374, 384 (1978) ("the right to marry is of fundamental importance for all individuals"); Turner v. Safley, 82 U.S. 78 (1987); United States v. Windsor, 570 U.S. ___ (2013). Obergefell v. Hodges, 576 U.S. ___, slip op. at 16, 22, 27 (2015). *Windsor*, however, grounded on the equal protection guarantee read into the Due Process Clause of the Fifth Amendment, does not provide the same sort of ammunition for marriage-as-fundamental-right. *Obergefell* does.

14   *Bostic*, 760 F.3d at *68 (Niemeyer, J., dissenting); *see also DeBoer* No. 14–1341 at *30.

15   Transcript of Oral Argument at 46, Hollingsworth v. Perry, 133 S. Ct. 2652 (2013) (No. 12–144), http://www.supremecourt.gov/oral_arguments/argument_transcripts/12-144a.pdf; *see also* Ashley E. Morin, "Use It or Lose It: The Enforcement of Polygamy Laws in America," 66 *Rutgers Law Review* 497, 528–29 (2014).

16   *Obergefell*, 576 U.S., slip op. at 20–21 (Roberts, C. J., dissenting).

17   Martha C. Nussbaum, "A Right to Marry?" 98 *California Law Review* 667, 688 (2010). Legal commentators have subsequently responded to Chief Justice Roberts's poly charge (what distinguishes gender from numerosity once marriage is recognized as a fundamental right?), but with lackluster and little success. *See, e.g.,* Richard A. Posner, "The Chief Justice's Dissent Is Heartless," *Slate*, June 27, 2015, http://www.slate.com/articles/news_and_politics/the_breakfast_table/features/2015/scotus_roundup/supreme_court_gay_marriage_john_roberts_dissent_in_obergefell_is_heartless.html, accessed August 2015; William Saletan, "The Case against Polygamy," *Slate*, June 29, 2015, http://www.slate.com/articles/news_and_politics/politics/2015/06/is_polygamy_next_after_gay_marriage_chief_justice_roberts_obergefell_dissent.html, accessed August 2015; Cathy Young, "Polygamy Is Not Next," *Time*, June 30, 2015, http://time.com/3942139/polygamy-is-not-next/, accessed August 2015.

18   William Saletan enumerates other ways, not discussed here, in which plural marriages differ from same-sex marriages: *inter alia*, gayness is immutable whereas nonmonogamy is not; denial of same-sex marriage consigns gays and lesbians to loneliness whereas denial of plural marriage does not consign polyamorists to loneliness; there is more marital conflict with more persons in a marriage; there is less loyalty to intimate partners when loyalty is distributed across a greater number of people. Most of these distinctions are speculative, untrue, or irrelevant, as well as constitutionally unsound. *See* Saletan, "The Case against Polygamy."

19  *Cf.* Cassiah M. Ward, "I Now Pronounce You Husband and Wives: *Lawrence v. Texas* and the Practice of Polygamy in Modern America," 11 *William & Mary Journal of Women & the Law* 131, 149–50 (2004).

20  For a summary rebuttal of the "responsible procreation" arguments held by opponents of same-sex marriage, *see*, for example, Zach Ford, "How the 'Responsible Procreation' Argument Sugarcoats Anti-Gay Prejudice," *ThinkProgress*, October 29, 2013, http://thinkprogress.org/lgbt/2013/10/29/2855271/responsible-procreation-argument-marriage-equality-sugarcoats-anti-gay-prejudice/, accessed December 2014.

21  *See, e.g., Windsor*, 570 U.S. at *23; *Baskin*, 766 F.3d at 654.

22  *See* Morin, "Use It or Lose It: The Enforcement of Polygamy Laws in America," 525; Adrienne D. Davis, "Regulating Polygamy: Intimacy, Default Rules, and Bargaining for Equality," 110 *Columbia Law Review* 1955, 2025 (2010); Den Otter, *In Defense of Plural Marriage*, pp. 148–49.

23  *Cf.* Ward, "I Now Pronounce You Husband and Wives: *Lawrence v. Texas* and the Practice of Polygamy in Modern America," pp. 145–48; Maura I. Strassberg, "Distinctions of Form or Substance: Monogamy, Polygamy, and Same-Sex Marriage," 75 *North Carolina Law Review* 1501, 1615–18 (1997).

24  John Stuart Mill, "The Subjection of Women," in *John Stuart Mill: On Liberty and Other Essays*, John Gray, ed. (Oxford: Oxford University Press, 1998), pp. 469, 502–23.

25  John Stuart Mill, "On Liberty," in *John Stuart Mill: On Liberty and Other Essays*, John Gray, ed. (Oxford: Oxford University Press, 1998), pp. 5, 101–2.

26  *See, e.g.,* Mill, "The Subjection of Women"; Den Otter, *In Defense of Plural Marriage*, pp. 93–95, 121. Two orbital inveighs against institutionalized heterosexuality as eroticized dominance are, of course, Catharine A. MacKinnon, *Toward a Feminist Theory of the State* (Cambridge, MA: Harvard University Press, 1989); Adrienne Rich, "Compulsory Heterosexuality and Lesbian Existence," 5 *Signs* 631(1980). For a more recent broadside, *see* Mary White Stuart, *Ordinary Violence: Everyday Assaults against Women Worldwide* (Santa Barbara, CA: Praeger, 2014).

27  Posner, "The Chief Justice's Dissent Is Heartless."

28  Posner, "The Chief Justice's Dissent Is Heartless."

29  Planned Parenthood v. Casey, 505 U.S. 833 (1992); Romer v. Evans, 517 U.S. 620 (1996); Lawrence v. Texas, 539 U.S. 558 (2003). In the United States, political, medical, and cultural antipathy to polygamy is not *ex nihilo*, but rather historically motored by anti-Mormonism, white supremacist ideology (associating polygamy—and thereby Mormonism—with racial/civilizational backwardness), and eugenic fears of white degeneration. *See* Martha M. Ertman, "Race Treason: The Untold Story of America's Ban on Polygamy," 19 *Columbia Journal of Gender and Law* 287 (2010).

30  *See* Davis, "Regulating Polygamy: Intimacy, Default Rules, and Bargaining for Equality"; Young, "Polygamy Is Not Next." However, what will most likely bar poly relations from statutory recognition in the foreseeable future is not any legal-

logical distinction (like administrative complexity), but the fact that poly persons have nothing like the social and political clout currently enjoyed by mainstream gays and lesbians. *See* Sean Trende, "Why *Obergefell* Is Unlikely to Lead to Polygamy," *Real Clear Politics*, July 6, 2015, http://www.realclearpolitics.com/articles/2015/07/06/why_obergefell_is_unlikely_to_lead_to_polygamy_127242.html.

31 Reed v. Reed, 401 U.S. 71 (1971).

32 Davis, "Regulating Polygamy: Intimacy, Default Rules, and Bargaining for Equality," p. 2005.

33 Davis, "Regulating Polygamy: Intimacy, Default Rules, and Bargaining for Equality," p. 1991.

34 For a schema of compelling state interests, *see* Eugene Volokh, "Freedom of Speech, Permissible Tailoring, and Transcending Strict Scrutiny," 144 *University of Pennsylvania Law Review* 2417, 2419–21, 2421 (1996).

35 *Baskin*, 766 F.3d at 657; *but see* Posner, "The Chief Justice's Dissent Is Heartless."

36 *Obergefell*, 576 U.S., slip op. at 3, 10–19.

37 For arguments favorably suggesting that *Obergefell* might lead to the constitutionalization of plural marriage, *see, e.g.,* William Baude, "Is Polygamy Next?" *New York Times*, July 21, 2015, http://www.nytimes.com/2015/07/21/opinion/is-polygamy-next, accessed August 2015; Fredrik deBoer, "It's Time to Legalize Polygamy," *Politico*, June 26, 2015, http://www.politico.com/magazine/story/2015/06/gay-marriage-decision-polygamy-119469.html#.VcI5sjBViko, accessed August 2015; for arguments suggesting that *Obergefell* does not unavoidably lead to the constitutionalization of plural marriage, *see, e.g.,* Posner, "The Chief Justice's Dissent Is Heartless"; Saletan, "The Case against Polygamy"; Young, "Polygamy Is Not Next." Four days after the *Obergefell* ruling, and spurred by Chief Justice Roberts's dissent, a Montana man sought a marriage license for a second wife. *See* Tanya Basu, "Montana Polygamist Seeks 'Legitimacy' after Supreme Court Ruling," *Time*, July 2, 2015, http://time.com/3944579/montana-polygamy-gay-marriage/, accessed August 2015.

38 *See Lawrence*, 539 U.S. at 604 (Scalia, J., dissenting).

39 On the moral and political import of "experiments of living," *see* Mill, "On Liberty," p. 63; *see also* Den Otter, *In Defense of Plural Marriage*, pp. 206–23.

40 Elizabeth F. Emens, "Monogamy's Law: Compulsory Monogamy and Polyamorous Existence," 29 *N.Y.U. Review of Law & Social Change* 277, 320–30 (2004).

41 Elisabeth Sheff, "Polyamorous Families, Same-Sex Marriage, and the Slippery Slope," 40 *Journal of Contemporary Ethnography* 487, 496 (2011).

42 Sheff, "Polyamorous Families, Same-Sex Marriage, and the Slippery Slope," p. 489.

43 Sheff, "Polyamorous Families, Same-Sex Marriage, and the Slippery Slope," p. 508.

44 Sheff, "Polyamorous Families, Same-Sex Marriage, and the Slippery Slope," p. 511.

45 Sheff, "Polyamorous Families, Same-Sex Marriage, and the Slippery Slope," p. 510; *see also* Den Otter, *In Defense of Plural Marriage*, pp. 216–18.

46 Sheff, "Polyamorous Families, Same-Sex Marriage, and the Slippery Slope," p. 513.

47 Sheff, "Polyamorous Families, Same-Sex Marriage, and the Slippery Slope," p. 511.

48  Dossie Easton and Janet W. Hardy, *The Ethical Slut* (Berkeley, CA: Celestial Arts, 2009), pp. 20–21, 108–30.

49  Easton and Hardy, *The Ethical Slut*, pp. 71–77.

50  Easton and Hardy, *The Ethical Slut*, pp. 133–47; *see also* Lauren Berlant and Michael Warner, "Sex in Public," 24 *Critical Inquiry* 547, 556 (1998).

51  Easton and Hardy, *The Ethical Slut*, pp. 56–70.

52  Courtney Bailey, "Love Multiplied: Sister Wives, Polygamy, and Queering Heterosexuality," 32 *Quarterly Review of Film and Video* 38 (2015).

53  Bailey, "Love Multiplied: Sister Wives, Polygamy, and Queering Heterosexuality," p. 39.

54  Bailey, "Love Multiplied: Sister Wives, Polygamy, and Queering Heterosexuality," p. 46.

55  Bailey, "Love Multiplied: Sister Wives, Polygamy, and Queering Heterosexuality," pp. 43, 47.

56  Emens, "Monogamy's Law: Compulsory Monogamy and Polyamorous Existence," p. 315.

57  Bailey, "Love Multiplied: Sister Wives, Polygamy, and Queering Heterosexuality," pp. 45–46.

58  *See, e.g.*, Hema Chatlani, "In Defense of Marriage: Why Same-Sex Marriage Will Not Lead Us down a Slippery Slope toward the Legalization of Polygamy," 6 *Appalachian Journal of Law* 101, 128–32 (2006).

59  Carlos A. Ball, "A New Stage for the LGBT Movement: Protecting Gender and Sexual Multiplicities," p. 158 of this volume. My modifications are styled from the Justice Scalia Playbook on Shoe-Dropping. *Windsor*, 570 U.S. at 16, 23 (Scalia, J., dissenting). Ball's parenthetical notwithstanding, the let-us-love current of the marriage equality movement is not redeemed in full by principles of equality and nondiscrimination; relational autonomy is at the movement's core. *See, e.g.*, "Why Marriage Matters," *Freedom to Marry*, http://www.freedomtomarry.org/pages/why-marriage-matters, accessed December 2014 ("Gay and lesbian couples want to get married to make a lifetime commitment to the person they love and to protect their families."). Lifetime commitments and family protection are not values limited to dyadic monogamous couples.

60  Joseph J. Fischel, *Sex and Harm in the Age of Consent* (Minneapolis: University of Minnesota Press, 2016); Joseph J. Fischel and Hilary O'Connell, "Disabling Consent, or Reconstructing Sexual Autonomy," 30 *Columbia Journal of Gender and Law* 428 (2016) (synthesizing legal, feminist, and political theoretic critiques of sexual and relational autonomy).

61  *Cf.* Laura Denis, "Sex and the Virtuous Kantian Agent," in *Sex and Ethics: Essays on Sexuality, Virtue, and the Good Life*, Raja Halwani, ed. (Basingstoke, UK: Palgrave Macmillan, 2007), pp. 37–48.

62  Carlos A. Ball, "This Is Not Your Father's Autonomy: Lesbian and Gay Rights from a Feminist and Relational Perspective," in *Feminist and Queer Legal Theories: Intimate Encounters, Uncomfortable Conversations*, Martha Fineman, et al., eds. (Farnham, UK: Ashgate, 2009), pp. 289, 311; for a magisterial account of au-

tonomy as relational, *see generally*, Jennifer Nedelsky, *Law's Relations: A Relational Theory of Self, Autonomy, and Law* (Oxford: Oxford University Press, 2011); for an account of the capabilities approach and its pertinence to gender justice, *see generally*, Martha C. Nussbaum, *Creating Capabilities: The Human Development Approach* (Cambridge, MA: Belknap, 2011).

63 *Obergefell*, 576 U.S., slip op. at 13; *but see Obergefell*, 576 U.S., slip op. at 19–20 (Roberts, C.J., dissenting); *Obergefell* 576 U.S., slip op. at 8 (Scalia, J., dissenting) ("one would think Freedom of Intimacy is abridged rather than expanded by marriage. Ask the nearest hippie.").

64 Ball, "This Is Not Your Father's Autonomy: Lesbian and Gay Rights from a Feminist and Relational Perspective," p. 303.

65 March, "Is There a Right to Polygamy? Marriage, Equality, and Subsidizing Family in Liberal Political Justification," p. 254.

66 March, "Is There a Right to Polygamy? Marriage, Equality, and Subsidizing Family in Liberal Political Justification," p. 254; *see also* Nussbaum, "A Right to Marry," p. 672.

67 March, "What Lies beyond Same-Sex Marriage? Marriage, Reproductive Freedom, and Future Persons in Liberal Public Justification," pp. 42–43; *see also* Elizabeth Brake, "Recognizing Care: The Case for Friendship and Polyamory," 1 *Syracuse Law & Civic Engagement Forum* (2014), http://slace.syr.edu/issue-1-2013-14-on-equality/recognizing-care-the-case-for-friendship-and-polyamory/# (arguing that justice under political liberalism requires the extension of marriage-like rights and benefits to other caring relationships); *but see* Stephen Macedo, *Just Married: Same-Sex Couples, Monogamy, and the Future of Marriage* (Princeton, NJ: Princeton University Press, 2015), pp. 145–203 (arguing that justice under political liberalism requires the denial of marriage-like rights and benefits to multiple-partner relationships).

68 Fischel, *Sex and Harm in the Age of Consent* (rehearsing feminist scholarly debates regarding intervention on spousal abuse).

69 Fischel, *Sex and Harm in the Age of Consent.*

70 *See* Fischel, *Sex and Harm in the Age of Consent.*

71 Although not his terms, "the capability to codetermine intimate and/or sexual relations" aligns with the principles promoted in Richard D. Mohr's *Gays/Justice: A Study of Ethics, Society, and Law* (New York: Columbia University Press, 1988).

72 Berlant and Warner, "Sex in Public," pp. 557–58.

73 Michel Foucault, "Friendship as a Way of Life," in *Hatred of Capitalism: A Semiotext(e) Reader*, Chris Kraus and Sylvère Lotringer, eds. (Cambridge, MA: MIT Press, 2001), pp. 297, 300.

74 *See, e.g., Against Equality: Queer Critiques of Gay Marriage*, Ryan Conrad, ed. (Lewiston, ME: Against Equality Publishing Collective, 2010); *Captive Genders: Trans Embodiment and the Prison Industrial Complex*, Eric A. Stanley and Nat Smith, eds. (Edinburgh: AK Press, 2011).

75 *See, e.g.*, Lisa Duggan, *The Twilight of Equality? Neoliberalism, Cultural Politics, and the Attack on Democracy* (Boston: Beacon, 2003); on same-sex marriage

as prefigured by and propellant of a racially "stratified welfare state," *see* Priya Kandaswamy, "State Austerity and the Racial Politics of Same-Sex Marriage in the U.S.," 11 *Sexualities* 706, 721–22; for a cogently carried brief for all three criticisms outlined above, *see* Michael Warner, "Beyond Gay Marriage," in *The Trouble with Normal: Sex, Politics, and the Ethics of Queer Life* (Cambridge, MA: Harvard University Press, 2000), p. 81.

76 *Cf.* Emma Goldman, "Woman Suffrage," in *Anarchism and Other Essays* (CreateSpace Independent Publishing Platform, 2013), pp. 75, 81.

77 *See* Cathy J. Cohen, "Punks, Bulldaggers, and Welfare Queens: The Radical Potential of Queer Politics?" 3 *GLQ* 437 (1997).

78 Cohen, "Punks, Bulldaggers, and Welfare Queens: The Radical Potential of Queer Politics?"; *cf.* Judith Butler, "Merely Cultural," 15 *Social Text* 265 (1997).

79 Rose Corrigan, *Up against a Wall: Rape Reform and the Failure of Success* (New York: New York University Press, 2013), p. 213 (my emphasis). Corrigan is referring to an actuarial risk-assessment survey allegedly designed to calibrate sex offender dangerousness, but the observation is applicable as social commentary.

80 I use "dominant" reservedly, acknowledging that institutional responses to rape vary widely depending on local stakeholders, circumstances, and exigencies. *See* Corrigan, *Up against a Wall: Rape Reform and the Failure of Success*, pp. 207, 209–10, 217.

81 *See* Corrigan, *Up against a Wall: Rape Reform and the Failure of Success*, p. 248.

82 *See* Corrigan, *Up against a Wall: Rape Reform and the Failure of Success*, pp. 228–33 (documenting how prosecutors will "substitute" registration and notification for conviction, thus appearing tough on crime).

83 For a more comprehensive rehearsal of SORN laws, *see* Fischel, *Sex and Harm in the Age of Consent.*

84 *See, e.g.,* Amanda Y. Agan, "Sex Offender Registries: Fear without Function?" 54 *Journal of Law & Economics* 207 (2011); J. J. Prescottt and Jonah E. Rockoff, "Do Sex Offender Registration and Notification Laws Affect Criminal Behavior?" 54 *Journal of Law & Economics* 161 (2011); Richard G. Wright, ed., *Sex Offender Laws: Failed Policies, New Directions* (New York: Springer, 2009). Prescott and Rockoff find that registration is a deterrent in some instances, and that notification may reduce *overall* crime rates.

85 Fischel, *Sex and Harm in the Age of Consent*, chapter 2.

86 "Myths and Facts about Sex Offenders," *Center for Sex Offender Management*, August 2000, http://www.csom.org/pubs/mythsfacts.html, accessed December 2014; *see also* "No Easy Answers: Sex Offender Laws in the U.S.," 19 *Human Rights Watch* 1, 25–32 (2007).

87 *See, e.g.,* Corrigan, *Up against a Wall: Rape Reform and the Failure of Success*, pp. 35–36, 212–13; Eric S. Janus, *Failure to Protect: America's Sexual Predator Laws and the Rise of the Preventative State* (New York: Cornell University Press, 2006), pp. 75–93.

88 Corrigan, *Up against a Wall: Rape Reform and the Failure of Success.*

89  Corrigan, *Up against a Wall: Rape Reform and the Failure of Success*, pp. 65–116.

90  Corrigan, *Up against a Wall: Rape Reform and the Failure of Success*, p. 65.

91  Corrigan, *Up against a Wall: Rape Reform and the Failure of Success*, pp. 69–74.

92  Corrigan, *Up against a Wall: Rape Reform and the Failure of Success*, pp. 82–95.

93  Corrigan, *Up against a Wall: Rape Reform and the Failure of Success*, p. 101.

94  Corrigan, *Up against a Wall: Rape Reform and the Failure of Success*, p. 115.

95  Corrigan, *Up against a Wall: Rape Reform and the Failure of Success*, pp. 42–51, 249–64.

96  For a list of RCCs in the United States, *see* "Search for a Local Crisis Center," *Rape, Abuse & Incest National Network*, http://centers.rainn.org/, accessed December 2014.

97  *See, e.g.*, *Women with a Vision*, http://wwav-no.org; *generationFIVE*, http://www. generationfive.org; *see also* Bench Ansfield and Timothy Colman, "Confronting Sexual Assault: Transformative Justice on the Ground in Philadelphia," 27 *Tikkun* 41 (2012).

98  *See, e.g.*, Leigh Goodmark, "Stalled at 20: VAWA, the Criminal Justice System, and the Possibilities of Restorative Justice," *CUNY Law Review* (2014), http:// www.cunylawreview.org/stalled-at-20-vawa-the-criminal-justice-system-and-the-possibilities-of-restorative-justice.

99  *See, e.g.*, Linda Gordon, "The Politics of Child Sexual Abuse: Notes from American History," 28 *Feminist Review* 56, 62 (1988); Callie Marie Rennison, "Privilege, among Rape Victims," *New York Times*, A27, December 22, 2014.

100  Assistant Secretary, Office for Civil Rights, "Dear Colleague Letter: Sexual Violence," *United States Department of Education*, April 4, 2011, http://www2.ed.gov/ about/offices/list/ocr/letters/colleague-201104.pdf, accessed December 2014.

101  *See, e.g.*, *Know Your IX*, http://knowyourix.org; *Michigan Sexual Assault Prevention & Awareness Center*, http://sapac.umich.edu; *University of New Hampshire Sexual Harassment & Rape Prevention Program (SHARPP)*, http://www.unh.edu/ sharpp; *Yale CCE Program*, http://cce.yalecollege.yale.edu.

102  One hopes that the collaborative, creative responses to sexual violence against college students will extend outward towards more vulnerable populations. *See* Rennison, "Privilege, among Rape Victims."

103  "Not Alone: The First Report of the White House Task Force to Protect Students from Sexual Assault," *Not Alone: Together against Sexual Assault*, April 2014, https://www.notalone.gov/assets/report.pdf, accessed December 2014; *see also* Assistant Secretary, Office for Civil Rights, "Questions and Answers on Title IX and Sexual Violence," *United States Department of Education*, April 29, 2014, http:// www2.ed.gov/about/offices/list/ocr/docs/qa-201404-title-ix.pdf, accessed December 2014.

104  *See* "A Brief History of Federal Funding for Sex Education and Related Program," *SIECUS*, http://www.siecus.org/index.cfm?fuseaction=page. viewPage&pageID=1341&nodeID=1, accessed December 2014.

105  "A Brief History of Federal Funding for Sex Education and Related Program."

106 *See generally*, Committee on Government Reform, Minority Staff, Special Investigations Division, "The Content of Federally Funded Abstinence-Only Education Programs," *U.S. House of Representatives*, December 2004, http://belowthewaist.org/podcast/2008/12/20041201102153-50247.pdf, accessed December 2014; Mathematica Policy Research, Inc., "Impacts of Four Title V, Section 510 Abstinence Education Programs," *U.S. Department of Health and Human Services*, April 2007, http://aspe.hhs.gov/hsp/abstinence07/report.pdf, accessed December 2014.

107 Al Vernacchio, *For Goodness Sex: Changing the Way We Talk to Teens about Sexuality, Values, and Health* (New York: HarperCollins, 2014), pp. ix–x.

108 *See* Michelle Fine and Sara I. McClelland, "Sexuality Education and Desire: Still Missing after All These Years," 76 *Harvard Educational Review* 297, 309–11 (2006); Nancy Kendall, *The Sex Education Debates* (Chicago: University of Chicago Press, 2013), pp. 151–223.

109 *See* "A Brief History of Federal Funding for Sex Education and Related Program"; Kendall, *The Sex Education Debates*, p. 2.

110 *See* Kendall, *The Sex Education Debates*, pp. 7–8.

111 Alexandra Sifferlin, "Why Schools Can't Teach Sex Ed," *Time*, http://time.com/why-schools-cant-teach-sex-ed/#by-alexandra-sifferlin, accessed December 2014, internal citation omitted.

112 *See* Kendall, *The Sex Education Debates*, pp. 6–7, 225–31; *see also* "Definition of Comprehensive Sex Education," *FoSE*, http://www.futureofsexeducation.org/definition.html, accessed December 2014.

113 Vernacchio, *For Goodness Sex: Changing the Way We Talk to Teens about Sexuality, Values, and Health*, p. 10.

114 *See, e.g.*, Dannielle Owens-Reid and Kristin Russo, "How to Talk to Your Gay Teen about Sex," *Time*, http://time.com/why-schools-cant-teach-sex-ed/#how-to-talk-to-your-gay-teen-about-sex, accessed December 2014.

115 *See generally* Vernacchio, *For Goodness Sex: Changing the Way We Talk to Teens about Sexuality, Values, and Health*.

116 *See* Kendall, *The Sex Education Debates*, p. 231; *see also* Jessica Fields, *Risky Lessons: Sex Education and Social Inequality* (New Brunswick, NJ: Rutgers University Press, 2008).

117 "Envisioning the Future of Sex Education: A Tool Kit for States and Communities," *FoSE*, http://www.futureofsexed.org/envisioningthefuture.html, accessed December 2014.

118 "The Future of Sex Education: A Strategic Framework (Executive Summary)," *FoSE*, http://www.futureofsexed.org/executivesummary.html, accessed December 2014.

119 "Youth Health and Rights in Sex Education," *FoSE*, http://www.futureofsexed.org/youthhealthrights.html, accessed December 2014.

120 *See* Sifferlin, "Why Schools Can't Teach Sex Ed"; Sharon Lamb and Zoë D. Peterson, "Adolescent Girls' Sexual Empowerment: Two Feminists Explore the Concept," 66 *Sex Roles* 703, 710 (2012).

121  See Kendall, *The Sex Education Debates*, pp. 224, 234–35.

122  Michel Foucault, *The History of Sexuality.* Vol. 1, *An Introduction* (New York: Vintage, 1990), p. 104.

123  Kendall, *The Sex Education Debates*, pp. 232–40; *see also* Vernacchio, *For Goodness Sex: Changing the Way We Talk to Teens about Sexuality, Values, and Health.*

124  On "gay teen" as the culturally intelligible shorthand for sexual-minority and gender-nonconforming youth, *see* Andrew Gilden, "Cyberbullying and the Innocence Narrative," 48 *Harvard Civil Rights–Civil Liberties Law Review* 357, 357 n.1 (2013).

125  Gilden, "Cyberbullying and the Innocence Narrative," pp. 360–61, 385.

126  Gilden, "Cyberbullying and the Innocence Narrative," pp. 363, 383.

127  Gilden, "Cyberbullying and the Innocence Narrative," pp. 390–94.

128  Gilden, "Cyberbullying and the Innocence Narrative," p. 381.

129  *See* Vernaccio, *For Goodness Sex: Changing the Way We Talk to Teens about Sexuality, Values, and Health*, pp. 179–80.

130  *See* Gilden, "Cyberbullying and the Innocence Narrative," pp. 377–80.

131  *See, e.g.*, C. J. Pascoe, *Dude, You're a Fag: Masculinity and Sexuality in High School* (Berkeley: University of California Press, 2011), p. 173.

132  *See* Lamb and Peterson, "Adolescent Girls' Sexual Empowerment: Two Feminists Explore the Concept," p. 710. These sorts of critical lessons might make apparent the way gender policing is the connective tissue across school sexual harassment, eating disorders, and other forms of gendered self-effacement, "mean girl"-ism, the exsanguination of boys' friendships, and so much of what registers as "gay bullying." *See, e.g.*, Pascoe, *Dude, You're a Fag: Masculinity and Sexuality in High School*; Jasbir K. Puar, "The Cost of Getting Better: Suicide, Sensation, Switchpoints," 18 *GLQ* 149, 157 (2011); Niobe Way, *Deep Secrets: Boys' Friendships and the Crisis of Connection* (Cambridge, MA: Harvard University Press, 2011).

133  "National Teacher Preparation Standards for Sexuality Education," *FoSE*, http://futureofsexed.org/teacherstandards.html, accessed December 2012.

134  *See also* John D'Emilio, "Capitalism and Gay Identity," in *The Lesbian and Gay Studies Reader*, Henry Abelove, Michèle Aina Barale, and David M. Halperin, eds. (New York: Routledge, 1993), pp. 467, 474.

# 8

## Diverging Identities

### *Gender Differences and LGBT Rights*

RUSSELL K. ROBINSON

This chapter argues that the debate over same-sex marriage and LGBT equality and inclusion more generally has incompletely and insufficiently considered the importance of gender. I hope to call attention to the salience of gender and demonstrate how it fractures the lived experiences of same-sex couples, and also to encourage scholars to grapple with the knotty reality of persistent gender differences. I predict that as same-sex marriage becomes more common, a gendered divide may become more apparent. Men may be less likely to form enduring relationships and less likely to marry. Moreover, men and women in same-sex relationships may face gendered challenges. Because men are less likely to be in committed relationships and men's relationships are less likely to be monogamous (as discussed below), men may become more likely targets of "the afterlife of homophobia."[1] At the same time, depictions of lesbians as child-centered partners suffering from "lesbian bed death" (discussed below) may reinforce the longstanding cultural invisibility of lesbians and lesbian sex.[2] I begin by examining two sites of gender difference within the LGBT community—relationship status and monogamy—and reveal how they tend to set queer men and women on different life paths.[3]

Despite these divergent patterns, which many LGBT people know of anecdotally, and which are supported by public health studies, many scholars and legal advocates have eschewed gender differences in their work. After providing a few illustrative examples, I attempt to explain the aversion to gender within LGBT scholarship and advocacy. My theory is that the push for gay rights, and especially same-sex marriage, has compelled many leaders of the gay and lesbian community to "closet" our gender differences. The need to present a unified and sympathetic "gay and lesbian" subject to the courts and the public as they contemplate same-sex marriage has motivated this obfuscation. However, now that the Supreme Court's *Obergefell v. Hodges* decision has recognized a fundamental right of same-sex couples to marry,[4] the pressure to produce a cohesive identity may dissipate. This turn may create space for more honest and complex depictions of LGBT people and relationships and also raise difficult normative questions about the gendered patterns within the LGBT community.[5] As challenging as these questions may be, I propose that we invite them in because they offer opportunities to interrogate the broader cultural socialization of men and women. In the conclusion, I provide a few examples of such critical gender analysis.

Let me begin with a few caveats. First, my view is that the gender differences that I discuss below are, in general, socially constructed.[6] We should be highly skeptical of claims that biology explains differences between men and women, which is not to say that biology is always irrelevant. Second, the empirical findings that I discuss below may be limited to particular segments of queer communities and may or may not persist over time. For example, studies that focus on middle-aged and mostly white LGB people may have limited applicability to adolescents, young adults, and people of color. Thus, we should approach such studies with caution. Some of my claims are necessarily tentative and subject to revision as better—and more inclusive—data emerge.

## Sex and Relationship Patterns

I begin by establishing significant gender differences within the LGBT community with respect to sex and relationship patterns in order to lay the foundation for my claim that many leaders of the LBGT community have glossed over gender differences to present a unified and sympathetic subject to the courts and the public in the quest for marriage equality. First, queer men and queer women are situated in communities that reflect divergent social norms regarding sex and relationships. Readers may be familiar with a common joke about lesbian relationship formation: "*Question*: What does a lesbian bring on a second date? *Answer*: A U-Haul."[7] Some versions of this joke append the followup: "*Question*: What do gay men do on the second date?" "*Answer*: Second date?"[8] As reductive as it may be, the U-Haul joke is a helpful heuristic for understanding the differential relationship paths of many, but not all, queer women and queer men. Queer men are more likely than queer women to meet on sex-saturated smartphone apps and websites such as Grindr or Manhunt, just two of the copious online hookup outlets that cater to gay men, or at a gay bar or bathhouse.[9] Queer women have fewer sex-focused outlets, whether online or "brick and mortar" establishments.[10] A central point of this chapter is to argue for critical thinking about gender norms in same-sex relationships. If these gendered patterns ring true with our experiences, why do they persist? How might these patterns impinge on romantic and sexual options for queer people who fail to conform to these gender norms (i.e., relationship-oriented gay men, queer women who want to hook up)? Do we want to change them? And how could we begin to do that?

Empirical studies confirm the gender differences suggested by the disparate structural environments that govern queer meeting and mating.[11] Queer women are more likely than queer men to enter into a same-sex relationship and to marry, and women and men in same-sex relationships are likely to engage in different sexual patterns.[12] As an initial matter, recent surveys indicate that queer women are more likely than queer men to be in relationships. A study by Gregory Herek found that "60% of gay men and 57% of bisexual men were *not* in a committed relationship, compared with fewer than one fourth of lesbians and bisexual women."[13] A more recent study by Gary Gates used National Health Interview Survey (NHIS) data and reported similar gender disparities. Half of lesbian-identified women reported that they were married or in a cohabiting relationship compared to about one-third of gay and bisexual men.[14] Other findings have focused more specifically on legal recognition of relationships. Lee Badgett and Christy Mallory's analysis surveyed ten states that offer legal recognition (*i.e.*, civil union, domestic partnership, or marriage) to same-sex couples. The authors found that 64% of the couples that received some form of legal recognition were female; and 62% of the married couples were female. Similarly, Herek found that of those in relationships, "significantly more lesbians than gay men said they were 'very likely' or 'fairly likely' to marry their partner (76% and 41%, respectively)."[15] A study by Christopher Carpenter and Gary Gates of California lesbian, gay, and bisexual people found that women were nearly three times as likely to be in a registered domestic partnership as men.[16] Their study also found evidence of racial disparities—nonwhite gay men and lesbians in California have significantly lower odds of having a committed partner than their white counterparts.[17] These disparities appear to carry over to domestic partnership registration.[18] The more recent Gates study, which expounded on these questions using a national sample derived from NHIS data, found that same-sex couples are whiter than different-sex couples. Specifically, 37% of unmarried different-sex couples were nonwhite, compared to 24% of unmarried same-sex couples.[19]

Not only are queer women more likely than queer men to be in committed relationships, but their conceptions of commitment appear to differ, at least as they pertain to sex and monogamy. In 2011, Gabriella Gotta and her coauthors published an important study that presents a stark picture of the differences between queer men and queer women regarding sex and monogamy.[20] The authors used archival data from an earlier study conducted by one of the coauthors.[21] The authors compared the 1975 data to data from a 2000 study, which asked similar questions.[22] This design allowed the researchers not only to compare relationship practices based on gender and sexual orientation but also to detect shifts over the twenty-five-year span of their archive.

The study demonstrates rather dramatic differences between queer men and women in terms of sexual behavior in relationships. Despite the highly publicized claim that queer women in relationships suffer from "lesbian bed death,"[23] in 2000, queer women were nearly as likely as queer men to report having had sex in the preceding year: 89.3% for women, and 93.2% for men.[24] Interestingly, in 1975, queer women were slightly *more* likely to have had sex with their partner than were queer men: 98.2% for women, and 95.3% for men.[25] The genders diverge, however, when it comes to monogamy. In 1975, the vast majority of queer men (82.6%) reported having had sex with at least one person other than their partner (which I will call "outside sex") since they became a couple, while just 28.4% of lesbians reported outside sex. In the next twenty-five years, reports of monogamy increased among all categories of couples (male, female, same-sex, and different-sex). Still, a substantial gender divide persisted among queer men and women. In 2000, 59.6% of queer men reported sex outside the relationship at some point in the past, while 8.2% of lesbians reported similarly. In addition to the gender divide among queer couples, the data demonstrate a convergence between queer female couples and heterosexual couples. In 1975, queer women (at 28.4%) were slightly more likely to report outside sex than heterosexual men (27.6%) and heterosexual women (22.9%). By 2000, queer women (at 8.2%) were slightly less likely to report outside sex than heterosexual men (10.1%) and heterosexual women (14.2%).[26] Notably, in both 1975 and 2000, queer women's sexual patterns were closer to those of heterosexual men and women than those of queer men.[27]

A question as to whether the subject "has had a meaningful love affair with someone else since they have become a couple"[28] produced results that are both similar to and different from the trends described above. On the one hand, in 1975, gay men were the *least* likely to report a love affair with someone outside the relationship—14.8%, compared to 31% for heterosexual women, 29.7% for queer women, and 26.9% for heterosexual men. When contrasted with their leadership in engaging in sex outside the relationship, it appears that in 1975, gay men tended to compartmentalize outside sex as "recreational," and it did not frequently lead to love affairs, which many would regard as more threatening to the relationship. By 2000, however, queer men were having less outside sex and fewer meaningful love affairs (7.3%) than in 1975. However, when compared to other categories, queer men in 2000 were most likely to have outside sex and slightly more likely to have a meaningful love affair.[29] The biggest shift appears to be a striking reduction in affairs among lesbians, heterosexual women, and heterosexual men.[30]

It is important to note the difference between sex outside the relationship that is permitted by a couple's agreement to be open versus that which violates an agreement to be monogamous. The Gotta study asked the subjects whether they had discussed monogamy with their partners and whether the couple reached agreement on the subject.[31] The results depict a gendered divide among queer men and women in 1975 and 2000. In 1975, nonmonogamy was normative among queer men—66.8% of queer men discussed the topic and agreed to be open, while another 5.1% agreed to be open without an explicit conversation. Just 13.5% of queer men pledged to be monogamous.[32] Meanwhile, queer women were much less likely than queer men to agree to have an open relationship (33.6% vs. 66.8%) but more likely to do so than heterosexual men (23%) and women (20.6%). By 2000, the prevalence of open relationships among queer women (5.1%) had dropped steeply and converged with that of heterosexual men (6%) and women (3.3%), while queer men continued to be the outlier at 43.7%.[33] The Gotta study convincingly demonstrates that gender differences in queer relationship patterns exist, or at least existed in 1975 and 2000, but future research is necessary to understand why they occur and how such patterns may change over time.

Finally, I briefly discuss gender differences regarding parenting, mainly because the discussion implicates my prior arguments about sex and relationship status. Herek's study found significant gender disparities: about one-third of lesbians were raising children, while just 8% of gay men were.[34] Bisexual women's and men's engagement in parenting differs substantially from each other—67.2% for women and 36.4% for men—and also surpasses their respective lesbian and gay peers.[35] Why does parenting matter? For one thing, *Obergefell's* emphasis on the link between marriage and children seems to place childrearing same-sex couples, which are disproportionately female, at the core of the constitutional right.[36]

But there are additional connections between parenting and relationship status. First, child rearing may motivate people to pursue relationships. Queer women who have children or want to have children may feel that the help of a partner is desirable. Relatedly, queer women with children may believe that obtaining legal recognition of their relationship is important for their children's sake, not simply because of the law's protections but also because of the social meaning of marriage.[37] In addition, the decision to parent often places constraints on one's sexual decision making. Coupled parents are likely to have less time for sex, and even if the couple is inclined to have open and active sexual involvement with others, it may not be feasible as a practical matter. Further, engaging in "disreputable" sexual conduct may hold consequences for one's child, including social judgment and the potential dissolution of the couple's relationship. An intriguing study suggests that queer fathers' sexual behavior may approximate that of queer mothers in that child care consumes energy that otherwise might be directed toward sexual activity.[38] This finding provides a reminder that the gendered patterns discussed above are not hard-wired in our DNA, but rather are shaped by social norms and roles.

## Struggling with Gender

Rather than confronting head-on the substantial differences between queer men and women with regard to sexual patterns and rates of non-monogamy, scholars and advocates tend to struggle with gender as they discuss and construct "gays and lesbians." First, much legal advocacy, including that in the marriage equality movement, simply ignores gender. In preparing an article on the racial politics of the marriage equality movement, I reviewed all of the legal briefs filed in the marriage equality movement during a ten-year period ending in 2013.[39] Virtually all of the briefs in favor of same-sex marriage ignored differences between gay men and lesbians. The opponents of same-sex marriage were more likely to engage gender in a significant fashion, but they tended to focus on differences between heterosexual men and women in romantic relationships (including the ostensible problem of "accidental procreation" and fathers abandoning their children)—*not* the differences between gay men and lesbians.[40] As I discuss more fully below, lawyers may have strategic reasons for avoiding gender to the extent that it would complicate their efforts to obtain rights for LGBT people. Yet scholars also tend to avoid fully engaging gender.

The second approach to gender, which is evident in some scholarly work, is to recognize gender differences but then try to gloss over or downplay them. Thus, the scholar's initial recognition of gender is followed by an effort to collapse men and women into a single category based on the conclusion that gender does not ultimately matter. Consider Michael Warner's book *The Trouble with Normal: Sex, Politics, and the Ethics of Queer Life*, a highly influential text in queer theory and politics.[41] In this book, Warner argues for a "queer ethic," which entails embracing sexual shame and seeing shame as something that connects all queer people, and even heterosexuals. Warner adamantly attacks the sexual hierarchy in the gay community that suggests that some sexual practices—particularly same-sex marriage—are more noble and dignified than others. Warner resists efforts to distinguish between queer men and women. For example, he repudiates Bill Eskridge's valorization of lesbians as sexually disciplined citizens, stating, "Never mind that many lesbians, far from standing as models of homey monogamy, were at that time fighting the feminist sex wars, or that many are even now developing a lesbian culture of experimentation."[42] Elsewhere in the book, Warner cites with approval claims by gay men that permitting gay men to marry will disrupt norms of monogamy, but then he hastens to include lesbians in this prediction.[43] Warner extensively discusses commercial public sex venues, yet he acknowledges the male-dominated nature of such spaces only implicitly and fleetingly.[44] Although he occasionally nods to gender differences, Warner strains to keep queer men and women under the same umbrella.

Bill Eskridge, perhaps the leading legal scholarly advocate for same-sex marriage, tells a very different story. He describes the AIDS crisis as tempering the sexual abandon of the 1970s and bringing gay men into lesbianic norms: "Whatever gravity gay life may have lacked in the disco seventies it acquired in the health crisis of the eighties. What it lost in youth and innocence it gained in dignity. Gay cruising and experimentation . . . a permanent obstacle to gay marriage, gave way somewhat in the 1980s to a more lesbian-like interest in commitment. . . . Part of our self-civilization has been an insistence on the right to marry."[45] Eskridge's narrative may be politically and legally effective in marshaling support for same-sex marriage, but the Gotta study suggests that it is factually wrong. Eskridge's description of gay men coming to embrace "lesbian-like" sexual norms seems to reflect Eskridge's personal aspiration for gay men rather than most gay men's lived realities.

Despite their vehement disagreements, Eskridge and Warner overlap in that they both conflate male and female experiences. For Eskridge, the conflation involves claiming that gay men have become like lesbians. For Warner, the conflation entails claiming that lesbians are just as sexually adventurous as gay men and implying that radical lesbian feminists are representative of all lesbians. Eskridge's claim serves to construct a unified "gay and lesbian" subject asking the state to bless same-sex unions. Warner fabricates an ostensibly gender-neutral "queer sexual culture"[46] to subvert Eskridge's marriage agenda. Despite the marked differences in sexual patterns among queer men and women described in the Gotta study and elsewhere,[47] scholars tend to conflate the two groups, speaking of "same-sex marriage" and "same-sex couples" as if male and female relationship practices are identical. The next part suggests that the movement for LGBT rights, particularly marriage equality, is largely responsible for the resistance to acknowledging fully the salience of gender within queer communities and that the recent success of marriage equality may open greater space for admitting and engaging divergent gender patterns.

Unlike Warner and Eskridge, the Gotta study is forthright in acknowledging gender differences. Still, Gotta's analysis at times rests on certain questionable normative assumptions as to how to reconcile the gender divide. This represents a final way in which scholars and advocates struggle with gender. The authors note with approval that "the shift of same-sex couples from 'outlaw' to 'in-law' status is giving same-sex couples more social and legal support for solidifying and maintaining their commitments," but they go on to worry that "our findings also suggest that this 'mainstreaming' may eventually draw same-sex relationships into the normative vortex of traditional expectations for couples in the realm[] of monogamy."[48] This statement relies on two questionable assumptions: (1) the sexual practices of same-sex couples before the law began to protect their sexuality and relationships[49] should be considered the ideal for queer people, if not for heterosexuals, and (2) heterosexuals' sexual norms threaten to invade queer relationships and sexual norms.[50] The valorization of 1970s sexual norms overlooks the fact that the 1970s was a much more homophobic era than today. That a mere 13.5% of queer men pledged to be monogamous probably reflects in part perceptions that maintaining an out, stable, and monogamous relationship was extremely difficult, if not impossible, during that era. Queer people had few visible role models for such relationships, and the law refused to protect and respect same-sex relationships. To the extent that a man desired such a relationship in the seventies, he also would have had to overcome the social norm of nonmonogamy among his peer group, rendering his pool of potential monogamous partners negligible. (Recall that a mere 13% of male couples in 1975 promised to be monogamous.) Thus, assumptions about sexuality in queer relationships were at least as likely to be shaped by homophobia as by "sexual liberation." Queer men today are in a much stronger position freely to decide whether to marry, have an open relationship, or have no relationship, although homophobia remains a factor.[51]

Further, it appears that queer women never behaved as sexually adventurously as queer men. Even in 1975, their sexual patterns were closer to those of heterosexuals than to gay men's . Does that mean that queer women have always been less "liberated" than queer men? Certainly society surveils and polices women's sexuality in ways that are rarely applied to men.[52] Nonetheless, that does not mean that male practices should set the standard for women. The peril of championing queer norms of nonmonogamy is that they may implicitly and inadvertently instantiate male sexual practices during a particular historical moment as the ideal and then use them to judge women's sexuality. There is a long history of scientists using male sexual patterns to measure the sexual performance of lesbians, and the Gotta study seems to perpetuate this pattern. The questions about sexual frequency that sexuality scholars pose to subjects have been trenchantly criticized as phallocentric.[53] In asking how many "times" the couple had sex, such studies seem to draw on background cultural norms that use male ejaculation as the measure of having sex. The very concept of "having sex," Marilyn Frye argues, is widely understood to constitute "male-dominant-female-subordinate-copulation-whose-completion-and-purpose-is-the-male's-ejaculation."[54] In such studies, it seems that "neither the women's pleasure nor the women's orgasms were pertinent in most of the individuals' counting and reporting the frequency with which they 'had sex.'"[55] Imagine the outcome of a study that declined to count male-female intercourse as "sex" where the female did not experience an orgasm. Recent scholarship has sought to shift the inquiry from frequency of sex to duration of sex. One such study found that the median duration of sex for queer women was thirty to forty-five minutes, compared to fifteen to thirty minutes for other couple types (male couples and male-female couples).[56]

The Gotta study authors—one of whom, Pepper Schwartz, is responsible for popularizing the term "lesbian bed death"[57]—perpetuate the theme of sexually stunted lesbians, and fail to think critically about gender.[58] "Although the causes of [lesbian bed death] remain unclear," they write, "couple therapists can help lesbian partners explore the dynamics of initiating and refusing sex in their relationships and the extent to which any inhibitions in initiating sex may be due to traditional gender role socialization."[59] This seems to reflect a stereotype of women as universally passive, although plenty of queer women identify as "butch" or "aggressive."[60] The authors are interested in exploring the possibility that the gendering of queer women helps to explain their ostensible sexual problems.[61] Yet they are unwilling to explore how the "traditional gender role socialization" of queer men may encourage them to see sex as disconnected from emotion and relationships,[62] may make monogamy particularly difficult, and might contribute to relationship disputes about sex. This asymmetry suggests that the Gotta study reflects an assumption that queer male sexual practices should be the norm for all queer people: women's sexuality needs to be fixed, but presumably men's sexuality is just fine.

## Identity Politics and the "Closeting" of Gender

Resistance from scholars like Eskridge to engaging gender differences in same-sex relationships illustrates how the movement for gay rights, including the right to marry, has long pursued a strategy of respectability.[63] As Sonia Katyal has observed, after the Supreme Court in *Bowers v. Hardwick*[64] refused to recognize a fundamental right to engage in consensual homosexual sex, the gay rights movement shifted from arguments based on sexual acts to those based on identity.[65] The movement sought to distinguish acts from identity to stanch the bleeding from *Bowers'* snide evisceration of the claim of sexual liberty, and to carve out the possibility of identity-based relief. As Devon Carbado has written, many gay rights campaigns, including the initial opposition to the military's "Don't Ask, Don't Tell" policy, have constructed and elevated images of "but for" gays.[66] In other words, Carbado writes, these advocates claim that gays are the same as everyone else but for their sexual orientation. Advocates for marriage equality have aligned gay and lesbian identity with plaintiffs who are predominantly white and affluent, reinforcing broader perceptions of gay, white, upper-class men as the essential face of the LGBT community. I have written elsewhere about the racial dimensions of respectability politics in the LGBT community.[67] However, close examination of a prominent Supreme Court case concerning same-sex marriage, *United States v. Windsor*,[68] shows that even an elderly white lesbian had to be tightly managed to ensure a respectable, gender-conforming, and desexualized image of lesbian and gay people. In *Windsor*, a divided Supreme Court ruled that the Defense of Marriage Act (DOMA) violated the Fifth Amendment's guarantee of equal treatment. After the Supreme Court marriage victory, the *New Yorker* magazine published a profile entitled "The Perfect Wife." The article reveals both Edith Windsor's lawyers' attempts to muzzle her and the three-dimensional personality that they hid from view.[69] In preparing her case for Supreme Court review, Roberta Kaplan argued within the marriage equality movement that Windsor was a superior client for a Supreme Court challenge to DOMA for a number of reasons. Namely, Windsor was (1) a widow—which meant she could not be caught in an affair, nor could her partner leave her during the course of the litigation; (2) a woman—which made her less likely to trigger stereotypes of gay promiscuity; and (3) in her eighties. Thus, "Windsor could be remade as a non-threatening little old lady."[70]

The *New Yorker* profile makes plain that much of this was an act. For instance, Windsor's relationship with Spyer was very sexual, and Windsor remains a sexually vital presence.[71] Yet Windsor's lawyers urged her not to talk about sex. Windsor was an appealing client precisely because of her gender conformity. Nothing about her long hair, pearls, and tastefully applied makeup signified anything other than a sophisticated elderly lady.[72] "Her [appearance], Kaplan knew, would make it easy for people across the country to feel that they understood her, that she embodied values they could relate to." At a deeper level, however, Windsor's relationship challenged gender norms by demonstrating that a woman (Windsor's spouse, Thea Spyer) could fully occupy a role historically reserved for men. Windsor and Spyer embodied traditional butch-femme roles. Windsor, who identifies as femme, said that "[e]very time somebody calls her my wife, I am furious. It's a fucking insult to her!" Spyer's faltering health involuntarily altered the gendered contours of their relationship. "As Spyer's body failed, she had to relinquish aspects of her [masculine] role. She hated not being able to carry grocery bags or heavy packages inside from the car—it upset her so much that she couldn't watch Windsor doing it."[73]

The desexing and degendering of Windsor and Spyer's relationship is not unique to their case. Marriage equality litigators routinely do this, first by weeding out potential clients who are deemed too deviant for prime time, and second by covering any residual traces of sexual and gender nonconformity from the judicial gaze. My review of the briefs in marriage equality litigation from 2003 to 2013[74] is consistent with Katherine Franke's summation: "The homosexual portrayed in these filings is the soccer mom, the partner who is a good provider, the loving father, the de-facto daughter-in-law, and the fellow who attends stamp-collecting conventions. The legitimate homosexual is he or she who is willing to keep quiet about the sex part of homosexual."[75] Moreover, this erasure of LGBT sexuality relies on gender. Marriage equality advocates who were fighting ballot initiatives that would have banned same-sex marriage concluded that when their advertisements featured gay people, "it was old-lady lesbians who . . . were the best messengers. . . . Nobody thought about sex when they saw them."[76] Although lesbians may thus have greater representation among "the strictly vetted, disciplined, sanitized faces the movement was putting forth,"[77] their access depends on the insulting stereotype that their relationships are not sexual. The flip side of the depiction of gay men as oversexed and unfit for marriage then is the representation of lesbians as sexless caretakers, which would reinforce an archaic conception of women and flatten the substantial diversity among queer women in terms of their sexual practices and beliefs.

## Conclusion: A Look to the Future

This analysis of the dynamics of marriage equality litigation helps to explain the gender struggles described in part 2. Marriage equality advocates may figure that engaging gender offers significant risks and little benefit. They know any acknowledgment that gay men are less likely to behave monogamously than heterosexuals could trigger the stereotype that gay men are sexually voracious and not marriage material. What is more surprising is that opponents of same-sex marriage generally do not claim that gay men are promiscuous. For example, I have not found a single legal brief that cites the Gotta study's findings.[78] Although there are many law review articles debating same-sex marriage, including some that critique same-sex marriage, I have found only one article that cites the Gotta study, and it is pro–marriage equality.[79] A number of factors might explain this, including the poorly researched nature of some briefs and the fear that raising claims about promiscuity will manifest "animus."[80] However, another motive may be that such studies hold limited strategic value to both sides of the marriage debate.[81] While the Gotta study could be read as confirming the stereotype that queer men are sexually deviant, it simultaneously shows that queer women's sexual patterns are similar to heterosexuals'. Thus, even if judges found queer men's sexual practices contemptible, they would have difficulty denying queer women the right to marry. Similarly, while drawing on studies that show convergence between queer women and heterosexuals in terms of monogamy and parenting might initially seem appealing, it might render the rights of queer men vulnerable or harm the entire class of "gays and lesbians."[82] So instead of dividing the class of "gays and lesbians" by gender, both marriage equality advocates and their opponents have tacitly agreed to act as if gender makes no difference. In addition, scholars who want to assert claims about same-sex marriage (such as Eskridge and Warner) may conflate gender because acknowledging that their argument applies only to half of the LGBT community would complicate the sweeping claims that they wish to make.

Although gender evasion and respectability politics have been very instrumental in securing marriage rights, we might very well see their limits in the coming decades. To the extent that the public feels that the Supreme Court has foisted same-sex marriage upon it rather than permitting the public to "evolve" gradually, the backlash could be considerable. But it may also be insidious. Since the public has gotten Justice Kennedy's memo in *Windsor* that animus toward gays and lesbians is morally wrong, we can expect reconstituted attacks to target conduct rather than status. In an ironic—or perhaps perverse—way, this strategy would invert the gay rights movement's decision to emphasize identity rather than conduct. Thus, critiques of LGBT people will be said to home in on how certain sexual minorities choose to behave, not their status as sexual minorities. And such critics can point to "upstanding" LGBT people, such as the plaintiffs in same-sex marriage litigation, to prove that they don't have a problem with LGBT people per se.

I expect that men may bear the brunt of these attacks because they are less likely to take advantage of the right to marry and less likely to maintain monogamous relationships. The same cultural logic that suggests that elderly white lesbians are ideal plaintiffs implies that men, especially those who lead active sex lives and men of color, who are additionally subject to sexualized racial stereotypes, might be the most natural targets of homophobia. Already, the media has published statistics showing that queer women are more likely to marry than queer men in some of the earliest states to permit same-sex marriage, and some such coverage has reflected a judgmental tone toward queer men who fail to wed.[83] Importantly, some studies have found that heterosexuals, especially heterosexual men, have more hostile attitudes toward gay men than toward lesbians. For example, Gregory Herek found that heterosexuals were more likely to perceive gay men than lesbians as mentally ill and as child molesters, heterosexuals were more likely to support letting a lesbian couple adopt than a gay couple, and heterosexual men were more likely to view gay men than lesbians as incapable of having a loving, long-term relationship.[84] A more recent study asked heterosexual subjects to assess a vignette in which two people met, expressed mutual attraction, dated, and eventually moved in together.[85] The researchers varied the vignette so that the couple was a male and a female, two females, or two males. Although the facts were identical—other than gender—the subjects determined that the gay male couple was less likely to be in love than the female couple and the male-female couple and, relatedly, that they were less deserving of certain rights.[86] The lesbian couple was perceived to be as in love as the heterosexual couple.[87] These studies indicate that the afterlife of homophobia will likely be gendered.

In closing, I want to highlight two examples of discourse that model the sort of intense engagement with and critical thinking about gender among LGBT people that I imagine. First, lesbian critiques of male domination in the gay rights movement of the 1970s and 1980s offer a critical eye on gender that seems absent in the recent marriage equality movement. For example, Liz Stanley wrote incisively about similarities between straight men and gay men in terms of how they treated women and other men.[88] In particular, Stanley called out gay male sexual practices, which she perceived as "treating each other as sexual objects, objectifying the young and stereotypically attractive, and making use of involvements with new members [of a gay rights organization] in order to exploit them sexually."[89] She deemed these practices sexist in nature and saw them as linked to these same gay men's patriarchal attitudes toward female colleagues in the movement for sexual liberation.

Second, David Frost and Michelle Eliason have produced an illuminating study on the question of whether queer women "fuse" when they enter relationships and lose their individuality.[90] Lesbian popular culture and psychological literature from the 1970s and 1980s is replete with claims that lesbian relationships tend to be overly intimate and that this dynamic creates problems for women in such relationships.[91] Drawing on feminist critiques of the fusion discourse, Frost and Eliason took on this conventional wisdom by asking subjects to describe the actual degree of intimacy in their relationship and their ideal degree of intimacy. Their sample included same-sex female couples, same-sex male couples, and male-female couples, which allowed them to compare intimacy across relationship types. Frost and Eliason found no significant difference between the reported degree of intimacy in female same-sex relationships and other relationship types. Nonetheless, women in same-sex relationships were significantly more likely to express a desire for less closeness in their relationships when compared to subjects in same-sex male and male-female relationships. Frost and Eliason suggest that "given the proliferation of fusion and merger discourses in the popular and psychological arenas, women in same-sex relationships have become sensitive to the 'threat' of fusion," but their sense of threat may be overstated.[92] The results of the Frost and Eliason study could be used to help reduce anxiety among queer women that fusion is a special problem afflicting women in same-sex relationships and more broadly undermine the gender stereotype of women/lesbian relationships as overly emotional.

My hope is that in having these difficult conversations about gendered patterns, LGBT people can connect gender differences within our community to gender differences in the broader society. Long before we come out as gay, lesbian, bisexual, or queer, our (mostly heterosexual) families and friends teach us what it means to be a man and what it means to be a woman. Coming out may create the opportunity to reconsider one's gender role and performance, but it does not automatically erase years of gender socialization, such as the expectation that women desire intimacy more than men. We need to look closely at such practices to understand the interaction between norms within sexual-minority communities and broader gender norms. It may turn out that the transactional sexual norms in much of gay male culture are not radically different from "hookup" norms among young heterosexual men before (and, for some, after) they marry.[93] To the extent that we are troubled by such norms, we should seek to redirect not just gay men but also straight men. Similarly, to the extent that we think that sexual norms among lesbian are overly relationship oriented and do not leave sufficient room for different engagements with sex and romance, we should link such conventions to the broader socialization of girls and women, which continues to fixate on marriage as the pinnacle of female development.[94] By drawing persuasive connections between the majority and minority communities,[95] we might demonstrate that the sexual and relationship patterns of queer men and queer women arise from their preexisting and ongoing socialization as men and women in addition to their status as sexual minorities. Ultimately, this chapter has sought to identify some of the gendered tensions and fissures that may fragment the LGBT community and calls for a frank intracommunity dialogue as a first step of resistance to the afterlife of homophobia.

NOTES

I am grateful to Kathy Abrams, Michael Boucai, Elizabeth Emens, Sonia Katyal, Steve Sugarman, Urvashi Vaid, UC Berkeley Law Faculty Workshop, UC Irvine Center on Law, Equality, and Race, and the New York City LGBT Law Workgroup for comments on earlier drafts. Shayla Myers, Jerome Pierce, Naomi Salas-Santacruz, Ryan Whitacre, and Abby Woodruff provided excellent research assistance.

1 Katherine Franke, "Public Sex, Same-Sex Marriage, and the Afterlife of Homophobia," in *Petite Mort: Recollections of a Queer Public*, Carlos Motta and Joshua Lubin-Levy, eds. (New York: Forever & Today, 2011), p. 158, available at http://www2.law.columbia.edu/faculty_franke/Franke_Public_Sex.pdf, accessed April 2015. This short chapter does not attempt comprehensively to survey all of the gendered burdens that may impact same-sex couples. For instance, studies suggest that female couples suffer from compounded gender inequality in that women are susceptible to enduring wage differentials. See M. V. Lee Badgett, *Money, Myths, and Change: The Economic Lives of Lesbians and Gay Men* (Chicago: University of Chicago Press, 2003). It is important to consider how economic privilege may bolster and insulate some male couples. My focus here, however, is different. I seek to call attention to gender-based differences that have received relatively little attention—relationship status and monogamy—and that are more likely to ensnare men. To the extent that female couples struggle with economic disadvantage or inadequate sexual satisfaction (discussed below), these burdens are unlikely to run afoul of puritanical public norms. Based on available empirical data, I predict that public criticism arising from failure to be in a committed relationship and failure to practice monogamy will fall disproportionately on men.

2 Here I want to distinguish between widespread depictions of heterosexual women dabbling in sex with women, which are generally geared toward titillating men, and representations of sex between women who identify as lesbian, bisexual, or queer and do not mimic heterosexual norms.

3  I use the term "queer" to refer to all sexual minorities, although I recognize that the term is imperfect. Many scholars use the term "gay men and lesbians," but this formulation erases bisexuals and sexual minorities who do not identify with the terms "gay" or "lesbian," both of which are significant communities. Some scholars use "queer" to refer to nonnormative sexual practices and see queer identity as extending beyond LGBT identity. In this chapter, I do not generally use "queer" in that sense, although there are a few contexts where I use "queer" in that sense to describe certain scholars' work. Although some LGBT people find the term "queer" offensive, since it was once widely used in a derogatory way, other sexual minorities have reclaimed the term, and younger people seem to prefer it. In the end, I use "queer" mainly because it is more concise than the terms "gay/bisexual/queer" or "sexual minority" and seems to erase fewer people. Unfortunately, few of the relevant studies and scholars consider transgender people, and thus, I am limited in my ability to opine on their experiences. There is a strong need for greater research with respect to the experiences of transgender people, and I am working on a forthcoming empirical study that will highlight the romantic relationship experiences of transgender people.

4  Obergefell v. Hodges, 135 S.Ct. 2584 (2015).

5  In this chapter, I do not take up how queer men and women perform gender in their relationships, including roles such as "butch," "femme," "top," and "bottom."

6  See generally Judith Butler, Gender Trouble: Feminism and the Subversion of Identity (New York: Routledge, 1990), pp. 24–25; Katherine M. Franke, "The Central Mistake of Sex Discrimination Law: The Disaggregation of Sex from Gender," 144 University of Pennsylvania Law Review 1, 98 (1995); Candace West & Don H. Zimmerman, "Doing Gender," 1 Gender and Society 125 (1987).

7  Shauna Miller, "Beyond the U-Haul: How Lesbian Relationships Are Changing," Atlantic, July 13, 2013, available at http://www.theatlantic.com/sexes/archive/2013/07/beyond-the-u-haul-how-lesbian-relationships-are-changing/277495/, accessed April 2015 (quoting actor Lea DeLaria and also tracing the concept to the popular novel Stone Butch Blues).

8  Michael C. LaSala, "Gay and Can't Find a Partner?" Psychology Today, September 6, 2014, available at https://www.psychologytoday.com/blog/gay-and-lesbian-well-being/201409/gay-and-cant-find-partner, accessed April 2015.

9  See, e.g., Michael Joseph Gross, "Has Manhunt Destroyed Gay Culture?" Out Magazine, August 4, 2008, available at http://www.out.com/entertainment/2008/08/04/has-manhunt-destroyed-gay-culture?page=full, accessed April 2015.

10  See Rachel Kramer Bussel, "Why Don't Lesbians Hook Up Online?" Village Voice, June 19, 2013, available at http://www.villagevoice.com/2013-06-19/news/lesbian-on-line/, accessed April 2015 (noting that even though several lesbian-focused smartphone apps have sought to follow in Grindr's footsteps, "None of the new apps have attracted the critical mass needed to make them cruisable" and "compar[ing] the 8,000 total users on FindHrr, one of the more successful lesbian

apps, to Grindr's claim of an astonishing 844,785 [male users] in New York City alone"). These structural differences probably influence the content of the connections that people make. Queer women appear more likely to meet a potential partner through a friend or ex-partner, and these thick social links may deter the bad behavior that tends to proliferate when strangers (of any sexual orientation) meet online.

11 On the role of structure in one's romantic decision making, see Russell K. Robinson, "Structural Dimensions of Romantic Preferences," 76 *Fordham Law Review* 2787 (2008); Elizabeth F. Emens, "Intimate Discrimination: The State's Role in the Accidents of Sex and Love," 122 *Harvard Law Review* 1307 (2009).

12 Most of these studies did not involve married same-sex couples, and it is possible that marriage changes one's sexual practices. Thus, my claim is necessarily speculative and awaits studies of sexual practices among same-sex married couples. However, many of the same-sex couples in the Gotta study (discussed below) had entered into civil unions, making them the closest possible comparison to a married same-sex couple.

13 Gregory Herek et al., "Demographic, Psychological, and Social Characteristics of Self-Identified Lesbian, Gay, and Bisexual Adults in a US Probability Sample," 7 *Sex Research & Social Policy* 176 (2010).

14 Gary J. Gates, "LGB Families and Relationships: Analyses of the 2013 National Health Interview Survey," *Williams Institute*, Oct. 2014, available at http://williamsinstitute.law.ucla.edu/wp-content/uploads/lgb-families-nhis-sep-2014.pdf, accessed April 2015. The Gates analysis found that bisexual women, at 32%, were less likely to be coupled than lesbians (51%) and more comparable to bisexual men (34%) and gay men (35%) in this regard.

15 Gates, "LGB Families and Relationships." The reasons for women's greater interest in marriage are probably complex. In addition to social norms that instill a taste for marriage in many women, women may have a greater perceived need for the legal protections and economic benefits that flow from marriage. The fact that female couples are more likely than male couples to raise children (*see infra*) seems to be an important factor.

16 Christopher Carpenter and Gary Gates, "Gay and Lesbian Partnership: Evidence from California," 45 *Demography* 573 (2008), p. 583.

17 Carpenter and Gates, "Gay and Lesbian Partnership," p. 580.

18 Carpenter and Gates, "Gay and Lesbian Partnership," p. 583 ("Gay men in registered partnerships are more likely to be white than other gay men."). The repercussions of these cleavages may intensify as LGB people age. A UCLA study found that half of aging gay and bisexual men (ages fifty to seventy) live alone, compared to 13.4% of heterosexual men and 28.3% of lesbian and bisexual women. Steven Wallace et al., *The Health of Aging Lesbian, Gay, and Bisexual Adults in California* (UCLA Center for Health Policy Research, 2011), p. 3, available at http://www.ncbi.nlm.nih.gov/pmc/articles/PMC3698220/pdf/nihms472438.pdf, accessed April 2015.

19 Among married couples, 28% of different-sex couples were nonwhite compared to 23% of same-sex couples, but this disparity was not statistically significant. *See* Gates, "LGB Families and Relationships," p. 5.

20 Gabriella Gotta et al., "Heterosexual, Lesbian, and Gay Male Relationships: A Comparison of Couples in 1975 and 2000," 50 *Family Process* 353 (2011). More recent studies, including those based on the National Survey of Family Growth, reveal aggregate information about a broader and more representative sample of men and women. However, such surveys do not ask the same questions as the Gotta study. They tend to focus on individual sexual behaviors rather than examining how people with particular sexual identities behave when they are in romantic relationships.

21 Gotta et al., "Heterosexual, Lesbian, and Gay Male Relationships," p. 356. This earlier study surveyed 972 gay men, 2,177 heterosexual men, 783 lesbians, and 2,150 heterosexual women in 1975.

22 The 2000 study included 195 gay men, 80 heterosexual men, 378 lesbians, and 129 heterosexual women. The authors of the 1975 study advertised in various mass media outlets and used bulletin boards and canvassing. The authors of the 2000 study gained access to all of the names and addresses of couples who entered into civil unions in Vermont. They began identifying subjects by inviting these couples to enroll in the survey, and then they asked the first four hundred of these couples who enrolled to refer them to a friend who was in a same-sex relationship but not in a civil union. They further asked the subjects for the contact information of a heterosexual married sibling. Although many of the subjects lived in Vermont, the methodology produced a national sample, in part because Vermont's civil unions were available to nonresidents. (That is not to say that the nonprobability sample was representative of the national population.)

23 Gotta et al., "Heterosexual, Lesbian, and Gay Male Relationships," p. 374.

24 Gotta et al., "Heterosexual, Lesbian, and Gay Male Relationships," p. 366.

25 Gotta et al., "Heterosexual, Lesbian, and Gay Male Relationships," p. 366.

26 Gotta et al., "Heterosexual, Lesbian, and Gay Male Relationships," p. 366.

27 However, despite being no more likely to engage in outside sex, queer women fought about outside sex more than heterosexuals. In general, queer men and women were more likely than heterosexuals to fight about outside sex. Gotta et al., "Heterosexual, Lesbian, and Gay Male Relationships," p. 367 ("When listed in rank order, gay men reported fighting the most about sex outside the relationship, then lesbians, then heterosexual men, and finally heterosexual women.").

28 Gotta et al., "Heterosexual, Lesbian, and Gay Male Relationships," p. 366.

29 Gotta et al., "Heterosexual, Lesbian, and Gay Male Relationships," p. 366.

30 The prevalence of meaningful love affairs in 2000 among heterosexual women was 5.5%; 4.0% for queer women; and 1.3% for heterosexual men. Some would attempt to dismiss the various disparities by positing that gay men are more honest about their sexual behavior. This claim is difficult to verify and also raises complicated questions. Are gay men more honest than lesbians? To the extent

that queer men in 2000 reported less sex outside the relationship than queer men in 1975, were queer men in 1975 simply more honest than queer men in 2000? Because it is very difficult to determine honesty rates among various groups over time, and because the researchers ensured subjects that their responses would be kept confidential, I do not discount particular findings based on intuitions about honesty. Finally, although my personal experience suggests that some gay men are quite vocal about their sexual behavior and preferences in certain gay settings, this honesty seems not to carry over to conversations with parents, siblings, and heterosexual friends. *See* Kenji Yoshino, *Covering: The Hidden Assault on Our Civil Rights* (New York: Random House, 2006) (discussing pervasive social pressure to downplay one's sexuality even after coming out as gay).

31 The authors analyzed data from only one partner in a couple. Thus, they were not able to compare responses of each member of the couple.

32 Gotta et al., "Heterosexual, Lesbian, and Gay Male Relationships," p. 368. Another 1.6% of queer men said that if they discussed monogamy with their partner, they would agree that the relationship is monogamous. In 1975, but not in 2000, heterosexuals were much more likely than queer people to assume monogamy.

33 Gotta et al., "Heterosexual, Lesbian, and Gay Male Relationships," p. 368. In 2000, queer men who discussed monogamy were evenly divided between those who agreed to be open (43.7%) and those who agreed to be monogamous (44.2%). The study's findings are subject to several limitations, of course. First, it concerned only people who were in committed relationships, not the many sexual minorities who are single or romantically and/or sexually involved in ways that diverge from conventional notions of a relationship. Gotta et al., "Heterosexual, Lesbian, and Gay Male Relationships," p. 356 (requiring that subjects "lived together and had a sexual relationship at least some time in their lives together" and that both "considered themselves a couple"). However, the fact that gender differences appear in the most conventional same-sex relationships seems telling. Second, the sample was heavily white and middle-class, perhaps in part because of the ties to Vermont. Thus, these patterns might not apply to communities of color or to working-class communities. I am working on an empirical study that will foreground the lives of people who are not in conventional committed relationships and people of color, groups that appear to overlap significantly.

34 Herek et al., "Demographic, Psychological, and Social Characteristics of Self-Identified Lesbian, Gay, and Bisexual Adults in a US Probability Sample," 7 *Sexuality Research and Social Policy*, 176, 194 (2000).

35 Herek et al., "Demographic, Psychological, and Social Characteristics of Self-Identified Lesbian, Gay, and Bisexual Adults in a US Probability Sample," p. 193; *see also* Gary J. Gates, "LGBT Parenting in the United States," *Williams Institute* (Feb. 2013), available at http://williamsinstitute.law.ucla.edu/wp-content/uploads/LGBT-Parenting.pdf, accessed April 2015 (stating that among LGBT people under fifty, nearly half of women are raising children, compared with 20% of men).

36 *See* Obergefell v. Hodges, 135 S.Ct. 2584, 2600–2601 (2015).

37  *See* United States v. Windsor, 133 S.Ct. 2675 (2013).

38  David M. Huebner et al., "The Impact of Parenting on Gay Male Couples' Relationships, Sexuality, and HIV Risk," 1 *Couple and Family Psychology: Research and Practice* 106 (2012).

39  Russell K. Robinson, "Marriage Equality and Postracialism," 61 *UCLA Law Review* 1010 (2014).

40  Opponents of same-sex marriage invoked "accidental procreation" to claim that law may rationally treat same-sex couples differently from different-sex couples, because only the latter can accidentally procreate.

41  Michael Warner, *The Trouble with Normal: Sex, Politics, and the Ethics of Queer Life* (New York: Free Press, 1999).

42  Warner, *The Trouble with Normal*, p. 94.

43  Warner, *The Trouble with Normal*, p. 131 ("Similarly, Claudia Card notes an under-recognized tradition among lesbians of having 'more than one long-term intimate relationship during the same time period.'").

44  Warner, *The Trouble with Normal*, pp. 169–70 (adding that "[t]he nascent lesbian sexual culture is threatened as well, including the only video rental club catering to lesbians"); Warner, *The Trouble with Normal*, p. 171 (asking—but not answering—the question, "Are my arguments against [a New York City bill that would restrict public sex venues] only going to protect gay male culture?"). At times, Warner slips and the "queer" practice of public sex is revealed to be a gay male practice. Warner, *The Trouble with Normal*, p. 175 ("Mohr defends the kinds of public sex common to gay male culture"); Warner, *The Trouble with Normal*, p. 177 (referring to "the gay male practice of public sex"). But he quickly returns to discussions of "the sexual cultures of gay men *and lesbians*" (emphasis added).

45  William Eskridge Jr., *The Case for Same-Sex Marriage: From Sexual Liberty to Civilized Commitment* (New York: Free Press, 1996), p. 58.

46  Warner, *The Trouble with Normal*, p. 218.

47  It is worth noting that in some other respects the Gotta study found that queer men and women were similar. They are more likely than heterosexual couples to share "masculine" and "feminine" housework equally and to have equal communication patterns. Gotta et al., "Heterosexual, Lesbian, and Gay Male Relationships," pp. 361–62.

48  Gotta et al., "Heterosexual, Lesbian, and Gay Male Relationships," p. 371.

49  *See, e.g.*, Lawrence v. Texas, 539 U.S. 558 (2003), United States v. Windsor, 133 S.Ct. 2675 (2013).

50  The latter strikes me as a curious inversion of the argument that opponents of same-sex marriage made in court—that legalizing same-sex marriage will destabilize norms in different-sex marriage.

51  For example, many LGB people remain closeted. J. Bryan Lowder, "The American Closet Is Bigger Than We Thought," *Slate*, Dec. 9, 2013, http://www.slate.com/blogs/outward/2013/12/09/how_many_men_are_gay_in_america.html, accessed April 2015. Those who are out may struggle with internalized homophobia, and

this tension impacts their romantic relationships. *See* David M. Frost and Ilan H. Meyer, "Internalized Homophobia and Relationship Quality among Lesbians, Gay Men, and Bisexuals," 56 *Journal of Counseling & Psychology* 1 (2009).

52  *See, e.g.*, Cynthia Grant Bowman, "Street Harassment and the Informal Ghettoization of Women," 106 *Harvard Law Review* 517 (1993); Kavita B. Ramakrishnan, "Inconsistent Legal Treatment of Unwanted Sexual Advances: A Study of the Homosexual Advance Defense, Street Harassment, and Sexual Harassment in the Workplace," 26 *Berkeley Journal of Gender, Law, and Justice* 291 (2011).

53  *See, e.g.*, Marilyn Frye, "Lesbian 'Sex,'" in *Lesbian Philosophies and Cultures*, Jeffner Allen, ed. (Albany: State University of New York Press, 1990), p. 305.

54  Frye, "Lesbian 'Sex,'" p. 305.

55  Frye, "Lesbian 'Sex,'" p. 308.

56  Karen L. Blair and Caroline F. Pukall, "Can Less Be More? Comparing Duration vs. Frequency of Sexual Encounters in Same-Sex and Mixed-Sex Relationships," 23 *Canadian Journal of Human Sexuality* 123, 133 (2014).

57  *See* Philip Blumstein and Pepper Schwartz, *American Couples* (New York: Morrow, 1983).

58  *See* Gotta et al., "Heterosexual, Lesbian, and Gay Male Relationships," p. 374. For scholarship that calls into question the methodology of studies finding "lesbian bed death," *see generally* Blair and Pukall, "Can Less Be More?"

59  Gotta et al., "Heterosexual, Lesbian, and Gay Male Relationships," p. 374.

60  As the Gotta study notes, it is true that other research has found that women in same-sex relationships had sex less frequently than married heterosexual women. *See, e.g.*, Sondra E. Solomon, et al., "Money, Housework, Sex, and Conflict: Same-Sex Couples in Civil Unions, Those Not in Civil Unions, and Heterosexual Married Siblings," 52 *Sex Roles* 561, 568 (2005) (stating that married heterosexual women reported having sex on average two–three times a month, while the average for coupled lesbians was about once a month). At least some of these studies, however, reflect a failure to think sufficiently about what constitutes "sex," focus inordinately on frequency while ignoring duration, and reflect rather reductive conceptions of women's sexuality. *See, e.g.*, Solomon, et al., "Money, Housework, Sex, and Conflict," p. 573 ("[W]hen couples consist of two women they lack someone socialized to be the sexual initiator. Lesbian couples, being female, may spend more time on romance than genital sex, but it is also true that in Western societies 'real' sex consists of genital activity.").

61  Gotta et al.'s analysis becomes quite garbled here. Almost as soon as they introduce gendered cultural norms as the source of queer women's ostensible sexual problems, they reimpose them as the solution. The problem, they suggest, is that women are "waiting to feel the kind of sexual urgency that males frequently require in order to initiate sexual encounters. That is, female sexuality in long-term relationships needs to be understood and normalized on its own terms— frequently more relational and frequently with somewhat slower arousal in the start-up phase." Gotta et al., "Heterosexual, Lesbian, and Gay Male Relationships,"

p. 374. Thus, they seem to say, women need to accept their essential gender difference and not measure themselves by male standards.

62 Consider the phrase "It didn't mean anything" to justify having sex outside one's relationship. Or President Bill Clinton's definition of "sex" when he was investigated for an inappropriate relationship with Monica Lewinsky.

63 *See, e.g.,* Katherine Franke, *Wed-Locked: The Perils of Marriage Equality* (New York: New York University Press, 2015).

64 478 U.S. 186 (1986).

65 Sonia Katyal, "Exporting Identity," 14 *Yale Journal of Law & Feminism* 97 (2002).

66 *See* Devon W. Carbado, "Black Rights, Gay Rights, Civil Rights," 47 *UCLA Law Review* 1467, 1506 (2000) (arguing that the movement has favored "'but for' gay people—people who, but for their sexual orientation, were perfectly mainstream").

67 *See* Robinson, "Marriage Equality and Postracialism."

68 133 S. Ct. 2675 (2013).

69 Ariel Levy, "The Perfect Wife," *New Yorker,* Sept. 30, 2013, available at http://www.newyorker.com/magazine/2013/09/30/the-perfect-wife, accessed April 2015.

70 Levy, "The Perfect Wife."

71 In the *New Yorker* profile, Windsor stated, "'I never wanted anybody inside me till Thea. And then I wanted her inside me all the time.'" Elsewhere in the article, a friend "said that she wanted to set Windsor up with a friend in town, a ninety-four-year-old redhead. 'Is she still sexual?' Windsor asked. 'Very,' Pomponio promised." As one commentator noted, "What's truly remarkable about the [*New Yorker*] story is that it treats lesbians as sexual creatures." June Thomas, "The Dirtiest, Sexiest Profile the *New Yorker* Has Ever Run," *Slate,* Sept. 23, 2013, available at http://www.slate.com/blogs/outward/2013/09/23/_edie_windsor_profile_in_the_new_yorker_the_dirtiest_in_the_magazine_s_history.html, accessed April 2015.

72 Windsor has been known to wear a t-shirt that says, "Nobody knows I'm a lesbian," at gay pride marches. Levy, "The Perfect Wife."

73 Levy, "The Perfect Wife." More could certainly be said about gender roles in same-sex relationships. I plan to tackle this issue in a future book project.

74 I conducted this review in connection with the article "Marriage Equality and Postracialism."

75 *See* Franke, "Public Sex, Same-Sex Marriage, and the Afterlife of Homophobia," p. 157.

76 Molly Ball, "How Gay Marriage Became a Constitutional Right," *Atlantic,* July 1, 2015, available at http://www.theatlantic.com/politics/archive/2015/07/gay-marriage-supreme-court-politics-activism/397052/, accessed August 2015.

77 Ball, "How Gay Marriage Became a Constitutional Right."

78 A search of the Westlaw database containing legal briefs found no citations. My review of same-sex marriage litigation briefs for "Marriage Equality and Postracialism" included only the briefs on the merits by the parties. I did not review

the various amici briefs, and it seems likely that some amici were more willing to make provocative arguments than the parties. Still, it is notable that only a handful of parties opposing same-sex marriage cited any empirical studies on same-sex couples and monogamy.

79  Nan D. Hunter, "Introduction: The Future Impact of Same-Sex Marriage; More Questions than Answers," 100 *Georgetown Law Journal* 1855 (2012).

80  Romer v. Evans, 517 U.S. 620 (1996).

81  By contrast, the Gotta study authors are scholars, not necessarily advocates for same-sex marriage, and thus may have been more interested in exploring gender differences. Nonetheless, it seems likely that most scholars of LGBT sexuality are aware of the political risks of studies that emphasize how LGBT people diverge from the mainstream. It may be that the Gotta authors did not regard their "lesbian bed death" analysis as problematic because depicting queer women as undersexed would probably help rather than hinder the struggle for LGBT rights.

82  As a practical matter, it is quite unlikely that a court would divide a class of "gays and lesbians," granting rights to just lesbians.

83  David K. Li "Gay or Straight, Guys Reluctant to Say I Do," *New York Post*, July 5, 2011 (citing "a stark, 3-to-2 ratio of lesbian marriages, compared to all-male unions").

84  Gregory M. Herek, "Gender Gaps in Public Opinion about Lesbians and Gay Men," 66 *Public Opinion Quarterly* 40, 49–52 (2002). Herek calls for greater attention to gender in assessing public attitudes about gays and lesbians. Surveys that treat "gays and lesbians" as a unified class, instead of asking about each group separately, may miss gender-based differences. Herek, "Gender Gaps," pp. 42–43. Herek's study suggests that linking lesbians to gay men may lead heterosexuals to express more hostile attitudes toward lesbians. Herek, "Gender Gaps," pp. 53–54.

85  Long Doan et al., "The Power of Love: The Role of Emotional Attributions and Standards in Heterosexuals' Attitudes toward Lesbian and Gay Couples," 94 *Social Forces* 401, 408 (2015).

86  Doan, "The Power of Love," pp. 412–13.

87  Doan, "The Power of Love," p. 412.

88  Liz Stanley, "'Male Needs': The Problems and Problems [sic] of Working with Gay Men," in *On the Problem of Men*, Scarlet Friedman and Elizabeth Sarah, eds. (Women's Press, 1982), pp. 190, 196.

89  Stanley, "'Male Needs,'" pp. 196, 207, 210 (critiquing the idea that men "need" to "behave in objectifying, unemotional, and entirely phallocentic ways" and arguing that men can and should change this culture). Other notable critics of gay male identity include Marilyn Frye, "Lesbian Feminism and the Gay Rights Movement: Another View of Male Supremacy, Another Separatism," in *The Politics of Reality: Essays in Feminist Theory* (Trumansburg, NY: Crossing Press, 1983), pp. 128–51; and Jacquelyn Zita, "Gay and Lesbian Studies, Yet Another Unhappy Marriage?" in *Tilting the Tower*, Linda Garber, ed. (New York: Routledge, 1994), pp. 258–76.

90 David M. Frost and Michelle J. Eliason, "Challenging the Assumption of Fusion in Female Same-Sex Relationships," 38 *Psychology of Women Quarterly* 65 (2013). The concept of lesbian fusion might be understood to reflect the heterosexual norm, once written into law, that a woman fuses into her husband's identity when she marries.

91 Frost and Eliason, "Challenging the Assumption of Fusion," pp. 65–66.

92 Frost and Eliason, "Challenging the Assumption of Fusion," p. 71.

93 Indeed, in future work, I want to examine potential connections between online hookups in gay male culture and hookup culture among younger people of various genders and sexual orientations on websites and smartphone apps such as Tinder. My focus on sex within relationships limits my ability more fully to engage pre–marriage/committed relationship sexual norms.

94 *See* Melissa Murray, "Marriage as Punishment," 112 *Columbia Law Review* 1 (2012).

95 *See* Russell K. Robinson, "Uncovering Covering," 101 *Northwestern Law Review* 1809 (2007).

9

## What Marriage Equality Teaches Us

*The Afterlife of Racism and Homophobia*

KATHERINE FRANKE

When I first set out to write about marriage equality almost twenty years ago, I began with the hypothesis that newly freed peoples' experience of the right to marry had a "be careful what you wish for" lesson for today's marriage equality movement.[1] I expected that just as marriage revealed itself to be a supple and effective means by which racism could reproduce itself through the state licensure of intimate relationships, it would be equally up to the task of reproducing homophobic bias in the contemporary context. Despite significant victories in the courts and legislatures gaining the right to marry, homophobia, I conjectured, would have an afterlife that would outlast the exhilaration of the first fabulous gay weddings.

In some respects my hypothesis was correct. And in others I was wrong, as events on the ground outpaced my working hypothesis.

How was I right? There has indeed been a backlash against the overwhelming success of the marriage equality movement. While there has been great success expanding marriage rights for same-sex couples in the Supreme Court, the voters in some states moved precipitously and preemptively to clarify a different local norm by passing laws that limited marriage to one man and one woman. Explicitly pursued in response to the success of the marriage equality effort, these clarifications or revisions of state marriage laws were undertaken either through the passage of an amendment to the law defining marriage or through a state constitutional amendment. California's Proposition 8, which put a referendum to voters to reverse a victory for marriage equality won before the California Supreme Court, is perhaps the most prominent example of this sort of measure.[2] But this kind of legal backlash against marriage rights for same-sex couples took place in thirty-one states. Twelve such measures barring marriage rights for same-sex couples were enacted in the November 2004 elections alone. A majority of these measures contain language explicitly denying recognition not only to marriages by same-sex couples but also to civil unions, domestic partnerships, or any other legal status.[3] Their aim was twofold: to clarify the essential heterosexual nature of the institution of marriage, and to make sure that marriage didn't have to compete with any other legal status that was "marriage-like."

Advocates who supported these measures used them as an opportunity to express a wide range of hostile attitudes toward gay people generally, toward their fitness as parents, and toward the notion of legal marriage for same-sex couples. In the spring of 2013 the president of the Southern Baptist Convention, along with a televangelist colleague, speculated that threats to the United States from North Korean president Kim Jong-Un might be attributable to the rise in marriage rights for same-sex couples in the United States: "Could our slide into immorality be what is unleashing this mad man over here in Asia to punish us?"[4] A pastor in New York City went on television and claimed that if same-sex couples are allowed to marry, they will "take a nine year old boy to an Arabic Nation" and marry him, then come back to the United States and force the state to recognize the marriage.[5] In response to President Obama's support of marriage rights for same-sex couples, Mississippi state representative Andy Gipson (R) posted a status update on Facebook citing a passage from Leviticus that calls for gay men to be "put to death," and then followed up with a response to a constituent's post:

[I]n addition to the basic principal that it is morally wrong, here are three social reasons it's horrific social policy: 1) Unnatural behavior which results in disease, not the least of which is its high association with the development and spread of HIV/AIDS; 2) Confusing behavior which is harmful to children who have a deep need to understand the proper role of men and women in society and the important differences between men and women, and fathers and mothers; and 3) Undermines the longstanding definition of marriage as between one man and one woman, a definition which has been key to all aspects of social order and prosperity. Anytime that definition is weakened our culture is also weakened. And yes, that is also true for other conduct which weakens marriage's importance in society.[6]

Latent and explicit hatred toward same-sex couples that exercised a new legal right to marry surfaced in another related context (before nationwide marriage equality was secured in *Obergefell v. Hodges*). In states that limited marriage to one man and one woman, the question arose as to whether the courts in those states had to recognize the marriages of same-sex couples entered into in states that allow them to marry. If, for instance, a lesbian couple living in South Carolina, a state that limited marriage to one man and one woman,[7] travelled to New York to marry legally and then returned to South Carolina to continue with their lives, what should the South Carolina courts have done when the couple later filed for divorce? Should they have recognized the marriage as valid under another state's law and proceeded with the divorce (as they would for any other couple validly married in another state), or refuse to recognize the validity of the marriage and dismiss the divorce action as a legal impossibility (you can't get divorced if you were never legally married)? Tobias Wolff has argued that when courts refused to recognize the validity of same-sex couples' marriages entered into lawfully in states that allowed such marriages, the courts were essentially sending a message to those couples: You are unwelcome here. The hostility against same-sex couples in courts in the South, he claims, was greater than it was against interracial couples. Even in states with the most draconian antimiscegenation laws, courts would sometimes recognize the validity of the marriage for at least some purposes, like inheritance. The categorical nature of the refusal to recognize same-sex marriages for any purposes was unprecedented, he insists. Rather than engendering respect for another state's law, these cases set off a kind of "social alarm" that justified harsh condemnation of the underlying immorality upon which these relationships rest.[8]

Particularly in jurisdictions that didn't sign up for this new civil rights revolution and that federal courts had to drag kicking and screaming to the point of making marriage available to same-sex couples, gay men and lesbians may find themselves suffering a kind of "price tag" for gay rights victories in other states. Gay people in Mississippi, Alabama, Georgia, Louisiana, Idaho, and Montana report an increase in hostility in their communities that negatively tracks the success of the marriage equality movement nation-wide. In their churches, in their workplaces, and at family dinners, they often bear painful witness to religious conservatives' need to hold the line on marriage equality while the rest of the nation goes to hell. This climate forces many gay and lesbian people, particularly people of color, even deeper into the closet. Advocates from Mississippi have told me that their low-income gay and lesbian clients are having more and more difficulty accessing social services delivered through churches (many state and local aid programs that provide food, housing, and other assistance contract with churches to provide these services). Rather than outing themselves to their fellow parishioners and enduring likely harassment or ostracism, many same-sex couples will lie about their relationships by telling people that they are cousins, not lovers. Or in small communities where this kind of lie would be impossible since everyone knows everyone else, they are forced to make a tragic choice between foregoing social services out of fear of the hostility they are likely to endure or closeting themselves so deeply that a normal relationship is impossible.

The story of Tom Wojtowick and Paul Huff being kicked out of their church chillingly illustrates the kind of backlash some couples are experiencing when they get married. After living together as a couple for over thirty years, Wojtowick and Huff, ages sixty-six and seventy-three, respectively, decided to get married and traveled from their small town in Montana to Seattle, Washington, for their nuptials. When they returned home they expected to take up their lives as they had lived them before—living together, known in the community as gay and active in their church, the Kiwanis Club, and other civic organizations. They had set an example to their community of how gay people are not all that different from everyone else. Yet a little over a year after their marriage, a new priest assumed the pulpit at their church, and he summoned them to the church for a conference. He told them that they could no longer sing in the church choir or participate in any other church rituals or functions, including communion. He demanded that they get divorced, stop living together, and sign a statement affirming that marriage was a sacrament of one man and one woman.

This incident divided the parishioners at their church, roughly half opposing the priest's excommunication of the gay couple and half supporting it. Meanwhile, the Episcopalians in town offered to take them in. What's remarkable about this incident is the fact that the church and half of its membership had no problem with Wojtowick and Huff, an openly gay couple, being part of the parish. It was their marriage that set them off. As Frank Bruni put it on the opinion page of the *New York Times*: "I do" means you're done.[9]

To be sure, law can't fix all of the backlash against same-sex couples who marry. The Supreme Court's 2015 decision in *Obergefell v. Hodges* (finding same-sex marriage bans unconstitutional), along with earlier courts that ruled that same-sex couples cannot be denied the right to marry, created a clear nation-wide legal norm supporting same-sex couples' right "to enjoy private intimacy and to share a household in which they can hold themselves out to their community as participants in a committed relationship."[10] Nevertheless, this condemnation of hostility toward gay people asserted in legal precedents has been met with a NIMBY-like response in more conservative parts of the country: You can have your marriage rights in San Francisco, New York, and other sinful cities, but not in our backyard and not in my church! In this sense, some communities approach the claims to marital legitimacy that same-sex couples present as a kind of public nuisance. And some churches, while able to love the sinner, find the sin intolerable when same-sex couples marry.

Ironically, in a number of cases, married gay men and lesbians have taken advantage of enduring homophobic sentiment by seeking to exploit disdain for gay people when their marriages end. Just as people with spouses of a different sex have sought to have their divorces adjudicated in a state that would give them the most advantageous financial leverage in dividing up joint assets or would favor them as a parent, some gay people have engaged in similar "forum shopping," seeking to have their marriages dissolved in states that are hostile to the very idea of same-sex couples marrying. A court order annulling the marriage on the grounds of its illegality might be a highly favorable disposition for the more affluent person in the couple—it's like the marriage never happened, so he or she can just walk away, owing the spouse/partner nothing. Or where a married couple is raising a child, the biological parent of a child could seek to have custody and visitation issues adjudicated in a jurisdiction that is hostile to the idea of lesbian or gay coparenting. This was surely the strategy of Lisa Miller, the biological parent of a child she was raising with Janet Jenkins. After they entered a civil union in Vermont, they broke up and Miller fled with their daughter to Virginia, where the courts are substantially less friendly to the custody and visitation rights of a nonbiological lesbian mother.[11]

All of these examples testify to the shared experience of a newly won right to marry for both recently emancipated black people in the nineteenth century and same-sex couples today: the enduring potency of bigotry, a bigotry that justified a longstanding exclusion from civil marriage, survives the repeal of that exclusion, and fuels a backlash against these new rights holders. In this sense, one of the lessons to be drawn from today's marriage equality movement from African Americans' early celebration of the ability to legally marry is that homophobia, like racism, will have an afterlife. Same-sex couples would be well counseled to prepare for the ways in which a marriage license inaugurates new forms of state discipline and regulation that can be easily deployed in the service of a durable and crushing homophobic itinerary. Just as the institution of marriage has been a sufficiently supple body to host both emancipatory and racist ends for African Americans, so same-sex couples are likely to find marriage to be a worthy standard bearer for both new forms of citizenship and familiar forms of disgrace and exclusion.

* * *

Surely some dots are amenable to connecting when we compare the afterlives of racism and homophobia and how these resilient social blights have been sustained by and through the institution of marriage. Yet the discontinuities between the experiences of African Americans and those of same-sex couples in marriage are striking and are worthy of careful consideration as well.

The examples I gave earlier of a backlash against married same-sex couples might be best understood as the exceptions that prove the rule. They are significantly less representative of the consequences of the rollout of marriage equality today than I had expected. Quite contrary to my predictions of a systemic homophobic recoil in response to the successes of the struggle for marriage equality (predictions that have earned me a reputation in the gay community as a kind of "turd in the punchbowl," to borrow a less than flattering moniker I learned from my mother), the trend has been in favor of embracing the right to marry for same-sex couples, even in sectors where it seemed unlikely just a few years ago. Same-sex marriage rights have found support from prominent conservative political actors and celebrities such as David Blankenhorn, the star witness against marriage equality in the trial challenging Proposition 8; former Bush-era solicitor general Ted Olson; Ken Mehlman, former head of the Republican National Committee; Meg Whitman, who supported Proposition 8 when she ran for California governor; Representatives Ileana Ros-Lehtinen of Florida and Richard Hanna of New York; Stephen J. Hadley, a Bush national security advisor; Carlos Gutierrez, a commerce secretary to Mr. Bush; James B. Comey, a top Bush Justice Department official; David A. Stockman, President Ronald Reagan's first budget director; and actor Clint Eastwood.[12] Their change of heart on this issue says something about their hearts, I suppose, but also about how the appeal for support has been framed. Many of these conservative leaders have seen a convergence of their deep *traditionalist* commitments with the arguments in favor of marriage equality. As they observed in a brief submitted to the Supreme Court in the Prop 8 case,

> Many of the signatories to this brief previously did not support civil marriage for same-sex couples . . . [but] amici have concluded that marriage is strengthened, not undermined, and its benefits and importance to society as well as the support and stability it gives to children and families promoted, not undercut, by providing access to civil marriage for same-sex couples.[13]

Like President Obama's, their views on marriage rights for same-sex couples have evolved.[14]

Why, then, have gay men and lesbians been able to find a kind of redemption in marriage that has eluded African Americans? Why have marriage rights been such a successful tool for gay people to achieve greater standing as full and equal citizens while marriage has remained a potent tool to shame, punish, and discipline African Americans? Why, in other words, have gay people been so successful at using marriage to redeem their good name, while marriage continues to be a site of failure and dysfunction for many African Americans?

I pose the questions in this manner not to ratify the premises that underlie them (for instance, that marriage is redemptive for gay people and dysfunctional for African Americans) but to acknowledge the kind of social reputation that these two groups enjoy or suffer in relation to marriage. So, too, I pose the questions this way not to ignore that these two social groups overlap with one another (there are plenty of African

Americans who are lesbians or gay men) but rather to acknowledge the social reputation that the gay rights movement and its subsidiary, the marriage equality movement, enjoy as white, and the African American community enjoys as heterosexual. By design or not, the gay community has been able to leverage its social capital in whiteness to its advantage in the marriage equality movement, yet African Americans have received little benefit in any endowment they might enjoy from the stereotype that most black people are heterosexual.

The juxtaposition this chapter aims to take on, and particularly the discontinuities it illuminates, tell us something very important about the relative mark of inferiority soldered to blackness as compared with that of homosexuality.

Advocates advancing the cause of marriage equality for same-sex couples have drawn from this powerful metaphor, arguing that the injury they suffer inflicts a similar badge of inferiority on same-sex couples who cannot marry or who are discriminated against for having done so. Invoking a clear analogy to the history of racial inequality in the United States, Ted Olson and David Boies argued in their brief to the Supreme Court in the Prop 8 case,

> Although opening to [same-sex couples] participation in the unique and immensely valuable institution of marriage will not diminish the value or status of marriage for heterosexuals, withholding it causes infinite and permanent stigma, pain, and isolation. It denies gay men and lesbians their identity and their dignity; it labels their families as second-rate. That outcome cannot be squared with the principle of equality and the unalienable right to liberty and the pursuit of happiness that is the bedrock promise of America from the Declaration of Independence to the Fourteenth Amendment, and the dream of all Americans. This badge of inferiority, separateness, and inequality must be extinguished. When it is, America will be closer to fulfilling the aspirations of all its citizens.[15]

Similarly, a group of law professors urged the Illinois legislature to reject a religious exemption in the Illinois marriage equality bill and condemned such a license to discriminate in the name of religion on the ground that it "stamps a badge of inferiority on married same-sex couples that permits their exclusion wherever they go."[16]

The invocation of the notion of a "badge of inferiority" as a way to denounce state policies that offend overarching principles of equality or liberty, whether on the grounds of racism or homophobia, suggests careful thought about the work that must be done to either resist that stamp or remove its mark once imprinted. What notions of the self in relation to larger societal stereotyping, violence, exclusion, and abjection are deployed in efforts to cleanse bodies marked with the moral stain of inferiority? Is there anything peculiar about a strategy that turns to law to remove a mark that is the remainder of law itself?

The badge of inferiority born by people of color is, to be sure, central to the logic that makes blackness intelligible and black bodies legible in a larger racist society. Testifying to the spectacular and violent way in which the signature of race becomes written on the body, Langston Hughes wrote in 1949, "They've hung a black man . . . For the world to see."[17] Once this endorsement of blackness is accomplished, it evokes a particular response, most often one violent in nature. And so the circuit is complete, as the violence of this reading marks the black body once again with a signature, or badge of inferiority. The shooting of Michael Brown in Ferguson, Missouri, in the summer of 2014 is only one recent iteration of these acts of signing and signification. Franz Fanon similarly suggested the spectacular way in which race is written on the body: "'*Maman,* look, a Negro; I'm scared!'"[18] This signature is not one written by black people, but its mark is truly "theirs" in the sense of belonging to them, as being a property of their blackness. Yet Fanon, among so many others, provides the analysis necessary to understand how race is more a moral category than one biological in nature, more an indictment than a fact: "I am overdetermined from the outside," he writes.[19]

When advocates for marriage equality today have conjured a "badge of inferiority" in their arguments to courts, are they mobilizing a notion of injustice that works in ways similar to the writing of race on black bodies? Judge Vaughn Walker, ruling in the case challenging California's Proposition 8's ban on same-sex marriage, credited expert testimony (from an economist, oddly enough) that the marriage ban "conveys a message of inferiority."[20] An Iowa trial court similarly found that

[p]laintiffs suffer great dignitary harm because the State's denial to Plaintiffs of access to an institution, so woven into the fabric of daily life and

so determinative of legal rights and status, amounts to a badge of inferiority imposed on them and Minor plaintiffs. Plaintiffs are continually
reminded of their own and their family's second-class status in daily in-
teractions in their neighborhoods, workplaces, schools, and other arenas
in which their relationships and families are poorly or unequally treated,
or are not recognized at all.[21]

Presumably, winning these cases, particularly after naming the injury of
suffering as a "badge of inferiority," resulted in the removal of that badge
and the signature of disgust and perversion suffered by homosexuals
in its name. Motivating these victories was the notion that gay couples
don't deserve such a degrading signature, that they have been wrongly
mistaken for those who do.

This is what distinguishes the work done by the marriage equality
cases for gay people that has not been and cannot be accomplished
for people bearing the signature of racial inferiority. In the marriage
cases, lesbians and gay men have accomplished a rebranding of what
it means to be homosexual. They have been awarded a kind of "dignity of self-definition" that law and culture have never recognized in
African Americans. In this sense, the dignity at stake in the marriage
cases is not that conferred by the blessings of marriage but rather a kind
of self-possession that has allowed them to tell a counternarrative of
"who gay people are." If the marriage equality cases have been about
anything, they've been about the insistence that gay people have been
misrecognized by law and society and that the time has come to tell a
more respectable, decent story that, if believed, justifies a city official's
signature on a marriage license. Marriage, it turns out, has been not only
an end in itself for the gay community but the container for a rebranding
project as well.

The success of this political project is truly stunning, particularly
when viewed in contrast to the challenges faced over time by the cause
for racial equality. For two social movements organized around particular identity-based claims to justice and equality, both seeking to escape
the subordinating consequences of a conception of difference anchored
in a biological difference from the norm, gay people have enjoyed astonishing success in revealing the irrelevance of biology and the injustice
done in its name.

Hughes's invocation of a lynching, "They've hung a black man . . . For the world to see," might be contrasted with "They've held a wedding . . . For the world to see." The difference between these two events and the subjects they spectacularly produce is to be found in the power, or dignity, of redefinition to be found in the gay wedding. It both reflects and then reproduces a new form of respectability so yearned for in many sectors of the gay community. It enunciates a new norm and a new normal. In an earlier era, a same-sex commitment ceremony or "marriage" elicited disgust, incredulity, or even violence. It operated as a kind of pastiche that mimicked the original but where the joke, if there was one, was on the couple doing the imitation insofar as the gap between the imitation and the original bore witness to the blasphemous nature of this inferior version of the sacred. Now, the marriages of same-sex couples are neither pastiche nor parody of the original, as they *are* the real deal.

In this sense, gay people have been able to reshape the response elicited by these spectacular performances, from disgust to empathy or even identification—something African Americans have never been allowed. Instead, in many cases marriage for African Americans has been a vehicle for reinforcing their inferiority and for eliciting familiar responses that assign a badge of inferiority. Made explicit in the Freedmen's Bureau records, in the rulings of postbellum southern judges, and in the Moynihan Report, marriage has been and largely remains a kind of test that the African American community is seen as failing.

What the marriage equality movement has shown is how lesbian and gay people have been better able to use a form of legal pleading to redefine what it means to be gay than have African Americans to redefine what it means to be black. Blackness, we learn, is both a durable badge *and* a badge of inferiority. What it marks is the residue of racism that no legal victory has been able to dissolve. At best, legal victories for African Americans award restitution for an injury, reinscribing an inferior status at the same time that it compensates for it. By comparison, the gay marriage cases have pulled off something altogether different, by converting marriage into a badge of superiority. Of course, this badge is awarded or "enjoyed" only by those members of the gay community who are willing or able to present their relationships within a logic of respectability. The work that badge does in redeeming the social reputation of "good gays" depends on a contrast with "bad gays" who don't want to marry or discipline their sexual selves into a tidy couple form.

How has this been possible? How has the gay community been so successful in deploying marriage to remake its public reputation so convincingly?

First of all, the team for marriage equality has been enormously successful in shaping their struggle as essentially conservative in nature. They don't seek to destroy marriage or to radicalize it, they have insisted, but rather aim to fold same-sex couples into the institution on its own terms. The claim for marriage rights for same-sex couples offers a stunning lesson in how a social justice movement has effectively and relatively swiftly transformed the perception of its agenda from radical and beyond the pale to essentially traditional in nature.

When the conservatives sign up for marriage equality, they do so because it dawns on them that their interests in traditional family values, in the nuclear family, in privatizing dependency, and in bourgeois respectability are stronger than their homophobia. As marriage equality advocates make the plausible case that they share with conservatives the same basic values about marriage, conservatives come around to seeing same-sex couples who wanted to marry as "just like us," or enough like us to recognize a shared identity. "My brother is gay and I know what he goes through and went through when he was younger. I don't see the problem with gay marriage. They are just like us but they like the [same] sex. That's no problem," writes a straight ally of the gay community in an on-line debate on marriage rights for same-sex couples.[22] Country western singer Dolly Parton took the comparison one step further when she quipped, "I think gay couples should be allowed to marry. They should suffer just like us heterosexuals."[23]

But if the "just like us" argument is what made a significant difference in turning the marriage equality argument into such a raging success, then why hasn't a similar argument worked for African Americans? They are just as able to deploy a narrative of traditional, family values as the gay community—perhaps even more so. In fact, the peculiar American commitment to a notion of racial equality grounded in the idea of "color-blindness" is, in significant respects, another version of the "just like us" claim made by gays and lesbians. It posits that skin color should be irrelevant in determining a person's worth and that we all share a basic humanity and dignity that should not be inflected or diminished by considerations of race or color.

Yet the argument from color-blindness has never been effective in diminishing indelible notions of difference and inferiority for African Americans. It certainly hasn't worked to remove a badge of inferiority for people of color in the way the appeal to a shared traditional notion of marriage and "just like us" arguments have functioned in the marriage equality cases.

Here we might note the unanticipated up side of not having gained "suspect class" status in U.S. constitutional jurisprudence. The odor of suspicion that underlies this most exacting of constitutional rules—a rule that requires the state to come forward with an exceedingly important justification for any classification deemed suspect in nature—is ostensibly aimed at the (il)legitimacy of the state's action. Yet it may also be the case that a form of suspicion is cast upon those classes of people intended to be protected by heightened scrutiny. In this curious way, the enjoyment of suspect class status may afford people of color heightened constitutional protection while also reinscribing an indelible identity as different and, tragically, as suspect in that difference.

Gay rights advocates have long argued that homosexuals are entitled to suspect class status on a par with classifications based on race, yet most courts have rejected this equivalence, preferring instead to analyze sexual orientation–based discrimination according to a lower level of scrutiny. Some legal commentators have criticized the courts' unwillingness to regard sexual orientation–based classifications with the same degree of suspicion as race-based classifications. Yet the lower constitutional status enjoyed by LGBT people may reflect something deeper and, ultimately, more beneficial to the cause for gay rights: a conception of gayness that is, in the end, more indelible than race.

Even more, it's worth noting that the successes of the marriage equality movement may have been won precisely because of the negative reputation African Americans suffer when it comes to marriage. The racial endowment as white from which the marriage equality movement has benefited (even if not grounded in reality, since many of the members of the LGBT community who sought marriage rights were people of color) surely helped conservatives courts, legislators, and others come to see an affinity of interest with this cause.

When the lawyers and clients in the gay marriage cases stand on the steps of the Supreme Court after arguing their case for marriage equality, all, or nearly all, of them are white. When the *New York Times* published a piece in fall 2014 by Adam Liptak, its chief reporter on the Supreme Court, speculating about which of the several competing same-sex marriage cases are likely to be taken up by the Supreme Court, the *Times* ran a photo to capture this horserace in the gay community. It featured three photographs, one of Ted Olson and the two male plaintiffs in "his" case, Paul Katami and Jeff Zarrillo; one of Jeffrey L. Fisher, the lawyer in the Oklahoma marriage case; and one of Roberta Kaplan, the lawyer in the Utah case who also argued the case for Edie Windsor in the Supreme Court in 2013. All of these people are white.[24] The heads of the biggest gay rights organizations—Lambda Legal, the Human Rights Campaign, the ACLU Lesbian Gay Bisexual & Transgender Project, the National Gay and Lesbian Task Force, the National Center for Lesbian Rights— are all white. Organizations in the LGBT community that have elevated people of color into leadership tend to be more grassroots oriented, and have not prioritized marriage equality to the same degree as the "Big Gay" shops, if they have prioritized it at all.

For this reason, it's not surprising that "gay marriage" is publicly perceived to be a white issue. As Kenyon Farrow writes, "in order to be mainstream in America, one has to be seen as white."[25] "Being seen as white" is a task the marriage equality movement could pull off, while African Americans, by definition, just can't.

Rightly or wrongly, homosexuality in general and the marriage equality movement specifically enjoy a kind of racial privilege that has underwritten the plausibility of this positive transformation in the meaning of gay identity. Here, as elsewhere, the project of identifying with another group, of seeing a shared sameness, is accomplished on the level not only of acknowledging a shared identity but also of recognizing a shared sense of what you are not. As a result, identities are constituted through, not outside, difference. When judges, policymakers, or the media are persuaded that same-sex couples are sufficiently similar to different-sex couples when it comes to marriage, that recognition of shared identity is premised upon the specter of a constitutive outsider that gay couples are *not* like. And what they are not like is African Americans (even though, of course, many lesbians and gay men *are* African American).

This is what we see at work when the marriage equality movement enjoyed unimagined success at the same time that the Family Leader, a right-wing policy and lobbying organization, injected a racialized form of "family values" into the 2012 presidential campaign. The Family Leader challenged candidates running for public office to endorse a "marriage vow" that included a promise that signers "solemnly vow to honor and cherish, to defend and uphold the institution of marriage as only between one man and one woman"; to remain faithful to their spouses; to oppose any "redefinition" of marriage, such as that between same-sex couples; and to embrace a federal marriage amendment to the U.S. Constitution.[26] The "marriage vow" went further and advanced the idea that black people were better able to maintain stable, two-parent households when they were enslaved than they are today.[27]

A conservative agenda that demonized unmarried African American mothers as "welfare queens" and disparaged African American fathers as deadbeats is not undermined, and indeed might be furthered, by supporting marriage rights for same-sex couples. At the same time, the claims of same-sex couples to marriage rights are enhanced to the degree that they can differentiate themselves from dysfunctional, broken families. Of course, none of the advocates for marriage equality have argued this dissimilarity by explicitly referring to African American families. But they don't need to, as that work is being done more than competently by groups such as the Family Leader and their ilk. But, in many ways, that work is already part of the historical framing of and ongoing moral imagination about marriage in the United States. A conception of marriage as the pinnacle of mature personhood and mutual responsibility is so saturated with racial and gender stereotypes that some things do not even have to be said to convey the feeling of truth and obviousness.

One of the challenges for the supporters of the marriage equality movement is to appreciate the costs to others of same-sex couples gaining rights in this context. This entails careful consideration of the negative externalities of certain arguments being made in the gay marriage cases, and attention to minimizing those externalized costs. Appeals to dignity, respectability, and the virtues of marriage figure prominently in the inventory of arguments that are likely to offload stigma from gay couples to their constitutive outside, African American families most prominently.

* * *

One lesson we can draw from the early experience of same-sex couples with the right to marry is that marriage may not be for all of us. While we might all support the repeal of an exclusion from marriage as a matter of basic constitutional fairness, we need not all jump into marriage to demonstrate our new rights-bearing identity. Perhaps we ought to slow down, take a breath, and evaluate whether marriage is "for us."

Yet, for some members of the lesbian and gay community, the financial and legal advantages of marriage are too compelling. I have a platform of action for the "nose-holding" pragmatists who marry to protect their legal and economic interests but do so "under protest"; who bear the weight of a new kind of dual consciousness and get married, but do so ambivalently; and who suffer a guilty queer conscience, with their queer tails between their legs. Most of my friends and colleagues find themselves in this situation. They promise to keep up their critiques of marriage and their defense of nonmarital forms of family even though they're getting married. They all have good economic or legal reasons to get married. And they insist that they have not surrendered their critique of marriage—it's just that their lawyers or financial advisors convinced them that it is foolish not to avail themselves of the advantages of marriage now that they are available. Or maybe their employers told them they had to marry or else their partners would be kicked off the health plan.

Without minimizing the importance of these reasons to marry, I find that too often the promises these folks make to keep up their critiques of marriage are just empty words that soothe a guilty conscience. To them I issue a challenge: that *you*, even more than those of us who aren't marrying, need to make real your promise of progressive engagement with marriage from its inside. It will not only assuage your guilt; it will make those who aren't marrying less resentful, and most importantly, you will make a real difference.

I have eight important things you can, you should, and you must do to make your ongoing commitment to a critique of marriage real. All of them will help nurture queer counterpublics in the era of same-sex marriage.

## A Progressive Call to Action on Marriage in the Era of Marriage Equality

1. Defend against the repeal of domestic partner benefits programs (for both same- and different-sex couples) at the same time that you advocate for marriage rights.

2. Refuse to give your support to marriage equality laws that surrender other rights in the name of religion. Many statutes granting marriage rights to same-sex couples include gaping religious-exemption clauses that create a new kind of license to discriminate against same-sex couples in the name of religion. Some advocates lobbying for marriage equality have seen this bargain as worth making. New York's law has a truck-size religious exemption in its 2011 "Marriage Equality Act."[28] Resist the urge to make this bargain. The more we accede to the legitimacy of religion-based exemptions to civil rights laws, the more acceptable and common they will be—not only as a tactic to undermine the right of same-sex couples to marry but as a means to attack reproductive-rights and racial-equality laws as well.[29]

3. Think hard about the degree to which you are expecting to have it all when you marry on terms that work best for you, but in so doing may sacrifice important advances in gender equality for others. When you ask your lawyer to draft a prenuptial agreement that exempts your relationship from all of the default rules of marriage, consider first why those rules exist and how the enforcement of your marriage contract may have negative spill-over effects for others—particularly women—who may not enjoy equal bargaining power when entering a marriage.

4. Cease defending arguments in support of marriage rights for same-sex couples that (1) turn on the dignity that marriage confers to qualifying couples, (2) turn on the benefits to children of having two parents who are married, and (3) advertently or inadvertently make it easier to disparage nonmarital and nonreproductive sexual activity. While it may be tempting to pitch these arguments to judges and policymakers to gain ground for the cause of marriage equality, these positions gain credibility for the cause largely by

reinforcing the stigma suffered by other people whose identities and behaviors don't look marital in form.

5. Pledge to think about how strategies to fight homophobia might be linked to other causes, such as antiracist organizing or defending reproductive rights. That harder thinking ought to include a sensitivity to the ways in which the same-sex-marriage movement has been the beneficiary of a racial endowment, and how some arguments made in furtherance of marriage equality may have amplified the ways in which marriage has not been a liberating experience for many people of color. Similarly, that hard thinking must include a sensitivity to the intersection of interests between the gay rights movement and the reproductive rights movement.

6. Resist defending arguments in support of marriage rights that rest on a negative judgment toward paying taxes. While it is unfair for same-sex couples to be taxed differently and more highly than different-sex couples (particularly when it comes to estate taxes), a progressive agenda should embrace the payment of taxes, estate taxes in particular. Too often the arguments made in favor of marriage equality echo a kind of Tea Party cynicism toward paying taxes. Commit to a progressive queer critique of the state *and* of the private accumulation of property and wealth by abandoning and repudiating any antitax ethos haunting some corners of the same-sex marriage movement.

7. Calculate the tax benefits you receive from being married, including estate taxes, and rather than pocketing it, give the money away to a worthy cause.

8. Think about what it means to gain an economic advantage through marriage, passing money tax-free to "preferred relatives" such as spouses rather than to the broader kin networks so prevalent in the lesbian and gay community. Find other creative ways to support the needs of our extended kin/family *even if* the state does not recognize them as "family" and there is no tax benefit for doing so.

NOTES

A version of this chapter appears in the book *Wed-Locked: The Perils of Marriage Equality* (New York: New York University Press, 2015).

1 See Katherine Franke, "Becoming a Citizen: Post-Bellum Regulation of African American Marriage," 11 *Yale Journal of Law & the Humanities* 251 (1999).

2 While Prop 8 was found by a federal judge in 2010 to violate the constitutional rights of gay people, *see* Perry v. Schwarzenegger, 704 F.Supp.2d 921 (N.D.Cal. 2010), its passage through a popular vote in 2008 illustrates a troubling fact surrounding many of the victories for marriage equality: In many cases the courts (both state and federal) were out ahead of the majority of the people on the question of same-sex couples' entitlement to marriage rights. Accordingly, the case for same-sex marriage illustrates well the "countermajoritarian difficulty" inherent in a social movement that relies heavily on courts to bring about change that the majority of the people have not yet embraced. For an early elaboration of the idea of a "countermajoritarian difficulty" see Alexander Bickel, *The Least Dangerous Branch: The Supreme Court at the Bar of Politics* (New Haven, CT: Yale University Press, 1986), pp. 16–22.

3 National Conference of State Legislatures, *Defining Marriage: State Defense of Marriage Laws and Same-Sex Marriage*, http://www.ncsl.org/research/human-services/same-sex-marriage-overview.aspx, accessed April 2015; Moritz College of Law, *Research Guides: Same-Sex Marriage Laws*, http://moritzlaw.osu.edu/library/samesexmarriagelaws.php, accessed April 2015.

4 "Southern Baptist President Fred Luter Links Gay Marriage to North Korean Threats," *On Top Magazine*, April 1, 2013, http://www.ontopmag.com/article.aspx?id=14839&MediaType=1&Category=26#, accessed April 2015.

5 Available at http://www.youtube.com/watch?v=U-ET9p-haBs, accessed April 2015.

6 Andy Towle, "MS Lawmaker Andy Gipson Says Gays Spread Disease, Suggest They Should Be Put to Death," *Towleroad Blog*, May 18, 2012, http://www.towleroad.com/2012/05/ms-lawmaker-andy-gipson-says-gays-spread-disease-suggest-they-should-be-put-to-death.html, accessed April 2015.

7 S.C. Code Ann. §§ 20-1-10 & 15 (Law. Co-op. Supp. 2004).

8 Tobias Barrington Wolff, "Interest Analysis in Interjurisdictional Marriage Disputes," 153 *University of Pennsylvania Law Review* 2215 (2005).

9 David Murray, "Church Discusses Gay Parishioners," *Great Falls Tribune*, September 21, 2014; David Murray, "Gay Montana Couple Responds to Controversy," *Great Falls Tribune*, September 25, 2014; Frank Bruni, "'I Do' Means You're Done," *New York Times*, September 23, 2014.

10 Wolff, "Interest Analysis in Interjurisdictional Marriage Disputes," p. 2227.

11 Miller v. Jenkins, 912 A.2d 951 (2006), cert. denied, 131 S.Ct. 568 (2010).

12 Sheryl Gay Stolberg, "Republicans Sign Brief in Support of Gay Marriage," *New York Times*, February, 26, 2013; Cary Franklin, "Marrying Liberty and Equality: The New Jurisprudence of Gay Rights," 100 *Virginia Law Review* 817, 820–23 (2014).

13 *Brief for Kenneth B. Mehlman et al. as Amici Curiae Supporting Respondents* at 2–3, Hollingsworth v. Perry, 133 S. Ct. 2652 (2013) (No. 12–144).

14 Sheryl Gay Stolberg, "Obama's Views on Gay Marriage 'Evolving,'" *New York Times*, June 18, 2011.

15  Hollingsworth v. Perry, *Brief for Respondents on Writ of Certiorari to the United States Court of Appeals for the Ninth Circuit*, http://www.afer.org/wp-content/uploads/2013/02/2013-02-21-Plaintiffs-Brief.pdf, accessed April 2015. The ACLU attorney challenging Oregon's ban on same-sex marriage similarly invoked "a badge of inferiority" as the injury of exclusion from marriage: "Oregon's Marriage Equality Lawsuit: Attorneys Argue Marriage Ban Is Unconstitutional," *Love: Oregon United for Marriage*, April 23, 2014, http://www.oregonunitedformarriage.org/oregons-marriage-equality-lawsuit-attorneys-argue-marriage-ban-is-unconstitutional/, accessed April 2015.

16  "Letter from Dale Carpenter et al. to Illinois Legislature on Same-Sex Marriage," *Chicago Tribune*, October 23, 2013, available at http://blogs.chicagotribune.com/files/five-law-professors-against-changing-sb-10.pdf, accessed April 2015.

17  Langston Hughes, "Silhouette," in *Selected Poems of Langston Hughes* (New York: Knopf Doubleday, 1990), p. 171.

18  Franz Fanon, *Black Skin, White Masks* (London: Pluto Press, 1986), p. 91.

19  Fanon, *Black Skin*, p. 95.

20  Perry v. Schwarzenegger, *Pretrial Proceedings and Trial Evidence Credibility Determinations Findings of Fact Conclusions of Law Order*, 704 F.Supp.2d 921, 974, 980 (N.D.Cal. 2010).

21  Varnum v. Brien, *Ruling on Plaintiffs' and Defendant's Motions for Summary Judgment*, 2007 WL 2468667 (Iowa Dist.) (Trial Order)(2007).

22  "Should Gay Marriage Be Legalized?" *Debate.org*, http://www.debate.org/opinions/should-gay-marriage-be-legalized, accessed September 2015.

23  Sarah Muller, "Dolly Parton: Gays 'Should Suffer Just Like Us Heterosexuals,'" *MSNBC.com*, May 1, 2014, accessed August 2015.

24  Adam Liptak, "Seeking a Same-Sex Marriage Case Fit for History," *New York Times*, September 22, 2014, p. A19.

25  Kenyon Farrow, "Is Gay Marriage Anti-Black?" June 14, 2005, available at http://kenyonfarrow.com/2005/06/14/is-gay-marriage-anti-black/, accessed April 2015.

26  "Marriage Vow: A Declaration of Dependence upon Marriage and Family," *Family Leader*, http://www.thefamilyleader.com/wp-content/uploads/2011/07/themarriagevow.final_.7.7.111.pdf, accessed April 2015.

27  "Slavery had a disastrous effect upon African-American families, yet sadly a child born into slavery in 1860 was more likely to be raised by his mother and father in a two-parent household than was an African-American baby born after the election of the USA's first African-American president." "Marriage Vow: A Declaration of Dependence upon Marriage and Family."

28  See the amendment adding a broad religious exemption to the New York marriage equality bill, http://www.governor.ny.gov/assets/GPB_24_MARRIAGE_EQUALITY_BILL.pdf, accessed April 2015.

29  See the work of the Public Rights/Private Conscience Project here: http://web.law.columbia.edu/gender-sexuality/public-rights-private-conscience-project, accessed April 2015.

PART III

Post–Marriage Equality in Other Nations

# 10

## Canadian LGBT Politics after Marriage

DAVID RAYSIDE

In the long protest wave that swept across Europe and North America in the 1960s, few activist movements can claim as great an impact on public policy and popular beliefs as advocates fighting against the social and political marginalization of sexual minorities. This is particularly true in Canada, where the lesbian, gay, bisexual, transgender movement secured major gains from the mid-1980s onward. Although I do not claim that the LGBT movement has eliminated inequity and prejudice based on sexual difference, or that all observers agree on how much has been won, the Canadian case raises important questions about what happens to social movements when they score major policy victories and shift popular beliefs significantly toward acceptance.

In 1960s Canada, sexual minorities labored under a regime that criminalized male homosexuality and extended no rights to anyone on the basis of sexual orientation or gender identity.[1] Public disapproval of homosexuality was intense and widespread.[2] Politicians and the media treated gay men and lesbians as pariahs dangerous to public order, and especially to children. Half a century later, a great deal has changed.

In mid-2003, an Ontario appeal court declared that the longstanding common law exclusion of same-sex couples from civil marriage was unconstitutional (*Halpern v. Canada*).[3] This had the immediate effect of opening up gay marriage to anyone who could travel to Ontario, from anywhere in the world. Through its ruling, the court created the world's first fully equitable marriage right, without the limitations on parenting that had been encoded in statutory changes introduced slightly earlier in the Netherlands and Belgium. Courts in other Canadian provinces had already been moving in that direction, but others soon followed in giving immediate effect to similar rulings. Within two years, the federal Parliament had passed legislation explicitly opening up marriage to same-sex couples, and by the end of 2006, a new Conservative government made it clear that the issue was settled.

Decades of advocacy have also resulted in massive shifts in public opinion, more perhaps than in any policy area. In response to survey questions asking for expressions of personal views of homosexuality, the percentage of Canadians who "disapproved" plummeted from 55 percent in 1987 to 15 percent in 2013.[4] Support for same-sex marriage increased dramatically over a short five-year period from 34 percent in 1996 to 68 percent in 2010.[5] While this was happening, Toronto, Montreal, and Vancouver were building reputations as among the most LGBT-friendly cities in the world.

These enormous changes provide a very particular opportunity to reflect on the impact of significant gains on the political and strategic character of the LGBT movement in Canada. Hidden behind this lies the "prior" question of the extent to which the struggle over relational and family rights, and marriage in particular, had itself reshaped or dominated the overall Canadian movement.

The first stage of responding to such questions is to consider whether activism has declined, losing energy as a result of complacency and (over a longer period) a preoccupation with mainstream "normalization." In fact, there are indications of movement decline, especially in the capacity of advocacy groups to mobilize grassroots activism on a large scale. That said, any analysis of such evolution has to consider the life cycles typically experienced by social movements and the groups comprising them, and in particular the difficulty of sustaining volunteer-based groups over long periods. Account must also be taken of the diffusion of the Canadian movement, and the increasing proportion of LGBT advocacy embedded in largely disconnected institutional settings.

The second stage of considering the impact of "success" on the LGBT movement is to explore the extent to which issues other than relationship recognition have gained higher priority, and here the focus of the analysis is on gauging changes on the ground rather than on what some critics of the movement would wish to see. What we find is increased attention to a variety of issues, schooling being a prime example. We also find more voice being assumed by sexual-minority communities historically on the margins of the movement, including trans people and LGBT members of the large diasporic communities in Canada's major cities. In addition, in the years since winning marriage equality, the movement is grappling with a wide range of competing rights claims on sexual and religious grounds, some familiar and others new. And finally, increasing attention is being paid to the challenges facing sexual minorities in other regions of the world. Such issues were already rising in prominence during the years of battle over family rights, and indeed the campaign for marriage never dominated the overall activist agenda in the way it has in the United States and in some parts of Europe and Latin America. Since the mid-2000s such issues have increased in profile, more so as the expanded rights regime starkly exposed those instances where only modest change had been effected.

## The Advocacy Context

There are distinctive features to the Canadian landscape that have shaped the organizational character of the LGBT movement, and the extent to which it was focused on marriage. The first logical step here, though, is to clarify what is meant here by a social movement. The essential characteristics are issue breadth and structural range. Movements are made of clusters of staffed and purely voluntary organizations, informal networks, advocacy groups within allied institutions, and committees lobbying for change in their workplaces.[6] They are often strongest at the local level, some parts focused on cultural or social activity, other parts on political change. Some groups and individuals are opposed to working inside large existing institutions representing (for them) the status quo, and others are ready to work with and within such institutions. Some have radically transformative agendas; others do not. Some focus on direct action, others on the strategies more commonly associated with the mainstream. This variety is inherent in all activist movements, though the balance of approaches and structural "forms" in the Canadian movement has been shaped by the passage of time and the gains it has made.

### The Comparatively Low Profile of Marriage within the LGBT Movement

In Canada, the issue of same-sex marriage had only a comparatively brief period in the advocacy spotlight, and even in that period it did not dominate the movement's agenda as much as has been true in the United States. It is true, as Paul Gallant has argued, that from 2003 until 2006, the issue was the top priority of the national group Egale Canada, which brought together those who sought the respectability of fitting in, straight allies who sympathized with the argument that exclusion created second-class relationships, and more experienced LGBT activists who may have questioned the very institution of marriage but who recognized that this was a rights battle that had to be won.[7]

However, before same-sex couples gained the right to marry, the vast majority of the rights and responsibilities associated with marriage in Canada had been extended to cohabiting couples (with varying minimum durations in the conjugal relationship).[8] In fact, the movement for legal and policy recognition of lesbian and gay couples was long focused, not on marriage but on extending to lesbian and gay couples the substantial rights and obligations already secured by heterosexual common law couples. Major gains on this front were registered through the 1990s, culminating in a 1999 ruling by the Supreme Court of Canada (*M. v. H.*) declaring that discrimination against same-sex couples in family law was unconstitutional.[9] In the meantime, courts had been ruling that denying parental rights to lesbian and gay couples was also unconstitutional, an issue that would dog activists in most U.S. states and almost all countries in otherwise progressive Europe for some years to come.

As a result of these gains in substantive "recognition," it was only at the end of the 1990s that the exclusion from full marriage rights loomed large. Even then, advocacy at first was focused entirely on the pursuit of court challenges in various provinces, including Quebec, Ontario, and British Columbia. Until the Ontario court ruling of 2003, therefore, the campaign was comparatively low key. Gallant is right that the Ontario victory led to large-scale mobilization among religious conservatives, and the LGBT activist movement then had more capacity to build resources and profile.[10] However, even during the peak of that struggle, there were many community members who believed it inevitable that the courts would prevent any serious political backsliding, so the campaign did not permeate overall community advocacy in the same way that it has, for example, in the United States.

## The Lack of Central Dominance in Canada's LGBT Movement

The geographic size of the country, the strong sense of regional identity in parts of it, the need for groups claiming a cross-country mandate to operate in two languages, and the extent of governmental decentralization all conspire to reduce the prominence of groups claiming such a cross-Canada profile. This means that Egale's place in the broader movement is less influential than the Human Rights Campaign and the National Gay and Lesbian Task Force in the United States, Stonewall in Britain, COC in the Netherlands, or the Federación Argentina LGBT.

Even more than in most other countries, then, LGBT politics in Canada have always been dominated by local or regional groups and networks. The overwhelming majority of such groups supported the campaign for marriage once it was so opposed by the Religious Right, though often without intervening actively in the struggle. However, that support and the resources mobilized by the fight for marriage equality did not necessarily hamper those groups in the pursuit of their unique agendas. To argue this would imply a zero-sum view of social movement energy, and that the gains made by one group or around one issue take away from others. The "steamrolling" view that a crisis or intense struggle over one issue area can push other issues to the side has had some plausibility at times during the evolution of the movement, for example, during the middle and late 1980s when the AIDS crisis loomed so large, but that phenomenon was not so obviously at play in relation to marriage.

## The Question of Movement Decline

Has success led to a diminished movement? Here we confront two major arguments. One is that success produces complacency. The second argument is that the movement has weakened itself by narrowing its focus to "normalizing" issues like marriage.

### Victory Breeds Complacency

The complacency argument has two closely related parts. The first is that major gains in public policy, institutional practice, and public opinion all too easily generate among LGBT people and their supporters a belief that advocacy is no longer necessary. This source of potential movement decline seems on the face of it to have particular relevance in the Canadian case, because of the breadth and speed of change on a variety of legal and policy fronts and over a relatively short period. The same is true of changes in public beliefs about homosexuality (more than gender identity), with sea changes occurring among younger people, including younger religious conservatives.[11]

The second part of the argument, very much related to the first, is that activist solidarity and mobilizational capacity can be weakened by real or perceived declines in the political influence of opponents—in this case the Religious Right. This too seems to have particular relevance to Canada, where the Religious Right, in the years since marriage equality was won, has been widely perceived as a spent force, at least in its pursuit of an antigay agenda. Religious conservatives were already a pale shadow of their American counterparts, but still able to mobilize on an impressive scale, and thereby energize pro-equity activism.[12] Even if many people in LGBT communities and their allies were unconvinced that changes to human rights codes and marriage laws would be transformative of their lives, they recognized that the seizure of these issues by moral conservatives made them effectively a referendum on the very idea of recognizing sexual diversity. The level of activist mobilization possible in such circumstances is difficult to sustain if the principal source of opposition is seen to be much weaker. Some observers disagree that the Religious Right is significantly weaker, most notably Marci McDonald, who maintains that evangelical Protestants still wield considerable political influence, but my view is more in line with those of Jonathan Malloy in seeing mobilization around same-sex marriage as the peak of the Religious Right's ability to marshal mass movement resources.[13] More importantly, I would argue that much of the leadership of the Canadian Religious Right sees campaigning on major LGBT issues as a lost cause, and that conservative parties at the federal and provincial levels are increasingly reluctant to play antigay cards by promising to roll back the clock on sexual-minority rights.[14] Crucially, many LGBT activists see the Religious Right as weaker than it was.

The changes in law and policy that have been secured by LGBT advocates in Canada also eliminate many of the starkest examples of official policy discrimination against sexual minorities, either in employment or in access to the public recognition of same-sex relationships. Issues like marriage were in some sense simple to understand for a wide set of LGBT constituencies and allies.[15] Many of the issues that remain unaddressed or that have arisen more prominently since marriage was won, on the other hand, entail more complex sources of marginalization, entailing a more diffuse or multidimensional activist agenda. For example, addressing LGBT Aboriginal issues necessarily requires engaging the Gordian knot of Aboriginal poverty and marginalization. The inclusion of diasporic communities requires attending to the difficulties faced by new waves of immigrants in securing employment, and to the care needed in addressing religiously based condemnation of sexual difference in socially marginalized communities. The challenge here is that multidimensional or ambitious agendas can pose challenges in securing consensus among existing and potential LGBT supporters, and in generating the kind of optimism that fuels the involvement of so many potential activists.

Does the evidence support these arguments about complacency? Egale Canada appears to have had significantly less community fundraising capacity since the end of the marriage struggle.[16] The 2009 dissolution of the Coalition for Lesbian and Gay Rights in Ontario (CLGRO), at the time the only multi-issue group claiming a province-wide mandate in Canada's largest province, was in part a result of the broader movement's gains. This is also part of the reason why its successor, Queer Ontario, has had difficulty retaining a public profile. Quebec is a partial exception, to some extent because of access to government grants, but in the rest of the country, where provincial-level organizations in Canada have had to depend largely or entirely on volunteers, such groups have had difficulty sustaining political presence, born in some measure of the absence of single unifying issues embroiled in contention with forceful opponents.

The complacency argument, however, is problematic in part because significant mainstream gains for LGBT advocates have in theory as much potential to energize as to deflate. Earlier successes in basic human rights, for example, created a "platform" of legitimacy on the basis of which additional campaigning resources could be mobilized. In fact, gains in policy and in public opinion can be used to focus attention on areas in which little or no change has occurred.[17] As we shall see, new issues were arising even before marriage rights were won, and new sites of advocacy have been continuously generated over many years, including the last decade.

One difficulty in taking the current pulse of the overall LGBT movement is that social movement groups often go through what might be termed an "energy" cycle, regardless of success or failure. Social movements as a whole rise and fall as part of "long waves" of contention, and that also applies to individual groups.[18] Organizational decline or exhaustion is especially likely for groups that depend primarily on volunteers and informal operational processes, difficult to sustain beyond moments of crisis or intense confrontation with opponents. The maintenance of activist energies is also difficult for groups with transformative goals requiring long-term devotion, and those opting for forms of direct action that entail recurrent mass mobilization. In each of these cases, the radicalism of a group's appeal can also narrow the size of the supportive constituency.

Those groups with a capacity to institutionalize or an ability to secure resources for maintaining a permanent staff are often able to extend their lives, and such groups could, in the right circumstances of contention, build or retain a capacity to mobilize large numbers of followers. Institutionalized or volunteer-based groups taking up specific issues that are widely understood to require continuing advocacy, or that mobilize especially marginalized LGBT communities, may still have opportunities for generating activist energy, particularly if the issues are widely understood, and at least some remedies widely agreed upon. The Canadian movement, always a decentralized one, has proliferated more than ever into specialized groups, often working in settings (institutional and geographic) quite separated from one another. We will return to this point.

### The Role of Mainstream Normalization in Narrowing Agendas and Desiccating Grass Roots

There is a longstanding critique of the LGBT movement's preoccupation with marriage that is linked to a broader analytical warning about the "normalization" of LGBT politics. Associated with this argument is the claim that governmental shifts toward neoliberal agendas have intensified the draw toward the respectable politics of the mainstream.

The normalization argument is usually framed as driven in significant measure by "internal" choices of LGBT leadership to prioritize formal legal rights and the entry of LGBT claimants into existing social and political institutions. This view is found in the widely cited work of Michael Warner and Urvashi Vaid.[19] It is also evident in Canadian writing by Gary Kinsman, Tom Warner, and Peter Knegt.[20] In respect to marriage in particular, such authors point to a campaign focused on the respectability of rights claimants, the similarities between them and heterosexual couples, and the absence of threat this poses to the irretrievably traditional institution of marriage. All this, they argue, signals a shift of the LGBT movement away from transformative goals and toward assimilationism.

Writing about the American LGBT movement from the vantage point of wide-ranging experience within it, Vaid has criticized limitations that have become more evident as gains have accelerated.

> The LGBT movement has been coopted by the very institutions it once sought to transform. Heterosexuality, the nuclear family, the monogamous couple-form are our new normal. In place of activism and mobilization, with a handful of notable exceptions, LGBT mainstream organizations have become a passive society of spectators, following the lead of donors and pollsters rather than advocating on behalf of sectors of the community that are less economically powerful and politically popular.[21]

The mainstream movement, in her view, has increasingly worked in isolation rather than in coalition with other justice-seeking movements; it also marshals the energies of professionals and financial contributions from onlookers rather than nurturing genuine grassroots engagement. The logical extension of this argument is that the movement is vulnerable if the big ticket struggles around which it has mobilized end up in victory. It will have lost the kinds of networks and connections required to address remaining issues, including the inequalities within LGBT communities, leaving only those interest groups that can sustain themselves through "checkbook activism."

It is fair to say that LGBT advocacy in Canada has become more dominated by professionals, in an evolution that began as early as the 1980s but that was accelerating at the time when marriage rights were being secured. As opportunities opened up for advocacy within mainstream institutions, activists inevitably became enmeshed in processes that privileged those with the skills to work in those environments. Exercising influence within government departments, major parties, and courts requires not only expertise but also a willingness to play by rules not of advocacy groups' making. This is not as powerfully true in Canada as it is in the highly complex institutional environments of Washington, DC, and the capital cities of large U.S. states, but it is an important change in the character of the movement. Canadian LGBT advocacy has depended to a considerable extent on litigation, taking advantage of a Charter of Rights and Freedoms that, in the late 1980s and early 1990s, was being interpreted broadly, and this at a crucial time in LGBT mobilization. This pushed legal experts to the forefront of the movement as much as in the United States, and tied parts of the movement to long-lasting litigation that was not dependent on popular mobilization. There are limits on what can be demanded or claimed within almost all mainstream settings, including labor unions, large employers, major cultural organizations, and social service agencies, but no more so than in the courts. Preoccupation with working by existing rules and within what is widely perceived as politically or legally possible can all too easily dislodge group leaders from the broader constituencies being served.

There are also "external" pressures that may well increase the gap between professionals in the movement and the most marginalized of sexual minorities, and narrow the range of what is deemed politically realistic. Economic inequality in Canada has increased considerably since the 1970s, and is only slightly less than in the United States, maintaining substantial inequities within sexual-minority communities and in some cases exacerbating them.[22] This may well reinforce the de facto exclusion of many trans people from the workforce, the socioeconomic marginalization of Canadian Aboriginals, the youth homelessness in Canada's largest cities, and the disadvantage reproducing itself in some ethno-racial minorities.

Over the last four decades, there have been major shifts toward neoliberalism in the public policies of federal and provincial governments. This has intensified pressure on funds for nongovernmental organizations, and at the same time increased the challenges for social movement activists seeking to address all forms of socioeconomic inequity, including those among LGBT communities. As Miriam Smith argues, Canada has seen much downloading of social policy, first by the federal government to provinces and territories, and in turn by those governments to localities and private agencies.[23] This has sometimes translated into an increased demand for social services provided by LGBT community groups, but potentially at the cost of their advocacy, or of their delivery of programs not favored by government funding. In addition, the federal government's elimination of the Court Challenges Program, designed to assist groups and individuals in seeking remedies on issues related to constitutional rights, substantially reduces the capacity of groups to pursue litigation.

Do these "assimilationist" arguments, however, capture the full story of how the LGBT movement has been evolving in recent years? In fact, they do not. Access to government officials and funding is not as closed off as this view suggests, and it is overly dismissive to assert that government support is available to only the "safest" and most respectable of causes. Egale has been able to secure project-specific funding from a variety of provincial and territorial governments, for example, in its campaign on schooling, and has had some cooperative dealings over refugee issues with particular ministries in the otherwise antagonist Conservative government in Ottawa. An extraordinarily homophobic Toronto mayor, elected in 2011, was part of a city council group that threatened funding for Pride Toronto's huge annual parade and festival, but was unable to prevail. Some groups have been able to counter a reduction in government funding with corporate and individual fundraising, though there are admittedly major differences across groups and causes for which nongovernmental fundraising has worked.

In truth, a full analysis of whether these internal and external pressures have fundamentally weakened the LGBT movement in Canada has to address the extent to which issues apart from relationship recognition have been taken up forcibly by the LGBT movement. Our analysis must also take into account that Canada's always-fragmented LGBT movement has become more specialized than ever, with important sites of advocacy more isolated from one another than ever but still important in their own right.

## Issue Prominence after Marriage

Several issue areas have risen in prominence since the mid-2000s, including those affecting young people and the elderly, trans people, ethno-racial LGBT minorities, refugee claimants, and the condition of sexual minorities in non-Western regions of the globe. These were never entirely absent from Canadian activist agendas, and in a few cases, the intensity of advocacy attention grew significantly in the 1990s, but the success in the area of marriage equality, and in the broader family-rights agenda behind it, created more capacity for advocates to draw public (and media) attention to the laggardly progress on other fronts.

### Schooling and Queer Youth

Demands from sexual minorities and their allies that schools be more inclusive of sexual and gender diversity have become an LGBT movement priority since the mid-2000s. Up to that point, the legal and political advances on family issues and marriage in Canada did not translate into a significant change in school inclusiveness. This is not unique to Canada, since the persistence of exclusionary cultures in public (and private) schools is widespread in the most progressive of U.S. states, as well as in the Netherlands, Britain, and other European countries in which there have been important changes in public attitudes and public policy.[24]

There was isolated advocacy aimed at greater school inclusiveness from the early 1990s, first in Toronto and then in cities like Calgary and Winnipeg, though widespread embrace of schooling issues by activists was evident only later on, picking up intensity in the late 1990s, and even more so in the mid-2000s.[25] The core propulsion behind school-focused advocacy was quite independent of the marriage campaign, and its key activists were not particularly central to the family-rights campaign, not least because their focus was at first local and then provincial, rather than federal. From the late 1990s on, too, much activist energy came from teacher unions such as the British Columbia Teachers' Federation and the Elementary Teachers' Federation of Ontario, which were not particularly engaged in the fight over marriage. While this was happening, activist ranks were expanded as the children of same-sex couples were approaching school age.[26] In the 2000s, a significant increase in Egale's attention to issues of school inclusiveness was built on this legacy but was also a direct effect of marriage claims being won. A large survey that it spearheaded on school climate in the late 2000s added considerable cross-country visibility to the problems facing queer youth, and widened openings for change in education ministries and school boards.[27]

There are signs that the significant expansion of activist attention to schooling has been accompanied by attention to broader patterns of marginalization disproportionately affecting queer youth.[28] Their alarming numbers among the substantial ranks of the urban homeless has attracted the attention of youth advocacy groups and urban social service agencies, as well as groups like Queer Ontario and Egale. There are slim indications that this has attracted widespread interest in the broader LGBT population, but advocacy from within social service agencies, even in a period of governmental restraint, has the advantage of a stable organizational platform.

## Trans Inclusiveness

In Canada's three largest cities, Vancouver, Toronto, and Montreal, trans activism gained significant visibility in the mid-1990s, at the peak of activist mobilization on the family rights of same-sex couples. By this time, most provinces had explicitly included sexual orientation (not gender identity) in their human rights codes, and courts were ruling that discrimination based on sexual orientation was unconstitutional. The Canadian labor movement played a role in securing basic rights and relational recognition for lesbians and gay men, and by the end of that decade several of the largest unions were assertively pressing for the rights based on gender identity and expression.[29] The success of the campaign over marriage, in some ways "completing" the rights agenda for lesbians and gay men, further amplified claims from trans activists that they were being left behind. Egale itself became more substantively committed to trans issues, and workplace discrimintation was being pursued more assertively through formal grievances procedures and courts.

This doesn't necessarily mean that trans advocacy "took off" after the mid-1990s, or indeed after the struggle over marriage had passed, and there are real questions about how much activist energy is being marshaled from the very different segments of the trans population and from other parts of the LGBT movement. However, it can be said that the overall LGBT movement is significantly more prepared to include trans issues in their agendas than before, and media coverage (mostly sympathetic) has increased dramatically. There is no prominent national group of any permanence focusing on gender-identity issues, but the activist energy that has been mobilized has achieved some success. Gender identity was explicitly added to human rights codes in the Northwest Territories, Manitoba, Ontario, and Nova Scotia in the 2011–12 period, and human rights tribunals have extended their interpretation of other grounds to include gender identity and expression in British Columbia, Quebec, Alberta, Nova Scotia, Prince Edward Island, the Yukon Territory, and the federal arena.[30] Significant barriers to treatments for those seeking gender reassignment remain, as does prejudice, and hugely disproportionate levels of unemployment and poverty.[31]

### Workplace Advocacy beyond Formal Rights

Campaigning against workplace discrimination has been prominent in LGBT politics from the earliest years of the modern activist wave, and is an illustration of the kind of specialization in issue focus and sites of activism that often gets lost in overall claims about the movement.[32] Labor unions, and the LGBT caucuses working within them, played a vital role in securing basic rights for individuals and couples, through advocacy focused on workplace benefit packages. What is different in the "post–marriage equality" period is the increased emphasis on going beyond formal prohibitions on discrimination and aiming for more thoroughly inclusive work environments.

What sustains workplace activism in an era when so much in formal policy has been achieved, therefore, is an interest in pressing employers to treat the employment and promotion of LGBT people as a positive good. In some cases, this means adding sexual orientation and gender identity to affirmative action programs—in Canada, widely referred to as "employment equity" policy.[33] In other cases, this means pressing employers to support internal LGBT committees, promote community institutions (pride celebrations, educational programs, school initiatives, cultural events), and advertise their LGBT inclusivity to customers and the broader public. Labor unions, particularly in the public sector, remain prominent players in workplace-focused campaigns. LGBT employee groups in nonunionized settings have also joined in advocating more thoroughgoing employer engagement with sexual-diversity initiatives.

There are naturally specific work sectors in which activism is especially challenging, though here too the spotlight on "laggards" potentially increases with the acquisition of a full set of formal equity rights, culminating in marriage. The results here are mixed. Heavily male occupations such as policing, fire fighting, and other protective services have seen episodic activism, though with no obvious acceleration since the mid-2000s. There has been an increase in attention to the exclusionary cultures that prevail in male professional sports, highlighted by the occasional coming out of professional athletes in other countries as well as Canada, and by the work of groups like Outsports Toronto. Still, the exclusionary dreadfulness of most team sports environments, from high school on up to professional leagues, has not yet attained sustained visibility.

## Diasporic Communities and Immigration

Canada has one of the highest per capita rates of legal immigration in the world, and comparatively little in the way of partisan opposition to such rates.[34] Since the 1970s, much of that immigration has come from outside Europe, the foundation of earlier migratory waves, transforming the demographics of Canada's large cities. About half of the Greater Toronto area's population (and only slightly less of Greater Vancouver's) was born outside of the country, and Montreal, too, has a rapidly growing immigrant population.

Consciousness of ethno-cultural-racial diversity has come late to the Canadian LGBT movement, and there is a legitimate argument that insufficient attention is paid to questions of ethno-racial difference in groups claiming a broad mandate. One illustration is that the leading advocate "faces" of Canadian campaigns for relationship recognition and marriage were white, as they were in earlier campaigns against police attacks and in favor of individual rights.

Since the mid-2000s, though, there has been a notable increase in attention to immigration and refugee policy, and an expansion in the number and visibility of groups articulating the concerns of visible minorities. The spread of the AIDS epidemic had provided a significant incentive to organize in such communities, most prominently the Aboriginal, South Asian, Afro-Caribbean, and East Asian. Groups like the Black Coalition for AIDS Prevention, Asian Community AIDS Services, and the Alliance for South Asian AIDS Prevention, all in Toronto, were formed in the late 1980s. Their emergence built on earlier activism within those communities, though their AIDS focus also provided them access to government funding.

Since then, the growing numbers of openly LGBT members within minority communities, arguably emboldened by formal rights recognition, have created a critical mass essential for autonomous organizing, and for enhancing the prominence of ethno-cultural diversity. LGBT writers of color, and of Aboriginal background, have risen to considerable mainstream prominence in the last decade. Writers like Thomson Highway, Shyam Selvadurai, Shani Mootoo, Dione Brand, Wayson Choy, and the filmmaker Deepa Mehta, are now widely known far beyond LGBT publics. Some of these cultural producers align themselves with activism, but even those who do not participate in the movement directly contribute to a visibility that strengthens those particular communities and enhances overall awareness of "intersectionality."

### International Connections

The Canadian LGBT movement, aside from that focused on AIDS, has lagged behind a few European counterparts in its engagement with international networks and advocacy in other regions of the world. The size of Canada's diasporic communities, and the visibility of queer organizing within them, would have made a natural bridge to international work, and in some cases activist groups and individuals have forged their own transnational linkages. For well over a decade, too, union activists have developed networks with counterparts in other places, for example, through the international Workers Out conferences. Internationalization is also evident in legal networks and advocacy groups like Legit, working on Canadian immigration for same-sex partners, the Rainbow

Railroad, helping LGBT people in hazardous situations come to Canada, and the Iranian Railroad for Queer Refugees. The gradual strengthening of such advocacy began before the win on marriage, though the energy devoted by Egale to international work, including regular lobbying of federal officials on immigration and refugee policy, can certainly be attributed to the completion of its marriage work.[35]

## Challenges Facing the "Post–Marriage Equality" Movement

Activism that is based in large and stable institutional systems, such as the labor movement, is sustaining itself where there are sufficiently obvious inequities with a core of activist champions who are already union members (trans issues in the workplace, for example). Advocacy on school issues will continue to expand in part because increasing numbers of students and teacher unions have been supportive. LGBT litigation may well be harder to sustain with so many core human rights issues settled, but for issues still calling for legal challenge, it can be carried on in part by the contribution of lawyer time in firms with ample paying clients. AIDS activism will continue to be driven by the high proportion of LGBT cases among new infections in Canada, and sustained by the fundraising potential that remains in that sector and the availability of government funding for social service provision.

Activism in some other sectors is being sustained, or enhanced, by the ability of groups to raise money from governments or private donors. This is now true of a number of organizations in the cultural sector—LGBT film and theater festivals, pride celebrations, literary events, archival collections, and conferences—now able to garner corporate sponsorships. It is also true of some institutions providing social services, for example, in support of queer youth.

### Advocacy for the Marginalized

That said, groups that depend on LGBT community support have been experiencing difficulties. The well-established Egale has less fundraising capacity since the marriage fight, even with its highly visible campaigning on school issues. The group's leadership has also acknowledged the particular challenges in raising money for campaigning on the needs of the most marginalized segments of the LGBT community.[36] True, there is more local attention to LGBT youth homelessness than there has ever been, growing activism within ethno-racial minority communities, and an expansion of LGBT-related advocacy within Aboriginal communities.[37] But socioeconomic and ethno-racial inequality needs more attention from the movement, and the resources available for such work are often limited. The same could be said in relation to issues of aging in the LGBT population. The lack of recognition of sexual diversity in most institutions and services directed at the aged is not new, but the dramatic increase in numbers of LGBT elders who are "out" poses a challenge that is only beginning to be addressed.

Do gains in relational and marriage rights sharpen the distinctions between "respectable" and "assimilated" gays and lesbians on the one hand, and on other hand those who do not conform to traditional models of monogamous stability? There is a false dichotomy built into this question, of course, since those who have fought for marriage are not necessarily conformist, and those who actually get married do not necessarily fit their behavior to traditional heterosexual norms.

There is no question that stark inequities remain within LGBT communities. Prejudice against gender ambiguity or gender crossing runs deep, and it is not yet clear that the political and legal influence of Canada's LGBT movement, even in the realm of rights based on gender identity, has yet challenged the fundamentals of that prejudice. The overall reduction in the movement's capacity to mobilize grassroots energy is manifest most clearly when the needs of the most needy under the LGBT umbrella are at stake. It does not help those causes to point out that this is not a new phenomenon. Nevertheless, we need to avoid exaggerating the role of "normalizing" in explaining unmet needs. However large and deplorable the inequities, there is little evidence that LGBT movement successes have led to an intensification of scrutiny directed at those who do not fit the category of "respectable," or to a perpetuation of neglect.

## Movement Fragmentation

The overall make-up of Canada's LGBT movement has been altered by its success. Within many sexual-minority communities, and the larger public that has so often provided allies in the movement, complacency is a challenge. So too is the waning of activist energy that inevitably affects volunteer-driven groups. All this allows some groups to survive, others to prosper, and still others to decline. This combination of factors also contributes to the kind of activist specialization that has long been a feature of most LGBT movements, and perhaps especially the Canadian. Where once the advocacy landscape might have been dominated by multi-issue groups, over time their work is paralleled (and sometimes siphoned off) by other groups with more focused mandates. This evolutionary pattern is enhanced by political success and shifting public opinion, as well as by the opening up of new spaces in which advocacy can occur.

Such changes may actually mean that more people than ever are engaged in one or another form of advocacy, but often in groups or institutions isolated from one another. Especially with the gains in law and public policy since the early 1990s, groups armed with a wide-ranging mandate are more difficult to sustain, since there are fewer potential supporters prepared to believe that the environment they live in is comprehensively oppressive. The apparent weakness of the anti-LGBT opposition makes it harder for activists to rally support and broaden alliances.

In Canada particularly, these fragmenting tendencies are enhanced by the tendency for activism in one region to be isolated from that in others. This is most dramatically evident in the case of Quebec, where language differences and a strong sense of nationalist distinctiveness have weakened the already-limited links between activists there and those in other provinces. That sense of distinctiveness, however, is almost as great among British Columbian and Albertan activists, and across at least some parts of the Atlantic region. It was always difficult in Canada to talk of a cross-country LGBT movement, and it is significantly more so today.

## Complex Issues at the Intersection of Religion and Sexual Diversity

LGBT-rights claims have opened up a number of legal and policy questions related to the collision, or perceived conflict, between rights assertions based on sexual diversity and those based on religious faith.[38] At some level this is not new, since religious conservatives were regularly at the forefront of campaigns opposing LGBT rights. What has made a difference with the LGBT movement's rights gains is that a number of these areas of potential conflict have "crystallized" enough to land in appellate courts or in the laps of legislators. Among the issues raised in the process are the extent to which hate crimes legislation extends to antigay pronouncements based on scripture; the extent to which faith-based groups can discriminate in hiring and firing employees on the basis of sexual orientation, gender identity, and sexual practice; the lee-way granted to marriage commissioners and health workers in excluding themselves from performing some acts on conscience grounds; and the capacity of faith-based schools to exclude themselves from legislation aimed at recognizing sexual diversity. LGBT-activist groups, including Egale, have therefore had to respond to a growing number of cases launched either by religious groups or by LGBT activists themselves.

What can be complicated about this? One potential difficulty is that LGBT advocacy so long based on constitutional rights claims will be insufficiently sensitive to rights claims of others, including protections against religious discrimination that are important to a wide range of ethno-cultural communities. In cases in which homophobic and trans-phobic speech is attacked on the grounds that its hatefulness runs afoul of federal or provincial human rights codes, which seems on the face of it to be straightforward, there is also a risk that the leverage secured by the LGBT movement will be deployed in favor of what amounts to censorship—a tool once so commonly used against it. Writing about the American movement, Richard Kim worries about a tendency that he sees in this and other movements to build on success by "taking down" enemies.[39] That is no less a risk in Canada than in the United States.

When the conservative evangelical William Whatcott distributed fiercely antigay leaflets in Saskatchewan in the 1990s and early 2000s, a human rights complaint against him was widely (though not univer-sally) cheered. And when his 2005 conviction under the hate speech provisions of Saskatchewan's Human Rights Code was challenged in the Supreme Court of Canada, Egale intervened in defense of the earlier judgment. There were dissenting voices, to be sure, including the *Xtra* magazines in Toronto, Vancouver, and Ottawa, and the prominent con-stitutional law expert Brenda Cossman.[40] However, it is fair to estimate that most LGBT activists wanted Whatcott punished, and the compara-tively broad wording of the Saskatchewan statute upheld.

Another issue provoking similar response is the case of Trinity Western University, an evangelical university located in the Greater Vancouver area that required its students to adhere to a code of behavior that prohibited same-sex activity. After it created a teaching certification program in 1995, the British Columbia College of Teachers imposed a requirement that its graduates complete one additional year at another university before certification, a requirement widely supported among LGBT activists. TWU challenged this, and in 2001 the Supreme Court of Canada sided with them (*Trinity Western University v. British Columbia College of Teachers*), in part on the basis that no evidence had ever been introduced that graduates of TWU in fact discriminated against sexual minorities.[41]

The Whatcott and TWU cases raise complex questions. They appear simple to many, it seems, because the protagonists are predominantly white evangelicals, with whom LGBT advocates have good reason to retain bitter memories of past struggles. Even then, expectations that rights based on sexual orientation and gender identity be taken seriously require at least some care in the treatment of rights based on religion and conscience, even if a continuing wariness is required in confronting repeated attempts to unreasonably expand the reach of such rights.

The theoretical and legal issues evoked in such cases also affect the faith claims of some ethno-religious minorities, and this deserves reflection. In the Canadian case especially, faith is deeply entwined with multiculturalism, since religion plays such an important role for ethno-cultural minorities, and among recent immigrants in particular, as vehicles for cultural survival and social connection. Recent immigration waves have also substantially boosted the size of Canada's non-Christian religious minorities. Muslims now constitute more than 2 percent of the population, and the number of Hindus and Buddhists is increasing rapidly. The religiosity of minority faiths, and the Christianity of many ethno-cultural minorities, is not necessarily more conservative on questions of sexual diversity than the faith of most white Canadians. But it is the case that many first-generation migrants from regions of the world where sexual diversity is little recognized hold to comparatively traditional "family" views. This may be particularly true of Muslims, in part because of the recentness of their migration and their origins in countries that are especially oppressive of sexual minorities (rather than anything inherently related to Islam).[42] Claims based on demands for multicultural recognition are to some extent strengthened by a constitutionally entrenched commitment to multiculturalism, and of course by protections afforded to religious minorities. None of this suggests that the LGBT movement should relax its opposition to rights claims that use faith to mask prejudice, but it does suggest that treating religious claims with respect is more important than ever.

## Conclusion

Winning equal access to marriage was not transformative for Canada's LGBT movement, since that issue never completely dominated the advocacy landscape. However, success on marriage equality and on the broader set of family rights that had been an important focus for activism for twenty years did allow groups working on other issues to gain more visibility, and provided an incentive for the national group Egale to give more priority to issues like schooling and trans rights. The gains made in Canada also helped enhance interest in transnational networks, and provided a platform for a range of community groups in this country to expand connections to activists in more disadvantaged settings.

This survey of the Canadian movement has confronted questions about whether the "mainstreaming" of the LGBT movement, and its success, have undermined its capacity to mobilize on the exclusion and inequality that remain. There are no simple answers here. The dramatic gains made by LGBT activists in Canada have not comprehensively weakened the movement as a whole, and new issues have arisen that were previously underplayed. Securing recognition in law and institutional policy inevitably leaves many deep-seated inequities in place, but it does create a platform that can be used by LGBT advocates to shine spotlights on segments of the community still facing sexuality-based prejudice or socioeconomic hardship.

There are challenges in addressing such persistent disadvantage. Complacency has been a factor in widening the gap between forms of activism most able to secure financial and institutional resources and those that depend more completely on volunteer commitment or that speak to the concerns of the most marginalized in LGBT communities. As well, the capacity of social movement groups to address those communities least likely to benefit from equal formal rights is constrained in a political environment dominated by neoliberal frameworks. The movement appears, for now at least, to have lost some of its capacity to mobilize genuinely grassroots action, and the struggles to address the interests of those on the radical or nonconformist fringes of LGBT communities are often carried on by small groups with only sporadic visibility. As a whole, the movement may well not have the kind of "energy" that it has had at times of intense confrontation or crisis in the past.

All that said, the shifts in public acceptance of sexual diversity, and the rights platform created by gains in law and policy, may expand the political openings for change, and the overall legitimacy of activists demanding it. The movement as a whole remains a strikingly complex array of regionally differentiated political groups, social networks, individual advocates, and cultural producers, with many distinct sites of advocacy, operating within an extraordinary range of social and institutional settings. It exists inside labor unions, social service agencies, universities, high schools, corporate offices, law associations, government offices, ethno-racial minority groups, faith communities—all of these in addition to the LGBT-focused advocacy groups we traditionally associate with the movement. As an uncoordinated whole, with activism in one sector often isolated from activism in others, the movement's strengths and priorities are as difficult as ever to assess. That said, LGBT advocacy is still able to challenge stereotypes and press for the visibility of its many communities, and at its best for the well-being of the disadvantaged among them.

## NOTES

This chapter has benefited from conversations with various colleagues and activists, most notably Brenda Cossman, director of the Mark S. Bonham Centre for Sexual Diversity Studies at the University of Toronto and professor of law. Gerald Hunt also commented helpfully on an earlier draft of this manuscript, as did Audrey L'Espérence during a session at the annual meeting of the Canadian Political Science Association, May 2014.

1 Gary Kinsman, *The Regulation of Desire: Homo and Heterosexualities*, 2nd ed. (Toronto: Black Rose Books, 1996); Barry Adam, *The Rise of a Gay and Lesbian Movement*, rev. ed. (Boston: Twayne, 1987).

2 David Rayside and Scott Bowler, "Public Opinion and Gay Rights," 25 *Canadian Review of Sociology and Anthropology* 649 (1988).

3   *Halpern et al. v. Canada (Attorney General)*, [2003] O.J. No. 2268. For overviews of legal and policy change, see David Rayside, *Queer Inclusions, Continental Divisions: Public Recognition of Sexual Diversity in Canada and the United States* (Toronto: University of Toronto Press, 2008); Miriam Smith, *Lesbian and Gay Rights in Canada: Social Movements and Equality-Seeking, 1971–1995* (Toronto: University of Toronto Press, 1999).

4   The 1987 survey is reported in Amy Langstaff, "A Twenty-Year Survey of Canadian Attitudes towards Homosexuality and Gay Rights," in *Faith, Politics, and Sexual Diversity in Canada and the United States*, David Rayside and Clyde Wilcox, eds. (Vancouver: UBC Press, 2011), p. 51. The 2013 survey comes from a similar question used by the Pew Research Center's "Global Attitudes" survey. The latter asked respondents a series of questions phrased as, "Do you personally believe that homosexuality is morally acceptable, morally unacceptable, or is it not a moral issue?"

5   *See* Rayside, *Queer Inclusions*, p. 47; Langstaff, "A Twenty-Year Survey"; and Michael Adams, "Pro Gay Rights, Because We Know Each Other," *Globe and Mail*, July 2, 2013.

6   In *Power in Movement*, Sidney Tarrow highlights the breadth and variety of movements when he defines them in terms of "collective challenges, based on common purposes and social solidarities," and underlying social networks able to maintain sustained challenges against powerful opponents. *See* Sidney Tarrow, *Power in Movement: Social Movements and Contentious Politics*, 3rd ed. (Cambridge: Cambridge University Press, 2011, pp. 4–5.

7   Paul Gallant, "Over the Rainbow: Marriage Certificates in Hand, Middle-Class Gays and Lesbians Have Drifted Away from the Fight over Gay Rights," *This Magazine*, September/October 2009, p. 16.

8   There were variations across provinces and territories in the recognition given to cohabiting couples, with Quebecers having the least rights, though statute law and court rulings have been narrowing those differences across regions.

9   *M. v. H.*, [1999] 2 S.C.R. 3. Courts were central players in these advances, but labor unions also played an important role in pressing employers, on which subject see Gerald Hunt, ed., *Laboring for Rights* (Philadelphia: Temple University Press, 1999).

10  Gallant, "Over the Rainbow."

11  Clyde Wilcox and Rentaro Iida, "Evangelicals, the Christian Right, and Gay and Lesbian Rights in the United States," in *Faith, Politics, and Sexual Diversity*, Rayside and Wilcox, eds., pp. 101–20.

12  See my own *Queer Inclusions*; Tom Warner, *Losing Control: Canada's Social Conservatives in the Age of Rights* (Toronto: Between the Lines, 2009); Jonathan Malloy, "Canadian Evangelicals and Same-Sex Marriage," in *Faith, Politics, and Sexual Diversity*, Rayside and Wilcox, eds., pp. 144–65; and Jonathan Malloy, "Between America and Europe: Religion, Politics, and Evangelicals in Canada," 12 *Politics, Religion, and Ideology* 317 (2011).

13  Malloy, "Canadian Evangelicals and Same-Sex Marriage." Marci McDonald's argument is focused on the federal Conservative Party. *See* Marci McDonald, *The Armageddon Factor: The Rise of Christian Nationalism in Canada* (Toronto: Random House Canada, 2010).

14  David Rayside, "The Conservative Party of Canada and Its Religious Constituencies," in *Faith, Politics, and Sexual Diversity*, Rayside and Wilcox, eds., pp. 279–99; Malloy, "Between America and Europe."

15  This helpful observation was contributed by Audrey L'Espérence, 2014.

16  Jeffrey Luscombe, "Egale Canadian Human Rights Trust," *Pink Play Magazine*, Autumn 2013.

17  This is similar to an argument made decades ago by Frances Fox Piven, about gains by the women's movement, in the face of arguments that seeking change in the political mainstream was itself not a contributor to transformative change. *See* Frances Fox Piven, "Women and the State: Ideology, Power, and the Welfare State," 74 *Socialist Review* 11 (1984).

18  Karl-Werner Brand, "Cyclical Aspects of New Social Movements: Waves of Cultural Criticism and Mobilization Cycles of New Middle-Class Radicalism," in *Challenging the Social Order: New Social and Political Movements in Western Democracies*, Russell J. Dalton and Manfred Kuechler, eds. (Cambridge: Polity, 1990), pp. 232–50; Claus Offe, "Reflections on the Institutional Self-Transformation of Movement Politics: A Tentative Stage Model," in *Challenging the Social Order*, pp. 232–50; Sidney Tarrow, *Strangers at the Gates: Movements and States in Contentious Politics* (Cambridge: Cambridge University Press, 2012), p. 128; Charles Tilly, *Social Movements: 1768–2004* (Boulder, CO: Paradigm, 2004).

19  Michael Warner, *The Trouble with Normal: Sex, Politics, and the Ethics of Queer* (New York: Free Press, 1999); Urvashi Vaid, *Virtual Equality: The Mainstreaming of Gay and Lesbian Liberation* (New York: Doubleday, 1995); Urvashi Vaid, *Irresistible Revolution: Confronting Race, Class, and the Assumptions of LGBT Politics* (New York: Magnus Books, 2013).

20  Tom Warner, *Never Going Back: A History of Queer Activism in Canada* (Toronto: University of Toronto Press, 2002); Kinsman, *The Regulation of Desire*; Peter Knegt, *About Canada: Queer Rights* (Halifax: Fernwood, 2011).

21  Vaid, *Irresistible Revolution*, p. xiv.

22  Tavia Grant, "Canada Lags Only U.S. in Income-Gap Growth," *Globe and Mail*, May 1, 2014.

23  Miriam Smith, *A Civil Society? Collective Actors in Canadian Political Life* (Peterborough: Broadview, 2005), p. 179.

24  Elizabeth Saewyc, et al., "The Hazards of Stigma: The Sexual and Physical Abuse of Gay, Lesbian, and Bisexual Adolescents in the U.S. and Canada," 85 *Child Welfare* 195 (2006); Rebecca Haskell and Brian Burtch, *Get That Freak: Homophobia and Transphobia in High Schools* (Halifax: Fernwood, 2010); Catherine Taylor and Tracey Peter, *Every Class in Every School: Final Report on the First National Climate Survey on Homophobia, Biphobia, and Transphobia in Canadian Schools*

(Toronto: Egale Canada Human Rights Trust, 2011); and Don Shortt, *"Don't Be So Gay!" Queers, Bullying, and Making Schools Safe* (Vancouver: UBC Press, 2013).

25  Warner, *Never Going Back*; Rayside, *Queer Inclusions*; Tim McCaskell, *Race to Equity: Disrupting Educational Inequality* (Toronto: Between the Lines, 2005).

26  Rachel Epstein, ed., *Who's Your Daddy: And Other Writings on Queer Parenting* (Toronto: Sumach Press, 2009).

27  Taylor and Peter, *Every Class in Every School*. It is worth adding that changes in provincial policy in Ontario stopped short of significant curricular change on sexual health education for a time. A major controversy over an updated curriculum, in 2010, resulted in the province delaying full implementation until September 2015.

28  Daniela Costa, "Raising the Roof," *Xtra!* April 3–16, 2014. Queer youth are estimated to comprise 20 percent or more of those who use Toronto's homeless shelters, and 25–40 percent of homeless youth more generally in the city.

29  Gerald Hunt and Jonathan Eaton, "We Are Family: Labour Responds to Gay, Lesbian, Bisexual, and Transgender Workers," in *Equity, Diversity, and Canadian Labour,* Gerald Hunt and David Rayside, eds. (Toronto: University of Toronto Press, 2007), pp. 130–55.

30  Among the cases at the provincial level are *Québec (Commission des Droits de la personne) c. Anglsberger,* [1982], 3 C.H.R.R. D/892 (Que. Prov. Ct.); *Québec (Commission des Droit de la personne) c. Maison des Jeunes À-Ma-Baie Inc. (No. 2),* [1998] 33 C.H.R.R. D/263 (Que. H.R. Trib.); *Gill v. Fairview Chrysler Dodge Ltd.* [1996] O.J. No. 4681 (QL) (Gen. Div); *Ferris v. O.T.E.U, Local 15* [1999] 36 C.H.R.R. D/329 (B.C.H.R.); and at the federal level *Montreuil v. National Bank of Canada* [2004] C.H.R.D. No. 4 (QL). *See* Hunt and Eaton, "We Are Family."

31  Trans Pulse, "Trans Pulse Project Survey, 2011," http://transpulseproject.ca/resources/trans-pulse-survey/ (accessed December 2014); Viviane Namaste, *Sex Change, Social Change: Reflections on Identity, Institutions, and Imperialism,* 2nd ed. (Women's Press, 2011).

32  Hunt, ed., *Laboring for Rights*; Warner, *Never Going Back*.

33  Gerald Hunt, David Rayside, and Don Shortt, "The Equity Landscape for Sexual Minorities in Canada," in *Employment Equity in Canada: The Legacy of the Abella Report,* Carol Agocs and Michael Lynck, eds. (Toronto: University of Toronto Press, 2014), pp. 156–75.

34  Jeffrey Reitz, et al., *Multiculturalism and Social Cohesion* (Dordrecht: Springer, 2009); Inder Marwah, Triadafilos Triadafilopoulos, and Stephen White, "Immigration, Citizenship, and Canada's New Conservative Party," in *Conservatism in Canada,* James Farney and David Rayside, eds. (Toronto: University of Toronto Press, 2013), pp. 95–119.

35  Gallant, "Over the Rainbow."

36  Luscombe, "Egale Canadian Human Rights Trust"; Elah Feder, "When the Money Dries Up," *Xtra!* May 1–14, 2014.

37 Aileen Murphy, et al., *Between the Cracks: Homeless Youth in Vancouver* (Burnaby: McCreary Centre Society, 2002); Warner, *Never Going Back*, p. 330.

38 Warner, *Losing Control.*

39 Richard Kim, "Close Down the Gay Movement?" *Nation*, April 16, 2014. *See also* Justin Ling, "Bully Pulpit," *Xtra!* April 17–30, 2014.

40 *See* Brenda Cossman, "Censor, Resist, Repeat: A History of Censorship of Gay and Lesbian Sexual Representation in Canada," 21 *Duke Journal of Gender Law and Policy* 62 (2013). In its 2013 decision, the Supreme Court of Canada held unanimously that hate speech provisions were reasonable limits on the freedoms of speech and religion, if particular instances could be found to be so hateful and extreme as to pose the threat of real and lasting harm to minority groups. *Saskatchewan (Human Rights Commission) v. Whatcott* [2013] 1. S.C.R. 467.

41 *Trinity Western University v. British Columbia College of Teachers*, [2001] 1 S.C.R. 772. Years later, TWU was back in the news when LGBT advocates and their allies demanded that provincial bar associations refuse to accredit a new law program, but that case has still not been finally resolved ("B.C. Government Pulls the Plug on Trinity Western University's Law School Plan," *Vancouver Sun*, December 12, 2014).

42 Momin Rahman and Amir Hussain, "Muslims and Sexual Diversity in North America," in *Faith, Politics, and Sexual Diversity*, Rayside and Wilcox, eds., pp. 255–74; and David Rayside, "Muslim American Communities' Response to Queer Visibility," 5 *Contemporary Islam* 109 (2011).

11

# The Pitfalls of Normalization

## *The Dutch Case and the Future of Equality*

JAN WILLEM DUYVENDAK

In *Beyond the Closet: The Transformation of Gay and Lesbian Life*, Steven Seidman, one of America's leading sociologists of sexuality, wrote the following on the future of the LGBT struggle:

> Gaining equal rights . . . will not bring about full *social* equality. . . . Until our workplaces celebrate events such as Coming Out Day and the anniversary of Stonewall . . . *civic* equality will remain an unrealized promise. We need a movement that broadens rights activism to include an agenda of across-the-board *institutional* equality and *cultural* justice.[1]

As the battle for equal rights for gays and lesbians has seen some significant victories since the publication of *Beyond the Closet* in 2002, it is time to take stock of what these legal victories mean—and what still remains to be done.

Seidman claims that the battle for legal equality has largely been championed by the assimilationist wing of the LGBT movement, sidelining the aspirations of queer activists. He argues that the struggle-beyond-the-legal should have a truly transformative impact on the American mainstream by challenging heteronormativity in everyday life. Although I agree with Seidman that on its own the legal battle is not enough, I also believe that he is too pessimistic about what has been achieved. Does it make empirical sense to separate the legal/political side of the LGBT movement (or, for that matter, of any other emancipation movement) from its social, civic, institutional, and cultural dimensions? I argue that these spheres cannot so easily be separated, and that we need to pay more attention to the performative effects of legal challenges, such as the actual opening of marriage to same-sex couples. Second, and related to this, I examine the claim that we need a transformative agenda to combat heteronormativity in all fields of life. Here I argue that Seidman is right, but that we have to be aware of the context in which new agendas are developed. Although battles for equality—and their performative effects—may appear alike in different countries, their meanings clearly differ, depending on what constitutes the main political cleavage in any given country.

Put differently, the meaning of the LGBT struggle is defined not only by those who are part of the struggle but often and as much by others who can embrace or reject our agenda for their own reasons. "Success" often depends on how our agenda fits into a broader one—not necessarily transforming the social mainstream but fitting in, sometimes even reinforcing its main characteristics. I will show how this has worked in the case of the Netherlands, the first country to open marriage to same-sex couples, and where acceptance of homosexuality has become a defining feature of the Dutch national self-image. While this may suggest that the LGBT movement has had an enormous transformative impact on all spheres of life, it also shows how well a certain homosexuality fits within the dominant mainstream, a mainstream that depicts other minorities—most prominently Muslim immigrants in the country—as backwards, uncivilized, and not Dutch. This obviously poses substantive and strategic challenges for the gay and lesbian movement, as a minority can evidently become too much a part of a mainstream that marginalizes another minority.

Since pursuing an LGBT agenda in many countries is almost exclusively a task taken up by progressive parties, it is often hard to explain what has happened in the Netherlands, where the goals of the movement have been embraced by almost all political parties from the Left to the Right—making gay emancipation a cornerstone of Dutch identity. Becoming the embodiment of Dutchness has not made the position of the LGBT movement exactly easy. On the one hand, the full support of the political spectrum seems to suggest that all native Dutch are totally emancipated and homosexuality is fully accepted. As I will show in the last part of this chapter, this is not the case. On the other hand, the fact that gay emancipation has become a cornerstone of Dutch identity has perversely reified the position of Muslims as the alleged "Other," as if no

Muslim can support LGBT rights. In other words, the normalization of homosexuality as something Dutch makes Muslims into the abnormal. Moreover, in this process of normalization of homosexuality as Dutch, homosexuality is itself normalized: it has to fit into a certain understanding of "proper sexuality."

## The Meaning of the Legal

Changes in laws are often considered the final outcome of much longer sociohistorical developments. Political scientists who espouse the logic of "policy cycles" assume that changes start in society, are picked up by policymakers, and are then translated and made into laws. But recent research in numerous domains suggests a different dynamic in which legal change is often not so much the outcome of societal changes and/ or popular protest but a result of protest being "produced" by policymakers who provide space for change.[2] Put differently, the relationship between society and politics is much more "interactive" than a simple "input-throughput-output" model of political decision making suggests. While policymakers sometimes do indeed respond to developments in society, they also often establish rules or laws that precede rather than follow public opinion.[3]

But even when new laws mirror changes in popular beliefs, the former may still have a performative effect upon the latter. Take the example of "gay marriage." Those who opposed opening the institution to same-sex couples claimed that the meaning of marriage would change, particularly for those who consider it a sacrosanct bond between one man and one woman. Instead of objecting to this objection (as some gay groups did, both in the United States and in Western Europe), we should acknowledge that marriage has indeed come to mean something different: a bond between two consenting adults, irrespective of their genders.

But opening marriage to same-sex couples also had unanticipated consequences: many people who previously opposed gay marriage now found it difficult to maintain their positions. As law-abiding citizens, they wanted to respect the law. And as the unthinkable became thinkable, it became more difficult for them to object: the mere fact that civil servants, acting according to the new law, married same-sex couples in the name of the state "normalized" practices that had previously seemed strange. This also complicates the rolling back of laws permitting same-sex marriage—although such a roll-back is not impossible, as we have seen.

Those in the gay and lesbian movement who never considered opening marriage to same-sex couples an important goal—as they were warning against the normalizing effect of gay marriage on homosexuality—may have overlooked the fact that state-sanctioned same-sex marriage has—at least somewhat—changed a mainstream institution. Lesbians and gays are now part of the core institutions of society (true not only for marriage but for the army as well, at least in both the Netherlands and the United States). In other words, "the legal" can have quite big—and ongoing—impacts on the social, cultural, insti-tutional, and civic aspects of people's lives, for both straight people and LGBT people, as well as for both the opponents and the proponents of gay marriage. In this sense, I think that the correct action is not to ques-tion what to do "after marriage" but to examine gay marriage's broader consequences for the possible normalization of homosexuality. And although the opening of marriage to same-sex couples may appear a similar phenomenon across countries, different societies, as I will show, have their own story to tell.

## The Depoliticization of Gay Identities

It should come as no surprise that the Dutch were the first to permit same-sex couples to marry. Following a long period in which Dutch society was markedly conservative, it witnessed significant trans-formations in the 1960s and 1970s, including a sexual revolution that had far-reaching effects on society. While surveys show that there was strong opposition to homosexuality, prostitution, pornography, abor-tion, divorce, and pre- and extramarital sex until the late 1960s, a decade later the *majority* of Dutch citizens had adopted a position of tolerance on these issues. Encouraged by the NVSH (Dutch Society for Sexual Reform) and the COC (Center for Recreation and Culture, a code name for what would be baptized in 1971 as the Dutch Society for the Inte-gration of Homosexuality), and by anti-authoritarian trends in society more generally, the Netherlands in the 1970s emerged as the most lib-eral nation in the world on issues of sexual morality.[4] Compared to the

United States, where "culture wars" rage to this day, substantial disagreement on "moral" issues, such as sexuality, drug policies, abortion, and euthanasia, almost completely vanished from Dutch society in the 1980s and 1990s.

Discourses of sexual freedom played a central role in the transformation of the Netherlands from one of the most religious societies in the world to one of its most secular.[5] As shown in surveys, large segments of the Dutch population after the 1960s distanced themselves from moral—sexual, family, and gender—traditionalism.[6] The percentage of Dutch citizens who now agree with the proposition that "homosexuality is normal" and who support gay marriage exceeds that in other countries.[7] More than most other Europeans (not to mention Americans), the Dutch disagree with conservative propositions such as "women must have children to be happy," "a child should respect its parents," and "we would be better off if we returned to a traditional way of life."[8] Surveys show that the Dutch are among the most ardent supporters in Europe of the right to freedom of speech and expression,[9] of gender equality, and of civil rights for sexual minorities. Opinions moreover differ little by level of education; when it comes to ideas about sexual freedom and gender equality, the Netherlands is among the three least polarized countries in Europe.[10] This progressive consensus has given the Netherlands, and especially the city of Amsterdam, a worldwide reputation as a place of sexual freedom, almost a haven. (For the record, this is not to claim that there has been a straight line from Amsterdam's seventeenth century [the "Golden Age"] to the sexual freedoms of today, as Russell Shorto does in his book *Amsterdam: The History of the World's Most Liberal City*).[11]

As homosexuality became increasingly "integrated" into Dutch society, *equality* rather than the celebration of *difference* became the main goal. As a result, gay identity became less politicized, with many gay men and some lesbian women claiming that the struggle was over since acceptance, broadly speaking, had been won. Indeed, discrimination against Dutch homosexuals decreased, which also allowed for increased visibility. Homosexuality was normalized within the progressive moral majority, and no radical queer identities or other significant forms of difference were celebrated, either within the LGBT movement or in the mainstream. Radical identities tend to develop under repressive conditions, and the Dutch context was anathema for more radical and diverse mobilization.[12] Registered partnerships between couples of the same sex were legalized in 1998. This was followed three years later, in 2001, by full marriage for same-sex couples. The legal battle was over.

As gays and lesbians won equal rights under the law, their emancipation seemed complete, and emancipatory ideals became less important in the political arena. But homosexuality returned to the foreground of public and political debate in the early millennium, tied to "problems with the integration of immigrants" and especially the alleged political and social tensions between gay and Muslim communities. To understand this more recent repoliticization of homosexuality in the Netherlands, I analyze the nationalist discourse that has developed over the past years. What do these developments mean for the future agenda of the LGBT movement?

## LGBT within a Nationalist Context: Dealing with Homo-Nationalism

Since the 2000s, we have witnessed a wave of abhorrence against Islam. In Dutch society, Islam is framed as the "Other" and as irreconcilable with universal liberal values.[13] In this context, almost all political parties, including the right-wing populists, define progressive values—particularly in the field of gender and sexuality—as core Dutch characteristics. The acceptance of homosexuality serves as an ideological benchmark to test whether Muslims have entered "modernity," the singular condition according to which they are allowed to belong to Dutch society.[14]

Recent analyses of new political cleavages in Western Europe have often overlooked the pivotal role played by the rhetoric of sexual and gender progress.[15] The rise of populism in Western Europe is then mistakenly analyzed as a shift towards conservatism, as if populists on both sides of the Atlantic want to conserve the same "culture." This misunderstanding is due to the conflation of progressiveness and pro-immigration viewpoints. My analysis, however, shows that populists combine the framing of Dutch national culture as morally progressive with a virulent anti-immigration agenda. As a result, when commentators such as Kriesi et al. conclude that the considerable decline in the "cultural liberalism of the most educated . . . probably reflects . . . the general hardening of the Dutch attitude to immigration,"[16] they miss the crucial point that Dutch anti-immigration discourse goes hand in glove with a rhetoric of sexual emancipation and gender equality.

Muslim immigration is seen as a threat to the stability of the Dutch progressive moral order, and cultural protectionists have set out to guard Dutch cultural and sexual liberties against the dangers allegedly posed by Muslim immigrants.[17] Gay rights and gender equality have thus become a normative framework within which to shape the critique of Islam and multiculturalism, rendering Muslim citizens "knowable" and making them the objects of critique. The central tropes of this discourse—individualism versus the lack thereof, "tolerance" versus "fundamentalism"—frame an imagined modern self against an imagined traditional (Muslim) other. Such tropes are especially powerful because they put progressives who oppose this populist discourse, but who are attached to the achievements of sexual and feminist progressive politics, in a serious bind. Taking up the defense of lesbian and gay rights comes to be associated with anti-Muslim populism, while solidarity with Muslims against Islamophobic rhetoric is represented as trivializing the homophobia of conservative Muslim communities.

The influential populist politician Pim Fortuyn, who emerged on the political scene in 2001, capitalized on the trope of sexual progress as essentially Dutch and managed to ingrain it deeper into the Dutch self-image. Fortuyn was openly and flamboyantly gay, and spoke of Muslims as backwards and rural. In the aftermath of 9/11 and the ascent of the "War on Terror," he argued that his sexually expressive lifestyle and his liberties and joys as a gay man were threatened by backwards Muslims.[18] Fortuyn managed to reframe the Dutch political landscape by entangling traditionally "new left" themes—secularism, gender equality, and gay liberation—with a neoliberal and anti-immigration populist agenda, and antipathy towards Islam with a politics of sexual freedom.[19] His party won almost 35 percent of the vote in his hometown of Rotterdam in the March 2002 municipal elections,[20] and 17 percent nationally in May of that year in elections held only days after his assassination. Fortuyn attacked the established political Right for not heeding widespread frustrations among the native Dutch, and proposed closing the borders to most asylum seekers and taking a tough stance towards the Muslim community.[21] Unlike Islam, Fortuyn argued, Judaism and Christianity had been transformed by the Enlightenment, during which essential "Western" values developed: individual responsibility, the separation of church and state, and the equality of men and women: "I refuse to start all over again with the emancipation of women and gays."[22]

Portraying Muslims through the lenses of gender and sexual equality has remained publicly salient since Fortuyn was dramatically assassinated in 2002. The member of Parliament Ayaan Hirsi Ali frequently claimed that Islam constitutes a violation of the rights of women, lesbians and gays, and children,[23] while the populist political leader Geert Wilders has repeatedly evoked violent antigay incidents in Dutch cities to score points against Muslims, Moroccan-Dutch youth, and cultural diversity. It has become almost impossible to discuss lesbian and gay emancipation without it being associated with immigration and the "problem" of multiculturalism. Indeed, so well entrenched is this schema that it has become common sense in the Netherlands to represent homophobia, even homophobic violence, as alien to white Dutch culture and society and as the unique attribute of young Moroccan-Dutch men and Muslims. Whereas lesbian and gay rights have a rather short history in the Netherlands, they are nonetheless now mobilized as exemplary of a Dutch "tradition of tolerance."[24]

Immigrants to the Netherlands—especially Muslims—form a tangible, visible "constitutive outside"[25] for the Dutch majority and as such play a key role in creating and reinforcing the Dutch self-image of cultural and sexual progressiveness. Progressive values are espoused today from the far Left to the populist Right, rendering the Netherlands one of the most homogeneous societies in the world when it comes to expressed values and attitudes on sexual and moral issues. The discourse of Dutch sexual tolerance plays a central role in transposing homophobia onto the immigrant and religious other, a transposition that erases from the national imagination the recent homophobic past and the continued heteronormativity of Dutch society.

Many Dutch citizens now demand that immigrants accept the official discourse of sexual and moral "progressiveness." In other words, when it comes to issues of public morality and personal values, citizens in liberal countries do not always value diversity in opinions and cultural repertoires.[26] Indeed, sexual progressiveness and tolerance may be employed as discourses of power,[27] producing immigrants and religious minorities as cultural others and excluding them by redrawing the contours of the national community.

> [S]exual politics, rather than operating to the side of this contestation, is in the middle of it, and . . . very often claims to new or radical sexual freedoms are appropriated precisely by that point of view—usually enunciated from within state power—that would try to define Europe and the sphere of modernity as the privileged site where sexual radicalism can and does take place. Often, but not always, the further claim is made that such a privileged site of radical freedom must be protected against the putative orthodoxies associated with new immigrant communities.[28]

Sexual freedom is thus used to frame Dutch society as the "avatar of both freedom and modernity."[29] In order to understand gay politics in the Netherlands, we must analyze how they have been implicated in the Dutch "progressive" narrative.[30] According to this narrative, Dutch society is characterized by liberal values such as gender equality, freedom of speech, sexual emancipation, and tolerance towards gay rights. Populists, in particular, and political leaders, in a broader sense, "have reconfigured what had been values of liberal citizenship into values of cultural distinctiveness: 'Dutch values' versus 'Islamic values.'"[31] The revival of nationalism defines these values in opposition to a perception of Islam as irrational, intolerant, illiberal, and backwards. Islam is framed as belonging to a different time and place, as a premodern state of mind and lifestyle.

Constructing an antagonistic relationship between Islam and homosexuality, of course, has a marginalizing effect on gay Muslims.[32] Within the heated debates around Islam and homosexuality, gay Muslims—and, doubly, lesbian Muslims—are largely invisible as agents[33] as they get subsumed into the larger, undifferentiated, and putatively straight Muslim populace. Where gay Muslims do figure in nationalist discourse, it is to express the claim that they are illiberal and premodern along with the rest of the Muslim community, and that so long as they continue to identify with Islam, they will remain oppressed. To be recognized as gay, Muslim LGBT individuals are thus called upon to break with their religious selves and communities. This notion of queer Muslims as being oppressed and alienated from their "true selves" is fueled by a "homo-normative model of sexuality" that dictates that the proper way to be homosexual is to embrace progressive and liberal values.[34] The proper gay is individualistic and lets go of tradition. Following this model, explicit "coming-out practices" are implicitly represented as the only natural way of being gay.[35] "Those queer Muslims that come out and match this paradigmatic model can be absorbed into 'Dutchness' and indeed be held up as mascots: the 'performative' Muslim gay as an embodiment of emancipated gayness, symbolizing modernity, no longer really Muslim."[36]

Expecting gay Muslims to publicly come out forces them to choose between their culture and kinship loyalty, on the one hand, and Dutch culture—where openly taking on a gay identity is seen as freedom—on the other.[37] We should also not overlook the fact that the impossibility of being a "gay Muslim" is also asserted from within the Moroccan and Turkish communities in the Netherlands, where homosexuality is still a highly embattled topic—particularly among influential orthodox community leaders whose defense of religious-minority rights intersect with antihomosexual rhetoric.

The kind of "homo-nationalism"[38] that I have described here is not as novel as it may appear. Since the 1960s, the Dutch have convinced themselves that their progressiveness is an example for everyone else, both for not-yet-emancipated groups within the Netherlands and for the rest of the world. While this mono-cultural progressive moral majority in the 1970s still tolerated those who did not (yet) share their opinions, this began to change in the late 1980s and early 1990s[39] as the native Dutch grew increasingly intolerant of those in Dutch society who allegedly did not share in the progressive consensus—particularly "guest-workers" from Morocco and Turkey, and their children.

In the Netherlands, homosexuality is now higher on the public and political agenda than ever before. At present it is often instrumentalized in nationalist discourse as a means to "educate" new immigrants, particularly Muslims, on the "normal Dutch way of life." Many politicians aspire to be movement allies. This has a puzzling effect on LGBT mobilization, particularly since the politicization of homosexuality is pitting the "native Dutch" (now including black, postcolonial immigrants who are seen to be rather progressive on gender and sexuality) against

Muslims. The different positioning of postcolonial immigrants, on the one hand, and Muslim immigrants, on the other, particularly regarding topics of gender and sexuality, makes solidarity among people of color extremely difficult, both within and outside the LGBT movement.

Although the Dutch situation differs from that of the United States when it comes to organizing among people of color, the mechanisms turn out to be largely the same. Internal LGBT organizing is largely determined by dominant views on identity and diversity in society at large. In this sense, it doesn't make much difference whether the government is an ally or an adversary of LGBT organizations: the identities that do mobilize—that are lived and experienced as important and distinctive—draw their meanings from the broader society. The marginal position of Muslims in the Netherlands is mirrored in the quasi-absence of Muslim LGBT organizations.

The effect of all this is that the LGBT movement is sometimes associated with verbal "Muslim bashing," and this indeed is partly what has happened. Whereas many LGBT activists were part of left-wing political parties until the 2000s, an important segment of the activists, and even more so of the gay electorate, started voting for right-wing populists parties in the 2000s. Another consequence is that antigay discrimination among the native Dutch is overlooked.

In the end, the future agenda of the LGBT movement must thus address these two sides of "homo-nationalism": the overemphasis on Muslims in debates on (homo)sexuality, which blinds us to the internal diversity among Muslim immigrants regarding gender and sexuality, and the neglect of continued heteronormativity among the native Dutch. Let me now turn to that part of the future agenda.[40]

## A Future Agenda

The emancipation of LGBTs is at a crossroads: LGBTs have been highly successful, both legally and in winning general social acceptance. At the same time, homophobic violence continues (whether it has actually increased is uncertain owing to factors such as different means of reporting within police statistics and the fact that surveys are often unrepresentative of LGBTs). And while the number of people who claim to accept homosexuality may be high, this acceptance is far lower when it comes to specific issues such as men kissing in public. Other research indicates that gay men in particular are only accepted under certain conditions, such as not behaving in an unmasculine manner and not being too sexually explicit or visible.[41] The invisibility of homosexuality asked for by some Muslims is thus also demanded by some white Dutch: we accept you as long as we don't have to see that you exist or have to see what you do. For their part, lesbians continue to remain far less visible in public life and in the media.

How have gays and lesbians responded to these developments, and how should the LGBT movement respond? Some younger gays and lesbians prefer to keep their homosexuality as "normal" and "private"—and thus invisible—as possible. They resist strong identities and communities; young lesbians attribute dyke styles like short hair, masculine clothing, and masculine behavior to an older generation.[42] Coming out as gay or lesbian takes on average three to four years from first awareness to telling somebody, and this among those who have actually come out—not a sign of widespread acceptance.[43] The incidence of psychological problems among male and female homosexuals is still much higher than among heterosexuals.[44] This is also the case among young gays and lesbians,[45] where 16 percent of girls and 9 percent of boys have tried to commit suicide.[46] Aggarwal has found social pressure to behave "normally" (i.e., like straight guys) and continuing experiences of discrimination to be important explanations for the psychological problems experienced by gay men.[47] In the dominant self-congratulatory discourse—praising the Dutch for their exceptional tolerance—these kinds of data don't get the attention they deserve. They do show, however, that the Dutch "tolerance" is often limited to the rather general notion that "everybody has the right to choose his or her lifestyle," whereas far less acceptance is shown when homosexuality comes closer to one's personal life.

In other words, although the Netherlands may seem exemplary in its acceptance of homosexuality, this applies more to the discursive level than to other aspects of life. As argued by Steven Seidman,[48] the work necessary to definitively break through heteronormativity remains, while many straight citizens see no need for change. Straight norms are furthermore deeply embedded in gender relations, which are in practice far less equal than one would expect given the Dutch political and public discourse.[49] In reality, Dutch women and men are, for instance, quite traditional in allocating responsibilities between them for paid work (most men work full-time while most women work only part-time) and household tasks (mostly a female domain). These structural inequalities among the "native" Dutch are, however, understood as the outcome of individual and autonomous "choices" of emancipated individuals, whereas gender imbalances among Muslims are almost by definition attributed to their repressive "culture."

Many Dutch wonder where sexual emancipation is headed. Broad support for gays and lesbians seems to indicate that there is still space for forward movement, and here we can point to several promising initiatives: gay-straight alliances in schools, strong assurances by the police to fight antigay violence, and certain policy investments in LGBT emancipation. On the other hand, school curricula on topics related to homosexuality or sexual and gender diversity—although legally mandated—remain controversial and embattled, not least because the Dutch public school system financially supports a majority of religious (many Christian and some Islamic) schools, and because the so-called black and white schools are highly segregated. In religious and "black" schools, teachers often do not dare touch upon "difficult" topics such as homosexuality or AIDS.[50]

The heteronormative discourse is adopted by some gays and lesbians as well, who are eager to act "normally" by shunning behavior that is unmasculine (for men), unfeminine (for women), and explicitly erotic (for both). Heteronormativity then becomes homonormativity, compelling both gay men and lesbian women to behave like straight people, making them afraid of showing any "gay" or "lesbian" signs.

Some gay men and lesbians share, for example, the ambivalent feelings of some straight Dutch people regarding Amsterdam's annual Canal Pride Parade due to its ostentatious seminudity, drag, and leather.[51] The homo-norm has become not to behave in public like an effeminate fag, a bull dyke, or an erotically explicit queer. Although such invisibility may indeed be strategic, it may hamper further sexual emancipation.

The agenda for sexual emancipation in the Netherlands is thus far from complete, and numerous strategic questions remain to be answered. The country is witness to puzzling developments. On the one hand, the Dutch majority embraces gay and feminist rights (as described above, mostly in the context of the debate on multiculturalism). On the other hand, social acceptance of nonheteronormativity remains thin and sometimes opportunistic. Although most Dutch share a "progressive" sexual morality, the existence of antigay violence shows that general "acceptance" exists alongside visceral opposition to homosexuality.

The opening of marriage to couples irrespective of their gender was as much about diversifying marital practice as it was about mainstreaming gays and lesbians. To give just one telling example, a famous gay couple—one the mayor of a large Dutch city, his husband a television entertainment star—were criticized for being married while both partners were openly not monogamous. In the newspapers, they were urged to "conform" to the "fundamentals of marriage" as understood in the days when marriage was still the preserve of straight couples: adhere to monogamy! Even though many gays wondered whether straight people were living up to the ideal of monogamy, little debate ensued about other possible interpretations of marriage.

In sum, a rather "normalized" homosexuality is embraced in the Netherlands, often in opposition to (Muslim) immigrants who are depicted as the absolute "Other." To escape this deadly polarization, I propose that LGBTs focus on strengthening diversity in the movement and in society at large. In the first place, LGBTs have to confront the native Dutch population on their remaining homophobia. This can be accomplished by asking publicly which homosexuality/ties are acceptable: only assimilated, normalized LGBTs who basically don't show their homosexuality, or a diverse range of people who visibly diverge from heteronormative standards regarding gender and sexuality? Second, the movement needs to create more space for people of color and strengthen alliances with immigrant organizations. One important implication of this shift is that white LGBTs need to acknowledge that emancipation can have many faces: "coming out" is just one of the strategies one can follow. These types of changes will bring greater diversity to the LGBT movement and help demystify the belief that all Muslim immigrants are homophobic. Acknowledging promising developments regarding gender and sexuality within Muslim organizations will also allow the LGBT movement to more effectively address the homophobia that exists within the Muslim population.

All this won't be easy since, as I discussed at the beginning of this chapter, we can't define our goals and strategies in isolation. What we can strive for largely depends on political opportunities, which are in turn at least partly determined by the dominant cleavages in society and politics. Another way to make progress, then, is to try to change the dominant cleavages in society—in the Dutch case, the opposition between self-congratulatory natives who consider themselves the embodiment of the Enlightenment and religious minorities who are equated with the dark times of the past. To make inroads here won't be easy either. But when our choice is becoming part of the mainstream (which includes the marginalization of other minorities) or trying to change the mainstream, I resolutely prefer the second option.

NOTES

1  Steven Seidman, *Beyond the Closet: The Transformation of Gay and Lesbian Life* (New York: Routledge, 2002), p. 16 (italics added).

2  Christian Bröer and Jan Willem Duyvendak, "Discursive Opportunities, Feeling Rules, and the Rise of Protests against Aircraft Noise," 14(3) *Mobilization* 337, 356 (2009); Ruud Koopmans and Jan Willem Duyvendak, "The Political Construction of the Nuclear Energy Issue and Its Impact on the Mobilization of Anti-Nuclear Movements in Western Europe," 42(2) *Social Problems* 235, 251 (1995).

3  Ellen Grootegoed, Christian Bröer, and Jan Willem Duyvendak, "Too Ashamed to Complain: Cuts to Publicly Financed Care and Clients' Waving of Their Right to Appeal," 12(3) *Social Policy and Society* 475, 486 (2013).

4  Gert Hekma and Jan Willem Duyvendak, "Queer Netherlands: A Puzzling Example," 14(6) *Sexualities* 625, 631 (2011).

5  Peter van Rooden, "Oral history en het vreemde sterven van het Nederlands Christendom," 19 *Bijdragen en Mededelingen Betreffende de Geschiedenis der Nederlanden*, 524, 51 (2004).

6  Netherlands Institute for Social Research, *25 Years of Social Change* (The Hague: Netherlands Institute for Social Research, 1998); Wilfried Uitterhoeve, *Nederland en de Anderen: Europese Vergelijkingen uit het Sociaal en Cultureel Rapport 2000* (Nijmegen: Uitgeverij SUN, 2000); Wilhelmus Antonius Arts, Jacques Hagenaars, and Loek Halman, *The Cultural Diversity of European Unity: Findings, Explanations, and Reflections from the European Values Study* (Leiden: Brill, 2003); Jan Willem Duyvendak, *Een Eensgezinde, Vooruitstrevende Natie: Over de Mythe van dé Individualisering en de Toekomst van de Sociologie* [A Unanimous, Progressive Nation: The Myth of Individualisation and the Future of Sociology] (Amsterdam: Vossius pers, 2004); Loek Halman, Ruud Luijkx, and Marga van Zundert, *Atlas of European Values* (Leiden: Brill, 2005); Dick Houtman and Jan Willem Duyvendak, "Boerka's, boerkini's en belastingcenten: culturele en politieke polarisatie in een post-Christelijke samenleving," in *Polarisatie: Bedreigend en Verrijkend,* Raad voor Maatschappelijke Ontwikkeling, eds (Amsterdam: Uitgeverij SWP, 2009), pp. 102, 19.

7  Jürgen Gerhards, "Non-Discrimination towards Homosexuality: The European Union's Policy and Citizens' Attitudes towards Homosexuality in 27 European Countries," 25(1) *International Sociology* 5, 28 (2010).

8  Jan Willem Duyvendak, *Een Eensgezinde, Vooruitstrevende Natie: Over de Mythe van dé Individualisering en de Toekomst van de Sociologie* (2004), Inaugural Lecture, University of Amsterdam.

9  Ronald Inglehart and Wayne Baker, "Modernization, Cultural Change, and the Persistence of Traditional Values," 65 *American Sociological Review* 19, 51 (2000); Ronald Inglehart and Christian Welzel, *Modernization, Cultural Change, and Democracy: The Human Development Sequence* (Cambridge: Cambridge University Press, 2005).

10  Peter Achterberg, *Considering Cultural Conflict: Class Politics and Cultural Politics in Western Societies* (Maastricht: Shaker, 2006), p. 55.

11  Russell Shorto, *Amsterdam: The History of the World's Most Liberal City* (Amsterdam: Doubleday, 2013).

12  Jan Willem Duyvendak, "The Depoliticization of the Dutch Gay Identity, or Why Dutch Gays Aren't Queer," in *Queer Theory/Sociology*, Steven Seidman, ed. (Cambridge: Blackwell, 1996), pp. 421, 438; Ronald Holzhacker, "The Europeanization and Transnationalization of Civil Society Organizations Striving for Equality: Goals and Strategies of Gay and Lesbian Groups in Italy and the Netherlands," *EUI Working Papers*, RSCAS/36.

13  Justus Uitermark, *Dynamics of Power in Dutch Integration Politics* (Amsterdam: Amsterdam Institute for Social Science Research/University of Amsterdam, 2010).

14  Gloria Wekker, "Van homo nostalgie en betere tijden: multiculturaliteit en post-kolonialiteit," *George Mosse Lecture Amsterdam* 1, 20 (2009).

15  This paragraph and the following four are strongly based on Justus Uitermark, Paul Mepschen, and Jan Willem Duyvendak, "Populism, Sexual Politics, and the Exclusion of Muslims in the Netherlands," in *European States and Their Muslim Citizens*, John Bowen, Christophe Bertossi, Jan Willem Duyvendak, and Mona Lena Krook, eds. (Cambridge: Cambridge University Press, 2014), pp. 235–55.

16  Hanspeter Kriesi, Edgar Grande, Romain Lachat, Martin Dolezal, Simon Bornschier, and Timotheos Frey, *West European Politics in the Age of Globalization.* (Cambridge: Cambridge University Press, 2008), p. 171.

17  Peter van der Veer, "Pim Fortuyn, Theo van Gogh, and the Politics of Tolerance in the Netherlands," 18(1) *Public Culture* 111, 124 (2006); Oscar Verkaaik and Rachel Spronk, "Sexular Practice: Notes on an Ethnography of Secularism," 59 *Focaal* 83, 88 (2011).

18  Van der Veer, "Pim Fortuyn, Theo van Gogh, and the Politics of Tolerance in the Netherlands."

19  Dick Pels, *De Geest van Pim: Het Gedachtengoed van een Politieke Dandy* (Amsterdam: Ambo, 2003); Van der Veer, "Pim Fortuyn, Theo van Gogh, and the Politics of Tolerance in the Netherlands."

20  Justus Uitermark and Jan Willem Duyvendak, "Civilizing the City: Populism and Revanchist Urbanism in Rotterdam," 45(7) *Urban Studies* 1485, 1505 (2008).

21  Van der Veer, "Pim Fortuyn, Theo van Gogh, and the Politics of Tolerance in the Netherlands."

22  Pim Fortuyn quoted in *De Volkskrant*, February 9, 2002.

23  Hirsi Ali, "Fundamentalisme is niet af te kopen met diplomatie. Maandag een half jaar geleden werd Theo van vermoord. Critici van de islam treft het verwijt van huisvredebreuk," *De Volkskrant*, May 4, 2005.

24  Paul Mepschen, Jan Willem Duyvendak, and Evelien Tonkens, "Sexual Politics, Orientalism, and Multicultural Citizenship in the Netherlands," 44(5) *Sociology* 962, 979 (2010); Suhraiya Jivraj and Anisa de Jong, "The Dutch Homo-Emancipation Policy and Its Silencing Effects on Queer Muslims," 19 *Feminist Legal Studies* 143, 158 (2011); Wekker, "Van homo nostalgie en betere tijden: multiculturaliteit en postkolonialiteit."

25  Francisco Panizza, "Introduction: Populism and the Mirror of Democracy," in *Populism and the Mirror of Democracy,* Francisco Panizza, ed. (London: Verso, 2005); Chantal Mouffe, *On the Political* (London: Routledge, 2005).

26  Sune Laegaard, "Liberal Nationalism and the Nationalisation of Liberal Values," 13(1) *Nations and Nationalism* 37, 55 (2007); Unni Wikan, *Generous Betrayal: Politics of Culture in the New Europe* (Chicago: University of Chicago Press, 2002).

27  Judith Butler, "Sexual Politics, Torture, and Secular Time," 59(1) *British Journal of Sociology* 1, 23 (2008); Jasbir Puar, *Terrorist Assemblages: Homonationalism in Queer Times* (Durham, NC: Duke University Press, 2007).

28  Butler, "Sexual Politics, Torture, and Secular Time," p. 2.

29  Butler, "Sexual Politics, Torture, and Secular Time," p. 2.

30  This analysis is based on and further developed in Nicholas Boston and Jan Willem Duyvendak, "People of Color Mobilization in the Dutch and US LGBT Movements," forthcoming in David Paternotte and Manon Trembley eds., *Ashgate Companion to Lesbian and Gay Activism* (Surrey, UK: Ashgate, 2015).

31  Uitermark, Mepschen, and Duyvendank, "Populism, Sexual Politics, and the Exclusion of Muslims in the Netherlands"; Wekker, "Van homo nostalgie en betere tijden: multiculturaliteit en postkolonialiteit."

32  Jivraj and De Jong, "The Dutch Homo-Emancipation Policy and Its Silencing Effects on Queer Muslims."

33  Fatima El-Tayeb, "Gays Who Cannot Properly Be Gay: Queer Muslims in the Neoliberal European City," 19(1) *European Journal of Women's Studies* 79, 95 (2011).

34  Mepschen, Duyvendak, and Tonkens, "Sexual Politics, Orientalism, and Multicultural Citizenship in the Netherlands."

35  Wekker, "Van homo nostalgie en betere tijden: multiculturaliteit en postkolonialiteit."

36  Jivraj and De Jong, "The Dutch Homo-Emancipation Policy and Its Silencing Effects on Queer Muslims," p. 152.

37  Jivraj and De Jong, "The Dutch Homo-Emancipation Policy and Its Silencing Effects on Queer Muslims."

38  Puar, *Terrorist Assemblages: Homonationalism in Queer Times.*

39  Menno Hurenkamp, Evelien Tonkens, and Jan Willem Duyvendak, *Crafting Citizenship: Negotiating Tensions in Modern Society* (Basingstoke: Palgrave Macmillan, 2012).

40  This agenda is strongly based on Hekma and Duyvendak, "Queer Netherlands: A Puzzling Example."

41  Laurens Buijs, Gert Hekma, and Jan Willem Duyvendak, *Als ze maar van me afblijven* (Amsterdam: Amsterdam University Press, 2009).

42  Katherine Fobear, *Beyond a Lesbian Space? Public Lesbian Social Spaces as Sites for the Production of Visibility, Identity, and Community* (University of Amsterdam, MA thesis, 2010).

43  Jantine van Lisdonk and Diana van Bergen, "Homojongeren en hun seksuele voorkeur: invulling en uiting," in *Steeds gewoner, nooit gewoon*, Saskia Keuzenkamp, ed. (The Hague: Netherlands Institute for Social Research, 2010), p. 143.

44  Theo Sandfort, Ron de Graaf, Ron Bijl, and Paul Schnabel, "Same-Sex Sexual Behaviour and Psychiatric Disorders: Findings from the Netherlands Mental Health Survey and Incidence Study NEMESIS," 58(1) *Archives of General Psychiatry* 85, 91 (2001).

45  Diana van Bergen and Jantine van Lisdonk, "Psychisch welbevinden en zelfacceptatie van homojongeren," in *Steeds gewoner, nooit gewoon*, Saskia Keuzenkamp, ed. (The Hague: Netherlands Institute for Social Research, 2010), pp. 174, 196.

46  Lisdonk and Bergen, "Homojongeren en hun seksuele voorkeur: invulling en uiting," pp. 191–93.

47  Sanjay Aggarwal, *Between Rejection and Belonging: Exploring Mental Health Disparities between Homosexual and Heterosexual Men in Amsterdam* (University of Amsterdam, MA thesis, 2010).

48  Seidman, *Beyond the Closet.*

49  Tim Savenije and Jan Willem Duyvendak, "De relatie tussen opvattingen over gender en homoseksualiteit," 3(9) *Sociologie* 318, 344 (2013).

50  Daphne van de Bongardt, *Teaching Sexuality Education in the Netherlands: Just Another Topic . . . ?* (University of Amsterdam, MA thesis, 2008); Daphne van de Bongardt, Ineke Mouthaan, and Henny Bos, "Seksuele en relationele vorming in het voortgezet onderwijs," 29(1) *Pedagogiek* 60, 77 (2009).

51  Gert Hekma, Saskia Keuzenkamp, David Bos, and Jan Willem Duyvendak, "Samenvatting en slotbeschouwing," in *Gewoon doen: Acceptatie van homoseksualiteit in Nederland*, Saskia Keuzenkamp, David Bos, Jan Willem Duyvendak, and Gert Hekma, eds. (The Hague: Netherlands Institute for Social Research, 2006), p. 234.

12

# The Power of Theory

*Same-Sex Marriage, Education, and Gender Panic in France*

BRUNO PERREAU

On April 23, 2013, the French National Assembly adopted the law known as "Marriage for All," which gives gay and lesbian couples the right to marry and jointly adopt children.[1] After review to ensure that it did not violate the 1958 French Constitution, the law was promulgated on May 17, 2013. The passing of this law was preceded by intense debates in Parliament, in the media, and on the streets, during an eventful year characterized by the large-scale mobilization of its opponents. The demonstrations that took place on the streets of Paris and other large cities in France came as a surprise to the rest of the world:[2] how could France, perceived as a socially liberal country, be the site of such resistance to same-sex marriage and adoption?

What I will show in this chapter is that the resistance to "marriage for all" is in fact not at all surprising, but belongs within a long tradition of street protests by Catholic and other conservative movements in France. It is only the forms these protests have taken that are novel: what conservative and religious movements have now begun to do is to borrow a number of the activist tactics of leftist movements (discourse that uses the language of labor movements, zaps, partial nudity in public spaces, and so on). I argue that these borrowings have become possible because the Socialist Party has deserted the sphere of activism and is increasingly disconnected from critical intellectual activity. The executive branch's vacillation during the debates over the proposed law is one example of this: the Socialist president, François Hollande, repeatedly sought to limit its scope, for example by reminding the country's mayors that they possessed "freedom of conscience" and thus were not personally obligated to perform same-sex marriages.[3] The term "freedom of conscience" originates in a clause of the Public Health Code that excuses doctors opposed to abortion from performing that procedure. It was quite naturally taken over by opponents of "marriage for all," many of whom began their careers as activists in the anti-abortion campaign.

Moreover, the law of May 17, 2013, discriminated in important respects between married heterosexual and married homosexual couples. There is, for example, no automatic presumption that same-sex married couples are related to each other's children: they are required to go through the process of adopting a partner's biological child. When such biological children are born by means of medically assisted reproduction performed outside France, some courts have refused to permit their adoption, on the ground that the parents have contravened a 1994 bioethics law that restricts medically assisted reproduction to heterosexual couples. It is only recently that the highest civil court has considered these adoptions legal.[4] To that example we can add the continuing existence of other forms of discrimination against LGBT people, such as the ban on surrogacy and the way that transsexuals who seek to change their officially registered gender are treated as medical cases. It is also interesting to note that the preamble to the law of May 17, 2013, supports extending the right to marry to same-sex couples by adducing examples from other countries, but never invokes the principles of equality, liberty, or dignity. In other words, this law should in no way be viewed as a genuine recognition of sexual minorities, but rather as a form of concession to their complaints, much like its predecessor the Civil Solidarity Pact (PaCS), which was made into law in 1999 after many years of lobbying by same-sex organizations and of the fight against AIDS.

In a social context in which equality is still withheld, that the protests against "marriage for all" would persist even after the law was passed seemed almost inevitable.[5] If the law continues to discriminate, why not continue to put pressure on the government? The chief movements that opposed the law of May 17, 2013, have quite naturally continued their strategy of occupying the space of public debate, targeting especially the teaching of so-called gender theory. Adopting a form of argument first developed by the Vatican in the mid-1990s, these movements claim that the growth of the academic study of gender created the conditions that made same-sex marriage and adoption possible, and that as a result it poses a risk to young people. In their view, the denaturalization of sexual categories is an "ideology" that aims to destabilize the "traditional French family." This denunciation of "gender theory" is thus impregnated with nationalist overtones (both racist and anti-Semitic, as I will show), and most prominently with anti-Americanism. What is actually meant by "gender theory" is essentially American queer theory, and most especially the work of philosopher Judith Butler. Fear of the transmission of homosexuality, the development of transsexualism, and the corruption of youth emerges from a moral register that these protesters are at home with. But I will show that the force they are able to exert in the public sphere is due above all to the fact that they denounce the damage being done to France's traditional heritage by a transnational community. They thus mirror the republicanism of the Socialist Party, a republicanism that allows for no other community than the nation, and that denounces "identity politics" (*communautarisme*) as a national scourge. This explains why, after several weeks of protest by the anti–"marriage for all" groups against programs to combat sexism in the schools (including Les ABCD de l'égalité, promoted by Najat Vallaud-Belkacem, the minister for women's rights), the Socialist government decided in February 2014 to withdraw a planned reform of family law in order to "appease" French society. This reform would have accorded legal status to step-parents, a status that French law has now withheld from them, whether heterosexual or homosexual.

From this perspective, there appears to be no radical break between the "before" and "after" of same-sex marriage in France. The inquiry I will pursue here thus includes a critical analysis of recent history. The understanding of the chronology of events is not only variable, but is itself the object of normative conflicts: where the opponents of "marriage for all" see this reform as a dangerous beginning, the supporters of equal rights are convinced that it is just one stage in an ongoing process. The social conservatives of the Left, meanwhile, hope that in passing this law they have dealt once and for all with the claims of the lesbians and gays. Understanding our relation to chronology is thus a key issue for the LGBT population today. We ought certainly to start by discarding the very idea of "post-marriage." This means rejecting the mythology of the "battle won." This seems to me all the more necessary in that LGBT communities have not been built up via simple linear progression over time, a fact that could well be forgotten in the absence of a critical reading of history.[6] Of course, the history of legal change does provide one possible narrative. The law gives recognition and security to many same-sex families with respect to naming, inheritance rights, health care, and so on. Its impact is thus both real and important. The relationship of LGBT populations to the law has itself changed, notably in their more frequent recourse to the judicial system. But does this mean that the law on gay marriage has transformed citizenship itself? Indeed, it is because they fear this understanding will change that the opponents of the law began to protest and continue to do so. Ultimately, the celebration of same-sex marriages is not their primary issue. Even the most aggressive of them have never sought to disrupt actual wedding ceremonies—because their protest is focused on the *idea* of marriage, seen as a vehicle of moral meaning and moral values. As I will show, this history not only began long before 2013, but it also did not end then.

This brings up another issue central to the future of LGBT populations both in France and in the United States—"reverse" relativism. While the traditionalist Right continues to denounce so-called postmodern and relativistic values that treat heterosexuality and homosexuality as equivalent, at the same time a new phenomenon has arisen, one created in the name of abstract universalism. Conservative movements in effect see themselves as in a "subordinate" position, given the new recognition of LGBT rights, and demand that their own worldview be recognized in turn. In other words, they appropriate the idea of moral relativism for their own purposes and present themselves as the majority victims of a system supposedly designed to suit minorities. In the name of the neutral treatment due to all citizens, they seek recognition on an equal footing with LGBT struggles. It is therefore not surprising that in France they try to get people to see LGBT rights as the outcome of a specific theory, because in this way they can gain legitimacy for their own principles (religious values in particular). I propose to take these conservative movements at their word: I argue for a strongly minoritarian democracy, by which I mean a political system that treats the protection of minorities as a primary objective and takes their situation as an index of the common good. Such a system is distinct from moral relativism, since it is based on the fact not only that every minority is produced via relations of domination but also that its experience of domination gives rise to an ethic of generosity.[7]

## Heterogeneous Protests

The movement in opposition to "marriage for all" came into existence in early fall 2012, arising out of several circles of zealous Christians close to the Vatican and the French Catholic Church. In spite of the cliché according to which Catholic circles are reluctant to demonstrate in public, they turn out in fact to be highly organized and to view the street as a place for "a referendum at the initiative of the people."[8] These networks have acquired real experience in activist techniques as a result of their previous protests against the law on free schools, against the voluntary interruption of pregnancy (that is to say, abortion), against the PaCS, and so on. Following the call to protest issued by several members of the Catholic hierarchy in the summer of 2012—in August 2012, for example, Cardinal Philippe Barbarin, the archbishop of Lyon, declared that "Parliament is not God the Father!"[9]—a collective opposed to "marriage for all" was quickly formed, calling itself the "Manif pour tous," or "the demonstration for all." It was founded in September 2012 and headed by Frigide Barjot,[10] a devout Catholic who had previously been a well-known visitor to the gay nightclubs of Paris. After the failure of the movement opposed to the PaCS, which had been led by parliamentary deputy Christine Boutin (a consultant to the Holy See's Pontifical Council for the Family and close to the fundamentalist Catholic group Opus Dei),[11] Frigide Barjot's leadership sought to "modernize" the opposition to "marriage for all," especially with respect to media relations (the Manif pour tous presented itself as nondenominational). Her takeover did not happen without creating its own internal tensions, since the majority of the Manif pour tous membership belonged to traditional Catholic groups, including its spokesman, Tugdual Derville,[12] the leader of Alliance VITA, an anti-abortion group founded by Christine Boutin in 1993. In May 2013, Frigide Barjot was replaced at the head of the Manif pour tous by Ludovine de la Rochère,[13] a former communications officer at the Conference of French Bishops and at the Lejeune Foundation, a group linked to Opus Dei that passionately supported the more militant anti-abortion protesters

The second movement to oppose "marriage for all" is the Printemps français (French Spring). It came into being in March 2013, when several members of the Manif pour tous refused to follow the movement's leaders and condemn the involvement of groups of skinheads on the fringes of the demonstration that had just been organized in Paris. Among these dissidents was Béatrice Bourges,[14] formerly a parliamentary attaché belonging to the Gaullist party and the founder of the Collectif pour l'enfant (Collective for the Child). Bourges is close to the extreme Right (the National Front deputies Marion Maréchal-Le Pen, Gilbert Collard, and Jacques Bompard regularly express their support for her), and she took charge of this new movement. The Printemps français was deliberately named in imitation of the popular uprisings of the Arab world in 2011, on the ground that like them it represents the real people against the decadent elite.

Another far right organization whose significant involvement should be noted is France Jeunesse Civitas. This group, founded in the 1970s, was extremely critical of the festive atmosphere of the Manif pour tous; it organizes public prayers in the street outside government offices and, more broadly, uses the opposition to "marriage for all" as a platform from which to attack republicanism and secularism.

While the Manif pour tous and the Printemps français have a national following as well as some international connections via French expatriates,[15] many other groups were formed in the context of particular demonstrations, often numbering only a few people who in most cases had no history of activism but were mobilized around a slogan, a form of action, or a dress code. There thus exists a whole galaxy of opponents of the same-sex marriage law. Though predominantly Catholic, they have been joined by some Muslim groups such as the Collectif des musulmans de France—a group given much prominence by the leaders of the movement although no more than a hundred or so of its members took part in the demonstrations. The UMP (Union for a Popular Movement), the conservative party now in opposition to the Socialist government, was in the throes of a leadership crisis (in November 2012, Jean-François Copé became the leader of the party with a contested 50.03 percent victory over former prime minister Jean-François Fillon); seeing the protests as an opportunity to regain some activist energy, the UMP has expressed support for the Manif pour tous on numerous occasions.[16] Many far-right groups (Jeunesses nationalistes, Groupe Union Défense, and others) also participated in the demonstrations and were the source of much of the trouble associated with the spring 2013 marches.

Civitas: Demonstration and prayers against "marriage for all."

Many of these ad hoc groups, especially those whose members are under twenty-five, actually borrow numerous activist tactics from the LGBT and feminist movements, for example by using "pride" as a key term in their attacks on "marriage for all." Following the example of World Youth Day (an event for young Catholics created by Pope John Paul II in 1985 and organized in Paris in 1997), they laid claim to "Catho Pride" and readily adopted new activist tactics in public while also making extensive use of social media (Facebook, and Twitter in particular) to expand their ranks. In the same way, the Veilleurs group organized vigils (readings and meditations) in the manner of flash mobs. Many protesters took up the idea of male-female parity, a principle of political representation in France, and claimed that it applied to the parental couple. After Femen (a Ukrainian feminist group that typically performs shock happenings in public) gave its support to "marriage for all," several groups opposed to it decided to respond directly: the Antigones, dressed in white, claim they are restoring the pride that comes from being feminine rather than feminist; the Hommen seek to "protect children" by highlighting the protective power of the male body, which in their view has been perverted by the public exposure of the naked female body (as symbolized by the Femen). Masked and bare-chested,

Extreme-right group Jeunesses nationalistes demonstrating against gay marriage and adoption in Lyon, April 17, 2013.

their young, slim, white bodies are almost indistinguishable from one another, differentiated only by the colors of the pants they wear. They call for a society in which men control the public space through their homosociality, that is to say, solidarity among heterosexual men that is defined by the proscription of homosexuality.[17] They frequently suggest parallels between the existing political establishment and Nazism, claiming that they themselves are the "resistance" (for example, by hijacking the image of Jean Moulin, the French Resistance leader), and demand that desecrated French masculinity be restored to its proper standing, as it was at the Liberation.

Opposition to the law has thus been extremely heterogeneous, and marked by internal tensions. However, all of these movements have had one theme in common: the protection of children. All of them routinely play on the ambiguity of "the desire for children": that is to say, they deliberately conflate the desire to be a parent with sexual desire for children. This implied equation of homosexuality with pedophilia makes it easier to present traditional gender roles as a bulwark against decadence and perversion.[18] It also gives support to the idea that homosexual practices are contagious, in that they can literally be reproduced through

Screen capture from the Antigones' video presentation: http://antigones.fr/.

filiation from same-sex parents. Opposition to the commercialization of the body (as allegedly reflected in the use of assisted reproduction technologies and surrogacy, but also prostitution and the use of sexual imagery in advertising), seen as the unnatural practice par excellence, thus lies at the heart of all the protest movements against "marriage for all."

The sensational nature of the argument against the commercialization of the body was widely exploited by the media, even as they claimed to be preserving balance and neutrality by presenting opinions (presumably equivalent) from all sides. Moreover, the absence of a clear social (in the economic sense) and liberal (in the political sense) position on marriage and filiation among the parties of the Left, and especially the Socialists, ended up encouraging rather than curbing this moral panic.

## The Socialist Party Drifts toward Republicanism

Throughout the debates over "marriage for all," the Socialist government followed the guiding principle pronounced by the president of the republic, François Hollande: do not divide the country.[19] Both proponents and opponents of extending marriage and joint adoption to same-sex couples were frequently consulted over the fall and winter

The Hommen: *above*, demonstration outside the Palais de Chaillot in Paris, June 7, 2013; *below*, a poster evoking Jean Moulin. Translations: "No to gay marriage," "We will never yield."

Posters from the Manif pour tous. *Left to right*: "And you, which one do you prefer?" "Neither for rent nor for sale." "Children going cheap."

(in parliamentary hearings[20] and meetings with the president).[21] The government also chose to adopt euphemistic wording for this extension of the right to marry and adopt jointly, by referring to the text of the law as "Marriage for All." Initially hostile to the institutions of the Fifth Republic, in the 1970s the Socialist Party in effect developed a strategy for getting into power based on accepting the rules of the republicanist game,[22] to the point where it felt obliged to carry some of the republican principles and symbols even further than its opponents. This explains why, when the first Socialist president of the republic was elected in 1981, the Socialists made it a point of honor to identify the nation as the sole community to which all French citizens belonged. This change was accentuated during the rise of the far Right in the 1980s. In 1983, the municipal elections in Dreux saw the Gaullist party (Rassemblement pour la République) allied for the first time with the National Front. The response was a visible ideological shift within the Socialist Party, which believed that the best way to distinguish itself from the clientelist attitude of the Right was to develop an anti-"communalist" rhetoric.

By doing so, it not only cut itself off from the legacy of anti-authoritarianism going back to the 1960s, when it was still opposed to the institutions of the Fifth Republic, but also distanced itself from those minority groups (racial and sexual minorities in particular) that had helped bring it to power. Criticizing what they see as their tendency to self-centeredness, Socialist governments are no longer willing to recognize minority groups unless they discard their own identity and history.[23] The Socialist Party's original voices, often rooted in the experience of local politics, have found themselves marginalized. This has been true of key figures working for recognition of LGBT rights, such as Françoise Gaspard (former Socialist mayor of Dreux, a deputy in the French and the European parliaments, who worked for the establishment of a women's division within the Socialist Party in 1979, eliminated by François Mitterrand from the list of ministers in his first government because of her sexual orientation) and Patrick Bloche (a deputy from Paris, former member of the organization Homosexualité et Socialisme, and coauthor of the PaCS legislation along with Jean-Pierre Michel). It is this fear of "communalism" that has led Socialist majorities to move forward only in tiny steps. On October 9, 1998, too few Socialist deputies were present in the National Assembly to vote the PaCS into law, thus causing the first version of the law to be rejected. In 1999, the Socialist government of Lionel Jospin refused to allow the PaCS to have any impact whatsoever on filiation.[24] In 2012, François Hollande supported the extension of assisted reproduction to single women and lesbian couples, only to back down in 2013 by deciding instead to defer to the opinion of the National Consultative Committee on Ethics, a body that had always been adamantly opposed to this procedure.[25] In this two-steps-forward-one-step-back manner, the Socialist Party has constantly left itself open to the suspicion of clientelism. The opponents of "marriage for all" criticize it for precisely what it seeks to refrain from. It is thus not surprising that the Manif pour tous and Printemps français have given such prominence to the figure of Marianne (the symbol of the French republic, whose image is used on all official documents, engraved on French euro coins, etc.) in all their demonstrations (in addition to the fact that she props up traditional gender roles, with women reduced to a symbolic function while men exercise real power).

Another striking feature of the debate on marriage was the absence of economic or social arguments for marriage equality. Two days after the National Assembly took the final vote on the law that would open up marriage and joint adoption to same-sex couples, France's prime minister, Jean-Marc Ayrault, told the newspaper *20 Minutes*, "We are not going to start a debate on a new subject every day. Every reform happens at its own pace. I do not want to force through reforms. More than ever, what I want is to bring the French people together in the fight for more jobs." Philippe Doucet, deputy for the Val d'Oise, made the point rather more explicitly:

> We have won the prize for the world's longest debate over marriage for all! Close to eight months, compared to 24 hours in New Zealand! It has all taken far too long. Let's get back to the real issues, our economic and social problems. . . . [Marriage] is an additional right, it's a very good thing. But it is not one of the real concerns of the French people. The truth has to be told: nobody gives a damn about marriage for all.

Christophe Caresche, a Paris deputy, added, "It was time we were done with this. We're glad to be moving on to other matters."[26] A candidate for mayor of Marseille, Patrick Mennucci, even claimed that his defeat in the 2014 municipal elections was the fault of the adoption of the law on "marriage for all."[27]

The idea that marriage is merely a social reform and as such not a high priority for "the French people," who are really concerned with the economic crisis, underpins a number of stereotypes. First, it excludes gays and lesbians from the category of citizens, as if they did not belong within the meaning of the term "the French people" (and precisely when it is their inclusion in the legal system that is at issue!). Next, it reiterates the traditional prejudice on the Left that homosexuality is a "bourgeois" practice. Lastly, it assumes that marriage is a purely social relationship, when its primary implications are economic (taxation, property, common residence, inheritance, etc.). In the absence of arguments in favor of "marriage for all" as a matter of ensuring equality on the economic front,[28] it was easy for the opponents of the law to claim they were defending the "voiceless," and to do this by drawing on imagery taken directly from workers' and trade unions' struggles. Their banners claimed kinship with the urchin Gavroche, the nineteenth-century poster child for abandoned and impoverished children. Many children were actually dressed up as street urchins, and a group of adult protesters began calling themselves the Gavroches to denounce the repressive measures of Interior Minister Manuel Valls (spelled ValSS on this occasion).

On other posters, raised fists painted with the colors of the French flag were accompanied by the slogan "Touche pas au mariage, occupe-toi du chômage" (Hands off marriage, do something about unemployment), while a drawing of a factory was captioned "On veut du boulot, pas du mariage homo" (We want jobs, not gay marriage), and signs read "La priorité c'est Aulnay, pas le mariage gay" (The priority is Aulnay [a Peugeot Citroën industrial site, scheduled to be closed in 2015], not gay marriage) and "Fraternité pour la croissance" (Fraternity for Economic Growth).

## Fantasizing "Theory"

Marriage and adoption were "test" debates for French society, being the occasion for supporters as well as opponents to affirm their moral values in a context deeply marked by questions relative to identity (immigration, religion, bioethics, etc.). In *The Politics of Adoption*, I argued that

Demonstration, February 2, 2014. Women dressed as Marianne with children dressed as street urchins.

Demonstration, February 2, 2014. The "Gavroches" group.

"We want jobs, not gay marriage"

"Kid's Rights"

"The priority is Aulnay, not gay marriage"

"Fraternity for Economic Growth"

"Hands off marriage, do something about unemployment"

for the past thirty years, reform of family law in France has been guided by the desire to uphold the sense of membership in a nation. Policies relative to filiation are first and foremost designed to manufacture the future "children of the nation" (evoking the opening words of the French national anthem).[29] Consequently, where pragmatic debates on these issues have taken place in Belgium, Spain, the UK, and Portugal, France has seen exchanges on the theoretical level, focused on the concept of civilization, anthropological principles, and the meaning of French identity. This approach is the outcome of a firm belief in the power of abstract conceptions of citizenship to direct or affect individual behavior. It is thus not surprising that in France the opponents of "marriage for all" should have searched for the underlying causes of this reform in what they call "gender theory."

Fear of gender theory was first fueled in 1995 by the Vatican at the Fourth World Conference on Women in Beijing.[30] Acting like a state in opposition to the "individualism of rights," the Vatican then sought to derail several UN projects, including the worldwide decriminalization

*Above*: Demonstration in Paris, February 2, 2014: "No to gender theory." Used with permission of Reuters/Benoît Tessier. *Below*: Poster by the France Jeunesse Civitas group: "Stop to gender theory."

of homosexuality. In 2004, Josef Ratzinger, at that time the pro-prefect of the Congregation for the Doctrine of the Faith, sent a letter to the dignitaries of the Catholic Church, warning them of the danger of disconnecting male and female roles from the "natural" attributes of the body, since such a theoretical position would make heterosexuality and homosexuality morally equivalent.[31] This return to the body is what the Vatican soon came to call "human ecology," a theory that it opposed explicitly to "gender theory."[32] Opponents of "marriage for all," who were steeped in these texts, were denouncing the evils of "gender theory" even before the law on "marriage for all" had been officially proposed. In spring 2011, several Catholic parents' associations filed objections to biology textbooks that suggested that sex and social behavior might be disconnected. These associations saw this suggestion as a dangerous denial of sexual difference, taken straight out of gender ideology. Their resistance was organized online in forums and blogs. In August 2011, eighty UMP deputies requested that the then minister of education, Luc Chatel, remove the textbooks in question from the schools. In order to keep his political majority happy, Chatel set up a committee to examine the textbooks. In other words, the future activists opposed to "marriage for all" were first mobilized around the question of what *national* education ought to mean.

It is not surprising that the denunciation of "gender" (a term often left in English) took the form of anti-Americanism. "Gender theory" was supposedly invented in the United States, a society that is viewed as constructed on a consumerist, identity-politics model, whose "political correctness" renders it fundamentally incompatible with the French tradition of the "commerce between the sexes."[33] U.S. society is also alleged to promote an irreligious culture, that of mass entertainment. In 2004 the U.S. show "Queer Eye for the Straight Guy" was imitated in France and shown on the main TV channel, TF1, under the euphemistic title "Queer. Cinq Experts dans le vent" (Queer: five hot experts), the first occurrence of the word "queer" in a show meant for general audiences. France, in short, is supposedly threatened by invasion, and queer theory and practice are the enemy's chief weapons. While this position is not without its inconsistencies—many of the key queer studies from the United States draw on French writers—it also arouses the suspicion that a foreign conspiracy is attacking the national interest, a conspiracy in which sexual minorities inside France are complicit. This fantasy of

A blog for "lay Catholics," the Salon Beige: "The scandal of gender theory."

betrayal by a "Sexual International" has very deep roots in the thinking of the Right and extreme Right in France.[34] During the 1930s the press used cartoons and articles to portray the "invert" as feminized, governed by an irresistible desire for the triumphant masculinity of enemy forces, and predisposed to denunciation, corruption, and, needless to say, treason. The invert belongs at once to an inferior race and an international conspiracy. As analyzed by Proust in his passages on the "accursed race," the invert is the enemy within, like the figure of the stateless Jew. The political leaders of the Left, such as Léon Blum, were also frequently caricatured as inverts.

Current attacks on "gender theory" tend to sing from the same hymn book: Judith Butler, the only queer author widely translated in France,[35] is attacked as a woman, an American, a lesbian, an intellectual, a Jew, and a leftist.[36] She is portrayed as the Antichrist by the anti–"marriage for all" movement. The link with the United States is also due to the fact that the rejection of "gender theory" is described as a true crusade, one that will prove to be beneficial for Americans too. In a talk addressed to the National Organization for Marriage in Washington in June 2014,[37] Ludovine de la Rochère, the leader of the Manif pour tous, declared that France was coming to the aid of the United States, to help reassert the universal definition of parenthood based on the male/female couple united in matrimony.

Image from a Facebook page: "The whole truth about the inventor of Gender Studies." "Gender theory, here we come!"

Lastly, it is important to note that groups opposing the alleged invasion by "gender theory" have attached themselves to other protests that are even more openly nationalistic and anti-Semitic. On January 26, 2014, a "Day of Rage" was organized in Paris. The demonstration brought together a miscellaneous assortment of extreme-right and populist groups (including Civitas and the Hommen); although the pretext was an attack on the government's fiscal policy, in fact it was the scene of belligerent public expressions of anti-Semitism. Fascist groups (such as Bloc Identitaire) marched chanting, "Jew get out, France doesn't belong to you." Many fans of the former comedian Dieudonné, who has repeatedly been convicted for making anti-Semitic statements, took the opportunity to perform the "quenelle" in public: the "quenelle" is the name given by Dieudonné to a downward thrust of the arm, which symbolizes humiliation by sexual penetration ("fuck the system") and also looks like an upside-down "Heil Hitler" salute. In this way, the general idea of foreign invasion becomes the focus for unlikely alliances among groups that demand the right to freedom of thought and expression from a republic that they view as corrupted by internationalized minorities and foreigners. These alliances have developed because the groups in question share the demand for a public platform, but they also prove deeply contradictory, as is shown for instance by the fact that not all use racist language to the same degree.

## Queer Monstrosity

While the debates over marriage and filiation have routinely linked homophobia and anti-Semitism via the image of the enemy within, they also draw on the imagery of the monstrous, the utterly strange (which in turn builds on racial stereotypes). The chief promoter of the "marriage for all" law in the government was the justice minister, Christiane Taubira. Taubira comes from a Guyanese background and belongs to the party of the Radical Left; both in the National Assembly and in the Senate she expounded a defense of "marriage for all" that broke with the Socialist Party's republicanist language. She drew on Aimé Césaire and Léon-Gontran Damas to speak about the contribution of minorities to the public good, stressing the expansive rather than reductive nature of identity politics. The Manif pour tous quickly targeted Taubira: she was depicted as the powerful, castrating black woman, beating children with the law code, destroying the natural order, a half-human, half-Godzilla mongrel, the monstrous symbol of the destruction of the French family.

This symbol was meant to mirror the monstrous character of the law itself, which supposedly sought to turn citizens, decently divided into two sexes, into animals: androgynous creatures (represented by the snail) who threaten to devour children, primitive beasts such as the mammoth, the symbol of the "theory of evolution" that threatens creationism. It all came to be seen as the menacing advance of bestial forces. Conversely, the Virgin Birth celebrated by Christianity became the ideal example of true civilization.[38]

The rhetoric of animality reached its peak during a visit by Taubira to Angers: children brought along by an anti–"marriage for all" group greeted the justice minister hooting like monkeys, waving bananas, and shouting, "Eat your banana, monkey lady."[39] On November 13, 2013, the far-right newspaper *Minute* ran a headline: "Maligne comme un singe. Taubira retrouve la banane" (Crafty as a monkey, Taubira gets her banana grin back).[40] These racist comments were made a few days after a National Front candidate, Anne-Sophie Leclère (who was convicted of racist abuse in July 2014), had published two photographs on her Facebook page comparing the minister to a monkey; these were widely copied by neo-Nazi groups like Hitler Boulevard, who also apologized to the monkey for comparing it with Taubira. Leclère was expelled from

Manif pour tous posters. *Above*: poster calling for demonstrations on May 26, 2013 ("Monster demonstration"). *Left*: "When Taubira appears, filiation disappears." *Right*: "Save our children from the Taubira law."

Manif pour tous posters calling for a demonstration on February 2, 2014. *Left*: "Sex education in elementary school: hands off our kids" (an allusion to the 1980s antiracist slogan "Hands off my buddy"). *Right*: "Gender theory in the schools: Stop."

the National Front on December 1, 2013, but the party has since supported her appeal against the conviction.

Najat Belkacem-Vallaud, who as minister for women's rights had worked on the introduction of materials about male-female equality in the schools, is another victim of these attacks. Her appointment as minister of education in August 2014 is seen by the anti–"marriage for all" cohorts as a deliberate provocation. Ludovine de la Rochère declared,

> In the department of National Education the State may, under the pretext of equality, impose indoctrination, requiring us to treat schoolchildren as neuter, undifferentiated beings. Najat Vallaud-Belkacem is living in an anthropological utopia, fighting in the sex struggle the way others used to fight in the class struggle. This is a serious matter. We may wonder what Hollande had in mind when he made such a controversial nomination. It's absurd, shocking.[41]

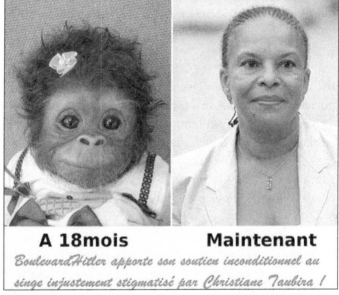

*Above*: Cover of the magazine *Minute* for November 13, 2013. *Below*: Poster created by the Hitler Boulevard group, borrowing an image used by National Front deputy Anne-Sophie Leclère: "Hitler Boulevard offers its unconditional support to the monkey unfairly stigmatized by Christiane Taubira!"

A few days later, the Catholic newspaper *Valeurs Actuelles* ran the headline "L'ayatollah: enquête sur la Ministre de la Rééducation natio-nale" (The ayatollah: investigating the minister of national reeducation), conflating the minister's Moroccan origins with religious fanaticism and insinuating in barely disguised language ("reeducation") that "gender theory" is a form of child abuse. The day before, the newspaper *Minute* ran the headline "Une marocaine musulmane à l'Éducation nationale: la provocation Vallaud-Belkacem" (A Moroccan Muslim in the National Education Ministry: the Vallaud-Belkacem provocation), stripping the minister of her French nationality and playing deliberately on Islamo-phobic prejudices.[42]

As these racist comments pile up, what in effect they do is to expose one of the implicit goals of the Manif pour tous and Printemps français: a France that is racially, religiously, and sexually pure. Nonetheless, it is crucial to recognize the paradox lurking within this fantasy of purity. The monster, by definition bestial and impure, delimits the symbolic frontiers of civilized humanity.[43] But if it is dangerous, this is because it is fueled by brutal, destructive energy. Hence, paradoxically, its super-human powers have to be acknowledged. It gives rise at once to a kind of fascination and a kind of revulsion. From this perspective, the figure of the "strong woman," as exemplified by Christiane Taubira and Najat Vallaud-Belkacem, directly parallels that of the "queer child" (and thus reinforces the idea of conspiracy). Opponents of so-called gender theory do in fact denounce the threat that they believe it poses to children: once children's assumptions about sexuality have been undermined, they too risk becoming sexually undifferentiated. Katherine Bond Stockton has shown how literature and film have made use of the oneiric force of the character of the queer child.[44] Both feared and admired, such a child provides a glimpse of a different world, since its very existence dem-onstrates that no kind of social necessity underpins the insistence on a predetermined model (whereas conservative groups see the assertion of a heterosexual model as necessary for reproduction itself). It is not surprising that one of the popular targets of the Manif pour tous and the Printemps français was Cécile Sciamma's film *Tomboy*, released in 2011. In the film, a ten-year-old child moves with her family to a new town; when she is taken for a boy by her schoolmates she makes no attempt to put them right.

Demonstration in Paris, April 21, 2013: a banner attacking the
film *Tomboy*. "Gender theory and its movies: Stop! April 2013:
my daughter was forced to watch this movie in fourth grade."

This fantasy of the queer child also functions as an inverted image
of the infantilized adult homosexual. While I do not have space here
to review the many theories that describe homosexuality as a form of
arrested sexual development stuck at an infantile stage, deconstructing
this prejudice seems to me to be particularly important for the LGBT
movement today. The fact that some gays and lesbians are parents and
are recognized as such by various state institutions does not mean that
the association of infantilization with homosexuality has been addressed. But marriage and filiation have introduced an exception to
this equation: they grant homosexuals a kind of social worth that they
would never have managed to acquire by the mere fact of their exis-

tence. In this context, rethinking the status of single and childless people and putting an end to the legal discrimination they endure would open up a new normative reality. Why does marriage entail rights that other forms of relationship do not? Why can couples who choose the PaCS not adopt jointly? Why should a childless married couple receive tax benefits denied to childless single people? Why should it be unthinkable to be married to one person and PaCSed with another? Or to be married to several people at once?

The second outcome of this deconstruction of the fantasy of the queer child would be the removal of sex identification from documents such as birth certificates (which would mean removing the requirement of surgical gender reassignment, now imposed on transsexuals in France) and the acceptance by the legal system of the possibility of multiple identities. A gay man who defines himself in terms of his sisterhood with other gay men can perfectly well, and simultaneously, define himself as the father of a child, a child to whom the specificity of this relationship matters. Many children live every day with several parents and step-parents, whose roles are sometimes interchangeable and sometimes mutually exclusive. Transsexual women can become mothers using their own sperm, preserved before they made the transition. These examples, to name but a few, show that a law that recognizes multiple identities has yet to be invented.

## Minors and Minorities: A Question of Education

School is one of the primary places where children develop their relationships with others. The Manif pour tous and Printemps français have concentrated their attacks on the schools, for two reasons. The first is that many of their members belong to Catholic parents' organizations. The second is that there is a residual distrust of the republican state school system among Catholic activists, a distrust inherited from the late nineteenth century and voiced on many occasions, for example in 1984 during demonstrations for "free schools" (these demonstrations were in fact attacking a proposed law that sought to increase state oversight of private schools, many of which are Catholic). Historian Grégoire Kauffmann speaks of "nostalgia" for a "pre-industrial world" in which Catholicism still essentially controlled the teaching of values.[45] In a society with very few practicing believers (the CSA—Conseil, Sondage, Analyse—institute estimates that today the regular practice of religion is found among only 4.5 percent of the French population), schools are still perceived as dangerous agents of secularization. Unlike in the United States, it is the call for freedom of conscience rather than for religious freedom that fuels the opposition to "gender theory." Presented as an ethical issue (especially in the light of the transformations made possible by biotechnology), this appeal to freedom of conscience enables alliances across religious affiliations. Several media commentators (Alain Finkielkraut, Marcel Gauchet, Michel Onfray, and others) have thus added their weight to the battle against "gender theory" in the schools, in the name of the preservation of childhood, the human body, and the traditional curriculum.

The rejection of "gender theory" is thus a rejection of school itself. For the past few years, Farida Belghoul has organized the opposition on the Internet and in public meetings. A teacher at a vocational college, a militant communist in the 1970s and antiracist in the 1980s, she is now close to Dieudonné and various right-wing circles[46] and denounces "LGBT propaganda" and the perverting of children. She propagates baseless rumors, going so far as to claim that "gender theory" has led to teaching kindergarten children to masturbate.[47] She especially targets the ABCD de l'égalité program. This experimental curriculum was introduced in nearly six hundred classes in September 2013, and consisted of lectures and exercises designed to get children to think about the inequalities between men and women; it implemented the July 8, 2013, law on the reorganization of the school, whose goal is to "convey the values of equality and respect between girls and boys, women and men." To oppose this program, Belghoul launched a "boycott school day" in December 2013, encouraging parents to keep their children at home once a month instead of sending them to school. The first of these days was scheduled for January 24, 2014. Enlisting networks via email and text message, Belghoul sought support from parents who, themselves often socially disadvantaged and discriminated against, have developed a degree of fear and distrust of the schools. Her initiative thus formed a complement to the actions of the organizations of Catholic parents: the latter, possessed of a wealth of cultural and economic capital, placed more emphasis on the transformation of pedagogy itself. This is expressed in the Vigi Gender network,[48] the appeal by the AFC (a Catholic family organization) to the Conseil d'Etat to reject the new education law,[49] and the pressure exerted on several public libraries identified by activists connected with the Printemps français as "ideological."[50] These same militant groups also protested against the antisexism demonstration by boys in a Nantes high school, who wore skirts to school in May 2014.[51]

Confronted with these assorted protests, the government has repeatedly backed down. In June 2013 Vincent Peillon, the minister for national education, claimed to be "against gender theory," admitting a few days later that no such theory exists. In February 2014, the day after a new protest by the Manif pour tous, then prime minister Jean-Marc Ayrault withdrew the proposed family law reform that would have simplified adoption and granted legal status to all step-parents. In June 2014, Benoît Hamon, the new minister for national education, announced the cancellation of the ABCD de l'égalité program. He viewed its outcome as positive overall and declared that more should be done in this direction, by educating teachers about male/female equality. But the ABCD de l'égalité curriculum intended for the students themselves was thrown out the window. In 2014 the government also reaffirmed its absolute opposition to extending medically assisted reproduction to single women and lesbian couples, and to surrogacy of any sort. The new prime minister, Manuel Valls, reiterated his opposition to medically assisted reproduction during a visit to the Vatican in April.

## Conclusion: Toward a Minoritarian Understanding of Democracy

In France, the fantasy of invasion by "gender theory" both precedes and prolongs the legislative debates on giving same-sex couples the right to marry and adopt jointly. In *The Politics of Adoption* I showed that this fantasy reveals the existence of what I call "pastoral governance," which is oriented toward future generations and depends on the idea of the present as "risk."[52] Here I would like to suggest another idea, one that politicizes the issue of our relation to time even further, thus repositioning the debates about the idea of the "future" that have featured in American queer theory since the publication of Lee Edelman's *No Future*.[53] The question of the future is in fact the vector connecting two related concepts: the "minor" and the "minority." Education may be defined as the totality of the activities that shepherd children (minors) through the process that leads to adulthood (majority), sometimes continuing beyond that. But all too often education conflates reaching one's majority and joining the majority: it assigns children strictly hierarchical social roles in accordance with their ability to blend into a predetermined, dominant social model.[54] There is of course some enjoyment and learning to be had through the acquisition of the social roles identified with the majority, but being limited to these not only creates lasting inequalities among children but also greatly diminishes the quality and diversity of the relations they will develop as adults. In a sense, those who protest against "marriage for all" and so-called gender theory are afraid that this "majority" education, which still dominates today in France, will be overtaken by a form of learning that also incorporates the experience and knowledge of minority cultures. They then stigmatize the minority by playing on the fantasy of pedophilia. After conflating reaching one's majority and joining the majority, they pretend to conflate being part of a minority and being a minor.

In September 2014, the former Gaullist prime minister, Alain Juppé, dismissed "marriage for all" by saying, "Let us focus on real problems. . . . Let us leave aside these debates, which after all are only of interest to minorities." I would like to make the diametrically opposite argument. A minoritarian democracy is not one that inverts the numerical relation between the more and the fewer, or between one norm and another; it is not a "tyranny of the minority." Rather, what it does is to acknowledge the minority character of any majority's exercise of power. The philosopher Condorcet demonstrated that when a choice is not a simple binary alternative (for/against, yes/no), no decision is mathematically possible (in other words, it is possible to prefer A to B and B to C but also C to A).[55] A complex democracy is thus a paradox: it gives rise to combinations that are internally coherent taken in isolation but contradictory on the macropolitical level. Condorcet does not reject decision making by majority vote (that is, by replacing it with a decision procedure in which the minority always prevails), but simply draws our attention to the fact that a majority is simply an imperfect and transitory conglomeration of minority experiences. To insert this perspective into every political system (rather than seeking to get beyond it by appealing to absolute, transcendental republican values) is an essential task for LGBT populations, for no matter how much legal recognition they achieve, they will always be a minority. What is needed, then, is not only to counteract discrimination (the liberal response par excellence), nor to gain recognition for one's community (the communalist response), nor to create gay-only spaces (the multicultural response), but constantly to challenge norms themselves. This minoritarian response involves thinking about norms from the perspective of the critical experience of minorities who, in their relation to the existence of the majority, must at some point be thinking against themselves. This is what makes speaking of an ethics of generosity possible. Unlike the editor of this volume, Carlos A. Ball, who proposes an ethics based on openness, mutuality, and pleasure,[56] I do not associate any such generic features with LGBT experience. However, what seems to me to be essential for a minoritarian democracy is its critical perspective on those norms that it has itself produced. Needless to say, marriage is one of those norms.

NOTES

1 My thanks to Linda Gardiner for her beautiful translation work.

2 "Why Did It Take France This Long to Allow Gay Marriage?" *Washington Post*, February 12, 2013; "Why Did France Take So Long to Approve Gay Marriage? Aren't the French Ultra-Liberal?" *Slate.com*, April 24, 2013; Alexander Stille, "An Anti-Gay-Marriage Tea Party, French Style?" *New Yorker*, March 18, 2014.

3 "Mariage pour tous: Hollande tente de rassurer," *L'Express*, November 21, 2012.

4 Tribunal de Grande Instance of Versailles, April 29, 2014, 13/00168. However, the Cour de cassation has since found that these adoptions do not contradict any fundamental principles of French law, since assisted reproduction (even if restricted to heterosexual couples) already exists in France. Cour de cassation, opinions G1470006 and J1470007, September 23, 2014.

5 "Gay Marriage Is Protested in France," *New York Times*, May 26, 2013.

6 See Judith Halberstam, *In a Queer Time and Space: Transgender Bodies, Subcultural Lives* (New York: New York University Press, 2005).

7 This argument in support of an ethics of generosity was first put forward by the philosopher Didier Eribon in *Une morale du minoritaire. Variations sur un thème de Jean Genet* (Paris: Fayard, 2001).

8 Danielle Tartakowsky, *Les droites et la rue. Histoire d'une ambivalence de 1880 à nos jours* (Paris: La Découverte, 2014), pp. 166 et seq.

9 "Mgr Barbarin contre le mariage gay: 'Le Parlement n'est pas Dieu le Père,'" *Le Progrès*, August 1, 2014.

10 Available at http://www.parismatch.com/Actu/Societe/Frigide-Barjot-au-7e-ciel-511970, accessed March 2015.

11 Christine Boutin at the Manif pour tous, with Gilberte Collard (Front National MP). Available at http://rue89.nouvelobs.com/2013/04/22/gilbert-collard-a-manif-tous-ump-y-es-241680, accessed March 2015.

12 "Frigide Barjot—Tugdual Derville. Une alliance contre nature," *Le Monde*, April 20, 2013.

13 Ludovine de la Rochère meets with the Pope (June 12, 2014), available at http://www.famillechretienne.fr/var/fc/storage/images/media/images/pape-ludovine-de-la-rochere/10774486-1-fre-FR/pape-ludovine-de-la-rochere_article_large.jpg, accessed March 2015.

14 "Béatrice Bourges, l'autre égérie des anti-mariage gay," *M Le Magazine du Monde*, April 19, 2013. To see Béatrice Bourges participating in a "vigil" at the Invalides, see http://upload.wikimedia.org/wikipedia/commons/e/ef/B%C3%A9atrice_Bourges_et_les_Veilleurs_aux_Invalides_-_21_avril_2013.jpg, accessed March 2015.

15 Available at http://www.lamanifpourtous.fr/fr/notre-reseau-hors-metropole, accessed September 2014.

16 "Une antenne de la Manif pour tous à l'UMP," *Le Figaro*, April 29, 2014.

17 Eve Kosofsky Sedgwick presents a truly excellent discussion of this homosocial paranoia in *Between Men: English Literature and Male Homosocial Desire* (New York: Columbia University Press, 1985).

18 *Le Petit Journal*, May 27, 2013, accessed September 2014.

19 François Hollande, press conference, November 14, 2012.

20 These hearings can be accessed on the National Assembly website: http://www.assemblee-nationale.fr/14/dossiers/mariage_personnes_meme_sexe.asp, accessed September 2014.

21 "Hollande reçoit les associations opposées au mariage gay," *L'Express*, January 25, 2013.

22 Olivier Duhamel, *La gauche et la Cinquième République* (Paris: Presses Universitaires de France, 1980).

23 Didier Eribon, *D'une révolution conservatrice. Et de ses effets sur la gauche français* (Paris: Léo Scheer, 2007).

24 Daniel Borrillo and Pierre Lascoumes, *Amours égales? Le Pacs, les homosexuels et la gauche* (Paris: La Découverte, 2002).

25 Bruno Perreau, "Comité national d'éthique: gardien de la famille?" *Libération*, February 6, 2013.

26 Quoted in "Mariage pour tous, les députés socialistes veulent revenir aux 'vrais sujets,'" *Le Figaro*, April 23, 2013.

27 Patrick Mennucci, "Le mariage pour tous nous a coûté des voix," *Le Monde,* April 1, 2014.

28 Numerous studies have shown how majoritarian social norms have produced the impoverishment of LGBT communities. *See, e.g.,* M. V. Lee Badgett, Laura E. Durso, and Alyssa Schneebaum, *New Patterns of Poverty in the Lesbian, Gay, and Bisexual Community* (Williams Institute, June 2013).

29 Bruno Perreau, *The Politics of Adoption: Gender and the Making of French Citizenship* (Cambridge, MA: MIT Press, 2014).

30 Mary Anne Case has traced this history in detail in "After Gender the Destruction of Man: The Vatican's Nightmare Vision of the 'Gender Agenda' for Law," 31(3) *Pace Law Review* 802–17 (2011). She particularly notes the Vatican's opposition to the idea of gender during the Beijing Conference, *see Report of the Fourth World Congress on Women, Beijing, September 4–15, 1995*, p. 162. Available at http://www.un.org/womenwatch/daw/beijing/pdf/Beijing%20full%20report%20E.pdf.

31 *Letter from Cardinal Joseph Ratzinger, Prefect, Congregation for the Doctrine of the Faith, to the Bishops of the Catholic Church on the Collaboration of Men and Women in the Church and in the World*, May 31, 2004. Available at http://www.vatican.va/roman_curia/congregations/cfaith/documents/rc_con_cfaith_doc_20040731_collaboration_en.html.

32 In 2003 the Pontifical Council was to issue a detailed report on "gender ideology": *Lexicon: Ambiguous and Debatable Terms regarding Family Life and Ethical Questions* (Human Life International, 2006).

33 Éric Fassin, "The Purloined Gender: American Feminism in a French Mirror," 22(1) *French Historical Studies* 113–38 (Winter 1999).

34 Florence Tamagne, "Caricatures homophobes et stéréotypes de genre en France et en Allemagne: la presse satirique, de 1900 au milieu des années 1930," *Le Temps des Médias*, no. 1, 2003, pp. 42–53.

35 "Théorie du genre: Judith Butler répond à ses détracteurs," *Le Nouvel Observateur*, December 15, 2013. Eve Kosofsky Sedgwick, Gayle Rubin, Donna Haraway, Teresa de Lauretis, David Halperin, and others have also been translated, but often only in part, and have not attracted the same attention from the media.

36 See the presentation by Claude Timmerman, a lecturer close to the extreme Right and to royalist factions, at a conference held on October 1 and 2, 2011, at the monastery of Saint-Gildard in Nevers, organized by the Centre d'Études et de Prospective sur la Science, an organization whose purpose is to reconcile "faith" and "science." Timmerman asserted that "gender theory" is "an ethnic theory that seeks to legitimize homosexuality. That's all. It is the product, and solely the product, of American Jewish lesbians." Available at http://www.youtube.com/watch?v=w8esfEoqLkE, accessed September 2014.

37 Available at http://www.youtube.com/watch?v=gKqhCluosHE#t=4517, accessed September 2014.

38 Christopher Peterson speaks of the "disavowal of human animality" in *Bestial Traces: Race, Sexuality, Animality* (New York: Fordham University Press, 2012), p. 7.

39 "Taubira traitée de 'guenon': la vidéo qui le prouve," *Libération*, November 2013.

40 In French, a wide smile or grin can be called "*la banane*," normally with no racial or derogatory overtones.

41 "La Manif pour tous 'horrifiée' par la nomination de Najat Vallaud-Belkacem," *Le Figaro*, August 26, 2014.

42  *Minute*, September 3, 2014; *Valeurs Actuelles*, September 4, 2014.

43  Mary Douglas, *Purity and Danger: An Analysis of Concepts of Pollution and Taboo* (London: Routledge, 1966), pp. 3–4.

44  Kathryn Bond Stockton, *The Queer Child; or, Growing Sideways in the Twentieth Century* (Durham, NC: Duke University Press, 2009), pp. 17–27.

45  Quoted in "La Manif pour tous, acte II," *Le Monde*, October 2, 2014.

46  Luc Cédelle, "Le catéchisme 'antipédago,' le 'gender' et la nouvelle extrême droite soralo-dieudonniste," *Le Monde.fr*, January 24, 2014.

47  Jonathan Parienté, "Cinq intox sur la 'théorie' du genre,"*Le Monde*, January 28, 2014.

48  Available at http://www.vigi-gender.fr, accessed September 2014.

49  "Les religions entendent calmer le jeu," *Le Figaro.fr*, January 31, 2014.

50  "'Théorie' du genre: Aurélie Filippetti dénonce des pressions contre des bibliothèques," *LeMonde.fr*, Agence France Presse, February 10, 2014.

51  Debates on this topic are reflected in Jean-Paul Lilienfeld's film *La journée de la jupe*, released in March 2009. *See* Christine Bard, *Ce que soulève la jupe. Identités, transgressions, résistances* (Paris: Autrement, 2010).

52  Perreau, *The Politics of Adoption*.

53  Lee Edelman, *No Future: Queer Theory and the Death Drive* (Durham, NC: Duke University Press, 2004).

54  René Schérer, *Vers une enfance majeure* (Paris: La Fabrique, 2006), pp. 17–18.

55  *Politique de Condorcet*, textes présentés par Charles Coutel (Paris: Payot, 1996), p. 140.

56  Carlos A. Ball, *The Morality of Gay Rights: An Exploration in Political Philosophy* (New York: Routledge, 2003), pp. 206–14.

# ABOUT THE CONTRIBUTORS

Carlos A. Ball is Distinguished Professor and Judge Frederick Lacey Scholar at the Rutgers University Law School. His books include *Same-Sex Marriage and Children: A Tale of History, Social Science, and Law* (2014); *The Right to Be Parents: LGBT Families and the Transformation of Parenthood* (NYU Press, 2012); and *From the Closet to the Courtroom: Five LGBT Lawsuits That Have Changed Our Nation* (2010).

Jan Willem Duyvendak is Distinguished Research Professor of Sociology at the University of Amsterdam. His books include *European States and Their Muslim Citizens* (2014; edited with John Bowen, Cristophe Bertossi, and Mona Lena Krook); *Crafting Citizenship: Negotiating Tensions in Modern Society* (2012; with Menno Hurenkamp and Evelien Tonkens); and *The Politics of Home: Nostalgia and Belonging in Western Europe and the United States* (2011).

Joseph J. Fischel is Assistant Professor of Women's, Gender, and Sexuality Studies at Yale University. He is the author of *Sex and Harm in the Age of Consent* (2016).

Katherine Franke is the Isidor and Seville Sulzbacher Professor of Law and Director of the Center for Gender & Sexuality Law at Columbia Law School. She is the author of *Wed-Locked: The Perils of Marriage Equality* (NYU Press, 2015).

Donald P. Haider-Markel is Professor of Political Science at the University of Kansas. His books include *Pulled Over: How Police Stops Define Race and Citizenship* (2014; with Charles Epp and Steven Maynard-Moody); *Transgender Rights and Politics: Groups, Issue Framing, and Policy Adoption* (2014; edited with Jami Taylor); and *Out and Running: Gay and Lesbian Candidates, Elections, and Policy Representation* (2010).

Nancy J. Knauer is the I. Herman Stern Professor of Law and Director of Law & Public Policy Programs at Temple University, Beasley School of Law. She is the author of *Gay and Lesbian Elders: History, Law, and Identity Politics in the U.S.* (2010).

Gary Mucciaroni is Professor of Political Science at Temple University. His books include *Same Sex, Different Politics: Issues and Institutions in Struggles for Gay and Lesbian Rights* (2008), and he is the author of "Are Debates about 'Morality Policy' Really about Morality? Framing Opposition to Gay and Lesbian Rights," 39 *Policy Studies Journal* 187 (2011) and "The Study of LGBT Politics and Its Contributions to Political Science," 44 *PS: Political Science and Politics* 17 (2011).

Bruno Perreau is the Cynthia L. Reed Associate Professor of French Studies at MIT. His books include *Queer Theory: The French Response* (forthcoming); *The Politics of Adoption: Gender and the Making of French Citizenship* (2014); and *Le choix de l'homosexualité. Recherches inédites sur la question gay et lesbienne* (2007).

Nancy D. Polikoff is Professor of Law at American University Washington College of Law. She is the author of *Beyond (Straight and Gay) Marriage: Valuing All Families under the Law* (2008).

David Rayside is Professor Emeritus of Political Science and was the founding director of the Mark S. Bonham Centre for Sexual Diversity Studies at the University of Toronto. His books include *Queer Inclusions, Continental Divisions* (2008); *On the Fringe: Gays and Lesbians in Politics* (1998); and *Faith, Politics, and Sexual Diversity in Canada and the United States* (2011; edited with Clyde Wilcox).

Russell K. Robinson is the Distinguished Haas Chair in LGBT Equity Professor of Law at UC Berkeley Law. His recent writings include "The Uncomfortable Relationship between Sexual Liberty and Sexual Oppression," in *Rewriting Homosexuality* (Shannon Gilreath et al., eds., 2015) and "Marriage Equality and Postracialism," 61 *UCLA Law Review* 1010 (2014).

Clifford Rosky is Professor of Law at the University of Utah's S.J. Quinney College of Law. His recent writings include "No Promo Hetero: Children's Right to Be Queer," 35 *Cardozo Law Review* 425 (2013) and "Fear of the Queer Child," 61 *Buffalo Law Review* 607 (2013).

Jami Taylor is an Assistant Professor of Political Science and Public Administration at the University of Toledo. She is the coeditor of *Transgender Rights and Politics: Groups, Issue Framing, and Policy Adoption* (2014; edited with Donald Haider-Markel).

# INDEX

ABCD de l'égalité, 334–35
Aboriginals, 267, 276
abortion, 45–46, 307
Abstinence Only Until Marriage (AOUM), 198
accidental procreation, 133–34, 218
ACLU LGBT Rights Project, 142
adoption: by African American same-sex couples, 144; denial of services, 47, 48; divorce and, 144; in French same-sex marriage, 307, 337n4; marriage-equality plaintiffs and, 139–40; in Michigan, 141–42; in New York, 143; second-parent, 130–31, 141–44
Affordable Care Act. *See* Patient Protection and Affordable Care Act
African American same-sex couples: adoption for, 144; children of, 138–39
African Americans, 57; children of, 137; color-blindness and, 249–50; social reputation of, 244–45; stereotypes of, 252. *See also* racism
African Americans' marriage: inferiority and, 246–47; marriage equality related to, 243–52
aging, 107–14. *See also* LGBT elders
AIDS. *See* HIV/AIDS
Ali, Ayaan Hirsi, 295
Alliance VITA, 310
American Community Survey, 140–41, 149
Americans with Disabilities Act, 28
American Unity PAC, 86
*Amsterdam: The History of the World's Most Liberal City* (Shorto), 292

animality, 327, 329
animus, 224–25
antidiscrimination laws: about bathrooms, 173–76; EEOC and, 27, 91–92; enforcement of, 29, 77; extent of, 75–76, 79–80; federal legislation for, 81–83; gender and sexual identities in, 166–72; race in, 167; in red states, 7–8; sexual orientation in, 9, 166–72, 250; state legislation for, 81, 83–87, 89–90; support for, 80; symbolism of, 77; value of, 76–81, 172
Antigones, 312, *314*
anti-immigration, 293–95
anti-Semitism, 325–26
AOUM. *See* Abstinence Only Until Marriage
Argentina, 265
Arizona, 31, 94
Arkansas, 94
Asian Americans, 137
assisted reproduction: in France, 314, 318, 337n4; sperm donation for, 143–45, 147, 150
assisted reproduction laws, 144–47
athletes, 275
autonomy, 123, 165. *See also* relational autonomy
Ayrault, Jean-Marc, 318

backlash, 49, 81; postmarriage movement and, 18–19, 30–31; RFRA, 46–48, 93–94; state marriage laws as, 238–42
Badgett, Lee, 214

CPSIA information can be obtained
at www.ICGtesting.com
Printed in the USA
BVOW08*1441220217
476910BV00007B/262/P